The Keynesian Heritage
Volume I

Schools of Thought in Economics

Series Editor: Mark Blaug
Emeritus Professor of the Economics of Education,
University of London and Consultant Professor of
Economics, University of Buckingham

For greater convenience, a cumulative index to all titles in this series will be published in a separate volume number 12.

The Keynesian Heritage Volume I

Edited by

G.K. Shaw

Rank Foundation Professor of Economics
University of Buckingham

EDWARD ELGAR

Published by
Edward Elgar Publishing Limited
Gower House
Croft Road
Aldershot
Hants GU11 3HR
England

Gower Publishing Company
Old Post Road
Brookfield
Vermont 05036
USA

British Library Cataloguing in Publication Data

The Keynesian heritage. — (Schools of thought
  in economics; 1).
  1. Economics. Theories of Keynes, John
  Maynard, 1883–1946
  I. Shaw, G.K. (Graham Keith), *1938–*
  II. Series
  330.15'6

Library of Congress-in-Publication Data

The Keynesian heritage.
  (Schools of thought in economics; 1)
  Includes indexes.
  1. Keynesian economics. I. Shaw, G.K.
(Graham Keith), 1938– II. Series.
HB99.7.K3955 1988
330.15'6   88–16528

ISBN 1 85278 053 3 (vol. I)
     1 85278 117 3 (2 volume set)

Printed and bound in Great Britain
by Bookcraft (Bath) Ltd.

for
Jina Pasban Dowlatshahi

'To understand my *state of mind, however, you have to know that I believe myself to be writing a book on economic theory which will largely revolutionize – not, I suppose, at once but in the course of the next ten years – the way the world thinks about economic problems. When my new theory has been duly assimilated and mixed with politics and feelings and passions, I can't predict what the final upshot will be in its effect on action and affairs. But there will be a great change, and in particular, the Ricardian foundations of Marxism will be knocked away.*

I can't expect you or anyone else, to believe this at the present stage. But for myself I don't merely hope what I say, – in my own mind I'm quite sure.'

John Maynard Keynes in a
letter to George Bernard Shaw,
1 January, 1935.

Contents

Acknowledgements

The editor and publishers wish to thank the following who have kindly given permission for the use of copyright material.

Academic Press Inc. (London) Ltd for article: Richard Kahn (1977), 'Malinvaud on Keynes: Review Article', *Cambridge Journal of Economics*, 1 (4), December, pp. 375–88.

American Economic Association for articles: Alan Coddington (1982), 'Deficient Foresight: A Troublesome Theme in Keynesian Economics', *American Economic Review*, 72 (3), June, pp. 480–7; James Tobin (1975), 'Keynesian Models of Recession and Depression', *American Economic Review*, 65, May, pp. 195–202; Franco Modigliani (1977), 'The Monetarist Controversy or Should We Foresake Stabilisation Policies?', *American Economic Review*, 67, March, pp. 1–19.

Basil Blackwell Ltd for article: Paul Davidson (1967), 'A Keynesian View of Patinkin's Theory of Employment', *Economic Journal*, 77, September, pp. 559–78.

Macmillan Publishers Ltd for: Robert W. Clower (1965), 'The Keynesian Counter-Revolution: A Theoretical Appraisal' from *The Theory of Interest Rates*, Hahn and Breechling (eds).

North Holland Publishing Co. for article: Oliver J. Blanchard and Lawrence Summers (1987), 'Hysteresis in Unemployment', *European Economic Review*, 31, February/March, pp. 288–95

The Review of Economics and Statistics for article: Paul Samuelson (1939), 'Interactions between the Multiplier Analysis and Principle of Acceleration', *Review of Economics and Statistics*, 21, May, pp. 75–8.

The Royal Bank of Scotland plc for article: A.P. Thirlwall (1981), 'Keynesian Employment Theory is Not Defunct', *Three Banks Review*, 131, pp. 14–29.

The Scandinavian Journal of Economics for article: Axel Leijonhufvud (1973), 'Effective Demand Failures', *Swedish Journal of Economics*, 75 (1), pp. 27–48.

M.E. Sharpe, Inc. for articles: J.R. Hicks (1980), 'IS-LM: An Explanation', *Journal of Post Keynesian Economics*, 3, Winter, pp. 139–54; P. Davison (1984), 'Reviving

Keynes's Revolution', *Journal of Post Keynesian Economics*, 6 (4), Summer, pp. 561–75.

The University of Chicago Press for articles: M. Kohn (1986), 'Monetary Analysis: The Equilibrium Method, and Keynes's "General Theory"', *Journal of Political Economy*, 94 (6), December, pp. 1191–224; Peter Diamond (1982), 'Aggregate Demand Management in Search Equilibrium', *Journal of Political Economy*, 90, pp. 881–894.

Unwin Hyman Ltd for: Richard Kahn (1976), 'Unemployment as Seen by the Keynesians' from *The Concept and Measurement of Involuntary Unemployment*, G.D.N. Worswick (ed.), pp. 19–34.

Western Economic Association International for article: Armen A. Alchian (1969), 'Information Costs, Pricing and Resource Unemployment', *Western Economic Journal*, VII (2), June, pp. 109–28.

John Wiley & Sons Inc. for articles: J.M. Keynes (1937), 'The General Theory of Employment', *Quarterly Journal of Economics*, 51, pp. 207–23; T. Mayer (1959), 'The Empirical Significance of the Real Balance Effect', *Quarterly Journal of Economics*, 73 (2), May, pp. 275–91; J.P. Neary and J.E. Stiglitz (1983), 'Towards Reconstruction of Keynesian Economics: Expectations and Constrained Equilibria', *Quarterly Journal of Economics Supplement*, 98, pp. 199–228.

Every effort has been made to trace all the copyright holders but if any have been inadvertently overlooked the publishers will be pleased to make the necessary arrangement at the first opportunity.

In addition the publishers wish to thank the Library of the London School of Economics and Political Science and the British Library Document Supply Centre for their assistance in obtaining these articles.

Publisher's note
Every effort has been made to reproduce exact copies of the articles and papers reprinted in this volume. Unfortunately, it proved impossible to find copies of Chapters 11, 14 and 16 in a sufficiently good condition for facsimile reproduction. These articles have been re-typeset in a style similar to the first printing. For ease of reference, the pagination in the original article has been printed in brackets [ ] in the text.

Introduction

The articles included in this volume are dubbed 'Keynesian' in the sense of being contributions to economics, whether theoretical or policy oriented, which may be thought of as being in the spirit of Keynes' *General Theory of Employment Interest and Money*. The immediate difficulty raised by such a criterion derives from the fact that there remains considerable controversy as to what was the real nature of the Keynesian revolution and what therefore is meant by the 'spirit of Keynes'. That such a question can be raised more than fifty years after the publication of the *General Theory* is in itself remarkable, particularly in view of all the ink that has been spilled in the interpretative debate that followed upon the Keynes versus the Classics controversies. One reason for this state of affairs lies in the fact that in the decade following the publication of the *General Theory*, prior to his death in 1946, Keynes participated hardly at all in the theoretical controversies stemming from his *magnum opus*. Illness – Keynes suffered a heart attack in 1937 – and then his involvement as a leading economic advisor to the wartime administrations limited his involvement in the purely theoretical disputes which he had initiated. Apart from his important 1937 *Quarterly Journal of Economics* article in which he defended his position against a series of critical reviews[1] published in the previous year, he stood apart from the major controversies and never attempted a revision or further edition of the *General Theory*. The difficulties of interpretation posed by Keynes were compounded by the manner in which the *General Theory* was written – by the deliberate avoidance of any formal mathematical model or even a systematic diagrammatic analysis and by the adoption of a style which, whilst satirical and often amusing, allows the reader to have a selective perception of what really constitutes the essence of the argument.

In the event, what emerged and continued to emerge over the years was a sequence of differing readings of the Keynesian revolution, each claiming to embody the essential message of the Messiah and each disputing the validity of alternative interpretations. The dominant orthodoxy was soon established by Hicks' seminal paper 'Mr Keynes and the Classics' (Hicks, 1937) which became the foundation of the Hicks–Hansen IS/LM analysis which was to dominate textbook discussion until the present day and which was to become the cornerstone of the so-called neoclassical synthesis whereby the articulate insights of Keynes were to be grafted onto the validity of classical economics to create a more general and all encompassing theory. In this scenario, Keynes' achievement in terms of pure theory is seen to be essentially trivial in character and limited to specific situations such as price and wage rigidity and liquidity trap conditions whilst his enduring value is seen to lie in having provided a framework for positive policy intervention in the macroeconomy. This conventional or orthodox view initiated by Hicks has been followed and extended by 'Keynesians' of the persuasion of Samuelson, Solow, Tobin, and others who would generally be considered critical of monetarism and inclined more positively towards fiscal intervention. The zenith of their influence at least in the United States was reflected in the composition of the US Council of Economic Advisors appointed by President Kennedy in 1960.

This limiting view of Keynes, at least from the perspective of his greatness as an economic theorist, has been challenged and strongly denounced as illegitimate by other schools of thought variously dubbed as neo-Keynesian, post-Keynesian or dis-equilibrium Keynesian who reject the Hicksian IS/LM simultaneous equation approach as emasculating the essence of Keynes. It should perhaps be stated that the latter has been increasingly disowned by Hicks himself in varying degrees of apologia as an accurate portrayal of the Keynesian message – see in particular Hicks (1980). Whilst it is comparatively easy to understand what these alternative Keynesian schools reject – in particular the equilibrium IS/LM framework – it is not always so clear what precisely is the alternative interpretation they advocate. On the one hand, there is the small but influential Cambridge School of Economics (Cambridge, UK) often referred to as neo-Keynesians, and whose major contributors have been Joan Robinson, Nicholas Kaldor and Luigi Pasinetti. They have also been strongly influenced by Piero Sraffa in his reappraisal of Ricardian economics and for this reason their reading of Keynes often possesses a certain neo-Ricardian or neo-Marxian flavour. The main focus of this school of thought has been to extend the essentially short-run Keynesian analysis into the longer term implications of economic growth and income distribution within an essentially Kaleckian framework of monopoly power. It is partly for this reason that the marginal productivity theory of distribution – the cornerstone of neoclassical economics – is denied and equally neoclassical static equilibrium concepts are replaced by what is considered more meaningful in a world of uncertainty – an historical and non-reversible dynamic process of adjustment through time.

Similar, although far from identical views, have also found expression in the United States, particularly in the interpretations stemming from Sidney Weintraub and Paul Davidson, co-founders of the influential *Journal of Post-Keynesian Economics* which seeks to promote those aspects of Keynesianism which have been lost or trivialized in the conventional IS/LM interpretation. Here the emphasis is very much upon the role of uncertainty and the unstable nature of long term expectations giving rise to the demands for liquidity and the fundamental importance of money. Emphasis is also placed upon the failure of the labour market to clear and the consequence of adjustment upon the side of output as opposed to wage rates. This emphasis has also been linked to another far reaching and radical interpretation of Keynes which suggests that Keynes was groping towards an explanation of unemployment in terms of disequilibrium economics, in which markets fail to clear because of inadequate information and more precisely because of misinformation generated by a 'false vector of relative prices' which moves the economy increasingly away from equilibrium. This interpretation is linked intimately with the monumental work of Leijonhufvud (1968) which in turn is deeply indebted to the seminal paper by Clower

(1965) which first applied the concepts of 'false trading' and 'dual decision hypothesis' to the Keynesian analysis of consumption and the multiplier. Various other refinements around this central theme have been proposed by economists such as Malinvaud, Patinkin, Lipsey, Okun and Tobin all of whom may justifiably claim to stand in the Keynesian tradition. Moreover, this aspect of the Keynesian reappraisal, emphasizing the difficulties of obtaining, processing and disseminating all relevant information has brought Keynesian economics into precisely the same arena as that occupied by Rational Expectations theorists. The growing gulf distancing the latter from the New-Classical Macroeconomics is intimately bound up with the informational base and characteristics of the economy – precisely those same issues which so occupied Keynes in this dis-equilibrium interpretation of his work.

How then are we to make any sense of this notion of 'the spirit of Keynes' which underlies the rationale of inclusion in the present volume? The answer provided here is that Keynesian economics is essentially interventionist in its philosophical orientation in that it is based upon the premise that the classical belief in the self correcting properties of the market economy was fundamentally flawed. Precisely why the Classical system is flawed, or more accurately why Keynes believed it to be flawed, remains the fundamental issue and controversy to which we have referred above. But no matter how we choose to answer this theoretical question, its answer leads to the need for intervention at the macroeconomic level and a macroeconomic intervention which is primarily demand oriented. Keynes was perfectly willing to accept, with minor exceptions, the resource allocating functions of the market economy as being reasonably efficient and beneficial – once the full utilization of resources had been assured. But there can be no guarantee that such utilization will be secured or will be secured in a time horizon sufficiently acceptable to allow the classical postulates to pursue their intended role. It is this sense of the inadequacy of market forces which unites Keynesians of all persuasions in the belief that judicious intervention can improve upon a non-interventionist stance. Even economists whose endorsement of the neoclassical synthesis is arguably more Classical than Keynesian, (as for example Patinkin), stressing as they do the virtues of price flexibility, are united in this respect:

> the propositions of Keynesian monetary theory are much less general than the *General Theory* and later expositions would lead us to believe. But this in no way diminishes the relevance of Keynesian unemployment theory for the formulation of a practicable full-employment policy.[2]

The contributions which follow all bear testimony to the inadequacy of the classical self adjustment mechanism and thus provide the provisional justification for interventionism and for the view that 'the State will have to exercise a guiding influence on the propensity to consume partly through its scheme of taxation' and also 'that a somewhat comprehensive socialization of investment will prove the only means of securing an approximation to full employment'.[3]

It is in this belief that the following papers possess a common theme and may be looked upon as comprising mainstream Keynesianism without necessarily having a common theoretical base. They reflect the virtues of demand management, a general distrust of monetarism and disdain of supply side economics whilst often providing limited sanction for income and price controls. Volume I of the *Keynesian Heritage* is primarily oriented towards theoretical considerations whilst Volume II deals more with the task of macroeconomic policy formulation and implementation – although as the reader will readily appreciate such a dichotomy can seldom be absolute. The actual decision of what to include remains very much the subjective choice of the editor, which may possibly account for a certain public finance bias, although due attention has been given to competing claims. However, it is perhaps necessary to emphasize that certain seminal and highly influential papers have been *deliberately* excluded upon the grounds that they are already so widely available in collected readings and compilations elsewhere that to include them would amount to needless duplication.

Acknowledgements

The present collection of papers has benefited considerably from the comments of the General Editor to this series, Professor Mark Blaug, and equally by the perceptive suggestions of my former colleague, Rod Cross of St Andrews University. Neither, of course, bear any responsibility for any idiosyncratic inclusion on the part of the editor nor equally any responsibility for a glaring sin of omission. As always, I am especially indebted to Mrs Linda Waterman of Buckingham University for her unfailing efficiency in conducting the secretarial and typing chores associated with such a venture.

G.K. Shaw
July, 1988

Notes

1   The critics were Leontief, Robertson, Taussig and Viner although Keynes chose to concentrate his defence upon the lengthy review of the latter entitled 'Mr Keynes on the Causes of Unemployment'. See Jacob Viner (1936), pp. 147–67.
2   Patinkin (1965), p. xxv.
3   J.M. Keynes (1936), p. 378.

Part I
Reflections
on the
General Theory

[1]

THE

QUARTERLY JOURNAL

OF

ECONOMICS

FEBRUARY, 1937

THE GENERAL THEORY OF EMPLOYMENT

SUMMARY

I. Comments on the four discussions in the previous issue of points in the General Theory, 209. — II. Certain definite points on which the writer diverges from previous theories, 212. — The theory of interest restated, 215. — Uncertainties and fluctuations of investment, 217. — III. Demand and Supply for output as a whole, 219. — The output of capital goods and of consumption, 221.

I

I am much indebted to the Editors of the Quarterly Journal for the four contributions relating to my General Theory of Employment, Interest and Money which appeared in the issue for November, 1936. They contain detailed criticisms, much of which I accept and from which I hope to benefit. There is nothing in Professor Taussig's comment from which I disagree. Mr. Leontief is right, I think, in the distinction he draws between my attitude and that of the "orthodox" theory to what he calls the "homogeneity postulate." I should have thought, however, that there was abundant evidence from experience to contradict this postulate; and that, in any case, it is for those who make a highly special assumption to justify it, rather than for one who dispenses with it, to prove a general negative. I would also suggest that his idea might be applied more fruitfully and with greater theoretical precision in connection with the part played by the quantity of money in determining the rate of interest.[1] For it is here, I think, that the homogeneity postulate primarily enters into the orthodox theoretical scheme.

1. Cf. my paper on "The Theory of the Rate of Interest" to appear in the volume of Essays in honor of Irving Fisher.

210   *QUARTERLY JOURNAL OF ECONOMICS*

My differences, such as they are, from Mr. Robertson chiefly arise out of my conviction that both he and I differ more fundamentally from our predecessors than his piety will allow. With many of his points I agree, without, however, being conscious in several instances of having said (or, anyhow, meant) anything different. I am surprised he should think that those who make sport with the velocity of the circulation of money have much in common with the theory of the multiplier. I fully agree with the important point he makes (pp. 180–183) that the increased demand for money resulting from an increase in activity has a backwash which tends to raise the rate of interest; and this is, indeed, a significant element in my theory of why booms carry within them the seeds of their own destruction. But this is, essentially, a part of the liquidity theory of the rate of interest, and not of the "orthodox" theory. Where he states (p. 183) that my theory must be regarded "not as a refutation of a common-sense account of events in terms of supply and demand for loanable funds, but as an alternative version of it," I must ask, before agreeing, for at least one reference to where this common-sense account is to be found.

There remains the most important of the four comments, namely, Professor Viner's. In regard to his criticisms of my definition and treatment of involuntary unemployment, I am ready to agree that this part of my book is particularly open to criticism. I already feel myself in a position to make improvements, and I hope that, when I do so, Professor Viner will feel more content, especially as I do not think that there is anything fundamental between us here. In the case of his second section, however, entitled "The Propensity to Hoard" I am prepared to debate his points. There are passages which suggest that Professor Viner is thinking too much in the more familiar terms of the quantity of money actually hoarded, and that he overlooks the emphasis I seek to place on the rate of interest as being the inducement *not* to hoard. It is precisely because the facilities for hoarding are strictly limited that liquidity preference mainly operates by increasing the rate of interest. I cannot agree that "in

THE GENERAL THEORY OF EMPLOYMENT   211

modern monetary theory the propensity to hoard is generally
dealt with, with results which in kind are substantially identical with Keynes', as a factor operating to reduce the
'velocity' of money." On the contrary, I am convinced that
the monetary theorists who try to deal with it in this way are
altogether on the wrong track.[2] Again, when Professor Viner
points out that most people invest their savings at the best
rate of interest they can get and asks for statistics to justify
the importance I attach to liquidity-preference, he is over-
looking the point that it is the *marginal* potential hoarder
who has to be satisfied by the rate of interest, so as to bring
the desire for actual hoards within the narrow limits of the
cash available for hoarding. When, as happens in a crisis,
liquidity-preferences are sharply raised, this shows itself not
so much in increased hoards — for there is little, if any, more
cash which is hoardable than there was before — as in a sharp
rise in the rate of interest, *i.e.* securities fall in price until
those, who would now like to get liquid if they could do so at
the previous price, are persuaded to give up the idea as being
no longer practicable on reasonable terms. A rise in the rate
of interest is a means *alternative* to an increase of hoards for
satisfying an increased liquidity-preference. Nor is my argument affected by the admitted fact that different types of
assets satisfy the desire for liquidity in different degrees. The
mischief is done when the rate of interest corresponding to
the degree of liquidity of a given asset leads to a market-
capitalization of that asset which is less than its cost of
production.

There are other criticisms also which I should be ready to
debate. But tho I might be able to justify my own language,
I am anxious not to be led, through doing so in too much
detail, to overlook the substantial points which may, nevertheless, underlie the reactions which my treatment has produced in the minds of my critics. I am more attached to the
comparatively simple fundamental ideas which underlie my
theory than to the particular forms in which I have embodied
them, and I have no desire that the latter should be crystal-

2. See below.

212   *QUARTERLY JOURNAL OF ECONOMICS*

lized at the present stage of the debate. If the simple basic
ideas can become familiar and acceptable, time and experience and the collaboration of a number of minds will discover
the best way of expressing them. I would, therefore, prefer to
occupy such further space, as the Editor of this Journal can
allow me, in trying to reëxpress some of these ideas, than in
detailed controversy which might prove barren. And I believe
that I shall effect this best, even tho this may seem to some as
plunging straight off into the controversial mood from which
I purport to seek escape, if I put what I have to say in the
shape of a discussion as to certain definite points where I seem
to myself to be most clearly departing from previous theories.

II

It is generally recognized that the Ricardian analysis was
concerned with what we now call long-period equilibrium.
Marshall's contribution mainly consisted in grafting on to
this the marginal principle and the principle of substitution,
together with some discussion of the passage from one position
of long-period equilibrium to another. But he assumed, as
Ricardo did, that the amounts of the factors of production in
use were given and that the problem was to determine the
way in which they would be used and their relative rewards.
Edgeworth and Professor Pigou and other later and contemporary writers have embroidered and improved this
theory by considering how different peculiarities in the shapes
of the supply functions of the factors of production would
affect matters, what will happen in conditions of monopoly
and imperfect competition, how far social and individual
advantage coincide, what are the special problems of exchange
in an open system and the like. But these more recent writers
like their predecessors were still dealing with a system in
which the amount of the factors employed was given and the
other relevant facts were known more or less for certain.
This does not mean that they were dealing with a system in
which change was ruled out, or even one in which the disappointment of expectation was ruled out. But at any given
time facts and expectations were assumed to be given in

THE GENERAL THEORY OF EMPLOYMENT   213

a definite and calculable form; and risks, of which, tho admitted, not much notice was taken, were supposed to be capable of an exact actuarial computation. The calculus of probability, tho mention of it was kept in the background, was supposed to be capable of reducing uncertainty to the same calculable status as that of certainty itself; just as in the Benthamite calculus of pains and pleasures or of advantage and disadvantage, by which the Benthamite philosophy assumed men to be influenced in their general ethical behavior.

Actually, however, we have, as a rule, only the vaguest idea of any but the most direct consequences of our acts. Sometimes we are not much concerned with their remoter consequences, even tho time and chance may make much of them. But sometimes we are intensely concerned with them, more so, occasionally, than with the immediate consequences. Now of all human activities which are affected by this remoter preoccupation, it happens that one of the most important is economic in character, namely, Wealth. The whole object of the accumulation of Wealth is to produce results, or potential results, at a comparatively distant, and sometimes at an *indefinitely* distant, date. Thus the fact that our knowledge of the future is fluctuating, vague and uncertain, renders Wealth a peculiarly unsuitable subject for the methods of the classical economic theory. This theory might work very well in a world in which economic goods were necessarily consumed within a short interval of their being produced. But it requires, I suggest, considerable amendment if it is to be applied to a world in which the accumulation of wealth for an indefinitely postponed future is an important factor; and the greater the proportionate part played by such wealth-accumulation the more essential does such amendment become.

By "uncertain" knowledge, let me explain, I do not mean merely to distinguish what is known for certain from what is only probable. The game of roulette is not subject, in this sense, to uncertainty; nor is the prospect of a Victory bond being drawn. Or, again, the expectation of life is only slightly uncertain. Even the weather is only moderately uncertain. The sense in which I am using the term is that in which the prospect of a European war is uncertain, or the price of copper and the rate of interest twenty years hence, or the obsolescence of a new invention, or the position of private wealth-owners in the social system in 1970. About these matters there is no scientific basis on which to form any calculable probability whatever. We simply do not know. Nevertheless, the necessity for action and for decision compels us as practical men to do our best to overlook this awkward fact and to behave exactly as we should if we had behind us a good Benthamite calculation of a series of prospective advantages and disadvantages, each multiplied by its appropriate probability, waiting to be summed.

How do we manage in such circumstances to behave in a manner which saves our faces as rational, economic men? We have devised for the purpose a variety of techniques, of which much the most important are the three following:

(1) We assume that the present is a much more serviceable guide to the future than a candid examination of past experience would show it to have been hitherto. In other words we largely ignore the prospect of future changes about the actual character of which we know nothing.

(2) We assume that the *existing* state of opinion as expressed in prices and the character of existing output is based on a *correct* summing up of future prospects, so that we can accept it as such unless and until something new and relevant comes into the picture.

(3) Knowing that our own individual judgment is worthless, we endeavor to fall back on the judgment of the rest of the world which is perhaps better informed. That is, we endeavor to conform with the behavior of the majority or the average. The psychology of a society of individuals each of whom is endeavoring to copy the others leads to what we may strictly term a *conventional* judgment.

Now a practical theory of the future based on these three principles has certain marked characteristics. In particular, being based on so flimsy a foundation, it is subject to sudden and violent changes. The practice of calmness and immobility, of certainty and security, suddenly breaks down. New fears and hopes will, without warning, take charge of human conduct. The forces of disillusion may suddenly impose a new conventional basis of valuation. All these pretty, polite techniques, made for a well-panelled Board Room and a nicely regulated market, are liable to collapse. At all times the vague panic fears and equally vague and unreasoned hopes are not really lulled, and lie but a little way below the surface.

Perhaps the reader feels that this general, philosophical disquisition on the behavior of mankind is somewhat remote from the economic theory under discussion. But I think not. Tho this is how we behave in the market place, the theory we devise in the study of how we behave in the market place should not itself submit to market-place idols. I accuse the classical economic theory of being itself one of these pretty, polite techniques which tries to deal with the present by abstracting from the fact that we know very little about the future.

I daresay that a classical economist would readily admit this. But, even so, I think he has overlooked the precise nature of the difference which his abstraction makes between theory and practice, and the character of the fallacies into which he is likely to be led.

This is particularly the case in his treatment of Money and Interest. And our first step must be to elucidate more clearly the functions of Money.

Money, it is well known, serves two principal purposes. By acting as a money of account it facilitates exchanges without its being necessary that it should ever itself come into the picture as a substantive object. In this respect it is a convenience which is devoid of significance or real influence. In the second place, it is a store of wealth. So we are told, without a smile on the face. But in the world of the classical economy, what an insane use to which to put it! For it is a recognized characteristic of money as a store of wealth that it is barren; whereas practically every other form of storing

wealth yields some interest or profit. Why should anyone
outside a lunatic asylum wish to use money as a store of
wealth?

Because, partly on reasonable and partly on instinctive
grounds, our desire to hold Money as a store of wealth is a
barometer of the degree of our distrust of our own calculations
and conventions concerning the future. Even tho this feeling
about Money is itself conventional or instinctive, it operates,
so to speak, at a deeper level of our motivation. It takes
charge at the moments when the higher, more precarious conventions have weakened. The possession of actual money
lulls our disquietude; and the premium which we require to
make us part with money is the measure of the degree of our
disquietude.

The significance of this characteristic of money has usually
been overlooked; and in so far as it has been noticed, the
essential nature of the phenomenon has been misdescribed.
For what has attracted attention has been the *quantity* of
money which has been hoarded; and importance has been
attached to this because it has been supposed to have a direct
proportionate effect on the price-level through affecting the
velocity of circulation. But the *quantity* of hoards can only
be altered either if the total quantity of money is changed or
if the quantity of current money-income (I speak broadly) is
changed; whereas fluctuations in the degree of confidence are
capable of having quite a different effect, namely, in modifying
not the amount that is actually hoarded, but the amount of
the premium which has to be offered to induce people not to
hoard. And changes in the propensity to hoard, or in the
state of liquidity-preference as I have called it, primarily
affect, not prices, but the rate of interest; any effect on prices
being produced by repercussion as an ultimate consequence
of a change in the rate of interest.

This, expressed in a very general way, is my theory of the
rate of interest. The rate of interest obviously measures —
just as the books on arithmetic say it does — the premium
which has to be offered to induce people to hold their wealth
in some form other than hoarded money. The quantity of

THE GENERAL THEORY OF EMPLOYMENT   217

money and the amount of it required in the active circulation for the transaction of current business (mainly depending on the level of money-income) determine how much is available for inactive balances, *i.e.* for hoards. The rate of interest is the factor which adjusts at the margin the demand for hoards to the supply of hoards.

Now let us proceed to the next stage of the argument. The owner of wealth, who has been induced not to hold his wealth in the shape of hoarded money, still has two alternatives between which to choose. He can lend his money at the current rate of money-interest or he can purchase some kind of capital-asset. Clearly in equilibrium these two alternatives must offer an equal advantage to the marginal investor in each of them. This is brought about by shifts in the money-prices of capital-assets relative to the prices of money-loans. The prices of capital-assets move until, having regard to their prospective yields and account being taken of all those elements of doubt and uncertainty, interested and disinterested advice, fashion, convention and what else you will which affect the mind of the investor, they offer an equal apparent advantage to the marginal investor who is wavering between one kind of investment and another.

This, then, is the first repercussion of the rate of interest, as fixed by the quantity of money and the propensity to hoard, namely, on the prices of capital-assets. This does not mean, of course, that the rate of interest is the only fluctuating influence on these prices. Opinions as to their prospective yield are themselves subject to sharp fluctuations, precisely for the reason already given, namely, the flimsiness of the basis of knowledge on which they depend. It is these opinions taken in conjunction with the rate of interest which fix their price.

Now for stage three. Capital-assets are capable, in general, of being newly produced. The scale on which they are produced depends, of course, on the relation between their costs of production and the prices which they are expected to realize in the market. Thus if the level of the rate of interest taken in conjunction with opinions about their prospective

218   *QUARTERLY JOURNAL OF ECONOMICS*

yield raise the prices of capital-assets, the volume of current investment (meaning by this the value of the output of newly produced capital-assets) will be increased; while if, on the other hand, these influences reduce the prices of capital-assets, the volume of current investment will be diminished.

It is not surprising that the volume of investment, thus determined, should fluctuate widely from time to time. For it depends on two sets of judgments about the future, neither of which rests on an adequate or secure foundation — on the propensity to hoard and on opinions of the future yield of capital-assets. Nor is there any reason to suppose that the fluctuations in one of these factors will tend to offset the fluctuations in the other. When a more pessimistic view is taken about future yields, that is no reason why there should be a diminished propensity to hoard. Indeed, the conditions which aggravate the one factor tend, as a rule, to aggravate the other. For the same circumstances which lead to pessimistic views about future yields are apt to increase the propensity to hoard. The only element of self-righting in the system arises at a much later stage and in an uncertain degree. If a decline in investment leads to a decline in output as a whole, this may result (for more reasons than one) in a reduction of the amount of money required for the active circulation, which will release a larger quantity of money for the inactive circulation, which will satisfy the propensity to hoard at a lower level of the rate of interest, which will raise the prices of capital-assets, which will increase the scale of investment, which will restore in some measure the level of output as a whole.

This completes the first chapter of the argument, namely, the liability of the scale of investment to fluctuate for reasons quite distinct (*a*) from those which determine the propensity of the individual to *save* out of a given income and (*b*) from those physical conditions of technical capacity to aid production which have usually been supposed hitherto to be the chief influence governing the marginal efficiency of capital.

If, on the other hand, our knowledge of the future was calculable and not subject to sudden changes, it might be justifiable to assume that the liquidity-preference curve was both stable and very inelastic. In this case a small decline in money-income would lead to a large fall in the rate of interest, probably sufficient to raise output and employment to the full.[3] In these conditions we might reasonably suppose that the whole of the available resources would normally be employed; and the conditions required by the orthodox theory would be satisfied.

III

My next difference from the traditional theory concerns its apparent conviction that there is no necessity to work out a theory of the demand and supply of output *as a whole*. Will a fluctuation in investment, arising for the reasons just described, have any effect on the demand for output as a whole, and consequently on the scale of output and employment? What answer can the traditional theory make to this question? I believe that it makes no answer at all, never having given the matter a single thought; the theory of effective demand, that is the demand for output as a whole, having been entirely neglected for more than a hundred years.

My own answer to this question involves fresh considerations. I say that effective demand is made up of two items — investment-expenditure determined in the manner just explained and consumption-expenditure. Now what governs the amount of consumption-expenditure? It depends mainly on the level of income. People's propensity to spend (as I call it) is influenced by many factors such as the distribution of income, their normal attitude to the future and — tho probably in a minor degree — by the rate of interest. But in the main the prevailing psychological law seems to be that when aggregate income increases, consumption-expenditure will also increase but to a somewhat lesser extent. This is a very obvious conclusion. It simply amounts to saying that

3. When Professor Viner charges me with assigning to liquidity-preference "a grossly exaggerated importance," he must mean that I exaggerate its instability and its elasticity. But if he is right, a small decline in money-income would lead, as stated above, to a large fall in the rate of interest. I claim that experience indicates the contrary.

220   *QUARTERLY JOURNAL OF ECONOMICS*

an increase in income will be divided in some proportion or
another between spending and saving, and that when our
income is increased it is extremely unlikely that this will have
the effect of making us either spend less or save less than
before. This psychological law was of the utmost importance
in the development of my own thought, and it is, I think,
absolutely fundamental to the theory of effective demand as
set forth in my book. But few critics or commentators so far
have paid particular attention to it.

There follows from this extremely obvious principle an
important, yet unfamiliar, conclusion. Incomes are created
partly by entrepreneurs producing for investment and partly
by their producing for consumption. The amount that is consumed depends on the amount of income thus made up.
Hence the amount of consumption-goods which it will pay
entrepreneurs to produce depends on the amount of investment-goods which they are producing. If, for example, the
public are in the habit of spending nine-tenths of their income
on consumption-goods, it follows that if entrepreneurs were
to produce consumption-goods at a cost more than nine times
the cost of the investment-goods they are producing, some
part of their output could not be sold at a price which would
cover its cost of production. For the consumption-goods on
the market would have cost more than nine-tenths of the
aggregate income of the public and would therefore be in
excess of the demand for consumption-goods, which by
hypothesis is only the nine-tenths. Thus entrepreneurs will
make a loss until they contract their output of consumption-
goods down to an amount at which it no longer exceeds nine
times their current output of investment goods.

The formula is not, of course, quite so simple as in this
illustration. The proportion of their incomes which the public
will choose to consume will not be a constant one, and in the
most general case other factors are also relevant. But there is
always a formula, more or less of this kind, relating the output of consumption-goods which it pays to produce to the
output of investment-goods; and I have given attention to it
in my book under the name of the *Multiplier*. The fact that

an increase in consumption is apt in itself to stimulate this further investment merely fortifies the argument.

That the level of output of consumption-goods, which is profitable to the entrepreneur, should be related by a formula of this kind to the output of investment-goods depends on assumptions of a simple and obvious character. The conclusion appears to me to be quite beyond dispute. Yet the consequences which follow from it are at the same time unfamiliar and of the greatest possible importance.

The theory can be summed up by saying that, given the psychology of the public, the level of output and employment as a whole depends on the amount of investment. I put it in this way, not because this is the only factor on which aggregate output depends, but because it is usual in a complex system to regard as the *causa causans* that factor which is most prone to sudden and wide fluctuation. More comprehensively, aggregate output depends on the propensity to hoard, on the policy of the monetary authority as it affects the quantity of money, on the state of confidence concerning the prospective yield of capital-assets, on the propensity to spend and on the social factors which influence the level of the money-wage. But of these several factors it is those which determine the rate of investment which are most unreliable, since it is they which are influenced by our views of the future about which we know so little.

This that I offer is, therefore, a theory of why output and employment are so liable to fluctuation. It does not offer a ready-made remedy as to how to avoid these fluctuations and to maintain output at a steady optimum level. But it is, properly speaking, a Theory of Employment because it explains *why*, in any given circumstances, employment is what it is. Naturally I am interested not only in the diagnosis, but also in the cure; and many pages of my book are devoted to the latter. But I consider that my suggestions for a cure, which, avowedly, are not worked out completely, are on a different plane from the diagnosis. They are not meant to be definitive; they are subject to all sorts of special assumptions and are necessarily related to the particular

conditions of the time. But my main reasons for departing
from the traditional theory go much deeper than this. They
are of a highly general character and are meant to be definitive.

I sum up, therefore, the main grounds of my departure as
follows:

(1) The orthodox theory assumes that we have a knowledge of the future of a kind quite different from that which
we actually possess. This false rationalization follows the
lines of the Benthamite calculus. The hypothesis of a calculable future leads to a wrong interpretation of the principles of behavior which the need for action compels us to
adopt, and to an underestimation of the concealed factors of
utter doubt, precariousness, hope and fear. The result has
been a mistaken theory of the rate of interest. It is true that
the necessity of equalizing the advantages of the choice
between owning loans and assets requires that the rate of
interest should be *equal* to the marginal efficiency of capital.
But this does not tell us at what *level* the equality will be
effective. The orthodox theory regards the marginal efficiency of capital as setting the pace. But the marginal
efficiency of capital depends on the price of capital-assets;
and since this price determines the rate of new investment, it
is consistent in equilibrium with only one given level of
money-income. Thus the marginal efficiency of capital is not
determined, unless the level of money-income is given. In a
system in which the level of money-income is capable of
fluctuating, the orthodox theory is one equation short of
what is required to give a solution. Undoubtedly the reason
why the orthodox system has failed to discover this dis-
crepancy is because it has always tacitly assumed that
income *is* given, namely, at the level corresponding to the
employment of all the available resources. In other words it
is tacitly assuming that the monetary policy is such as to
maintain the rate of interest at that level which is compatible
with full employment. It is, therefore, incapable of dealing
with the general case where employment is liable to fluctuate.
Thus, instead of the marginal efficiency of capital determin-

ing the rate of interest, it is truer (tho not a full statement of the case) to say that it is the rate of interest which determines the marginal efficiency of capital.

(2) The orthodox theory would by now have discovere' the above defect, if it had not ignored the need for a theor of the supply and demand of output as a whole. I doubt many modern economists really accept Say's Law that supp creates its own demand. But they have not been aware tha they were tacitly assuming it. Thus the psychological la; underlying the Multiplier has escaped notice. It has no been observed that the amount of consumption-goods whic' it pays entrepreneurs to produce is a function of the amoun of investment-goods which it pays them to produce. The explanation is to be found, I suppose, in the tacit assumptio: that every individual spends the whole of his income eithe on consumption or on buying, directly or indirectly, new' produced capital goods. But, here again, whilst the old economists expressly believed this, I doubt if many cc temporary economists really do believe it. They have d carded these older ideas without becoming aware of i consequences.

J. M. KEYNES.

KING'S COLLEGE, CAMBRIDGE

[2]

JOHN HICKS

IS-LM: an explanation

The *IS-LM* diagram, which is widely, but not universally, accepted as a convenient synopsis of Keynesian theory, is a thing for which I cannot deny that I have some responsibility. It first saw the light in a paper of my own, "Mr. Keynes and the Classics" (1937), but it was actually written for a meeting of the Econometric Society in Oxford in September 1936, just eight months after the publication of *The General Theory* (Keynes, 1936). (There I used different lettering but here I keep that which has become conventional.) And this is not my only connection with it; I also made use of it in some chapters (11-12) of my book *The Trade Cycle* (1950), and again in a paper which appears as "The Classics Again" in my *Critical Essays* (1967).[1] I have, however, not concealed that, as time has gone on, I have myself become dissatisfied with it. I said, in my contribution to the Festschrift for Georgescu-Roegen, that "that diagram is now much less popular with me than I think it still is with many other people" (1976, p. 140-1). In the reconstruction of Keynesian theory which I published at about the same time (1974), it is not to be found. But I have not explained the reasons for this change of opinion, or of attitude. I shall try, in this article, to do so.

The author is a Nobel Laureate in Economics and Professor Emeritus, Oxford University. This article was originally written for presentation to the Marshall Society in Cambridge, England, in November 1979 and repeated at a symposium at the European University Institute, Florence, Italy, in May 1980. It has undergone considerable changes between, and since, these presentations as a result of the discussions that took place on those occasions, and for other reasons.

[1] The date of this latter paper is really 1958, when it appeared, in an earlier version, in the *Economic Journal* as a review of Patinkin. I still believe that the use I made of *IS-LM* in that paper is perfectly legitimate. I am much less sure about the version in *The Trade Cycle* (1950).

140   JOURNAL OF POST KEYNESIAN ECONOMICS

I

I must begin with the old story. "Mr. Keynes and the Classics" was actually the fourth of the relevant papers which I wrote during those years. The third was the review of *The General Theory* that I wrote for the *Economic Journal*, a first impression which had to be written under pressure of time, almost at once on first reading of the book. But there were two others that I had written before I saw *The General Theory*. One is well known, my "Suggestion for Simplifying the Theory of Money" (1935*a*), which was written before the end of 1934. The other, much less well known, is even more relevant. "Wages and Interest: the Dynamic Problem"[2] was a first sketch of what was to become the "dynamic" model of *Value and Capital* (1939). It is important here, because it shows (I think quite conclusively) that that model was already in my mind before I wrote even the first of my papers on Keynes.

I recognized immediately, as soon as I read *The General Theory*, that my model and Keynes' had some things in common. Both of us fixed our attention on the behavior of an economy *during a period*—a period that had a past, which nothing that was done during the period could alter, and a future, which during the period was unknown. Expectations of the future would nevertheless affect what happened during the period. Neither of us made any assumption about "rational expectations"; expectations, in our models, were strictly exogenous.[3] (Keynes made much more fuss over that than I did, but there is the same implication in my model also.) Subject to these *data*—the given equipment carried over from the past, the production possibilities within the period, the preference schedules, and the given expectations—the actual performance of the economy within the period was supposed to

[2] See Hicks (1935*b*). The paper is reprinted in the supplement which was added to the second edition of my *Theory of Wages* (1963).

[3] It is true that when I came to "Mr. Keynes and the Classics" I did propose to make investment depend on current output (just as Kaldor was to do, three years later, in his "Model of the Trade Cycle" [1940]). But I have never regarded this as an essential part of the *IS-LM* construction. I have fully accepted, in later work, that a capital stock adjustment principle, or some equivalent, is a better expression of what one had in mind. But whatever view one takes about this, it is still the case that it has never been intended, in any of the versions for which I am responsible, that investment changes should be entirely explicable by changes in output, of whatever sort. Even in my *Trade Cycle* book (1950), there was autonomous investment. There was always a residual element, depending on expectations, and many other things, which could vary independently.

be determined, or determinable. It would be determined as an equilibrium performance, with respect to these data.

There was all this in common between my model and Keynes'; it was enough to make me recognize, as soon as I saw *The General Theory*, that his model was a relation of mine and, as such, one which I could warmly welcome. There were, however, two differences, on which (as we shall see) much depends.

The more obvious difference was that mine was a flexprice model, a perfect competition model, in which all prices were flexible, while in Keynes' the level of money wages (at least) was exogenously determined. So Keynes' was a model that was consistent with unemployment, while mine, in his terms, was a full employment model. I shall have much to say about this difference, but I may as well note, at the start, that I do not think it matters much. I did not think, even in 1936, that it mattered much. *IS-LM* was in fact a translation of Keynes' nonflexprice model into my terms. It seemed to me already that that could be done; but how it is done requires explanation.

The other difference is more fundamental; it concerns the length of the *period*. Keynes' (he said) was a "short-period," a term with connotations derived from Marshall; we shall not go far wrong if we think of it as a year. Mine was an "ultra-short-period": I called it a week. Much more can happen in a year than in a week; Keynes has to allow for quite a lot of things to happen. I wanted to avoid so much happening, so that my (flexprice) markets could reflect propensities (and expectations) as they are at a moment. So it was that I made my markets open only on a Monday; what actually happened during the ensuing week was not to affect them. This was a very artificial device, not (I would think now) much to be recommended. But the point of it was to exclude the things which might happen, and must disturb the markets, during a period of finite length; and this, as we shall see, is a very real trouble in Keynes.

In the rest of this article, I shall take these two issues separately, beginning with the fixprice-flexprice question, which is the easier.

II

It will readily be understood, in the light of what I have been saying, that the idea of the *IS-LM* diagram came to me as a result of the work I had been doing on three-way exchange, conceived in a

142   JOURNAL OF POST KEYNESIAN ECONOMICS

Walrasian manner. I had already found a way of representing three-way exchange on a two-dimensional diagram (to appear in due course in chapter 5 of *Value and Capital*). As it appears there, it is a piece of statics; but it was essential to my approach (as already appears in "Wages and Interest: the Dynamic Problem") that static analysis of this sort could be carried over to "dynamics" by redefinition of terms. So it was natural for me to think that a similar device could be used for the Keynes theory.

Keynes had three elements in his theory: the marginal efficiency of capital, the consumption function, and liquidity preference. The market for goods, the market for bonds, and the market for money: could they not be regarded in my manner as a model of three-way exchange? In my three-way exchange I had two independent price parameters: the price of A in terms of C and the price of B in terms of C (for the price of A in terms of B followed from them). These two parameters were determined by the equilibrium of two markets, the market for A and the market for B. If these two markets were in equilibrium, the third must be also.

Keynes also appeared to have two parameters—his Y (income *in terms of wage units*) and r, the rate of interest. He made investment depend on r and saving on Y; so for each value of r there should be a value of Y which would keep saving equal to investment—excess demand on the market for goods then being zero. This gave a relation between r and Y which I expressed as the *IS* curve. The demand for money depended on Y (transactions balances) and on r (liquidity preference). So for any given supply of money (*in terms of wage units*) there should be a relation between r and Y which would keep the money "market" in equilibrium. One did not have to bother about the market for "loanable funds," since it appeared, on the Walras analogy, that if these two "markets" were in equilibrium, the third must be also. So I concluded that the intersection of *IS* and *LM* determined the equilibrium of the system as a whole.

Now this was really, at that stage, no more than a conjecture, for I had not properly shown that the Walras analogy would fit. In Walras, all markets are cleared; but in *IS-LM* (following Keynes) the labor market is not cleared; there is excess supply of labor. Does this, by itself, upset the Walras model? I think that by now it is generally accepted that it does not. It will nevertheless be useful, for what follows, to check the matter over in detail.

In strictness, we now need four markets, since labor and goods will have to be distinguished. But before giving them those names, let us look at the matter in terms of a general Walrasian four-goods model.

We then say that commodities A, B, C, and X are being traded, with X as standard (*numéraire*). Prices p_a, p_b, p_c are reckoned in terms of the standard; $p_x = 1$. Demands and supplies on the ABC markets are functions of the three prices. The three equations $S_a = D_a$ and so on are sufficient to determine the three prices. Further, since

$$S_x = p_a D_a + p_b D_b + p_c D_c, D_x = p_a S_a + p_b S_b + p_c S_c,$$

when the supply and demand equations are satisfied for ABC, that for X follows automatically.

There is just this one identical relation between the four equations. We could use it to eliminate the X equation, as just shown, or to eliminate any one of the other equations, while retaining the X equation. Thus the system of three prices for ABC can be regarded as determined by equations for ABC, or by equations for BCX, CAX, or ABX.

Thus far Walras. But now suppose that one of the commodities is sold on a fixprice market, where the price is fixed in terms of the standard, but where the equation of supply and demand does not have to hold. The actual amount sold will be equal to the demand or to the supply, whichever is the lower. So let p_a be fixed, with the equation $D_a = S_a$ removed. The remaining (variable) prices can still be determined from the equations $S_b = D_b$, $S_c = D_c$, for the p_a which appears as a parameter in these equations is now a constant. If it turns out that at these prices $S_a > D_a$, it is only D_a that can actually be traded. When calculating S_x and D_x, we must use this *actual* D_a for both D_a and S_a. With that substitution, we have $S_x = D_x$, as before.

And it is still possible, using this construction, to let the equation for the standard, $S_x = D_x$, replace one of the equations otherwise used, as could be done in the all-round flexprice case. For with D_a substituted for S_a, $p_a(S_a - D_a) = 0$ is an identity. The only terms in $S_x - D_x$ that survive, on application of this identity, are those which relate to the flexprice commodities B and C. The subsystem of BCX will then work in the regular Walrasian manner. We can determine p_b and p_c from any pair of the three equations that are left.

In this way, the Walrasian analogy gets over its first hurdle; but there is another, close behind it, which may be considered more serious. We have so far been making demands and supplies depend only on prices; and for the pure case of multiple exchange with flexible prices, that may probably be accepted. But as soon as a fixprice market is introduced, it ceases to be acceptable. It must be supposed that the demands and supplies for B and C will be affected by what happens in the market for A. That can no longer be represented by the price, so it must be represented by the quantity sold. Assuming, as before, that there is excess supply in the A market, this is D_a. So demands and supplies for B and C will be functions of p_b, p_c, and D_a. The BCX subsystem would then *not* be complete in itself; but the whole system, with D_a included as a parameter, would still work in the way that has been described.

We would then have three variables to be determined, p_b, p_c, and D_a—and four equations. They are the demand-supply equations for BCX (the X equation being constructed with the *actual* D_a, as before); and there is also the demand equation for D_a, which makes D_a a function of p_b and p_c. As before, any one of the BCX equations can be eliminated. The system is determined, whichever equation we choose to eliminate.

The model is still very formal; but now it is the same kind of model as the *IS-LM* model. We could represent that as a three-way (ABX) model, in which there is just one price (p_b, which becomes the rate of interest) that is determined on a flexprice market, and one quantity (Y) which plays the part of D_a. I have deliberately taken a case which in the same formal terms is slightly more complicated, since I have admitted two flexprice markets, for B and for C. It may indeed be useful to show that there is, in principle, no difficulty in introducing a second flexprice market—or, for that matter, introducing several. It could be useful, even for macroeconomic purposes, to introduce a second flexprice market —for instance, a market for foreign exchange.

But that is not the reason I have introduced the extra market. The important use of a four-way model, in this connection, is that it enables us to consider the market for goods and the market for labor separately. And when we take them separately, quite interesting things happen.

One could construct a model in which only the market for labor was a fixprice market, and not only the rate of interest but also the price (or price level) of finished products was flexible. That would fit very exactly into the scheme which has just been outlined, with demand-supply equations determining D_a (employment) and the two flexible prices p_b, p_c. It is possible that Keynes himself sometimes thought in terms of that sort of model (see, for example, Keynes, 1936, ch. 21); but it cannot be this which *IS-LM* is supposed to represent. For Y is taken to be an index not only of employment, but also of output, so the prices of products also are supposed to be fixed in terms of the standard; and it is hard to see how that can be justified unless the prices of products are derived from the wage of labor by some markup rule. But if that is so, we have not one, but two, fixprice markets.

Say that A and B are fixprice markets, while C is flexprice. As long as we follow the Walrasian practice of working entirely in terms of price parameters, there is no trouble. p_a and p_b are then fixed, so that all demands and supplies are functions of the single variable p_c. p_c is determined on the market for C (or, equivalently, on the market for X) as before. And the actual amounts of A and B that are traded are D_a or S_a, D_b or S_b —whichever, at the equilibrium p_c, turns out to be the lower.

But now suppose that, as before, we change the parameters, making demands and supplies functions of D_a and D_b (assuming that there is excess supply in both markets), not of p_c only. One would at first say that at a (provisionally given) p_c, D_a would be a function of D_b and D_b of D_a; and there need be nothing circular about that. There are just these two "curves" in the $(D_a D_b)$ plane (like supply and demand curves); at their intersection, the equilibrium is determined.

It must be this which, in the *IS-LM* model, is supposed to happen. We are now to take A to be the labor market, C the market for loanable funds (as before), and B the market for finished products (consumption goods and investment goods not being, so far, distinguished). p_a is the fixed money wage; p_b, the fixed price level of the finished products; p_c, the rate of interest, the only price that is left to be determined on a flexprice market.

How, then, do we identify the "curves"? One, which makes D_b (effective demand for products) a function of D_a (employment) is easy to find in Keynes. D_b depends on D_a, since the consumption component of D_b increases when employment increases (the consumption function), while the investment component depends on the rate of interest, provisionally given. There is no trouble about that. But what of the other "curve"—the dependence of D_a on D_b, of employment on effective demand? Keynes took it for

146   JOURNAL OF POST KEYNESIAN ECONOMICS

granted that they must go together, but the matter needs looking into. For it is here that there is a danger of going seriously wrong by neglecting time.

III

It is not true, of course, that time has been wholly neglected. As I said at the beginning, all the prices and quantities that have figured in the analysis must belong to a period; the past (before the period) and the future (beyond the period) have always been playing their regular parts. What has been neglected is the flow of time within the period. It is here that the length of the period is important.

In my own version ("Wages and Interest: the Dynamic Problem" or *Value and Capital*), the period ("week") was kept very short, so that little could happen within it. The actual outputs of products and (probably also) the actual input of labor would be largely pre-determined. What could vary, considerably, would be prices. So for the study of price formation on flexprice markets, the "week" had something to be said for it.[4] But that was not what Keynes was interested in; so he had to have a longer period.

It is not unreasonable to suppose that the prices which are established in flexprice markets, during a "week" (or even at a point of time) do reflect the expectations of traders, their liquidity positions, and so on. That is to say (it is equivalent to saying), we may fairly reckon that these markets, with respect to these data, are in equilibrium. And one could go on, as we have in fact been seeing, even while maintaining the "week" interpretation, to admit that there are some markets which are fixprice markets, in which demands and supplies do not have to be equal. Then it is only to the markets which are flexprice markets that the equilibrium rule applies. Now it would be quite hard to say, in terms of such a model, that effective demand would determine employment. It is so tempting to say that there can be no output without labor input, so that an increase in demand must increase employment (as Keynes effectively did). But the question is not one of the relation between input and output, in general; it is a question of the rela-

---

[4] No more than something. I have myself become pretty critical of the *Value and Capital* temporary equilibrium method when applied to flow markets. (I do not question its validity for the analysis of markets in stocks.) See chapter 6 of my *Capital and Growth* (1965).

tion between current demand and current input, both in the current period. It is at once shown, on the "week" interpretation, that current output is largely predetermined; while, if the price of output is fixed, current demand may be greater or less than current output (stocks being decumulated or accumulated). How, then, is current input to be determined? We can only make it determinate, as a function of current demand, if we can bring ourselves to introduce some *rule*, according to which the extent of excess demand (or supply) in the current period will affect the employment that is offered, again in the current period. If we have such a rule, we can complete the circle, and show, in the current period, effective demand and employment simultaneously determined.

It is quite a question whether we would be justified, in general, in imposing such a rule.[5] For the effect on current input of excess demand or supply in the product market is surely a matter of the way in which the excess is interpreted by decision makers. An excess which is expected to be quite temporary may have no effect on input; it is not only the current excess but the expectation of its future which determines action. It may be useful, on occasion, to suspend these doubts, and so to make models in which current input depends on excess demands (or supplies) in the product markets according to some rule. But one can hardly get a plausible rule while confining attention to what happens within a single period. So it would seem that the proper place for such a proceeding is in sequential models, composed of a succession of periods, in each of which the relevant parameters have to be determined; there is then room for linkages between the periods, and so for lags. I have myself made some attempts at the construction of such models.[6] I think they have their uses, but they are not much like *IS-LM*.

If one is to make sense of the *IS-LM* model, while paying proper attention to time, one must, I think, insist on two things: (1) that the period in question is a relatively long period, a "year" rather

---

[5] My mind goes back to a conversation I had, a few years ago, with a distinguished economist, who might at an earlier date have been reckoned to be a Keynesian. I was saying to him that I had come to regard J. S. Mill as the most undervalued economist of the nineteenth century. He said, "Yes, I think I understand. *Demand for commodities is not demand for labour.* It is true, after all."

[6] In particular, in *Capital and Growth* (1965, chs. 7-10).

148   *JOURNAL OF POST KEYNESIAN ECONOMICS*

than a "week"; and (2) that, because the behavior of the economy over that "year"[7] is to be *determined* by propensities, and such-like data, it must be assumed to be, in an appropriate sense, *in equilibrium*. This clearly must not imply that it is an all-round flexprice system; the exogenously fixed money wage, and (as we have seen) the exogenously fixed prices of products must still be retained. But it is not only the market for funds, but also the product market, which must be assumed to be in equilibrium.

Though the prices of products are fixed, it is not necessary to suppose that there is disequilibrium in the product market. Even at the fixed price and fixed wage, when these are maintained over the relatively long period, it will pay producers to adjust supply to demand, as far as they can. For a loss is incurred in producing output that cannot be sold, and a profit is forgone when output that could profitably be sold is not produced. There are problems of adjustment, of which sequential analysis can take account; but there may be purposes for which it is legitimate to leave them to one side. We should then assume that the product markets, during the "year," are in equilibrium and remain in equilibrium. And since it is to be continuing equilibrium, maintained throughout the "year," this must mean that plans (so far as they relate to the proceedings of the year) are being carried through without being disturbed.

It is not, I think, inconsistent to suppose that the product markets are in equilibrium, while the labor market is not in equilibrium. For although there are some possibilities for adjusting supply to demand in the case of unemployment on the labor market (even while prices and wages remain unchanged), as by withdrawal of elderly labor from the market, or by departure of migrants, they are surely less than the corresponding possibilities in the market for products. A model which permits excess supply in the labor market, but no product market disequilibrium, is not inconsistent.

Once we allow ourselves to assume that product markets remain in equilibrium, things become easier. For once we assume that production plans, during the period, are carried through consistently, we have the relation between current input, during the period, and current output, during the period (which has been made equal to effective demand within the period) for which we have been looking. There are some difficulties about production processes which

---

[7] The *year* must clearly be long enough for the firm to be "free to revise its decisions as to how much employment to offer" (Keynes, 1936, p. 47, n. 1).

were begun before the commencement of the period, and others which will not be completed at the end of the period, but these, perhaps, may be overlooked. We can then proceed to the two "curves" in the (D_aD_b) plane, by which employment and effective demand are simultaneously determined.

The goal is reached, but at a considerable price. For how, after all, can this equilibrium assumption be justified? I do not think it can be justified for all purposes, maybe not for the most important purposes; but I have come to think that there is one purpose for which it may sometimes be justified. I have described this purpose in chapter 6 of my book *Causality in Economics* (1979); an abstract of the argument of that chapter may be given here.

We are to confine attention to the problem of explaining the past, a less exacting application than prediction of what will happen or prescription of what should happen, but surely one that comes first. If we are unable to explain the past, what right have we to attempt to predict the future? I find that concentration on explanation of the past is quite illuminating.

We have, then, facts before us; we know or can find out what, in terms of the things in which we are interested, did actually happen in some past year (say, the year 1975). In order to explain what happened, we must confront these facts with what we think would have happened if something (some alleged cause) had been different. About that, since it did not happen, we can have no factual information; we can only deduce it with the aid of a theory, or model. And since the theory is to tell us what would have happened, the variables in the model must be determined. And that would seem to mean that the model, in some sense, must be in equilibrium.

Applying these notions to the *IS-LM* construction, it is only the point of intersection of the curves which makes any claim to representing what actually happened (in our "1975"). Other points on either of the curves—say, the *IS* curve—surely do not represent, make no claim to represent, what actually happened. They are theoretical constructions, which are supposed to indicate what *would have happened* if the rate of interest had been different. It does not seem farfetched to suppose that these positions are equilibrium positions, representing the equilibrium which corresponds to a different rate of interest. If we cannot take them to be equilibrium positions, we cannot say much about them. But, as the diagram is drawn, the *IS* curve passes through the point of inter-

150   JOURNAL OF POST KEYNESIAN ECONOMICS

section; so the point of intersection appears to be a point on the curve; thus it also is an equilibrium position. That, surely, is quite hard to take. We know that in 1975 the system was not in equilibrium. There were plans which failed to be carried through as intended; there were surprises. We have to suppose that, for the purpose of the analysis on which we are engaged, these things do not matter. It is sufficient to treat the economy, as it actually was in the year in question, as if it were in equilibrium. Or, what is perhaps equivalent, it is permissible to regard the departures from equilibrium, which we admit to have existed, as being random. There are plenty of instances in applied economics, not only in the application of *IS-LM* analysis, where we are accustomed to permitting ourselves this way out. But it is dangerous. Though there may well have been some periods of history, some "years," for which it is quite acceptable, it is just at the turning points, at the most interesting "years," where it is hardest to accept it.

What I have been saying applies, most directly, to the *IS* curve; what of the other?

In elementary presentations of the *IS-LM* model, the *LM* curve is supposed to be drawn up on the assumption of a given stock of money (the extension to a stock of money given in terms of wage units comes in only when the level of money wages is allowed to vary, so I shall leave it to one side). It is, however, unnecessary to raise those puzzling questions of the definition of money, which in these monetarist days have become so pressing. For I may allow myself to point out that it was already observed in "Mr. Keynes and the Classics" that we do not need to suppose that the curve is drawn up on the assumption of a given stock of money. It is sufficient to suppose that there is (as I said)

> a given monetary system—that up to a point, but only up to a point, monetary authorities will prefer to create new money rather than allow interest rates to rise. Such a generalised (*LM*) curve will then slope upwards only gradually—the elasticity of the curve depending on the elasticity of the monetary system (in the ordinary monetary sense). (p. 157)[8]

That is good as far as it goes, but it does not go far enough. For here, again, there is a question of time reference; and it is a very tricky question. The relation which is expressed in the *IS* curve is a flow relation, which (as we have seen) must refer to a period, such as the year we have been discussing. But the relation expressed in

[8] In the reprint of this paper in my *Critical Essays* (1967), the passage appears on p. 140.

tne *LM* curve is, or should be, a stock relation, a balance-sheet relation (as Keynes so rightly insisted). It must therefore refer to a point of time, not to a period. How are the two to be fitted together?

It might appear, at first sight, that we must proceed by converting the stock relation into a relation which is to hold for the period—treating it, in some way, as an average of balance-sheet relations over the period. But this has to be rejected, not merely because it is clumsy, but because it does not get to the point. It has been shown that, if we adopt the equilibrium interpretation, on the *IS* side, the economy must be treated *as if* it were in equilibrium over the period; that means, on the *IS* side, that the economy must remain in flow equilibrium, with demands and supplies for the flows of outputs remaining in balance. It would be logical to maintain that on the *LM* side the economy must be treated similarly. There must be a *maintenance* of stock equilibrium.

I have examined the relation between stock equilibrium and flow equilibrium in chapter 8 of my *Capital and Growth* (1965), where I have shown that the maintenance of stock equilibrium over the period implies the maintenance of flow equilibrium over the period; so it is a sufficient condition for the maintenance of equilibrium over time, in the fullest sense. A key passage is the following:

> Equilibrium over time requires the maintenance of stock equilibrium; this should be interpreted as meaning that there is stock equilibrium, not only at the beginning and end of the period, but throughout its course. Thus when we regard a "long" period as a sequence of "short" periods, the "long" period can only be in equilibrium over time if every "short" period within it is in equilibrium over time. Expectations must be kept self-consistent; so there can be no revision of expectations at the junction between one "short" period and its successor. The system is in stock equilibrium at each of these junctions; and is in stock equilibrium with respect to these consistent expectations. That can only be possible if expectations—with respect to demands that accrue within the "long" period—are *right*. Equilibrium over time thus implies consistency between expectations and realisations within the period. It is only expectations of the further future that are arbitrary (exogenous) as they must be. (pp. 92-93)[9]

That is the formal concept of full equilibrium over time; I do

---

[9] I have made a few minor alterations in wording to make it possible to extract the passage quoted from the rest of the chapter.

not see how it is to be avoided. But for the purpose of generating an *LM* curve, which is to represent liquidity preference, it will not do without amendment. For there is no sense in liquidity, unless expectations are uncertain. But how is an uncertain expectation to be realized? When the moment arrives to which the expectation refers, what replaces it is fact, fact which is not uncertain.

I have suggested, in my most recent book (1979), a way of cutting the knot, but I do not have much faith in it.

> We must evidently refrain from supposing that the expectations as they were before April (some date in the middle of the "year") of what is to happen after April, were precise expectations, single-valued expectations; for in a model with single-valued expectations, there can be no question of liquidity. And we must also refrain from the conventional representation of uncertain expectations in terms of mean and variance, since that makes them different in kind from the experiences which are to replace them. There is, however, a third alternative. Suppose we make them expectations that the values that are expected, of the variables affecting decisions, will fall within a particular range. This leaves room for liquidity, since there are no certain expectations of what is going to happen; but it also makes it possible for there to be an equilibrium, in the sense that what happens falls within the expected range. A state of equilibrium is a state in which there are no surprises. What happens (during the period) falls sufficiently within the range of what is expected for no revision of expectations to be necessary (p. 85).

As far as I can see, that is the only concept of equilibrium over time[10] which leaves room for liquidity.

IV

I accordingly conclude that the only way in which *IS-LM* analysis usefully survives—as anything more than a classroom gadget, to be superseded, later on, by something better—is in application to a particular kind of causal analysis, where the use of equilibrium methods, even a drastic use of equilibrium methods, is not inappropriate. I have deliberately interpreted the equilibrium concept, to be used in such analysis, in a very stringent manner (some would say a pedantic manner) not because I want to tell the applied economist, who uses such methods, that he is in fact committing himself to anything which must appear to him to be so

[10] I should here make an acknowledgement to G. L. S. Shackle, who in much of his work has been feeling in this direction.

ridiculous, but because I want to ask him to try to assure himself that the divergences between reality and the theoretical model, which he is using to explain it, are no more than divergences which he is entitled to overlook. I am quite prepared to believe that there are cases where he is entitled to overlook them. But the issue is one which needs to be faced in each case.

When one turns to questions of policy, looking toward the future instead of the past, the use of equilibrium methods is still more suspect. For one cannot prescribe policy without considering at least the possibility that policy may be changed. There can be no change of policy if everything is to go on as expected—if the economy is to remain in what (however approximately) may be regarded as its *existing* equilibrium. It may be hoped that, after the change in policy, the economy will somehow, at some time in the future, settle into what may be regarded, in the same sense, as a new equilibrium; but there must necessarily be a stage before that equilibrium is reached. There must always be a problem of traverse. For the study of a traverse, one has to have recourse to sequential methods of one kind or another.[11]

[11] I have paid no attention, in this article, to another weakness of *IS-LM* analysis, of which I am fully aware; for it is a weakness which it shares with *The General Theory* itself. It is well known that in later developments of Keynesian theory, the long-term rate of interest (which does figure, excessively, in Keynes' own presentation and is presumably represented by the r of the diagram) has been taken down a peg from the position it appeared to occupy in Keynes. We now know that it is not enough to think of the rate of interest as the single link between the financial and industrial sectors of the economy; for that really implies that a borrower can borrow as much as he likes at the rate of interest charged, no attention being paid to the security offered. As soon as one attends to questions of security, and to the financial intermediation that arises out of them, it becomes apparent that the dichotomy between the two curves of the *IS-LM* diagram must not be pressed too hard.

The modern "post Keynesian" view of interest takes its origin from R. F. Kahn (1953). But I have done a good deal of work on it myself, in chapter 23 of *Capital and Growth* (1965), in lecture 3 of "The Two Triads" (1967), in the second chapter of *The Crisis in Keynesian Economics* (1974) and in the section on Keynes in *Economic Perspectives* (1977, pp. 77 ff).

REFERENCES

Hicks, J. R. *The Theory of Wages*. London: Macmillan, 1932; 2nd ed., 1963.

_____. "Suggestion for Simplifying the Theory of Money." *Economica*, 3. 1935. (*a*)

_____. "Wages and Interest: The Dynamic Problem." *Economic Journal*, 3. 1935. (*b*)

154   JOURNAL OF POST KEYNESIAN ECONOMICS

_____ "Mr. Keynes and the Classics." *Econometrica*, 5, 1937.

_____. *Value and Capital*. Oxford: Oxford University Press, 1939.

_____. *The Trade Cycle*. Oxford: Oxford University Press, 1950.

_____. *Capital and Growth*. Oxford: Oxford University Press, 1965.

_____. *Critical Essays in Monetary Theory*. Oxford: Oxford University Press, 1967.

_____. *The Crisis in Keynesian Economics*. New York: Basic Books, 1974.

_____. "Some Questions of Time in Economics." In *Evolution, Welfare and Time in Economics*, ed. by A. M. Tang et al. Lexington, Mass.: Lexington Books, 1976.

_____. *Economic Perspectives*. Oxford: Oxford University Press, 1977.

_____. *Causality in Economics*. New York: Basic Books, 1979.

Kaldor, N. "Model of the Trade Cycle." *Economic Journal*, 50, 1940.

Kahn, R. F. "Some Notes on Liquidity Preference." *Manchester School*, 1953.

Keynes, J. M. *The General Theory of Employment, Interest and Money*. New York: Harcourt Brace, 1936.

[3]

PAUL DAVIDSON

Reviving Keynes's revolution

Addressing *The General Theory* chiefly to his "fellow economists" (1936, p. v), Keynes insisted that

> the postulates of the classical theory are applicable to a special case only and not to the general case. . . . Moreover, the characteristics of the special case assumed by the classical theory happen not to be those of the economic society in which we actually live, with the result that its teaching is misleading and disastrous if we attempt to apply it to the facts of experience. (1936, p. 3)

Keynes (1936, p. 26) believed that he could *logically* demonstrate why "Say's Law . . . is not the true law relating the aggregate demand and supply functions" when we model an economy possessing real world characteristics; and until we get our theory to accurately mirror and apply to the "facts of experience," there is little hope of getting our policies right. That message is just as relevant today.

Keynes compared those economists whose theoretical logic was grounded in Say's Law to Euclidean geometers living in a non-Euclidean world,

> who discovering that in experience straight lines apparently parallel often meet, rebuke the lines for not keeping straight—as the only remedy for the unfortunate collisions which are taking place. Yet, in truth, there is no remedy except to throw over the axiom of parallels and to work out a non-Euclidean geometry. Something similar is required today in economics. (1936, p. 16)

To throw over an axiom is to reject what the faithful believe are "universal truths." The Keynesian revolution in economic theory was

The author is Professor of Economics, Rutgers University.

therefore truly a revolt since it aimed at rejecting basic mainstream tenets and substituting postulates which provide a logical foundation for a non–Say's Law model more closely related to the real world in which we happen to live. Unfortunately, since Keynes, mainstream macrotheorists, seduced by a technical methodology which promised precision and unique results at the expense of applicability and accuracy, have reintroduced more sophisticated forms of the very axioms Keynes rejected almost a half century ago. Consequently the Keynesian revolution was almost immediately shunted onto a wrong track as more obtuse versions of the axioms underlying a Say's Law world became the keystone of modern mainstream theory. Monetarists and the New Classical Economists, as well as Neoclassical Synthesis Keynesians, have reconstructed macrotheory by reintroducing the "universal truths" that Keynes struggled to overthrow.

The major neoclassical axioms rejected by Keynes in his revolutionary logical analysis were (1) *the axiom of gross substitution*, (2) *the axiom of reals*, and (3) *the axiom of an ergodic economic world*. The characteristics of the real world which Keynes believed could be modeled only by overthrowing these axioms are: (1) Money matters in the long and short run; i.e., money is not neutral—it affects real decision making.[1] (2) The economic system is moving through calendar time from an irrevocable past to an uncertain future. Important monetary time series realizations will be generated by nonergodic circumstances; hence decision making agents know that the future need not be predictable in any probability sense (see Davidson, 1982-83). (3) Forward contracts in money terms are a human institution developed to efficiently organize time consuming production and exchange processes (Davidson, 1980, p. 299). The money-wage contract is the most ubiquitous of these efficiency oriented contracts. Modern production economies are therefore on a money-wage contract based system. (4) Unemployment, rather than full employment, is a common *laissez-*

---

[1]Despite Friedman's use of the motto "money matters," he remains faithful to the axiom of reals (see below) and does not permit money to affect the long run real outcome of his system. In his own description of his logical framework, Friedman states:

> that changes in the quantity of money as such *in the long run* have a negligible effect on real income so that nonmonetary forces are "all that matter" for changes in real income over decades and money "does not matter". . . . I regard the description of our position as "money is all that matters for changes in *nominal income* and for *short-run* changes in real income" as an exaggeration but one that gives the right flavor to our conclusions. (Friedman, 1974, p. 27)

faire situation in a market oriented, monetary production economy.
  Only the Monetarists and the New Classical Theorists (like Ricardo)

> offer us the supreme intellectual achievement, unattainable by weaker
> spirits, of adopting a hypothetical world remote from experience as
> though it was the world of experience and then living in it consistently.
> With most of . . . [the Keynesians?] common sense cannot help breaking
> in—with injury to their logical consistency. (Keynes, 1936, pp. 192-193)

Spending, constrained demand, Say's Law and gross substitution

Keynes's *General Theory* is developed via an aggregate supply–aggregate demand function analysis which can be used to illustrate the
difference between Say's Law and Keynes's analytical structure
(Keynes, 1936, pp. 25-26).

  The aggregate supply function (Z) relates entrepreneurs' expected
sales proceeds with the level of employment (N) entrepreneurs will hire
for any volume of expected sales receipts. In Figure 1a this aggregate
supply (Z) function is drawn as upward sloping, indicating that the
higher entrepreneurs' sales expectations, the more workers they will
hire. The aggregate demand function relates buyers' desired expenditure flows for any given level of employment. In Figure 1b, the aggregate demand (D) function is drawn as upward sloping indicating that,
the greater the level of employment hire, the more buyers will spend on
goods and services.

  The aggregate supply and demand functions can be brought together
in a single quadrant to provide the equilibrium employment solution. In
Figure 2a the aggregate supply (Z) and aggregate demand (D) functions
are drawn as they would be developed in a Say's Law world where
supply creates its own demand. In a Say's Law world (as explained
below and as shown in Figure 2a), the aggregate supply and demand
functions are coincident throughout their entire length. Thus if at any
point of time the actual employment level is $N^a{}_1$, actual demand is
constrained to point G. Any coordinated expansion in hiring by entrepreneurs to provide additional output (say to point H in Figure 2a) will
increase actual demand concomitantly to point H and full employment
$(N^a{}_f)$ could be established. In a Say's Law world there is no obstacle to
full employment.

  In Figure 2b, on the other hand, the aggregate demand and supply
functions are distinguishable functions which intersect at a single

564   JOURNAL OF POST KEYNESIAN ECONOMICS

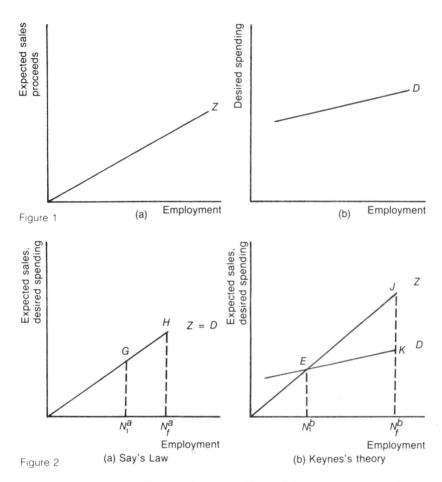

Figure 1   (a)   Employment   (b)   Employment

Figure 2   (a) Say's Law   (b) Keynes's theory

point, the point of *effective demand* (E); and in a manner consistent
with Keynes's theory (1936, p. 25) the equilibrium level of employment is N^b_1. At the full employment level (N^b_f in Figure 2b) there is a
deficiency in effective demand equal to the vertical distance *JK*, and
hence all of the full employment output cannot be profitably sold.

As defined by Keynes, Say's Law required that the aggregate supply
curve be coincident with the aggregate demand curve over its entire
length so that supply could create its own demand. Accordingly, *effective demand* "instead of having a unique equilibrium value, is an infinite range of values, all equally admissible" (Keynes, 1936, p. 26).
If, therefore, Say's Law prevails, then the economy is in neutral equilibrium where actual demand is *constrained* only by actual income
(supply). In other words, Say's Law requires that aggregate demand is
a *constrained demand function* (in the terminology of Clower, 1965,
or Barro and Grossman, 1976), and a "short-side of the market

rationing'' rule limits employment opportunities. This short-side rule is specifically adopted by Malinvaud (1977, pp. 12-35) to "explain" Keynesian unemployment. It has also been used by most of the "Keynesians" who have manned the Council of Economic Advisers under Democratic administrations to explain what their logical unconstrained model cannot.[2]

In the Clower–Leijonhufvud neoclassical synthesis version of the Keynesian system, which has been labeled the dual decision hypothesis with a coordination failure, purchasing decisions are always equal to, and constrained by, *actual* income (Clower, 1965). The economy is in neutral equilibrium at any level of actual income. There is no obstacle to full employment except that entrepreneurs do not receive a market signal that they would be able to profitably sell the full employment output if only they would coordinate and march together to the full employment hiring level. Unemployment is solely due to a "coordination failure" of the market system to signal entrepreneurs that, if they would only hire the full employment level of workers, actual income would equal *notional* (full employment) *income* and the spending decisions by income earners would be equal to, and constrained by, the full employment budget line and all markets would clear.[3] Hence, in contrast to Keynes (1936, pp. 30-31), these "Keynesians" argue that if only entrepreneurs would hire all workers there would never be an insufficiency of aggregate demand.

---

[2]These liberal Democratic Economic Advisers, however, have the difficulty that their logic is based on Say's Law, but their common sense tells them that unemployment is a problem which the system cannot solve without direct government interference. Thus they turned to *ad hoc* modifications of their neoclassical model—a short-side rule or a constrained demand function—to abrogate Say's Law and achieve a non-Walrasian equilibrium, at least in the short run.

[3]Since in this neoclassical world, engaging in a production process is assumed distasteful it would seem axiomatic that no agents would contribute to production unless they planned to spend all their income on producible goods. Consequently, full employment hiring decisions should always bring forth sufficient demand to buy all the products of industry.

This belief also underlies the rational expectations hypothesis via Lucas's aggregate supply analysis. Lucas believes there is no way of explaining real world unemployment patterns except via an analysis of intertemporal substitutability of labor by optimizing households (Lucas, 1983, p. 4). In order for households to achieve utility maximization solely in terms of the four arguments of Lucas's utility function— (1) today's consumption, (2) today's labor supply, (3) tomorrow's consumption, (4) tomorrow's labor supply—Lucas must assume that the intertemporal marginal propensity to spend on producible goods is unity. Say's Law therefore prevails by assumption. Unemployed workers are optimizing by preferring leisure today with rational expectations that they will get more real income per unit of effort tomorrow

Those who believe a short-side rule or constrained demand function limits employment opportunities should, if they follow their logic and not their common sense, support President Reagan's proposal for solving the unemployment problem. In the Spring of 1983 Reagan suggested that unemployment could be ended if each business firm in the nation immediately hired one more worker. Since there are more firms than unemployed workers, the solution is obviously statistically accurate—but unless the employment by each of these additional workers created a demand for the additional output at a profitable price (additional supply creating *pari passu* additional demand), it would not be profitable for entrepreneurs to hire additional workers.

Neoclassical Keynesians should applaud Reagan's clarion call for firms to coordinate increased hiring. If each firm does hire an additional worker so that full employment is (at least momentarily) achieved, then actual income flows earned would be equal to notional income and therefore aggregate demand would not be constrained short of full employment. There is no coordination failure—and no short-side rule limits job opportunities.

In a Keynes world, on the other hand, involuntary unemployment is due to an insufficiency or lack of effective demand (at full employment) as shown by the vertical distance *JK* in Figure 2b. The sales of the additional output produced by private sector entrepreneurs hiring workers above the N^b_1 level in Figure 2b cannot be profitable.

Keynes would never have endorsed Reagan's Say's Law solution to the unemployment problem. In a closed economy context, Keynes held that neither of the two private sector components of the aggregate demand function (D_1 and D_2 or aggregate consumption and investment spending) are constrained by actual income, although D_1 may be related to income earned! To put it bluntly and in its most irritating—thought provoking—form, the underlying axioms of Keynes's revolutionary theory of effective demand require that *the demand for goods produced by labor need never be constrained by income; spending is*

---

when they go back to work. Hence today's unemployed are not suffering any loss in permanent real welfare; i.e., the colliding lines that we observe are not really colliding—it is all apparently an optical illusion.

If, on the other hand, you believe, as Keynes did and Post Keynesian do, that today's unemployed know they are suffering a permanent loss in real well-being then you must throw off the classical axioms of gross substitution *and* the axiom of reals and enter the world of Keynes's non-Euclidean economics! In such a world, the desire to possess liquidity—liquid assets not producible by labor—is also an argument in any labor (factor owner) supply function.

constrained only by liquidity and/or timidity considerations. Thus the budget constraint, in a Keynes model, need never limit individual spending—or aggregate spending at less than full employment.

In the real world, planned spending need never be equal to, or constrained by, actual income as long as (a) agents who earn income by selling their labor (or goods produced by labor in the private sector) are not required to spend all of their earned income on goods produced by labor, and/or (b) agents who plan to spend on currently producible goods are not required to earn income (previously or concurrently) with their exercise of this demand (where by "demand" we mean "want" *plus the ability to pay*).

Hahn (1977, p. 31) has put point (a) as meaning that Say's Law is done away with and involuntary unemployment can occur whenever there are "resting places for savings in other than reproducible assets" so that all income earned by engaging in the production of goods is not, in the short or long run, spent on assets producible by labor. For savings to find such ultimate resting places, the axiom of gross substitution must be thrown over (see Davidson, 1980, pp. 303-305).

This axiom is the backbone of mainstream economics; it is the assumption that any good is a substitute for any other good. If the demand for good *x* goes up, its price will rise inducing demand to spill over to the now relatively cheaper substitute good *y*. For an economist to deny this "universal truth" is revolutionary heresy—and, as in the days of the Inquisition, the modern day College of Cardinals of mainstream economics destroys all nonbelievers—if not by burning them at the stake, then by banishment from the mainstream professional journals. Yet in Keynes's analysis (1936, Ch. 17) "The Essential Properties of Interest and Money" requires that the elasticity of substitution between all liquid assets including money (which are not reproducible by labor in the private sector) and producible (in the private sector) assets is zero or negligible. These properties which Keynes (1936, p. 241, n. 1) believed are *essential* to the concepts of money and liquidity necessitate that a basic axiom of Keynes's logical framework is that nonproducible assets that can be used to store savings are not gross substitutes for producible assets in savers' portfolios.

Instead, if the gross substitution axiom is true,[4] then even if savers

---

[4]Recent empirical work by Benjamin Friedman (1983) has demonstrated that the facts do not justify assuming gross substitutability among all assets in savers' portfolios.

attempt to use nonreproducible assets for storing their increments of wealth, this increase in demand will increase the price of non-producibles. This relative price rise in nonproducibles will, under the gross substitution axiom, induce savers to substitute reproducible durables for nonproducibles in their wealth holdings and therefore nonproducibles will not be ultimate resting places for savings (cf. Davidson, 1972, 1977, 1980). The gross substitution axiom therefore restores Say's Law and denies the logical possibility of involuntary unemployment.

In *Debate with His Critics*, Friedman could correctly attack Tobin and other Neoclassical Keynesians for logical inconsistencies involving "differences in the range of assets considered" as possible gross substitutes in savings portfolios. For Friedman the total spectrum of assets including "houses, automobiles, let alone furniture, household appliances, clothes and so on" (1974, p. 29) is eligible for savings. (After all in his *permanent income hypothesis*, Friedman deliberately defines savings to include the purchase of producible durable goods.) Thus, Friedman, in his logical world, remote from reality, can "prove" that savings does not create unemployment; for the Samuelsons, Tobins, and Solows of the world their common sense if not their logic tells them better.

To overthrow the axiom of gross substitution in an intertemporal context is truly heretical. It changes the entire perspective as to what is meant by "rational" or "optimal" savings, as to why people save or what they save. Recently Sir John Hicks noted that all Keynes needed to say was that income was divided between current consumption and a vague provision for the uncertain future. The mathematical assumption that "planned expenditures at specified different dates in the future have independent utilities [and are gross substitutes] . . . this assumption I find quite unacceptable. . . . the normal condition is that there is strong complementarity between them [consumption plans in successive periods]" (Hicks, 1979, pp. 76-77, n. 7). Indeed Danziger *et al.* (1982-83) have shown that the facts regarding consumption spending by the elderly are incompatible with the notion of intertemporal gross substitution of consumption plans which underlie both life cycle models and overlapping generation models currently so popular in mainstream macroeconomic theory.

In the absence of the axiom of gross substitution, income effects (e.g., the Keynesian multiplier) predominate and can swamp any hypothetical neoclassical substitution effects. Consequently, relative price changes via a flexible pricing mechanism will not be the cure-all "snake-oil" medicine usually recommended by many neoclassical doctors for the unfortunate economic maladies that are occurring in the real world.

Investment spending, liquidity, and the axiom of reals

Point (b) *supra* is that agents who planned to spend in the current period are not required to earn income currently or previously to their exercise of demand in the market. This implies that spending for D_2, the demand for fixed and working capital goods (or even consumer durables) reproducible by labor in the private sector, is constrained by neither actual income nor endowments. For Keynes, given animal spirits and not timidity on the part of entrepreneurs, D_2 is constrained solely by the *monetary*, and not the real, *expected return on liquid assets* (Keynes, 1936, Ch. 17). The rate of interest, which is strictly a monetary phenomenon in Keynes, rules the roost.

Keynes (1936, p. 142) believed that the "real rate of interest" concept of Irving Fisher was a logical confusion. In a monetary economy moving through calendar time towards an uncertain (statistically unpredictable) future there is no such thing as a forward looking real rate of interest. Moreover, money has an impact on the real sector in both the short and long run. Thus, money is a real phenomenon, while the rate of interest is a monetary phenomenon (cf. Kregel, 1983).

This is just the reverse of what classical theory and modern mainstream theory teaches us. In orthodox macrotheory the rate of interest is a real (technologically determined) factor while money (at least in the long run for both Friedman and Tobin) does not affect the real output flow. This reversal of the importance or the significance of money and interest rates for real and monetary phenomena between orthodox and Keynes's theory is the result of Keynes's rejection of a second neoclassical universal truth—the axiom of reals.

For the D_2 component of aggregate demand not to be constrained by actual income, agents must have the ability to finance investment by borrowing from a banking system which can create money. Such money creation is therefore inevitably tied to the creation of money (debt) contracts. This financing mechanism involves the heresy of overthrowing what Frank Hahn calls the "axiom of reals" (cf. Minsky, 1984). Hahn describes this axiom as one where:

> The objectives of agents that determine their actions and plans do not depend on any nominal magnitudes. Agents care only about "real" things such as goods . . . leisure and effort. We know this as the axiom of the absence of money illusion, which it seems impossible to abandon in any sensible sense. (Hahn, 1983, p. 44)

The axiom of reals implies that money is a veil so that all economic decisions are made on the basis of real phenomena and relative prices alone. Money does not matter!

To reject the axiom of reals does not require assuming that agents suffer from a money illusion. It only means that "money is not neutral" (Keynes, 1973, p. 411); money matters in both the short run and the long run, or as Keynes put it:

> The theory which I desiderate would deal . . . with an economy in which money plays a part of its own and affects motives and decisions, and is, in short, one of the operative factors in the situation, so that the course of events cannot be predicted in either the long period or in the short, without a knowledge of the behavior of money between the first state and the last. And it is this which we ought to mean when we speak of a *monetary economy*. (Keynes, 1973, pp. 408-409)

Can anything be more revolutionary? In this passage from an article entitled "The *Monetary* Theory of Production" (and I emphasize the word *Monetary*) Keynes specifically rejects the axiom of reals! The only objective for a firm is to end the production process (which takes time) by liquidating its working capital in order to end up with more money than it started with (Keynes 1979, p. 82).

Let me illustrate: suppose during the next great depression a firm has a production process gestation period of one year. At the beginning of the year it hires workers, buys materials, and so on, on forward money contracts for the entire production process and thereby has, except for acts of God, controlled its costs of production. Suppose that during the year, the CPI falls by 10 percent but the price at which the firm expected to sell its product at the end of the gestation period falls by only 5 percent. In relative real terms the firm is better off; but in the real world the firm is really worse off. Now change the numbers to say 50 percent and 45 percent respectively. The firm still has a 5 percent improvement in real terms, but in all likelihood if this continues the firm will soon have to file for bankruptcy. (Of course a good neoclassical economist would respond the firm will not go bankrupt if it can recontract without penalty—but such recontracts without penalties are not a characteristic of the world we live in.)

If on the other hand we had assumed the CPI goes up by 10 percent (or 50 percent) while the firm's product price went up by 5 percent (or 45 percent), although the firm's real position has deteriorated its real world position is better. As long as money contracts are used to efficiently plan the production process, production decisions will be affected by nominal values and money is a real phenomenon![5]

Once we admit that money is a real phenomenon, that money matters, then the traditional axiom of reals must be rejected. Hahn should realize this, since Arrow and Hahn have demonstrated that:

> The terms in which contracts are made matter. In particular, if money is the goods in terms of which contracts are made, then the prices of goods in terms of money are of special significance. This is not the case if we consider an economy without a past or future. . . . *If a serious monetary theory* comes to be written, the fact that contracts are made in terms of money will be of considerable importance. (1971, pp. 356-357, italics added)

Moreover Arrow and Hahn demonstrate (p. 361) that, if contracts are made in terms of money (so that money affects real decisions) in an economy moving along in calendar time with a past and a future, then *all existence theorems are jeopardized*. The existence of money contracts—a characteristic of the world in which Keynes lived and which we still do—implies that there need never exist, in the long run or the short run, any rational expectations equilibrium or general equilibrium market clearing price vector.

The pervasive ergodic axiom— precision vs. accuracy

Most neoclassical and New Classical economists suffer from the pervasive form of envy which we may call the "Economist's Disease"; that is, these economists want to be considered as first class scientists dealing with a "hard science" rather than be seen as "second class" citizens of the scientific community who deal with the non-precise "social" and "political" sciences. These economists, mistaking preci-

---

[5]It should be noted that Minsky (1982) has explicitly demonstrated the inapplicability of the axiom of reals for at least one major sector of the economy. In his work Minsky has emphasized that there are at least some entrepreneurs, we call them bankers, who are guided solely by money-cash flows and maintaining increasing nominal values of net worth in balance sheets even if this means lower real values. Thus at least for this very important sector of the economy, the axiom of reals cannot be applicable.

sion (rather than accuracy) as the hallmark of "true" science, prefer to be precise rather than accurate.

Precision conveys the meaning of "sharpness to minute detail." Accuracy, on the other hand, means "care to obtain conformity with fact or truth." For example, if you phone the plumber to come fix an emergency breakdown in your plumbing system, and he responds by indicating he will be there in exactly 12 minutes, he is being precise, but not exercising care to obtain conformity with fact or truth. If he says he will be there before the day is over, he is being accurate, if not necessarily precise.

Most economists, unfortunately, prefer to be precisely wrong rather than roughly right or accurate. The axiom of ergodicity permits economists to act "as if" they were dealing with a "hard" science where data are homogeneous with respect to time. In an ergodic world, observations of a time series realization (i.e., historical data) are useful information regarding the probability distribution of the stochastic process which generated that realization. The same observations also provide information about the probability distribution over a universe of realizations which exist at any point of time such as today, and the data are also useful information regarding the future probability distribution of events. Hence by scientifically studying the past as generated by an ergodic situation, present and future events can be forecasted in terms of statistical probabilities (cf. Davidson, 1982-83).

Keynes (1936, Ch. 12) rejected this view that past information from economic time series realizations provides reliable, useful data which permit stochastic predictions of the economic future. In a world with important nonergodic circumstances—our economic world—liquidity matters, money is never neutral, and neither Say's Law nor Walras's Law is relevant (cf. Davidson, 1982-83). In such a world, Keynes's revolutionary logical analysis is relevant.

Conclusions

Mainstream economic theory has not followed Keynes's revolutionary logical analysis to develop what Arrow and Hahn have called a "serious monetary theory" in which contracts are made in terms of money in an economy moving from an irrevocable past to an uncertain, nonergodic future (cf. Davidson, 1982-83). At the very beginning of his *Treatise on Money*, Keynes (1930, p. 3) reminded the reader that, in a modern economy, money exists only because there are contracts and therefore money is intimately related to the existence of money contracts.

In his writings Keynes explicitly assumed things which are incompatible with (a) the gross substitution axiom, (b) the axiom of reals, and (c) ergodicity. Unfortunately, many of the popularizers and professional interpreters of Keynes's analysis either did not read what he wrote, or did not comprehend his revolutionary logic requiring the overthrow of these fundamental neoclassical axioms. Nevertheless, Keynes's policy prescriptions made a great deal of common sense. Hence Keynes won the policy battles of the first three decades after the publication of *The General Theory*, even though "Keynesians" had erected a "neoclassical synthesis" microfoundation to Keynes's macroeconomics which could not logically support Keynes's general case.

From a logical standpoint the neoclassical synthesis Keynesians had created a Keynesian Cheshire Cat—a grin without a body. Thus, Friedman and the rational expectations—New Classical—theorists were able to destroy the rickety neoclassical Keynesian scaffolding and replace it with a technologically advanced, logically consistent, but irrelevant and inaccurate theory.

In this one-hundred-first year after Keynes's birth, it is surprising how few in the economics profession are willing or able to defend the logical basis of Keynes's analysis. It is almost as if many believed that, as Clower (1965, p. 120) indicated, "the *General Theory* is theoretical nonsense" unless Keynes believed in the constrained demand function, dual decision hypothesis. Yet, we have shown *supra* that this constrained demand function analysis implies Say's Law. Hence, if Clower is correct in his claim that Keynes had the dual decision hypothesis at the back of his mind, then Keynes was a theoretical charlatan in claiming his analysis eliminated Say's Law. Of course, it is Clower and the other neoclassical Keynesians who maintain axioms rejected by Keynes who are in error in trying to apply Keynes's label to their logical system.

At the Royal Economic Society's Centennial Celebration of Keynes's birth in July 1983, the detractors of Keynes on the program far exceeded those who were attempting to honor Keynes's accomplishments and build on the legacy he left. Some such as Professors Samuelson and Solow proudly labeled themselves as "reconstructed Keynesians" to differentiate their theory from the "unreconstructed" Keynesians of Cambridge, England. As Samuelson put it—a reconstructed Keynesian was one who found the Keynesian structure imperfect and had therefore to reconstruct it.

This "reconstructed Keynesian" appellation is, however, a misnomer when applied to the Neoclassical Synthesis Keynesian approach of Samuelson and Solow. These mainstream American "Keynesian" models never began with the same logical foundations and axioms as Keynes's model. Hence these Keynesians cannot, and will not, reconstruct Keynes until they throw over the neoclassical axioms rejected by Keynes.

The "unreconstructed" Keynesians—or Post Keynesians as I would call them—recognize that there may be many flaws in the Keynes superstructure and that the times have brought forth new and different pressing problems. Post Keynesians may not have worked out all the answers but at least they recognize that Keynes started with a logically different theoretical system—a system which accurately reflects the characteristics of the real economic world—those of Wall Street and the Corporate Board room, rather than those of Robinson Crusoe or the Medieval Fair.

Post Keynesians recognize that their logical model is neither fully developed, nor as neat and precise as the neoclassical one—after all, the number of person-hours put into developing the orthodox model exceeds those invested in the Post Keynesian analysis several million-fold. Nevertheless, Post Keynesians believe it is better to develop a model which emphasizes the special characteristics of the economic world in which we live than to continually refine and polish a beautifully precise, but irrelevant, model. Moreover, when one is dealing with human activity and institutions, one may be, in the nature of things, outside of the realm of the formally precise. For Keynes as for Post Keynesians the guiding motto is "it is better to be roughly right than precisely wrong!"

After the revolution comes evolution. Post Keynesians are trying to build on the logical foundations of Keynes's real world analysis to resolve modern day economic problems. They invite all who possess open minds to undertake the further evolution of Keynes's logical heresy and to explore a Keynesian (non-Euclidean) world where the axioms of ergodicity, of gross substitution, and of reals are not universal truths applicable to all economic decision making processes.

Unlike Samuelson's "reconstructed Keynesians," Post Keynesians do not believe that a regression to pre-Keynesian (Euclidean) axioms represents progress no matter how much technological garb these postulates are wrapped in. Only in the world of 1984 and Doublespeak can a regressive analytical structure be considered an advance!

REFERENCES

Arrow, K. S., and Hahn, F. H. *General Competitive Analysis*. San Francisco: Holden Day, 1971.

Barro, R. J. and Grossman, H. I. *Money, Employment, and Inflation*. Cambridge: Cambridge University Press, 1976.

Clower, R. W. "The Keynesian Revolution: A Theoretical Appraisal." In *The Theory of Interest Rates*. Ed. by F. H. Hahn and F. P. R. Brechling. London: Macmillan, 1965.

Danziger, S., van der Gaag, J., Smolensky, E., and Taussig, M. K. "The Life-Cycle Hypothesis and Consumption Behavior of the Elderly." *Journal of Post Keynesian Economics*, Winter 1982-83, 5(2), 208-227.

Davidson, P. *Money and the Real World*. London: Macmillan, 1972.

————. "Money and General Equilibrium." *Economie Appliquée*, 1977, *30*.

————. "The Dual-faceted Nature of the Keynesian Revolution." *Journal of Post Keynesian Economics*, Spring 1980, 2(3) 291-307.

————. "Rational Expectations: A Fallacious Foundation for Studying Crucial Decision-making Processes." *Journal of Post Keynesian Economics*, Winter 1982-83, 5(2), 182-198.

Friedman, B. "The Substitutability of Debt and Equity Securities." National Bureau of Economic Research Working Paper 1130, May 1983.

Friedman, M. "A Theoretical Framework for Monetary Analysis." In *Milton Friedman's Monetary Framework: A Debate with his Critics*. Ed. by R. J. Gordon. Chicago: University of Chicago Press, 1974.

Hahn, F. H. "Keynesian Economics and General Equilibrium Theory." In *Microfoundations of Macroeconomics*. Ed. by G. C. Harcourt. London: Macmillan, 1977.

————. *Money and Inflation*. Cambridge: MIT Press, 1983.

Hicks, J. R. *Causality in Economics*. New York: Basic Books, 1979.

Keynes, J. M. *A Treatise on Money*. London: Macmillan, 1930.

————. *The General Theory of Employment, Interest and Money*. New York: Harcourt, 1936.

————. *The Collected Writings of John Maynard Keynes*, Vol. 13. Ed. by D. Moggridge. London: Macmillan, 1973.

————. *The Collected Writings of John Maynard Keynes*, Vol. 29. Ed. by D. Moggridge. London: Macmillan, 1979.

Kregel, J. A. "The Multiplier and Liquidity Preference: Two Sides of the theory of Effective Demand." (Mimeo), 1983.

Lucas, R. E. *Studies in Business Cycle Theory*. Cambridge: MIT Press, 1983.

Malinvaud, E. *The Theory of Unemployment Reconsidered*. Oxford: Blackwell, 1977.

Minsky, H. P. *Can It Happen Again?* Armonk, N.Y.: M. E. Sharpe, Inc., 1982.

————. "Frank Hahn's *Money and Inflation*: A Review Article." *Journal of Post Keynesian Economics*, Spring 1984, 6(3), 449-457.

[4]

Cambridge Journal of Economics 1977, **1**, 375–388

REVIEW ARTICLE

Malinvaud on Keynes

Richard Kahn*

(reviewing: Edmond Malinvaud, *The Theory of Unemployment Reconsidered*, Basil Blackwell, Oxford, 1977; three lectures delivered for the Yrjö Jahnsson Foundation, Helsinki)

This book is likely to have a great success. There is something in it to please everyone—Walrasian equilibrium, unemployment that can be reduced by cutting real wages, unemployment that can be reduced by raising real wages, workers who prefer leisure to earnings, savings equal to investment and prices equal to marginal cost—all presented in an ostensibly precise and elegant model.† But the reader needs to keep his wits about him to follow the intricacies of the argument.

1. Introduction

The conundrum that Edmond Malinvaud sets himself is to see what modifications to Walrasian theory (which he calls classical) have to be made in order for it to deal with the Keynesian problem of unemployment:

The classical teaching, according to which prices quickly react to excess supplies or demands, is more and more inadequate for short-run macroeconomic analysis as we move into ever-higher degrees of organisation of society (p. 9).

A number of economists have been working on these lines in recent years. Malinvaud gives them full credit. Perhaps the most important article is 'Non-Keynesian disequilibrium theory' by Jean-Pascal Benassy (*Review of Economic Studies*, October 1975) which also contains a useful bibliography. But Malinvaud's book is a highly original presentation—far more than a synthesis of earlier contributions.

Malinvaud's proposal is to deal with the problem by assuming fixed prices and rationing:

Hence, the proper theoretical framework is one in which supplies are rationed both on the labour market and on the goods market. Moreover the two types of rationing are so tightly interdependent that, in order to study policies against involuntary unemployment, one feels justified in concentrating attention exclusively on the formation of demand on the goods market (p. 4).

This is quite inadequate, for there are many differences between a Walrasian model and a Keynesian one besides the speed of reaction of prices.

* King's College, Cambridge. I would like to express my gratitude to the editors of the *Cambridge Journal of Economics* for their generous help, and also to Robert Neild and Dick Goodwin.

† The problem of inflation is not faced: 'It is well understood that static equilibrium analysis has limited scope for a theory of inflation. But I do not claim to discuss here mainly the theory of inflation' (p. 32, n. 27).

376   R. Kahn

First of all, the modern version of the Walrasian model is set up to deal with instantaneous equilibrium in an economy where there are given 'endowments' of 'factors' while Keynes' theory deals with a world where production and accumulation are going on through time. Secondly, in the Walrasian model, individuals are free to decide how much work it is worth their while to do. The return per unit of work (corresponding to the real-wage rate) is determined by the demand for commodities and the amount of work offered, while, in the Keynesian world, the number of men to be employed is decided by industrial firms in the light of the state of demand. Moreover, the amount of work per man is fixed by collective agreements, say an eight hour day and a 300 day year. This may be changed from time to time. But, at any one moment, one agreement is in force and when there is a good deal of unemployment, a man who took more leisure than is provided in the collective agreement would soon be sacked. Thirdly, and most important of all, in the Walrasian world the equality of saving and investment is attained by variation in the rate of interest (and other appropriate prices), whereas in Keynes' analysis the equality is attained by variation in the level of income. Investment, which determines saving, is itself determined by a process quite different from the Walrasian notion of utility maximisation subject to constraint.

Malinvaud's conception of 'rationing' runs through the whole argument, but it is used in a sense all his own. When industry is working up to capacity, consumers are said to be rationed:

The immediate impact of changes in demand or supply is to be found in order-books, waiting lines, inventories, delivery dates, output, hours of work, employment. . . . Such quantitative adjustments are the first signals of changes in the demand-supply relationship. Shifts in relative prices come later and in a less apparent way (p. 9).

Where there is less than full employment, workers are said to be rationed. It is true that employers can often pick and choose whom to employ. This might be described as rationing jobs. But here the workers are all alike, the 'ration' of employment is simply the number of workers employed. When 'firms do not produce more because of lack of effective demand' (p. 31), they are said to be 'rationed in the goods market':

In business surveys, firms are regularly asked whether they would produce more if demand was higher, i.e. whether they are rationed in the market for output (p. 33).

This unnatural use of language clouds the whole argument, but with care and patience the reader can work out a commonsense interpretation of what it all means.

2. The basic model

In a non-Walrasian economy, with firms employing labour for money wages, the real wage is governed by the price of consumer goods. Malinvaud distinguishes two cases, one *Keynesian*, where a higher level of real wages brings about a higher level of employment, and one, which he calls *classical*, where higher real wages are associated with less employment. He regards the Keynesian case as the most prevalent and it is the less incomprehensible. I therefore start by examining this case in terms of his model.

He states:

It concerns the operations during one given period, which is analyzed independently of past and future periods (p. 38).

But this is not accurate. At the beginning of the period there is a stock of plant and of wealth which must have been inherited from the past, and investment and savings are going on during the period, which are affected by expectations of the future and will, in turn, affect the future.

The economy is capitalist. But little attention is paid to the organisation of production or of society. There are capitalists who seem rather amorphous. They produce goods; they make profits; but they do not appear to consume. There are no rentiers as such. The only other class consists of workers, who are sometimes called consumers. Each worker owns a certain amount of wealth at the beginning of the period. Employed workers may save. The unemployed live on their accumulated wealth.

This neglects the public transfer payment to the unemployed, which will not be considered in the present prototype (p. 45, n. 6).

Wealth is held in the form of money, on which no interest is received. Some of the wealth takes the form of shares, but the references to shares are cryptic: they play no active role in the analysis.

This suggests that consumers have no other income than wages. But I do not really mean this: the implicit assumption is rather that non-labour incomes are exogenous, i.e. independent of the employment level; this is certainly an admissible hypothesis to make in a first approximation of short-run income distribution (p. 39).

There is a government and an investment sector, the expenditures of which are aggregated in the exposition. The firms in the investment sub-sector are free to employ as much labour as they please. The government can make what expenditure it pleases. There is no taxation. All profits are saved. Net savings of the workers are equal to the excess of government expenditure and investment over profits, in accordance with the Keynesian principle that, given the propensity to save, the level of income is such that the flow of saving is equal to the budget deficit and the rate of investment.

It is convenient to suppose that money takes the exclusive form of bank deposits (although Malinvaud does not adopt that use of language). The firms deposit their profits and the workers their savings. The banks' deposits are equal to their loans to the government and the producers of capital goods.

The treatment is based on the assumption that government expenditure has

no utility for individuals; this is of course a simplification, but it is admissible for the study of short-term equilibrium. In any case removing it is not likely to change the conclusions reached here (p. 64, n. 15).

As utility plays an important role in Malinvaud's analysis, the removal of this assumption would make a great deal of difference.

3. The determination of employment

I now turn to the main topic—the determination of employment in the consumption-good sector. Malinvaud treats employment in the government and investment sectors as exogeneously given.

It is convenient to take the money wage per worker as given. Malinvaud prefers to take both money wages and the price of the commodity as variable. But diagrams are more perspicuous if the money wage is taken as given, with the price of the commodity on the y axis and the level of employment in the consumer-good sector on the x axis. A lower price represents a higher real wage rate.

378   R. Kahn

Since there are no other variable inputs, the prime cost of the output of the consumer-good sector is equal to its wage bill.

The flow of expenditure on consumer goods is the wage bill of both sectors *minus* saving by employed workers *plus* expenditure out of wealth of the unemployed. Since prime cost is equal to wages in the consumption-good sector, it follows that the flow of profit on the sale of the consumer good is equal to the wage bill of the government and investment sector, *minus* saving out of wages in both sectors *plus* expenditure by the unemployed.

The higher the price of the commodity, the lower the real wage and the lower the real value of workers' wealth held in money. The lower wealth, taken by itself, means a higher rate of saving. The lower real wage means a lower rate of saving. The lower level of employment means, taken by itself, a lower rate of saving. The higher level of unemployment which goes with it means more spending out of wealth. Purely in order to simplify the argument, I assume that these four influences on the rate of saving—one in the positive direction and three in the negative—cancel out. The object is to represent in a two-dimensional diagram the relationship between the real wage and employment

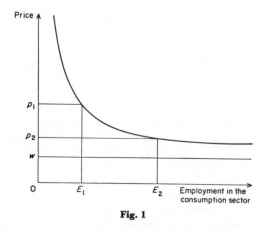

Fig. 1

in the consumption-good sector with a given money wage bill and given employment in the government and investment sectors. Otherwise it would be necessary in order to allow for the relationship between employment and saving in the consumption sector to use a third dimension.

Since the amount of saving by workers is independent of the level of employment, the flow of profits in the consumption-good sector is independent of the level of employment in that sector. The relationship between the real wage and employment in the consumption-good sector can then be represented by a rectangular hyperbola between the *y* axis and a horizontal line running above the *x* axis at the level of the money wage. At each point on the curve the area of the rectangle represents the flow of profits, which is the same at all prices. The profit per man employed is determined by the price of the commodity.

There are no overhead costs, no interest charges, no taxation, no uncertainty about future sales, and Malinvaud admits to being quite vague about the constitution and policy of firms. There is no theory here to account for the level of profit margins. We must follow Malinvaud in taking the price of the commodity (relatively to the money wage) to be arbitrarily given.

However, we can compare different prices. The higher is the price, the lower is the real wage and the lower the level of employment. This is shown in Fig. 1. The level of employment, E_1, corresponding to the higher price, p_1, is less than E_2, corresponding to the lower price. This model illustrates some Keynesian arguments. The greater is the propensity to save, the lower is the level of employment at a given price (the curve is shifted to the left). The higher is the level of government expenditure and investment, the greater is the amount of employment in the consumption-good sector (the curve is shifted to the right).

But this is a very thin representation of Keynes' theory. There is no mention of liquidity preference, no effect of uncertainty or of expectations about the future. The level of investment is arbitrarily fixed without any discussion of how it is determined. The only scope for policy is to vary government expenditure. However, the model brings out one clear point: in a given state of effective demand, a reduction in profit margins would raise real wages and increase employment. It is not clear whether this is really the moral which Malinvaud intended to draw.

4. Marginal costs

Malinvaud includes another element in his story that is incompatible both with Walras and with Keynes—an aggregate marginal cost curve, based in effect, on the assumption of perfect competition.†

A theory aiming at explaining the short-term determination of unemployment must take as given the equipment of firms. For each producer there is then a strict functional relationship between labour input and output; this assumption has indeed been made in section 8 of the first lecture. More precisely, we may say that the different types of available equipment differ with respect to the labour productivity achieved when they are used; they differ within each firm as well as between firms . . .

The easy hypothesis to make is that the allocation of labour and the distribution of sales among firms are efficient, i.e. do result in an overall efficient use of available equipment as they would if the price system was working under ideal conditions . . .

To go from this principle to a definite mathematical representation, one needs only to define the existing stock of equipment with its distribution according to productive capacity and labour requirements. A precise identification of firms is no longer necessary, since the most productive equipment will be used first irrespective of which firms use it (pp. 49–51).

Evidently, Malinvaud assumes a rising supply curve determined by marginal cost as in an old-fashioned textbook.

To follow his story we require a different diagram. With given money-wage rates, there is a supply curve of output in the consumer-good sector with marginal costs rising with employment, starting from the level of average prime costs with the most efficient plant. The amount of labour taken on is now governed by the price of the commodity, the real-wage rate being equal to output per man on the plant which is marginal at a particular level of demand. This relationship is depicted by the supply curve S in Fig. 2. The 'demand curve' D relates the price level and the level of effective demand. For ease of exposition I assume (as Malinvaud does in the Appendix to his book) that

---

† There was an element of 'rising supply price' in Keynes' aggregate supply function, but it is not essential to the main argument. It was criticised on empirical grounds as soon as the *General Theory* was published.

380   R. Kahn

the labour of each worker is fixed. The level of consumption compatible with full employment is indicated by $0E^*$.

With any given flow of money expenditure on the commodity, there is a price (and real wage) at which supply and demand are equal. There is then no 'rationing' in the goods market (see Fig. 2). The amount of employment in the consumer-good sector is governed by the plant available and the flow of expenditure, being such that the price of the commodity is equal to its marginal cost. Profits, or rather quasi-rents, in the consumer-good sector, are determined by the excess of marginal cost over average cost at the corresponding level of output. Malinvaud notes that a rise in the flow of expenditure (a shift of D to the right), which increases employment and lowers real wages, involves a conflict of interest. Workers already employed have a lower income, while there is a gain to the unemployed who now get jobs (p. 64).

Malinvaud devotes little attention to the possibility of equilibrium with the price equal to marginal cost. For him, the real wage is an arbitrary independent variable:

Given the short-run price rigidities that actually exist, the theory under consideration here is justified in assuming full price rigidity, i.e. in working with models in which prices and wage-rates are exogenous (pp. 11 and 12).

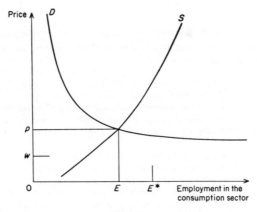

Fig. 2

He considers a number of cases. In his first case, the price is fixed above (and the real wage below) the level at which supply and demand would be in equilibrium; see p_1 in Fig. 3. This case is described by Malinvaud as Keynesian, in which a higher real wage would result in a higher level of employment.

Malinvaud's second case is what he calls the classical position. This is not classical in the sense of being a Walrasian equilibrium. It is a case in which the real wage has been set above the level that equates demand to supply (the price is too low). Now employment, and therefore output, in the consumer-good sector is restricted by the high real-wage rate—see p_2 in Fig. 3. There is a violent excess of demand for the commodity.

In order to know whether a classical equilibrium holds, we must check that there is an excess of supply of labour and an excess demand for goods (p. 79).

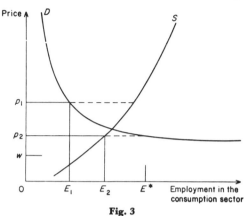

Fig. 3

Malinvaud regards this position as rare, but it should rather be described as impossible. Anyone who could succeed in buying some goods at the fixed price would resell them at a higher price and take a profit for himself. Workers would have to buy the commodity at black-market prices. The real wage could not be kept at the high fixed level.

There is also a case (which Malinvaud calls Walrasian equilibrium) in which both demand and supply just happen to be sufficient to maintain full employment. The level of effective demand is such that the plant which is marginal when the whole labour force is employed gives an output per man which determines the real wage rate. Marginal cost is equal to the demand price for the corresponding level of output. In terms of Fig. 2, above, the intersection would be at the level of full employment.

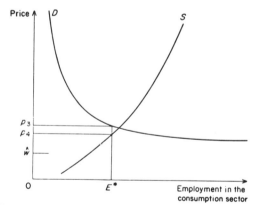

Fig. 4. *At price levels between p_3 and p_4 there is* repressed inflation

A final case is that in which the real wage is forced up higher than is consistent with full employment. There is a shortage of labour in the consumption sector and money wages would tend to be forced up by competition between employers. This is Malinvaud's case of 'repressed inflation' (see Fig. 4).

Malinvaud depicts these various cases in a kind of map, drawn in the space of the money wage and the price of the commodity (p. 85). As he draws the map, it is rather

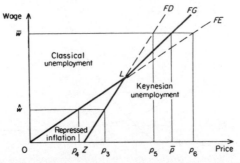

Fig. 5. *At the money wage rate $\bar{w}$, demand at p_5 is sufficient for full employment, but the real wage is higher than the output per man on plant which is marginal at full employment; p_6 covers marginal cost at full employment but gives a large defficiency of demand; at $\bar{p}$ marginal cost is equal to price at less than full employment. At $\hat{w}$ (cf. Fig. 4) prices corresponding to repressed inflation lie between p_4 and p_3. $Z = A/Y^*$*

obscure. It is more perspicuous if it is interpreted as in Figs 5 and 6. The real wage shown by the slope of the *FE* line is that which, on Malinvaud's assumptions, will be consistent with full employment demand for labour, being the product per man on the plant that is marginal when the whole labour force is employed. The line *FD* represents the flow of demand in real terms which would purchase the output produced at full employment. Effective demand for consumption goods is equal to consumption expenditure out of wages (*cwE*), where *c* is the propensity to consume, *plus* consumption expenditure out of wealth (A). The relationship between the wage level and the price level at full employment output of the consumer good (Y^*) is then

$$A + cwE^* = pY^*.$$

The line *FG*, which Malinvaud describes as the frontier between Keynesian and classical situations, represents positions at which supply is equal to demand.

The various cases can now be placed on Malinvaud's map.

In the upper triangle between the lines *FD* and *FE*, the real wage is higher than that corresponding to full employment demand for labour, and expenditure in real terms is

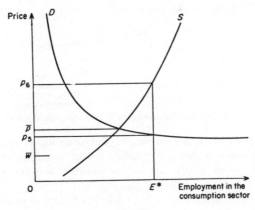

Fig. 6

less than that required to purchase the full employment output. Our first case, in which the price (relatively to the money wage) is such that supply and demand are equal at less than full employment lies on *FG*.

At the point of intersection of the lines, *L*, there is full employment and sufficient outlay to purchase the corresponding output. It is the case in which both demand and supply happen to be sufficient to establish full employment.

In the lower triangle the real wage is higher than corresponds to full employment and so is expenditure. This is the case of repressed inflation (compare with Fig. 4).

In the area below the lines ZL and *FG*, expenditure is too low to permit full employment. Although in the triangle between *FE* and *FG* real wages are too high as well as expenditure being too low, it is the expenditure constraint which is binding. This is what Malinvaud treats as the Keynesian case (his first case).

In the area above the lines *OL* and *FG*, the real wage rate is too high to correspond to full employment. Although in the triangle between *FD* and *FG* expenditure is too low as well as real wages too high, the real wage rate is the binding constraint. This is Malinvaud's second case—his classical case.

As I indicated above, I regard this case as impossible. It is the consequence of mixing assumptions about the shape of the cost curves and the degree of price flexibility which are inconsistent with one another.

Fixed or 'sticky' prices are found in manufacturing and distribution, where products are not homogeneous and labour costs are constant or decreasing up to the limits of capacity. The result, which has been well confirmed by various empirical studies and is widely known as Okun's Law, is that productivity in industry increases with short-run increases in output, while prices are sticky.

Flexible prices are found in those markets for a limited range of primary products where products are homogeneous, demand to the individual producer is almost perfectly elastic, and costs rise with output due to fixed natural resources.

Malinvaud mixes the two, assuming a single homogeneous commodity, many producers with rising cost curves, and yet prices which stay fixed in the face of excess demand. It is this that is impossible. For, on these assumptions, producers who are profit maximisers would not keep their prices fixed. The whole notion of sticky prices, based on the studies of the real manufacturing world to which Malinvaud refers early in his lectures, cannot be squeezed into the textbook notion of homogeneous products and rising cost curves. If, on the other hand, one wishes to justify the assumption of sticky prices by returning to reality, then one must assume constant or falling variable costs. Even if one ignores overheads, it follows that, if the real wage is at a level at which it pays a firm to produce, it will increase, not reduce, its profits by increasing output in response to extra demand. There will be no rationing of goods in Malinvaud's sense.

Ironically, 'rationing' can only be introduced into this setting, interpreted either way, if one gives the word its normal meaning and introduces a government which overrules the market forces.

5. Leisure

There is an elaborate treatment of the determination of the amount of work done (and of leisure) under the influence of a worker's psychology, and the amount of his wealth. This I discuss in the Appendix to this article.

384   R. Kahn

All this evidently belongs to the Walrasian world, in which the individual can decide how much work he wants to do. In a Keynesian world, the preference for leisure of the typical worker may influence collective agreements about hours and conditions in relation to the real wage and the average amount of wealth. But, under any given agreement, there is little choice for the individual about the amount of effort he can offer. The only effect of Malinvaud's psychological theory is to blur the distinction between unemployment and leisure. The number of men employed (for standard hours of work), and the number not employed, are objective facts. But, amongst those who are not employed, some may be in distress and very anxious to find a job while others, who have plenty of wealth, may not be particularly reluctant, for the time being, to remain out of work.

Malinvaud's picture of the social system, in which there is no spending out of profits, every worker has an arbitrary amount of wealth in the form of money, which yields no income, and the unemployed are provided with no means of support and are forced to live on their wealth, is too remote from reality to be of interest, though perhaps it will appeal to those who regard unemployment as being due to idleness.

6. Present-day economic problems

In the third lecture Malinvaud wanders around present-day economic problems, trying to illuminate them by reference to his three models, Walrasian, Keynesian and what he claims is classical; as though it was possible to move from one set of institutions and technical conditions to another merely by altering the real wage rate.

> One may first wonder how the short-term equilibrium would progressively shift if its environment did not change, i.e. if behaviour as well as policy were to remain unchanged for some time. A number of economists argue that a strong tendency toward a long-term full employment equilibrium does exist. According to them, policy measures, which may look favourable in the short run, actually disturb the spontaneous tendency toward full employment. Theory should permit an examination of such views (p. 77).

In the Appendix to this article I discuss Malinvaud's ideas about the influence of the passage of time, when production depends on the workers' willingness to earn. But the problem of introducing accumulation through time into the market economy is much more complicated than he seems to realise. In a Keynesian world, investment is going on, and the most important concomitants of the passage of time are changes in the amount of productive capacity. Also saving and dis-saving are going on so that the amount and distribution of private wealth is altering. Perhaps a number of economists are objecting to the rise in the national debt that results from continuous government borrowing, but they would have hard work to show that there is a spontaneous tendency to full employment under a regime of 'sound finance'.

This Malinvaud seems (partially) to recognise:

> Individual assets, autonomous demand and technical possibilities change through time for many reasons including capital accumulation, technical progress and frequent changes in the economic or non-economic environment. Since prices and wages are sticky, we cannot expect the growth path to coincide permanently with the changing Walrasian equilibrium of our short-term model (p. 93).

There is a curious passage in which he contrasts Keynesian with Walrasian accumulation:

In each period, whether it experiences repressed inflation or Keynesian unemployment, aggregate savings are equal to investment, i.e. to autonomous demand in our model. The short-run equilibrium always fulfils this basic requirement; moreover, the demand for investment being exogenous in the short run, the supply of savings must adapt to it, as it does in Keynesian economics (this is forced saving under repressed inflation). Hence, it cannot be said that the need for capital accumulation requires a shift of the income distribution in favour of those types of income that are most saved. The same amount of capital accumulation that is considered to be made in a stationary Walrasian equilibrium will also be made on average in a sequence of non-Walrasian short-run equilibria as long as the demand for investment is on average the same in both cases. Any argument in favour of a different price–wage constellation must involve the demand for investment rather than the supply of savings (p. 99).

This last sentence seems to indicate that he wishes to take off from Walras altogether and sail with Keynes, to a world where accumulation depends upon investment, not upon the desire of individuals to save. But he can never quite bring himself to cut the hawser.

He attempts to relax the assumption of a single market and allow for a multiplicity of goods. He suggests that there may then be Keynesian unemployment with 'classical contamination' (p. 110). This would mean that, while prices are in general too high to permit full employment, for some commodities prices are too low (real wages are too high) to secure full capacity operation. But if there is a demand for these commodities why should not prices be raised? At the same time, there may be a few industries working up to capacity, enjoying a seller's market, while most are suffering from slack demand.

Malinvaud's curious system of analysis leads him to make some excellent points, for instance that technical progress, which raises output per man employed, should be accompanied by rising real wages (p. 90).

The most important and sensational of his statements is that the nature of unemployment in the 1960s and early 1970s was classical.

Among the many conceivable combinations of events, the one most favourable to classical unemployment occurs when there is a sudden decrease in the quantity of final output per unit of labour, and when anticipations or social tensions lead to an abnormal increase in real wages (p. 107).

This combination of events would reduce the share of profit in the proceeds of industry and this is likely to lead to a reduction in plans for investment. Here is a highly important and completely Keynesian cause of recession. It is all very sad, but not at all 'classical'.[†]

Malinvaud towards the very end of his book states:

There is no doubt that the main features of the 1975 unemployment are again Keynesian (p. 109).

However he adds:

There are signs that the [substitution effect of the deterioration of the terms of trade] will soon again emerge (p. 109).

[†] Malinvaud cites a paper by H. den Hartog and H. S. Tjan as providing evidence for the existence of classical unemployment. This paper was discussed by R. A. de Klerk, H. B. M. van der Laan and K. B. T. Thio in their paper 'Unemployment in the Netherlands: a criticism of the den Hartog-Tjan vintage model', this *Journal*, September 1977, pp. 291–306 [eds].

386   R. Kahn

7. Conclusion

Ultimately Malinvaud's argument rests on two pillars: an elaborate utility analysis of the determination of the workers' propensities to consume and to supply labour; and the combination of a rising marginal cost curve of the textbook type with fixed prices. The first seems unnecessarily mystical, and the second has nothing to do either with Keynes or with the real world. On the fundamental difference between Keynesian and classical theory—the relationship between saving and investment—he has nothing to say. His faith in the Walrasian long run (p. 93) is simply wishful thinking.

Malinvaud evidently feels that he has seen a great light.

At the end of these lectures, we realise that a great many questions require further theoretical and econometric studies. The general equilibrium approach, in a world where prices are sticky in the short run, is not only highly relevant but also highly challenging. I do hope that economists will devote some of their best efforts to developing this approach and that, as a consequence, these lectures will soon be out-dated (pp. 115–116).

Actually, Malinvaud's commonsense observations, which are often acute, have been distorted by this approach and further development of it would distort them all the more. *The Theory of Unemployment Reconsidered* is a sad example of the effect which the study of orthodox economic theory can have upon a powerful mind.

Appendix

The purpose of this Appendix is to avoid cluttering up the main text of the article with algebra. The ingenuity and elegance of Malinvaud's equations determining the behaviour of workers are fascinating. They play an important role throughout the book.

The treatment applies to one certain period of time. The employed workers are assumed to be all alike in every sense. Each employed worker at the beginning of the period possesses the same amount of wealth, m_o in terms of money, and at the end of the period m. Over the period he buys and consumes a quantity x of the consumer good. He provides a quantity, l, of labour. The maximum quantity of labour that he could provide (without detriment to his efficiency) is L. This is independent both of his real wealth and of the real wage. L *minus* l is the amount of leisure which he decides to enjoy—at the expense of his earnings. This depends both on the worker's real wealth and on the real wage. The price of the good is p and w is the money-wage rate. The equations are (p. 42):

$$x = (m_o + wL)/2p, \tag{1}$$

$$l = (3wL - m_o)/4w, \tag{2}$$

$$m = \tfrac{1}{4}(m_o + wL). \tag{3}$$

The value of leisure (earnings forgone) in the period is

$$\tfrac{1}{4}(m_o + wL). \tag{4}$$

Savings amount to

$$\tfrac{1}{4}(wL - 3m_o). \tag{5}$$

The equations show how these decisions are related to the real wage and the amount of his wealth (money balance expressed in real terms); and also to the maximum amount of work which a worker is capable of doing. There is 'complete freedom of choice'. The only constraint is financial.

Equations are also given for cases in which certain constraints are imposed. Although I do not discuss them, they enhance the ingenuity and elegance of the algebraic treatment. One constraint is rationing of consumers. If a man is prevented from spending as much as he would like, he devotes less of his time to work (more to leisure). A constraint utilised in the main text of this article is one in which the hours of work a day and the number of working days a year are fixed (by the employers—perhaps in agreement with the workers' representatives). It is dealt with in the Appendix of the book.

Malinvaud points out that $3wL$ has to exceed m_o if there is to be any work at all (the initial holding of wealth must not exceed three times the maximum sum that could be earned in the period). This is absurd.

Equation (1) means that expenditure is one-half of the potential maximum possible expenditure (if the worker took no leisure and the whole of the initial wealth was spent). This is another peculiar assumption. But realism apart, it is an elegant result that, out of the potential maximum possible expenditure, not only is actual expenditure one-half, but the value of leisure (equation (4)) one-quarter. The remaining one-quarter is the terminal wealth, m (equation (5)), m_o *plus* saving.

It is impossible to believe that these remarkable behaviourist relationships have been based either on observations of how people behave in practice (e.g. by field studies) or on any attempt to combine the use of common sense with intuition. They are designed to secure simplicity and elegance. This is demonstrated by the fact that the parameters are 1, 2, 3 and 4—the four lowest integral numbers. In a sense this is perfectly legitimate. Malinvaud's intention is, I imagine, to demonstrate how the equations operate rather than to attempt to be realistic. Nevertheless it helps to bring out the implications of the equations by working out some numerical illustrations. Malinvaud states that 'working with actual numbers rather than parameters will simplify somewhat the formulae we shall have to consider' (p. 42).

The equations are derived from the simplest possible utility function of consumption, leisure and terminal wealth (p. 41). (The use of cardinal utility is an unnecessary metaphysical device which could be dispensed with.)

$$U = x^2 \, (L-l) \, m/p.$$

For the expenditure out of his wealth by an unemployed worker, the utility function results in the amazing conclusion that in the period he spends two-thirds of his initial wealth (irrespective of its amount) (p. 45, equation (28), $m = m_o/3$). If he remains unemployed for a second period, in that second period he spends two-ninths of his initial wealth. And so on until he dies of starvation.

The equations, in just one respect, make good sense (but it is common sense and does not call for the use of algebra). A higher initial amount of wealth means less saving, more leisure (less work and earnings) and more expenditure. A higher real wage means more saving, more leisure (less work but greater earnings) and more consumption.

A curious feature of the relationships is that the relative influences on behaviour of the amount of initial wealth and of the real wage depend on the length of the period. The trouble is that the dimensions of m and wl are different. One is a stock, the other a flow. If the period were very short, the real wage would have no influence—the influence would be exclusively that exercised by the real wealth. If the period were very long, vice versa. This is utter nonsense. Malinvaud fails entirely to discuss the length of period. The expenditure by an unemployed worker out of his wealth, two-thirds of it in the course of the period, makes less nonsense the longer the period. This is not only because a longer period means a lower standard of living—a higher degree of prudence—but because the prospect of becoming re-employed at the end of the period is higher the longer the period. Also, for employed workers a little arithmetic indicates that the equations make less nonsense the longer the period. But in the absence of any help from Malinvaud I feel that I must take a year for the purpose of the following arithmetical illustrations.

I begin with a case in which the real wage is £20 a week and the maximum possible amount of work is equivalent to 50 weeks a year (£1000 a year). I take a worker's initial wealth to be £600. From equation (5) the worker is dis-saving at the annual rate of £200. This is quite astonishing improvidence for a poor and badly paid man. The explanation provided by equation (4) is that the value of his leisure is at the annual rate of £400. It amounts to 20 weeks a year, out of the maximum of 50. He works 30 weeks a year. Thus his annual earnings amount to £600. And yet his annual expenditure (equation (1)) is £800. At the end of a year his wealth is down from £600 to £400. His annual rate of saving is now £50. The value of his leisure has come down to £350 in the second year. It amounts to $17\frac{1}{2}$ weeks. He works $32\frac{1}{2}$ weeks and earns £650. He spends £700. It is a sad story. Although there is no reason why Malinvaud should be attempting to be realistic, the departure from realism is disconcerting.

At a higher rate of wages and a smaller amount of wealth per head more sense would be made of the equations. The condition for zero saving is that the worker's wealth should be one-third of his maximum earnings. In the above case this would be £333$\frac{1}{3}$. To secure positive saving requires that the maximum possible annual earnings exceed three times each worker's wealth.

388   R. Kahn

The question is what assumptions have to be made in order to secure a rate of workers' saving equal to the excess of the sum of government expenditure, investment and expenditure of the unemployed over saving out of profits.

As an indication of the character of the problem I conclude by assuming a real wage of £40 a week and a maximum of 50 working weeks a year. Maximum possible earnings per head are then £2000 a year. I take the initial wealth of each employed worker as only £400. Each employed worker then saves £200 a year. His saving reaches zero when his wealth has risen to £666⅔, i.e. in a little over a year.

The obvious conclusion is that even those (of whom I am not one) who accept the general character of Malinvaud's behaviouristic relationships, must adopt very different parameters. Those who enjoy parlour games are given plenty of opportunity for fun.

[5]

Deficient Foresight: A Troublesome Theme in Keynesian Economics

By Alan Coddington*

The fact that John Maynard Keynes had made a distinguished contribution to the theory of probability (1921) no doubt predisposed many of his readers to imbue with great significance his subsequent remarks on the related topic of uncertainty in economic decision making. Among those who have provided commentaries on his work, there are those who have singled out this uncertainty theme not only for its special importance, but also for its potential for analytical subversion. The purpose of this paper is to scrutinize the ideas involved in this particular aspect of Keynes' work, together with the lines of argument that have emerged from those commentators who have pursued it. The result of this scrutiny will be to call into question the idea that there is anything peculiarly subversive in the analytical consequences of broaching problems of uncertainty in economic decision making. I shall argue, rather, that as an analytical issue it is —depending on how it is handled—either innocuous or else quite indiscriminately destructive.

I. Keynes on Uncertainty

Chapter 12 of Keynes' General Theory, "The State of Long-term Expectation," deals with the knowledge of the future that would be required to make correct decisions regarding the instigation of capital projects; in particular it revolves around the theme that, since infallible knowledge of the future is unattainable, the decisions to embark on capital projects must, in the nature of the case, be based on beliefs the epistemological foundations of which are more or less flimsy.[1] This chapter broaches, in other words, the

theme of uncertainty in the making of investment decisions, a theme that makes a much brisker reappearance in Keynes' 1937 article which appeared shortly after his General Theory. This article is of special importance in that it has been seized upon by a number of commentators on Keynes as providing the interpretative key to The General Theory and, indeed, to the whole tendency of his work of the 1930's, and perhaps even of his whole intellectual life.[2]

What is problematic about Keynes' discussion of uncertainty in his 1937 article is the question of what its scope is supposed to be. On the face of it, the object of attention is economic activity in its entirety; specific categories of decision are mentioned—in particular, the decisions underlying private sector investment expenditure and the (stock) demand for liquid assets[3]—but no reason

---

focused, and drifts into a discussion of trading on secondary securities markets where Keynes points out the difficulty of making short-term capital gains when everybody else is trying to do the same thing.

[2] For example:

...there were moments when we had some trouble in getting Maynard to see what the point of his revolution really was, but when he came to sum it up after the book [The General Theory] was published he got it into focus. [There follows a reference to the QJE paper.] On the plane of theory, the revolution lay in the change ...from the principles of rational choice to the problems of decisions based on guess-work and convention.
[Robinson, 1973, p. 3]

Again: "...Keynes himself declared in the Quarterly Journal of Economics that the General Theory was concerned with our mode of coping with, or of concealing from our conscious selves, our ignorance of the future" (Shackle, 1967, p. 6). See also Shackle (1973, p. 516).

[3] The radical implications for the theory of liquidity preference and the determination of money prices of Keynes' discussion of uncertainty, and especially of his notion of the resort to conventional bases of valuation in the face of changing expectations of future valuations of durable assets, were forcefully and succinctly expressed in Hugh Townshend (1937), a paper apparently provoked by J. R. Hicks' (1936) review of the General Theory, and aimed at challenging what Townshend took to be Hicks' traducing of Keynes' theory of interest.

---

*Professor of economics, Queen Mary College, University of London.

[1] In fact, as has been remarked by Joan Robinson (1971, pp. 31–32) this discussion is not at all well

480

VOL. 72 NO. 3   CODDINGTON: KEYNESIAN DEFICIENT FORESIGHT   481

is given why the considerations advanced should either be confined to these cases, or should apply with relatively greater consequence in these cases. Such differentiation, however, is precisely what would be required to sustain the argument that is being advanced, as I shall try to demonstrate in Section II.

As a matter of shorthand, it may be said, as many other commentators have done, that Keynes was, in the places referred to, broaching the theme of the *uncertainty* inherent in investment decisions. But although this is no doubt a convenient piece of shorthand, it fails to convey the root-and-branch quality of Keynes' discussion. For what Keynes is concerned to suggest is that the epistemological foundations of private sector investment are comprehensively flimsy. In elucidation of his conception of uncertainty, Keynes writes:

> The sense in which I am using the term is that in which the prospect of a European war is uncertain, or the price of copper and the rate of interest twenty years hence, or the obsolescence of a new invention, or the position of private wealth-owners in the social system in 1970. About these matters there is no scientific basis on which to form any capable probability whatever.
>
> [1937, p. 214]

From the viewpoint of economic theory, however, this position is both odd and unhelpful. For, to paraphrase George Orwell: All expectations are uncertain; but some are more uncertain than others. The price of copper twenty years hence is a thoroughly uncertain thing, and depends on so many circumstances the forecasting of which would be difficult and unreliable, that any one figure is, one might think, better seen as a guess than as anything more sophisticated. But it is worth pressing the example a bit further. For the belief, on any reasonable present understanding of the world, that the price of copper in 2002 will be greater at 1982 prices than 10 cents per ton and less than $1 billion per ton is not at all uncertain. And, pressing the example still further, it is even less uncertain that there will be a demand for copper in 2002; and even if this is to a degree uncer-

tain (a hitherto undreamt of copper substitute may be discovered, invented, or developed), it is less uncertain that there will be a demand in 2002 for metals of high electrical conductivity. And so on. Without pursuing the example any further, it should be apparent by now what I mean by the "root-and-branch" aspect of Keynes' discussion. I shall return to this issue in Section III, where an attempt will be made to characterize in more detail just what is unsatisfactory about this approach to uncertainty in economic affairs.

II. The Sources of Variation in Expenditure Aggregates

At the period of time in which Keynes was working on the *General Theory*, the concept of "the multiplier"—a means whereby autonomous variation in some category of expenditure could be transmitted, made pervasive, and possibly amplified in its effects—had already been developed (see R. F. Kahn, 1931). What Keynes needed to set his system in motion was a source of autonomous variation: some category of expenditure that is subject to fluctuations originating outside the model. As is well known, investment was the candidate chosen.

Investment decisions rest on beliefs about future circumstance, beliefs which in turn must be based on, if anything, present and past conditions. Accordingly, investment behavior could exhibit erratic patterns if either: (i) present conditions change erratically leading to erratically fluctuating beliefs about future circumstances; or (ii) beliefs change erratically without corresponding changes in their basis in conditions. It is the second of these possibilities that leads to *autonomous* variations in the aggregate of expenditure resulting from investment decisions.

Accordingly, if changes in private investment have their origins in the spontaneous and erratic workings of individual minds, a solution to Keynes' problem is to hand: such an account provides the reason why this category of expenditure will fluctuate autonomously rather than in response to changes in objective circumstances (circumstances that should have their counterparts elsewhere in the model). It is in this way that subjec-

482   THE AMERICAN ECONOMIC REVIEW   JUNE 1982

tivist ideas make their appearance in Keynes' *General Theory*. These ideas have the effect of driving a wedge between behavior and circumstances: they can be used, as it were, to detach behavior from the circumstances in which it takes place. It should be noted, however, that the wedge is supposed to have its effect only on the behavior of investors in the private sector of the economy.

This same wedge reappears in the theory of "liquidity preference" as the means whereby wealth-holding decisions are given analytical autonomy, and whereby the rate of interest is thereby cut loose from economic "circumstances." (Again, the application is evidently supposed to be restricted to the private sector of the economy.) For ease of exposition, attention has here been confined to the investment case, although the discussion could equally well be directed, *mutatis mutandis*, to that of liquidity preference.

It is worth emphasizing, in summary, that it is not the *fact* of uncertainty that is important for Keynes' argument, but rather how individuals are supposed to respond to the fact of uncertainty. Thus, if there is great uncertainty surrounding investment decisions, and producers respond to this by making, so far as possible, the same investment decisions this period as last period (since, after all, the results of previous decisions are the one thing they do know something about), this would not result in private sector investments being wayward and unruly; indeed, it might result in greater stability than would result from sophisticated calculations based on epistemologically privileged beliefs or an uncanny degree of foresight. Thus, the fact of uncertainty does not, of itself, establish the conclusion concerning the wayward and unruly behavior of particular macroeconomic variables. Indeed, it is not even evident that this argument helps to establish Keynes' conclusion rather than the opposite conclusion.

Unless there is some way of restraining the application of these subjectivist ideas and their associated implications of uncertainty, they cannot serve the purpose that is required of them within Keynes' scheme. In that case they become merely an analytical red herring. For what is required within

Keynes' scheme is not the uncertainty, as such, surrounding private sector investment decisions: it is the wayward and unruly behavior of the aggregates resulting from the decisions taken in the face of this uncertainty. Indeed, Keynes' system requires private sector investment to display this unruliness in two quite distinct senses: first, when compared with private sector *consumer* expenditure (this is required in order for Keynes' model to work); and, second, when compared with *public* sector investment expenditure (this is required in order for Keynes' policies to work). But since what is required is accordingly not the unruliness of private sector investment expenditure, but its *relative* unruliness when put into the context of the two comparisons to which we have just referred, it follows that, in the absence of some principle governing the relative influence of uncertainty on private vs. public investment and on private investment vs. private consumption (and hence saving), the uncertainty issue is, indeed, an analytical red herring. Given that the object of the exercise is to establish the relative unruliness of various expenditure aggregates, any discussion of pervasive, nonspecific uncertainty is actually beside the point (even allowing—what we have in fact been disputing—that greater uncertainty surrounding the decisions would lead to greater unruliness in their outcomes over time). In the great stream of interpretation and appraisal, reinterpretation and reappraisal of Keynes' work, this fact seems to have escaped attention.

Although subjectivist ideas do provide a wedge of sorts for driving between behavior and circumstances, it is apparent that it is a thoroughly unwieldy tool with which to operate: it cannot be satisfactorily used in a selective and discriminating way, to detach a certain class of behavior (or the behavior of a certain group of individuals) from the circumstances in which the behavior takes place.

III. Certainty and Fallibilism

What is unsatisfactory about focusing on the "uncertainty" of expectations is its way of seeing knowledge and beliefs as falling so far short of some ideal state of certainty. If "certainty" is interpreted in a way that makes

VOL. 72 NO. 3   *CODDINGTON: KEYNESIAN DEFICIENT FORESIGHT*   483

it unattainable, why should we be interested in the lack of it? To assess beliefs by their uncertainty is like assessing one's progress on a journey not by how far one has traveled, but by how far away the horizon is. The appropriate base line for assessing beliefs is ignorance, not omniscience. One may speculate on the progress that might have been made in geometry if the Greeks had succumbed to the temptation to measure distance by the extent to which it falls short of being infinite.

The state of certainty is in any case itself an ambiguous idea. For one could, firstly, regard certainty as a state of complete confidence in a belief, irrespective of whether that belief is correct (but how much confidence does one need for it to be "complete"?); or one could regard it as a state of complete confidence in a belief together with the correctness of this belief and perhaps even the believer having the grounds for entertaining the belief "with certainty."

Now, from the viewpoint of economic theory, the former concept of certainty as purely a state of complete confidence is evidently not much use. Perfect confidence in a belief is perhaps far better sustained by ignorance than by understanding. And one would not feel at all happy expounding a theory in which everyone could—repeatedly—be perfectly confident one moment and discover themselves to have been wrong the next. So it is to the second idea of certainty as correct foresight that we are driven.

It is recognized that there are analytical difficulties with the concept of correct foresight. There are problems, notably, of how a number of interdependently acting individuals may simultaneously enjoy correct foresight. This is a theme on which George L. S. Shackle has dwelt at length, arguing that general and simultaneous correct foresight is possible only to the extent that the conditional plans and intentions of the individuals have been—somehow—"pre-reconciled" within a state of general (market-clearing) equilibrium (1972). Now, this proposition can undoubtedly be rendered impregnable by the adoption of a sufficiently strong concept of market clearing in which it is required, *inter alia*, that the expectations of agents are of a particular type and are fulfilled. What is less

clear is whether such a way of proceeding is particularly helpful. For we may wish to recognize the fact that agents could become aware of the existence (or possibility) of non-clearing markets, and form expectations accordingly. The conditional plans that are pre-reconciled in the ("Walrasian") kind of general equilibrium that Shackle evidently has in mind are plans each of which is made on the assumption that all markets *will* clear (that is, no one makes any plans for responding to "trading difficulties"). But if the *form* of the expectations entertained by agents is restricted to this class, it is hardly surprising that they can be fulfilled only if a complete reconciliation is achieved, such as will avoid all the difficulties that—by the nature of the construction—the agents have disregarded in forming their expectations. If, however, the agents were allowed to form a wider range of plans, including plans conditional on the emergence of trading difficulties, then we have no reason at all to suppose that expectations of general market clearing are the only ones that are capable of being realized (i.e., of being self-fulfilling in the aggregate, when acted upon). The pursuit of this line of argument, however, would take us into far deeper analytical waters than is necessary for our immediate purposes.

To say, as I did previously, that certainty may be interpreted in a way that identifies it with some unattainable ideal, is, however, to gloss over the most important questions involved in deciding what one could reasonably mean by the term. Suppose that, proceeding along the lines of the preceding discussion, we were to provide an account of certainty in terms of correct foresight. Suppose, moreover, that we were to start with the (as it will turn out, naive) idea that foresight is correct if the future, when it arrives, *exactly* resembles what was forseen, in every particular, at every instant. If that is what is meant by "correct foresight", then its absence or nonattainment is a matter of utter triviality. But as soon as it is admitted that any *reasonable* conception of correct foresight must allow for some (reasonable) margins of error, we are on the beginnings of a slippery slope. For we then have to admit that there is no clear dichotomy between certainty and uncertainty (or between knowl-

484   *THE AMERICAN ECONOMIC REVIEW*   *JUNE 1982*

edge and ignorance, for that matter). Just to emphasize this point, we could go to the other extreme and claim that all foresight is "correct" (to some sufficiently lax standards of approximation), just as all foresight is "incorrect" (by the absurd standards of comprehensive exactness).

Accordingly, suppose we reject as absurd the idea that correct foresight is to be understood as foresight that is comprehensively exact in its correctness. We must then be driven to the notion that correctness must consist in the foresight's being within certain "reasonable" bounds of approximation, and, as a development of this, the scatter of actual cases within these bounds not exhibiting any *systematic* error. Accordingly, we wish to insist that part of what we mean—or what we should mean—by correct foresight is that the errors we make, even if they are all within the bounds of "reasonable approximation" are not "predominantly" in one direction: there are then further loose ends to be tidied up in elucidating what should count as predominantly in one direction. As soon as one gets this far, it is evident that the notion of correct foresight is crying out for statistical elaboration. It is very tempting to say that foresight is correct if the expected value of the error is zero. It is then a technical problem to devise tests to determine whether the expected value of the error in any particular case differs from zero by an amount that is statistically significant in the circumstances. (But I do not think that we would *really* accept that if the expected value of the error is zero this constitutes correct foresight irrespective of the variance; i.e., no matter how great the variance is.)

It is, on the argument I have been developing, a matter of no possible interest whether a particular belief or expectation is uncertain when compared with some—as it happens, unattainable—ideal state of omniscience. What *is* interesting is whether the belief or expectation is the best that one could arrive at in the circumstances: that is, does it make the best use of such information as is available to the agent concerned? If the best that can be done falls short of some ideal, that may lead to feelings of humility, but it cannot provide reasonable grounds for action or

for the revision of actions. By assessing beliefs and expectations in terms of the best use of available information rather than in terms of omniscience, one arrives at a framework of thought that is consistent with fallibilism. One concedes that mere mortals will continue to entertain expectations that will be mistaken in various particular ways; the reasonableness of these agents, however, will manifest itself in their unwillingness to persist in systematic patterns of error, once these have become apparent.

The fundamental mistake that is made in dealing with uncertainty in what we could now call a nonfallibilistic manner, is that it first conflates knowledge with certainty; it then argues, in effect, that since certainty is not attainable, neither is knowledge.[4] That is to say, it is to operate with the tacit presumption that knowledge, to count as such, must be demonstrable, provable, indisputable; which, given the way things are, means that any possibility of knowledge is confined to something like mathematics and formal logic. Philosophically, the position arrived at is known as "justificationist skepticism." Thus:

> Justificationism, that is, the identification of knowledge with proven knowledge, was the dominant tradition in rational thought throughout the ages. scepticism did not deny justificationism: it only claimed that there was (and could be) no proven knowledge and *therefore* no knowledge whatever. For the sceptics "knowledge" was nothing but animal belief. Thus justificationist scepticism ridiculed objective thought and opened the door to irrationalism, mysticism and superstition.   [Imre Lakatos, 1970, p. 94]

Justificationist skeptics present themselves, however, not in those terms, but simply as skeptics. What we are now in a position to see is that they at the same time both

---

[4] For example: "[Keynes] declares unequivocally that expectations do not rest on anything solid, determinable, demonstrable. 'We simply do not know'." (Shackle, 1973, p. 516).

VOL. 72 NO. 3   CODDINGTON: KEYNESIAN DEFICIENT FORESIGHT   485

guarantee and trivialize their skepticism by adopting unattainable standards for beliefs to qualify as knowledge. We have seen that Keynes, on occasion, wrote in a way that suggests the adoption of such unattainable standards, although even the most cursory acquaintance with the facts of his life show that he was not reduced to the state of puzzled indecision that a wholehearted adoption of such standards would entail. The contrast between the spirit and the letter of this aspect of Keynes' writing would be made all the more marked by those who attempt to impose on it the consistency of justificationist skepticism.

IV. Two Schools

Those commentators on Keynes who have been impressed by his forays into the realm of uncertainty in economic decision making give, as we have seen, canonical status to his 1937 article, where, in the opening passages, this theme is vigorously expounded. In doing so, however, these commentators may be taken to task for omitting to read the first half of the article in its proper context: namely, the second half. For having completed his brief essay on the incalculability of things in general, Keynes goes on to perform some comparative static exercises on the assumption that consumers' aggregate expenditure is a stable function of consumers' aggregate disposable income and that, furthermore, this stability is maintained in the face of the turbulence arising from the unruly behavior of private investment and the demand for money. (In the context of Keynes' policy proposals, it is also required that this stability be maintained in the face of arbitrary time paths for fiscal and monetary variables.) All this requires that consumers' expenditure is calculable on the basis of their current disposable incomes and that, therefore, their saving behavior, by subtraction, is also calculable on the same basis. Accordingly, those who have pointed to this article as an interpretative key owe us, at the very least, an explanation of why, immediately after having provided his key proposition, Keynes engages in analysis in flagrant contradiction with it.

Leaving on one side, however, this purely exegetical issue, we may turn to a consideration of the developments that have been inspired by this theme in Keynes' work.

Those who have been influenced by Keynes' forays into the realm of uncertainty and have tried to develop this theme in his work have taken it in one of two ways.[5] First, there are those who have continued to use notions of uncertainty, with its surrounding penumbra of subjectivism, in the same analytically opportunistic way that Keynes himself did. Here I have in mind the group who elect to be called "post-Keynesian,"[6] in the sense of aspiring to go a stage further in what they take to be the direction that Keynes himself was heading. Of paramount importance among those who see themselves as post-Keynesian in this sense is, of course, Joan Robinson. Second, there are those who have tried to follow in a consistent (and, indeed, relentlessly consistent) way the root-and-branch approach to uncertainty that Keynes on occasion adopted. Most notable among these are Shackle (1967, 1972, 1973, 1974) and Brian J. Loasby (1976).[7]

---

[5]Compare E. Roy Weintraub (1975) who, in his survey of this branch of literature, brings together all those who, for whatever reason, stress this aspect of Keynes' work. In concentrating on this apparent uniformity of subject matter, however, he obscures, I would argue, a more important opposition of purposes, and hence presents as a single interpretative "school" a group of commentators whose aims and outlooks are—as I shall try to show—irreconcilably diverse.

[6]I intend to provide a far more detailed exposition and appraisal of the Post-Keynesian School in a forthcoming paper.

[7]Thus:

If one can summarise in one sentence the theory of employment set forth by Keynes in his article 1937, it is this: unemployment in a market economy is the result of ignorance too great to be borne. The fully-specified macroeconomic models miss the point—which is precisely that no model of this situation can be fully specified.   [Loasby, 1976, p. 167]

Again:

The holder of cash...in return for giving up his right to the present possession of goods, retains unlimited discretion over the future use of...resources: he is absolved from giving any indication whatever of the timing or content of his future demands; and there is no automatic provision for meeting his future requirements. The problem is not one of communications, for there is nothing to communicate.   [Loasby, 1976, p. 166]

486   THE AMERICAN ECONOMIC REVIEW   JUNE 1982

The first group, the post-Keynesians, are interested in uncertainty insofar as it helps to show that, under capitalist institutions, the decentralization of production and investment decisions leads inevitably to chaos and waste. What this group needs to establish, then, is: (i) that the allegedly wayward and unruly nature of production and investment decisions under capitalist institutions is in some way a product of these institutions; and (ii) that under some alternative institutional arrangements things would be different (and better).

It is evident, however, that uncertainty and subjectivism in themselves have no bearing on the institution of private property in the means of production, nor on any other institution. The considerations that follow from these ideas are as applicable just as readily to members of parliament, Ministers and their officials within the civil service as to entrepreneurs within the private sector of the economy. Indeed, they are just as applicable to the actions of Comrade Prokin of the Reftninsky power station near Sverdlovsk in the Urals when he appears 1,000 miles away in Kharkov in search of truck number 4730092 and the generator that it contains. And, indeed, to his comrades at the Ministry of Railways who were unable to trace its whereabouts; and his further comrade, the director of the Reftninsky power station, whose plant had been reduced to a standstill by the absence of the missing generator and whose telegrams to his comrades at the Ministry of Railways had proved fruitless (The Times, April 25, 1980).

Anyone who has taken even a cursory interest in either the Concorde project, the U.K. nuclear power program, or the various schemes for a third London airport, will be well aware of the degree of uncertainty that may surround public sector investment projects. Post-Keynesians appear to favor some kind of tripartite institution to oversee investment programs at the national level, but they do not explain why this will not increase the degree of uncertainty surrounding aggregate investment, rather than reduce it. (See, for example, Alfred Eichner 1979, pp. 176–77, 179–81.)

The post-Keynesians are quite happy to make appeals to uncertainty insofar as this enables them to drive a wedge between behavior and circumstances in some cases; but if the wedge were to become comprehensive, they would be left with no theory at all, all behavior would appear equally capricious and unintelligible.

The second group has been led to a position that appears to be consistent but analytically nihilistic.[8] A consistent or all-embracing subjectivism is, analytically, a very self-denying thing.[9] If subjectivist logic is followed to the point of becoming convinced that there is nothing for economists to do but to understand certain (praxiological) concepts, then the only problem that remains is that of subjugating one's conscience long enough to draw one's salary in exchange for imparting this piece of wisdom. One could, of course, having got into this state of mind, spend a good deal of time and energy in trying to convince those who engage in macroeconomics, econometric model building, mathematical economics, general equilibrium theory, and so on, of the folly of their ways. But, that task accomplished, there would be nothing left but for the whole profession to shut up shop. This could become a real issue if the current revival of interest in Austrian economics should succumb to the messianic element that is to be found in some of the writing of Austrian subjectivists. We would then be faced with a situation akin to one in which there was an outbreak of Christian Science among the medical profession, or a passion for telekenesis among airline pilots.

V. Concluding Remarks

This paper has been concerned with a theme in Keynes' writing that it is convenient but—as we have seen—rather unsatisfactory to refer to as that of uncertainty in

[8] For example: "... Keynes' book [The General Theory] achieves its triumph by pointing out that the problems it is concerned with are essentially beyond solution" (Shackle, 1973), p. 516).

[9] See, for example, the exchange between Hicks and Lachmann in Mario Rizzo (1979).

economic decision making. It has been my purpose here to present Keynes' forays into this area as an opportunistic but mild flirtation with subjectivism. I have argued that those who have been impressed and influenced by this strand in Keynes' work fall into two groups: (i) those who fail to see that Keynes' encounter with subjectivism is only a passing one; (ii) those who fail to see that subjectivism, once introduced, cannot be confined within the limits that would suit their analytical purposes.

The first group has no doubt been influenced by Keynes' manner of writing, on occasion, in a way that takes a root-and-branch approach to the matter. I have argued, however, that, in taking this root-and-branch approach at all literally, they have got hold of the wrong end of the stick. I have also tried to explain the way in which the second group has been led into an unwarrantedly consistent interpretation of Keynes' work. There is probably a moral in all this, although if so, it is unlikely to differ very much from those derived in other contexts in which opportunistic flirtation has resulted in misunderstanding among onlookers.

REFERENCES

Eichner, Alfred S., *A Guide to Post-Keynesian Economics*, London: Macmillan, 1979.

Hicks, J. R., "Mr. Keynes' Theory of Employment," *Economic Journal*, June 1936, *46*, 238–53.

Kahn, R. F., "The Relation of Home Investment to Unemployment," *Economic Journal*, June 1931, *41*, 173–98.

Keynes, J. M., *A Treatise on Probability*, 1921; reprinted in his *Collected Writings*, Vol. VIII, London: Macmillan, for the Royal Economic Society.

_____, *The General Theory of Employment, Interest and Money*, 1936; reprinted in his *Collected Writings*, Vol. VII, London: Macmillan, for the Royal Economic Society.

_____, "The General Theory of Employment," *Quarterly Journal of Economics*, February 1937, *51*, 209–23.

Lakatos, Imre, "Falsification and the Methodology of Scientific Research Programmes," in his and Alan Musgrave, eds., *Criticism and the Growth of Knowledge*, Cambridge: Cambridge University Press, 1970.

Loasby, Brian J., *Choice, Complexity and Ignorance*, Cambridge: Cambridge University Press, 1976.

Rizzo, Mario J., *Time, Uncertainty and Disequilibrium*, Lexington: D.C. Heath and Co., 1979.

Robinson, Joan, *Economic Heresies*, London: Macmillan, 1971.

_____, "What has become of the Keynesian Revolution?," in her *After Keynes*, Oxford: Basil Blackwell, 1973.

Shackle, George, L. S., *The Years of High Theory*, Cambridge: Cambridge University Press, 1967.

_____, *Epistemics and Economics*, Cambridge: Cambridge University Press, 1972.

_____, "Keynes and Today's Establishment in Economic Theory: A View," *Journal of Economic Literature*, June 1973, *11*, 516–19.

_____, *Keynesian Kaleidics*, Edinburgh: Edinburgh University Press, 1974.

Townshend, Hugh, "Liquidity-premium and the Theory of Value," *Economic Journal*, March 1937, *47*, 157–69.

Weintraub, E. Roy, "'Uncertainty' and the Keynesian Revolution," *History of Political Economy*, Winter 1975, *7*, 530–48.

The Times, London, April 25, 1980.

[6]

Monetary Analysis, the Equilibrium Method, and Keynes's "General Theory"

Meir Kohn

Dartmouth College

Compared with the work of his contemporaries, Keynes's *General Theory* represented a radical change in theoretical method—from sequence analysis to the method of equilibrium. The nature of this change is discussed, together with its implications for the substance of Keynes's message and for the subsequent development of macroeconomics.

To understand the nature of the Keynesian revolution (and the significance of the new classical counterrevolution) one must realize that the *General Theory* (1936) was more a revolution of method than one of substance. Although Keynes represented his book as a new and dramatic break with what he called "classical economics"—Say's law, the separation of real and monetary phenomena, the stability of general economic equilibrium—that break was far from new. It went back at least to Marshall, Fisher, and Wicksell and had been widening steadily for over half a century in the work of Ohlin, Myrdal, Hayek, Hawtrey, Robertson, and Keynes himself, among others. While the *General Theory* did make significant new contributions of substance to this neoclassical tradition, it represented a truly startling revolution in method. This revolution lay in Keynes's abandonment of sequence analysis in favor of the method of equilibrium. Indeed, contrary to what one might have expected from reading the first few chapters of

I am grateful to Athanasios Asimakopulos, Björn Hansson, David Laidler, Axel Leijonhufvud, Ming-Yih Liang, George McCandless, Walter Salant, and two anonymous referees for helpful comments on earlier drafts and to the Lewis H. Haney Fund at Dartmouth College for financial support.

[*Journal of Political Economy*, 1986, vol. 94, no. 6]

1192   JOURNAL OF POLITICAL ECONOMY

the *General Theory,* no "classical" economist stepped forward to debate with Keynes the validity of Say's law. Instead, the debate raged over the instantaneous multiplier, the role of expectations, liquidity preference versus loanable funds, and, in general, over the nature and the validity of Keynes's concept of equilibrium.

The adoption of the equilibrium method was both the strength of the *General Theory* and its weakness. On the one hand, it gave Keynes's message the power and simplicity it needed to supplant the classical verities in the textbooks and to influence the making of policy. On the other, the internal contradictions of the *General Theory*—for the anticlassical message cannot be expressed in a logically consistent and nontrivial way using the equilibrium method—led to a nightmare of confusion among professional economists from which we are only now beginning to emerge. As this inconsistency has become increasingly clear, it is not the equilibrium method that has been repudiated, but the anticlassical message. To salvage this message and to give ourselves a fair chance of weighing its merits, we need a clear understanding of precisely how the *General Theory* departed from previous and contemporary work both in substance and in method.[1]

I.   Real Analysis and Monetary Analysis

In attempting to place the *General Theory* in the history of monetary thought, Schumpeter (1954, pp. 276–82) developed the very useful distinction between "real analysis" and "monetary analysis."

Real analysis begins with the assumption that all essential features of the economy may be understood in real terms—in terms of underlying tastes and technologies. The use of money in actual transactions should not distract us: money is a veil to be drawn aside. In essence, households trade real factor services for the goods they consume; firms convert real inputs into outputs; capital markets allocate real resources between consumption and investment. If the monetary mechanism functions properly—and it normally does—we may analyze the economic process *as if* it takes place in a barter economy. Monetary considerations may safely be relegated to an appendix, being irrelevant to the main theoretical structure.[2]

---

[1] Since the emphasis throughout will be on the change in theoretical method, there will be little discussion of other recent interpretations, which dwell largely on different aspects of the *General Theory.* Two interpretations that do stress the change in theoretical method are those of Milgate (1982) and Hansson (1983). Milgate reaches very different conclusions, however, on the implications of this change. Anyone doubting the importance for current work of a proper understanding of the nature of Keynes's change in method should read Lucas and Sargent (1978), especially p. 58.

[2] Cf. Clower (1975). This "virtual barter" economy is quite unlike any actual barter economy in that trade proceeds costlessly and smoothly.

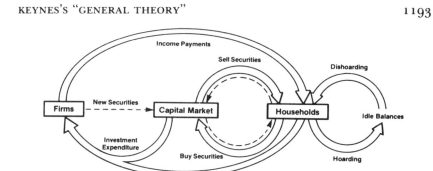

FIG. 1.—The circular flow of money payments

Monetary analysis concentrates precisely on that which real analysis considers secondary: the money flows that are the counterpart of all real transactions. The as-if-barter approach is rejected, and money is introduced "on the very ground floor of our analytic structure": "Money prices, money incomes, and saving and investment decisions bearing upon these money incomes, no longer appear as expressions—sometimes convenient, sometimes misleading, but always nonessential—of quantities of commodities and services and of exchange ratios between them: they acquire a life and an importance of their own, and it has to be recognized that essential features of the capitalist process may depend upon the 'veil' and that the 'face behind it' is incomplete without it" (Schumpeter 1954, p. 278).

Discussion of the issues between real and monetary analysis is made exceptionally difficult because, while we have a generally accepted theoretical framework for real analysis, there exists no such framework for monetary analysis. However, the basic "vision" of monetary analysis may be illustrated with the aid of a simple circular flow diagram, showing expenditure flows in a stylized monetary economy (see fig. 1).

Since the expenditure flows will generally be changing over time, any formal theory of this economy will have to be explicitly dynamic. The simplest approach is some sort of *sequence analysis* consisting of (*a*) a "single-period theory" that determines the state of the economy at a moment of time (the "current period") and (*b*) a "continuation theory" concerned with how the outcome of the current period determines the initial conditions of the next (see Hicks 1956). While the continuation theory will stress the money flow "hydraulics" of monetary analysis, it will have to pay attention, too, to other "mechanical" linkages (see Villard 1948): production takes time, so that more employment today means more output only in the future; the accumulation and decumulation of stocks of fixed and working capital will

1194   JOURNAL OF POLITICAL ECONOMY

matter. In addition to these mechanical linkages, attention will also have to be paid to expectational dynamics: if plans formed on current expectations are not mutually consistent, expectations, and so plans, will have to be modified; the resultant disappointment of expectations will involve profits and losses, and these too will affect the evolution of the system.

Many of these daunting complexities can be swept aside, however, if we are willing to restrict our attention to a *repetitive flow*—a situation in which behavior is unchanging over time. In such a situation, it is *as if* production is instantaneous and current production is currently consumed; the circulation of money is precisely suited to real activity and does not constrain it in any way; since nothing is changing, it is only natural that expectations are fulfilled and that there are no "windfall" profits or losses.

In a repetitive flow, the monetary aspects of exchange recede into the background. The static (stationary) relations that emerge may be analyzed as if they were the result of a frictionless and instantaneous exchange of goods for goods—"virtual barter." In a repetitive flow, money is indeed a veil: nothing is lost by drawing this veil aside, and the real foundations of economic behavior are revealed with great clarity.

Of course, the repetitive flow is an analytical fiction. There is no implication that any actual economy will ever be found in such a situation. The construct is justified by the enormous simplification it allows and by the assumption—usually implicit—that results carry over (perhaps with minor modifications) to actual economies, even though the latter are not in a repetitive-flow situation.[3]

It seems natural to regard the repetitive flow as a state of equilibrium: behavior is unchanging because individuals have no desire to change their plans, and no need either, since those plans are mutually consistent. This assumption allows us to use the *equilibrium method*. The state of the economy is characterized by a system of simultaneous

---

[3] Cf. Schumpeter (1954, pp. 555–70, 963–71, 1160–61), especially: "Here we are concerned with a different kind of stationary state, namely, with a stationary state that is not a future reality but only a conceptual construct or tool of analysis that serves to isolate, for the purposes of a preliminary study, the group of economic phenomena that would be observable in an unchanging economic process" (p. 562). Schumpeter saw this analytical construct, which he called the "stationary flow" or "stationary state" (creating confusion with a quite different concept of the same name), as the basis not only of classical value theory but also of the value theory of Marshall and Walras. More recent versions of real analysis, the Arrow-Debreu framework in particular, have extended real analysis to encompass changing behavior over time and even uncertainty. This extension is not without its conceptual problems, particularly with respect to the sort of monetary issues considered here. To simplify the discussion, I will ignore this sort of extension, which anyhow did not exist when Keynes was writing the *General Theory*.

equations expressing the necessary conditions for stationarity. These conditions are typically derived from rational individual behavior. The specification of such behavior is much simplified by considering only what is rational *in equilibrium* (in a repetitive flow). This "circularity" is harmless as long as discussion is restricted to the characterization of equilibrium. It becomes a major handicap, however, in considering issues of stability—how equilibrium is brought about or how the economy behaves outside of equilibrium.[4]

Monetary analysis, then, is general and complicated; real analysis is special and simple, the result of restricting the domain of the theory to an equilibrium repetitive flow. Despite its limitations, real analysis using the equilibrium method—what Keynes meant by "classical economics"—has been highly successful in analyzing problems of public finance, trade, distribution, and growth. For these issues, the special assumptions underlying the theory seem a reasonable and costless simplification. However, for one issue, and one that was becoming a major concern by the end of the nineteenth century, these simplifying assumptions are patently inappropriate. That issue is the short-run instability of the economy—the question of industrial fluctuations or business cycles. Here, *changing* flows of money income and expenditure are clearly of the essence, and some sort of explicit monetary analysis seems inescapable.[5]

II.   Where the "General Theory" Fits In

A.   *The Cycle of Real and Monetary Analysis*

The history of economic theory has seen alternating periods of real and monetary analysis. While this alternation has been related to an alternation in policy concern between stability and growth, it has also reflected the internal logic of theoretical development.

The first major "interlude" of monetary analysis—preceded by a long tradition of real analysis going back to Aristotle and succeeded by the real analysis of classical economics—reached its zenith with the work of Boisguillebert, Cantillon, and Quesnay. The chief concern of this Physiocratic monetary analysis was the stability of the economic system in the face of potential interference with the circular flow. The imposition of taxes and tariffs was criticized because it drew money out of the circular flow, hence restricting consumer expenditure. The

---

[4] What is required, of course, is a stationarity of *plans* rather than a stationarity of behavior (see Bode 1943). It is possible to talk of dynamic, as well as static, equilibrium (see n. 3 above).

[5] For somewhat different, and very illuminating, approaches to the relationship between equilibrium, real analysis, and the repetitive flow, see Hicks (1965) and Milgate (1982).

1196   JOURNAL OF POLITICAL ECONOMY

archvillain, however, was saving: "In this analytic schema the prompt onward flow of purchasing power is everything. Saving is believed to interrupt it. Hence saving is a sort of public enemy" (Schumpeter 1954, p. 287). Quesnay expressed these ideas formally in his famous *Tableau Économique* (1758).[6]

The shift to the real analysis of the classicals was principally the product of a change in policy concern from stability to growth, trade, and distribution. These latter could best be analyzed by ignoring the monetary epiphenomena of the short run and concentrating on the major real forces of the long run. The *Tableau* facilitated this shift in attention because, although it described the circular flow, it did so precisely in the state of *repetitive* flow that lends itself to as-if-barter analysis.[7] Concern with the issues of monetary analysis continued— witness the debate over Say's law—but in the absence of a workable analytical framework, interest waned. (The *Tableau* was little help in answering such questions because of its restriction to the repetitive flow: no analytical framework was available to deal with a *non*repetitive flow.) The classical mainstream had both analytical rigor and "relevance" on its side, and it "conquered England as completely as the Holy Inquisition conquered Spain" (Keynes 1936, p. 32).

B. Neoclassical Monetary Analysis

The rigid adherence of classical economics to real analysis, and its rejection of the concerns of monetary analysis, were not to last for very long. Already in Mill's *Principles* (1848), classical dogma was sufficiently diluted to allow Mill to write, "[In times of crisis] there is

---

[6] The *Tableau* was also the first general equilibrium model. As Schumpeter (1954, p. 243) notes, this method—however crude—retained some definite advantages over the later version of real analysis: "[Since] the idea of representing the pure logic of the economic process by a system of simultaneous equations was quite outside their range of vision, they represented it by a picture. In a sense, this method was primitive and lacking in rigor—which is, in fact, why it fell out of the running and why analysis historically developed on the other line. But in one respect it was superior to the logically more satisfactory method; it visualized the (stationary) economic process as a circuit flow that in each period returns upon itself. This is not only a method of conveying the fact that the economic process is logically self-contained, a distinct thing that is complete in itself, but it is also a method of conveying features of it—definite sequences in particular—that do not stand out equally well in a system of simultaneous equations." Indeed, these failings—or rather omissions—of real analysis were to lead to the resurgence of monetary analysis that culminated in the *General Theory*.

[7] The difficulty of dealing with the change implicit in growth with a purely static analysis was elegantly overcome with the device of comparative statics: the economy was analyzed through a succession of static depictions, with the economy at each time assumed to be in a stable repetitive flow. Problems of traverse from one such situation to the next were brushed aside as "uninteresting" (which they may well have been in terms of the larger issues addressed).

really an excess of all commodities above the money demand; in other words there is an under-supply of money . . . . Almost everybody is therefore a seller and there are scarcely any buyers" (quoted in Schumpeter 1954, p. 622). Marshall, Fisher, and, especially, Wicksell contributed to a growing resurgence of monetary analysis that was to peak in the 1920s and 1930s and that included the work of Robertson, Hawtrey, and Keynes in England; Mises and Hayek in Austria; and Myrdal, Lindahl, Ohlin, and Lundberg in Sweden.

Like Physiocratic monetary analysis before it, this new neoclassical version was principally concerned with the stability of the economic system. Its point of departure was the real equilibrium of classical and neoclassical real analysis. The economy of fact was believed to deviate from this ideal because real or monetary shocks could shift either the actual economy or the position of the equilibrium itself. While the veil of money could be safely ignored in characterizing the nature of the equilibrium, monetary factors were of the essence in understanding the movement of the economy toward or about the equilibrium state.

While real shocks required changes in the composition, and even in the intensity, of economic activity, these "appropriate fluctuations," as Robertson (1926) called them, were exacerbated by failures of the monetary-financial system to adjust as it should. The goal of monetary policy was to prevent this exacerbation and to help the actual economy track real equilibrium as closely as possible.[8]

The equilibrium method, which had been so fruitful for real analysis, seemed inappropriate in the situation of flux outside the repetitive flow that was the subject matter of neoclassical monetary analysis. For the first time, economists faced squarely the difficulties of dynamics, attempting various forms of period analysis or sequence analysis (see Schumpeter 1954, p. 1160).

The result was an embarrassment of riches, with each author devising a sequence analysis of his very own. The sheer complexity of the problem required a choice between mechanical and expectational approaches, with only lip service paid to the side neglected. The selection of the unit period depended on the approach taken and varied from theory to theory. Each author adopted his own set of definitions for common terms such as saving and investment and frequently invented a host of new terms specific to his own theory. The analysis being literary rather than formal, very few definite results emerged. Typically, the analysis would begin with equilibrium being disturbed

---

[8] This was called a policy of "neutral money." Just what such a policy would entail— whether stabilizing the price level, stabilizing the quantity of money, or something quite different—was the main question addressed by neoclassical monetary analysis (cf. Schumpeter 1954, p. 1089).

by some shock and go on to trace through the repercussions for one or two periods before becoming hopelessly tangled.[9]

Those involved in the endless debates over terminology and approach had a wonderful time, but they spoke mainly to one another. Because of its confusion and incoherence, neoclassical monetary analysis failed to displace classical real analysis as a policy tool. Many academic economists still clung to classical views, and consequently "the deep divergences of opinion between fellow economists [had] for the time being almost destroyed the practical influence of economic theory" (Keynes 1936, p. vi). Textbooks were still dominated by the classical view. Being less an ivory-tower academic and more a polemicist and commentator on public policy than most, Keynes found this inability to persuade and to influence particularly frustrating. He described his own contribution to the policy debate of the period as "the croakings of a Cassandra who could never influence the course of events in time" (Keynes 1933/1972, p. xvii).[10]

The policy message of neoclassical monetary analysis was simple enough. Whatever the root cause of economic disturbance, monetary factors could make the resulting dislocation worse, and suitable policy could help. The system might be self-righting eventually, but things could usefully be speeded up. While to some extent policy practice was running ahead of theoretical justification, it was constantly hampered by the intellectual resistance of those who, inappropriately, still based their policy advice on real analysis. It was Keynes's intention in the *General Theory* to overcome this intellectual resistance once and for all. He hoped to provide a formal treatment of monetary analysis simple and powerful enough to dominate the debate on countercycli-

---

[9] See Lundberg (1937) for an excellent critical review of the various theories. Villard's (1948) retrospective judgment on all this seems quite fair: "[One] can wish period analysis every success and yet remain skeptical as to whether it will prove fruitful within the immediate future" (p. 327). "For however much the careful step-by-step procedure of period analysis commends itself as the only way to attain *complete* knowledge of the operation of our economic system, to date most examples can best be described as methodological explorations rather than positive contributions" (p. 326).

[10] The most notable group of "holdouts" in England, with whom Keynes constantly found himself at odds, resided at the London School of Economics (see Winch 1969, chap. 8). On the continuing dominance of real analysis in undergraduate instruction, see Samuelson (1968), Salant (1978), and Austin Robinson (1983, p. 260). Keynes himself wrote: "Most treatises on the principles of economics are concerned mainly, if not entirely, with a real-exchange economy; and—which is more peculiar—the same thing is also largely true of most treatises on the theory of money. In particular, Marshall's *Principles of Economics* is avowedly concerned with a real-exchange economy; and so, I think, is by far the greater part of the treatises of Professor Pigou—to name those English works on which I have been brought up and with which I am most familiar. But the same thing is also true of the dominant systematic treatises in other languages and countries" (1973a, p. 409). Keynes had hoped that his own *Treatise* would fill the gap, but its reception had been disappointing, and it had failed to do so.

cal policy and to limit classical real analysis to the policy issues to which it was properly suited.[11]

C.   The "General Theory" as Monetary Analysis

There can be no question that Keynes saw his own work as a form of monetary analysis. The *Treatise* (1930) was a typical work of neoclassical monetary analysis and was seen as such by Keynes's contemporaries. In "doing it all over again" in the *General Theory*, Keynes's *purpose* had not changed.[12]

A particularly clear statement of that purpose appeared under the title "A Monetary Theory of Production" in a 1933 festschrift for Arthur Spiethoff:

> In my opinion the main reason why the problem of crises is unsolved, or at any rate why this theory is so unsatisfactory, is to be found in the lack of what might be termed a *monetary theory of production.*
>
> The distinction which is normally made between a barter economy and a monetary economy depends upon the employment of money as a convenient means of effecting exchanges—as an instrument of great convenience, but transitory and neutral in its effect. It is regarded as a mere link between cloth and wheat, or between the day's labour spent on building the canoe and the day's labour spent on harvesting the crop. It is not supposed to affect the essential nature of the transaction from being, in the minds of those making it, one between real things, or to modify the motives and decisions of the parties to it. Money, that is to say, is employed, but is treated as being in some sense *neutral.*
>
> That, however, is not the distinction which I have in mind when I say that we lack a monetary theory of production. An economy, which uses money but uses it merely as a neutral link between transactions in real things and real assets and does not allow it to enter into motives or decisions, might be called—for want of a better name—a *real-exchange economy.* The theory which I desiderate would deal, in contradistinc-

---

[11] Support for public works programs to combat unemployment was nonetheless quite widespread even among those who disagreed with Keynes on theory. He found this inconsistency quite exasperating, writing, "they insist on maintaining theories from which their own practical conclusions cannot possibly follow" (1973b, p. 259). See, too, Hutchison (1978, p. 165) and Salant (1978).

[12] Schumpeter's (1954) view is clear enough. He called the *General Theory* "the leading system of Monetary Analysis of today" (p. 278, n. 4); "Monetary Analysis has once more conquered in our own time" (p. 276).

1200   JOURNAL OF POLITICAL ECONOMY

tion to this, with an economy in which money plays a part of its own and affects motives and decisions and is, in short, one of the operative factors in the situation, so that the course of events cannot be predicted, either in the long period or in the short, without a knowledge of the behaviour of money between the first state and the last. And it is this which we ought to mean when we speak of a *monetary economy* . . . .

. . . It is my belief that the far-reaching and in some respects fundamental differences between the conclusions of a monetary economy and those of the more simplified real-exchange economy have been greatly underestimated by the exponents of the traditional economics; with the result that the machinery of thought with which real-exchange economics has equipped the minds of practitioners in the world of affairs, and also of economists themselves, has led in practice to many erroneous conclusions and policies. The idea that it is comparatively easy to adapt the hypothetical conclusions of a real wage economics to the real world of monetary economics is a mistake. It is extraordinarily difficult to make the adaptation, and perhaps impossible without the aid of a developed theory of monetary economics.

One of the chief causes of confusion lies in the fact that the assumptions of the real-exchange economy have been tacit, and you will search treatises on real-exchange economics in vain for any express statement of the simplifications introduced or for the relationship of its hypothetical conclusions to the facts of the real world. We are not told what conditions have to be fulfilled if money is to be neutral. Nor is it easy to supply the gap. Now the conditions required for the "neutrality" of money, in the sense in which this is assumed in— . . . to take this book as a leading example— Marshall's *Principles of Economics,* are, I suspect, precisely the same as those which will insure that crises *do not occur.* If this is true, the real-exchange economics, on which most of us have been brought up and with the conclusions of which our minds are deeply impregnated,. though a valuable abstraction in itself and perfectly valid as an intellectual conception, is a singularly blunt weapon for dealing with the problem of booms and depressions. For it has assumed away the very matter under investigation. . . .

Accordingly I believe that the next task is to work out in some detail a monetary theory of production, to supplement the real-exchange theories which we already possess. At any rate that is the task on which I am now occupying myself, in some confidence that I am not wasting my time. [Keynes 1973a, pp. 408–11]

In 1932, Keynes had changed the title of his Cambridge lectures from "The Pure Theory of Money" to "A Monetary Theory of Production," and it was this same title that he initially adopted for the new book he had just begun (1979, p. 49).[13]

D.   What Keynes Meant by "Classical Economics"[14]

Keynes's adoption of the term "classical economics" for the views he opposed led to much controversy and confusion. In the passage above it is clear that the theory from which he wished to distinguish his own, and which he associated with Marshall and Pigou, was the theory of the real exchange economy—the economy in which money is neutral by assumption, the economy of real analysis. In the *General Theory* he wrote: "The conviction, which runs, for example, through almost all Professor Pigou's work, that money makes no real difference except frictionally and that the theory of production and employment can be worked out (like Mill's) as being based on 'real' exchanges with money introduced perfunctorily in a later chapter, is the modern version of the classical tradition" (1936, pp. 19–20).

Keynes clearly did *not* include in the ranks of classical economists those who had, like himself, labored in the development of neoclassical monetary analysis: "I have never regarded Hawtrey, Robertson or Ohlin, for example, as Classical economists. Indeed, they have all been pioneers in the other line of approach" (1979, p. 270).

That Keynes believed the views of policymakers largely to have been molded by classical ideas is clear from a letter to Hawtrey in 1936:

> When you tell me that none of your colleagues at the Treasury have been brought up on the classical theory of interest, I can only assume that you have forgotten in what sense I have used the term "classical". . . . . I mean by the classical school, as I have repeatedly explained, not merely Ricardo and Mill, but Marshall and Pigou and Henderson and myself

---

[13] The early drafts of the introduction to the book (Keynes 1979, pp. 66–68, 76–102) were based on this distinction between monetary and real exchange economies. By the draft table of contents of mid-1934 (1973b, p. 423) this introduction had been dropped in favor of the one actually to appear in the *General Theory* based on the "postulates of the Classical economics" and the "principle of effective demand" (see 1973b, p. 421; 1979, pp. 49, 62, 63). A reason for this change is suggested in n. 19 below.

[14] The interpretation offered here of what Keynes meant by "classical" is very similar to that of Hutchison (1978, chaps. 5, 6).

1202   JOURNAL OF POLITICAL ECONOMY

until quite recently, and in fact every teacher of the subject in this country with the exception of yourself and a few recent figures like Hayek, whom I should call "neo-classicals". I should have thought that it was absolutely certain that all your colleagues, who had had any economic education at all, had been educated according to the classical school. [1973b, p. 24]

E.   The Meaning of "General" in "General Theory"

Logically speaking, the "monetary theory of production" (monetary analysis) represents the more general view of the economic process, with "classical economics" (real analysis) valid only for the special case of a repetitive flow (from which all problems of time, money, and coordination have been excluded by assumption). It is precisely in this sense that Keynes considered his theory to be a *general* theory.[15]

Such an interpretation makes unexceptionable the following passage in the *General Theory* that many disciples of Keynes have regarded as "remarkable backsliding": "Our criticism of the accepted classical theory of economics has consisted not so much in finding logical flaws in its analysis as in pointing out that its tacit assumptions are seldom or never satisfied, with the result that it cannot solve the economic problems of the actual world. But if our central controls succeed in establishing an aggregate volume of output corresponding to full employment as nearly as is practicable, the classical theory comes into its own again from this point onwards" (1936, p. 378). That is, if stability is assured by a policy grounded in monetary analysis, the real analysis characterization of equilibrium is quite valid.

Note, too, that what Keynes meant by trying "to bring the theory of prices as a whole back to close contact with the theory of value" (1936, p. 293) is precisely the *reverse* of what Hicks proposed in his "Suggestion for Simplifying the Theory of Money" (1935). While Hicks con-

---

[15] The evolution of the book's title certainly supports this view: 1932: The Monetary Theory of Production (1979, p. 49); 1933: The Monetary Theory of Employment (1979, p. 62); The General Theory of Employment (1973a, p. 421; 1979, p. 63); 1934: The General Theory of Employment, Interest and Money (1973a, p. 423). Both the shift in title from "monetary" to "general" and the introduction of the term "classical" for real analysis seem to date from Keynes's reading of, and strong reaction to, Pigou's *Theory of Unemployment* (1933) (see 1973a, pp. 309–13; 1979, pp. 27–33; and esp. 1973a, p. 420). The abandonment of the early introduction based on the distinction between real exchange and monetary economies in favor of the one finally adopted— "The Postulates of Classical Economics" and the awkward equilibrium analysis of chap. 3, "The Principle of Effective Demand"—seems also to have resulted from Keynes's preoccupation with Pigou's book. One may speculate that the *General Theory* would have been less confusing a book had Keynes ignored Pigou's work on unemployment entirely and stuck to what he himself had had to say.

sidered the theory of money to be no more than a particular chapter in the theory of value, Keynes believed just the opposite: that the whole of the theory of value was just a special case of the monetary theory of production.

F. *Keynes's Adoption of the Equilibrium Method*

The *Treatise,* while differing in many ways from other works of neo-classical monetary analysis, was like them in adopting the method of sequence analysis. All too aware of the difficulties of rigorous formali-zation, Keynes had tried to avoid controversy by being vague about the precise nature of his dynamics—the length of the unit period and the length and nature of the various lags involved. The ploy, how-ever, was unsuccessful, the vagueness itself drawing strong criticism. The issues could not be evaded:

> It was the *Treatise* more than any other volume that brought the problem of equilibrium to a head and repre-sented a crossroads in the development of monetary the-ory. . . . The *Treatise* was criticized both because of the ambi-guity of its discussion of [dynamics] and for the extent to which the time period in question could be expected to vary over the course of the business cycle. Against these criticisms there were two possible lines of defense: either the various factors influencing the [dynamics] could be examined, and explicit assumptions could be made regarding the time pe-riod in question; or a "timeless" analysis could be developed and the problem avoided in this fashion. In the first of these directions lies modern period analysis, with its explicit as-sumptions regarding lags and leads . . . in the other, the instantaneous analysis of Keynes' *General Theory of Employ-ment, Interest and Money.* [Villard 1948, pp. 325–26]

While Keynes did eventually take the "timeless" route, there is evi-dence in the early draft chapters of *The Monetary Theory of Production* that initially he had inclined, rather, toward a more explicit period analysis. In a letter to Hawtrey in June 1932 he wrote: "As I men-tioned to you, I am working it out all over again. . . . The main object of my treatment . . . will be to fill in the gap of which you complain that I do not follow up the actual genesis of change and am too content with a purely formal treatment of the first and final truisms" (1973a, pp. 172–73).

In the end, however, he repudiated both the "mechanical" money flow approach of Robertson and the "expectational" approach of the Swedes:

> While Keynes must at the time have understood and ac-
> quiesced in my step-by-step method, it is evident that it
> never, so to speak, got under his skin; for in his two succes-
> sive treatments of the savings-investment theme in his two
> big books he discarded it completely. [Robertson 1926/1949,
> p. xi]

> As regards the *ex post* and *ex ante* method, I shall certainly
> give further thought to its advantages. This is in fact almost
> precisely on the lines that I was thinking and lecturing some-
> where about 1931 and 1932, and subsequently abandoned.
> [Keynes (in a letter to Ohlin in January 1937) 1973*b*, p. 184]

Although Keynes is sometimes deprecated today as a formal theorist, his reason for abandoning sequence analysis seems to have been
that he was *too* demanding in terms of rigor and logical consistency.
(It is interesting that Robertson, the classicist, attempted a formal
analysis of money flows, while Keynes, the mathematician, found it
intractable.) He explained to Ohlin his abandonment of the ex ante/
ex post method in the following terms:

> My reason for giving it up was owing to my failure to
> establish any definite unit of time, and I found that that
> made very artificial any attempt to state the theory precisely.
> So, after writing out many chapters along what were evi-
> dently the Swedish lines, I scrapped the lot and felt that my
> new treatment was much safer and sounder from the logical
> point of view.
>   . . . When one comes to prove something truly logical and
> properly watertight, then I believe there are advantages in
> my method and that the *ex post* and *ex ante* device cannot be
> precisely stated without very cumbrous devices. [1973*b*, p.
> 184]

Whatever his reasons, Keynes abandoned sequence analysis in
favor of the equilibrium method. This attempt to apply the equilibrium method to monetary analysis represented a radical departure
and was regarded as such by contemporary commentators, most of
them themselves contributors to neoclassical monetary analysis. Indeed, many found the adoption of the equilibrium method to be the
most striking thing about the *General Theory*:

> The real hall-mark of the new theorizing is its setting in
> general equilibrium analysis. . . . Is the business cycle en-
> visaged as a movement *of* "general equilibrium" itself, or
> *around* equilibrium, or *from* one equilibrium to another? For-
> mally, at least, we seem to have the first. [Ellis 1938, p. 111]

Keynes further simplified his structure by avoiding, as much as possible, all complications that arise in process analysis. The exact skeleton of Keynes' system belongs, to use the terms proposed by Ragnar Frisch, to macrostatics, not to macrodynamics. . . . He had an aversion to "periods" and . . . he concentrated attention upon considerations of static equilibrium. [Schumpeter 1947, pp. 92–93]

Keynes' theoretical system is . . . "old-fashioned" in [one] respect which characterises recent economic theory— namely, the attempt to break away from an explanation of economic events by means of orthodox equilibrium constructions. No other analysis of trade fluctuations in recent years—with the possible exception of the Mises-Hayek school—follows such conservative lines in this respect. In fact, Keynes is much more an "equilibrium theorist" than such economists as Cassel and, I think, Marshall. [Ohlin 1937/1944, pp. 124–25][16]

The *General Theory* was, of course, replete with loose, literary references to implicit dynamics. There was no doubt in anyone's mind, however, that the formal analytical framework was strictly one of static equilibrium: "What is strictly static in *The General Theory* is the theoretical skeleton as precisely stated in several places in the book (e.g., p. 245 *et seq.* or p. 280 *et seq.*) and later formalized by Lange, Meade, and others. The text surrounding the theoretical statements in *The General Theory* contains, of course, many dynamic considerations. The frequent use made of the expectation concept shows the dynamic intent. But the dynamic elements are not incorporated into the theory. All the functions stated are strictly static" (Haberler 1946, p. 188, n. 3).

III. The Evolution of Keynes's Concept of Equilibrium

It is obvious from the quotations above that Keynes's espousal of the equilibrium method was greeted with less than enthusiasm. There were, first of all, many inconsistencies in his use of the equilibrium method in the *General Theory*, and I will trace how the resolution of these inconsistencies through debate with his critics pushed Keynes toward the particular formalization of his theory that has come to be known as the "Keynesian model." Beyond criticism of these inconsis-

[16] That this is typical of the reaction of the Swedish economists is documented in Hansson (1982, chap. 11). See also Haberler's reaction (1937/1963, p. 249).

1206   JOURNAL OF POLITICAL ECONOMY

tencies, however, many of Keynes's critics objected *in principle* to his adoption of the equilibrium method. Monetary analysis deals with an economy "out of equilibrium"; how can the equilibrium *method* be applied to such an economy? This objection to the dissonance between method and substance will be evident, below the surface, in the discussion that follows. At this deeper level the issue was never resolved in Keynes's own time. Resolution of the logical inconsistencies of his theory, the emergence of an equilibrium concept that "worked," seemed to leave his critics stumped. The deeper issue remained, however, and in the next section we will see its significance for the subsequent development of modern macroeconomics.

A. *The Origin in Kahn's Theory of the Multiplier*

The central idea of the *General Theory*, the idea that enabled the equilibrium method to be applied, was the existence of an equilibrium relationship between income and investment. In a letter to Robertson in December 1936, Keynes summed up the essence of his theory thus:

> Incomes are created partly by entrepreneurs producing for investment and partly by their producing for consumption. The amount that is consumed depends on the amount of income thus made up. Hence the amount of consumption goods which it will pay entrepreneurs to produce depends on the amount of investment goods which they are producing. If, for example, the public are in the habit of spending nine-tenths of their income on consumption goods, it follows that if entrepreneurs were to produce consumption goods at a cost more than nine times the cost of the investment goods they are producing, some part of their output could not be sold at a price which would cover its cost of production. For the consumption goods on the market would have cost more than nine-tenths of the aggregate income of the public and would, therefore, be in excess of the demand for consumption goods, which, by hypothesis is only the nine-tenths. Thus entrepreneurs will make a loss, until they contract their output of consumption goods down to an amount at which it no longer exceeds nine times their current output of investment goods.
>
> To my own thought the simple notion expressed in the above has been very greatly illuminating. To me at least it was a wholly new idea. [1973*b*, p. 90]

Of course, the concern with a balance between the consumption goods industry and the investment goods industry was not new: it had been at the heart of the *Treatise*. What was new was the proposition that there existed an *equilibrium* relation between the two that derived from the "habit" of the public in spending a given fraction of its income on consumption.

While the origin of this new idea was undoubtedly in Kahn's (1931) famous article on the multiplier, the transition from Kahn's analysis to Keynes's was far from immediate. In particular, Kahn's was a *sequence* analysis. It asked how much secondary employment would be generated by a permanent increase in government investment. It traced through the "rounds" of income generation and expenditure, considered the various "leakages" that would make each successive round progressively smaller, and worried about how the initial increase in investment would be financed before sufficient new saving had been generated. For Keynes, these dynamic considerations only obscured the much more important implicit relationship between income and investment—the potential linchpin of a powerful new *equilibrium* theory that could challenge "classical economics" on its own terms.[17]

B. The Two Notions of Equilibrium in the "General Theory"

The *General Theory* contained two quite different notions of equilibrium derived from the multiplier relationship, each of them in its own way designed to avoid the problems of sequence analysis. The first was a sort of "instantaneous" relationship that was supposed to hold at all times between income and investment. It derived from Keynes's definitions of income, saving, and investment and represented an attempt to avoid the dynamic problem by defining it away.[18] The second notion was a "short-period equilibrium," a sort of equilibrium over time. In terms of the Hicksian terminology of "single-period theory" and "continuation theory," the instantaneous relation represented a peculiar kind of single-period theory that was always true by

---

[17] Keynes acknowledged his debt to Kahn in the *General Theory* (1936, p. 113). For a careful discussion of the transition from Kahn's multiplier to Keynes's theory of effective demand, see Patinkin (1976, p. 68 et seq.). See also Patinkin and Leith (1978, pp. 18–20, 81–84) and Milgate (1982, p. 78 et seq.). Keynes did occasionally find Kahn's original version useful in discussing the effects of fiscal policy. See, e.g., his 1934 lecture to the American Political Economy Club (1973*a*, p. 459 et seq.). The *General Theory*, however, was only peripherally concerned with fiscal policy: it was above all a work of theory "chiefly addressed to [Keynes's] fellow economists" (1936, p. v).

[18] A methodological vice that Leontief (1937) called "implicit theorizing." He found it rampant among "the Neo-Cambridge School," a euphemism for Keynes and his pupils. Keynes had certainly been guilty of it before in the Fundamental Equations of the *Treatise*.

definition and could therefore be stated without a continuation theory. The short-period equilibrium represented an equilibrium over time, a sort of quasi-repetitive flow, in which a continuation theory was not required because nothing was changing.[19]

At the time the *General Theory* was published, Keynes seemed to favor the first notion, but certainly not to the exclusion of the second. The instantaneous relation drew tremendous criticism, and, under its weight, Keynes was forced to fall back on his second line of defense— the notion of equilibrium over time. Whether or not it was a deliberate strategy, this double line of defense proved highly successful. His critics seemed to expend all their fury on the essentially indefensible "outer fortifications" of the instantaneous relation. When Keynes fell back on the much more solid equilibrium over time, his critics seemed too spent to continue the debate.

Discussion of the attack on the instantaneous notion of equilibrium may usefully be divided into two parts, matching the two types of continuation theory Keynes failed to provide: the "mechanical" (money flows) and the "expectational."

C. Mechanical Problems with the Instantaneous Notion

In the *General Theory*, Keynes introduced a new set of definitions for income, saving, and investment that made saving and investment identically the same. He tried to connect the relation between investment and income implicit in these definitions, a relation "which holds good continuously, without time-lag, at all moments of time," with the "psychological" propensity to consume. As his critics were quick to point out, this attempt was not legitimate (see, e.g., Haberler 1936; Hawtrey 1937, p. 180 [and in Keynes 1973a, p. 584]; Lundberg 1937, pp. 37–39; Ohlin 1937/1944, p. 124). The definitional relation between income and investment could not be justified as the basis for any *causal* analysis. The multiplier so defined was unstable over time, it being an empirical commonplace that investment varied over the cycle much more than output. If the multiplier varied over the cycle, then either it bore no fixed relation at any given time to the psychological propensity to consume or the latter too had to be understood to vary over the cycle. Acceptance of the first possibility led directly to the notion of equilibrium over time: "Since the [instantaneous] multi-

---

[19] Precisely the same rationale underlies the equilibrium approach of real analysis, which also formulates a single-period theory and no continuation theory. It is not quite true that *nothing* is changing in Keynes's short-period equilibrium over time. In particular, the effect of investment on the capital stock is ignored as being "negligible." Removal of this simplifying assumption would soon lead to the development by Harrod, Kaldor, Hicks, and others of a new theory of economic growth.

plier must be assumed to vary with the different phases of the business cycle . . . we may instead refer to a 'normal' value for this coefficient, applying to a situation, where the conditions of the equilibrium system are satisfied. This can be said to occur when the total income of the firms is *correctly anticipated;* Then operations corresponding to given psychological 'propensities' may be supposed to be carried out according to the equilibrium equations" (Lundberg 1937, p. 38). Acceptance of the second possibility, of a cyclically varying propensity to consume, which itself had to be explained, would have involved the very sort of dynamics that Keynes wanted to avoid.[20]

The identical equality of saving and investment was also used by Keynes, again fallaciously, to evade the question of how new investment was to be financed. Since saving always equals investment, there must always be enough saving to finance any level of investment. Robertson, in particular, was outraged by this:

> (I never liked Kahn's s[hort]. p[eriod]. method in his public works article: but it did at least allow *time* (though unspecified in amount) for the "savings", corresponding to an act of investment financed (e.g.) by new bank money, to be elicited: whereas now, since there is no limit to the shortness of the time over which we are at liberty to apply your equations, they are simultaneous and identical.) It seems to me that the rehabilitation of the Grand Tautology takes us all back to pre-Withers, pre-Wicksell days, and obscures instead of clarifying what happens when an act of investment takes place. [Quoted in Keynes 1973a, p. 497]

Robertson (1936) argued that an increase in government investment would have to be financed initially by the creation of new money until income increased and saving rose to equal the new investment. Keynes later conceded this point (1973b, pp. 207–8), and this led to a further exchange on the consequent "finance motive" for holding money (1973b, pp. 227–33).

Once again, the way out was to limit the discussion to states of equilibrium over time, in which income *has* increased enough, and saving *is* available. The difficulties of transition from one equilibrium to another may be set aside as being of "secondary importance."[21]

---

[20] In his "Notes on the Trade Cycle" (1936, chap. 22) Keynes does entertain a cyclically varying propensity to consume, but this is part of the "literary" dynamics that has no part in his formal model. Keynes makes no attempt to deal with this formally.

[21] The whole issue was to be rediscovered in the "government finance constraint" literature of the 1960's (see, e.g., Christ 1968).

D. Expectational Problems

There are two distinct sets of expectations in the *General Theory:* short-period and long-period. Long-period expectations, which enter into the determination of the marginal efficiency of capital, are assumed, essentially, to be exogenous (their volatility underlies the shifts in the propensity to invest that drive the whole system). Short-period expectations are involved in the determination of effective demand. Keynes was less than clear on whether short-period expectations were to be taken as given exogenously, like long-period expectations, or whether they were to be taken as being correct—equilibrium expectations.[22]

This ambiguity was the source of further attacks on Keynes's instantaneous notion of equilibrium, particularly as expressed in chapter 3 of the *General Theory*. Robertson wrote:

> Income (later called *Y*) is the proceeds which result from giving a certain amount of employment; aggregate demand price (*D*) is the proceeds which are *expected* to result from giving that amount of employment; aggregate supply price (*Z*) is the proceeds the expectation of which will just make it worth while to give that amount of employment . . . (pp. 24–25). . . .
>
> But suppose that entrepreneurs (perhaps having heard at their last Rotary Club luncheon a lecture on J. B. Say) expand output in the *belief* that Δ*Y* will equal Δ*Z*. Their disappointment must surely not be represented, as is suggested in these pages, as due to a divergence between aggregate demand price and aggregate supply price; for in the case supposed these two are equal. It must be represented (as Mr. Keynes first discloses much later, on p. 78) as due to a divergence between aggregate demand price and income. Mr. Keynes in fact oscillates between using "aggregate demand price" to mean what he has defined it to mean, viz. what entrepreneurs *do* expect to receive, and using it to mean (p. 30, line 5) what they "can expect" to receive, i.e., what they can legitimately expect to receive, because that, whether they expect it or not, is what they *will* receive. In a world in which errors of anticipation are common, the distinction is not unimportant! [1936, pp. 168–69; page references to the *General Theory*]

In a private letter to Robertson (1973*b*, p. 89), Keynes accepted this criticism. As with the mechanical problems, there were two possible

---

[22] Hicks, in his review of the *General Theory* (1936/1982, p. 87), clearly understood the former.

ways out: bring in explicit dynamics or restrict attention to an equilibrium over time in which expectations *are* fulfilled.[23]

E.   The Instantaneous Notion Abandoned in Favor of Equilibrium over Time

Under the weight of criticism of his instantaneous notion of equilibrium, Keynes abandoned it in favor of the more logically consistent and defensible notion of equilibrium over time. The shift was clear in his 1937 lectures:

> I now feel that if I were writing the book again I should begin by setting forth my theory on the assumption that short-period expectations were always fulfilled; and then have a subsequent chapter showing what difference it makes when short-period expectations are disappointed.
>
> For other economists, I find, lay the whole emphasis, and find the whole explanation in the *differences* between effective demand and income; and they are so convinced that this is the right course that they do not notice that in my treatment this is *not* so. [1973*b*, p. 181]
>
> I'm more classical than the Swedes, for I am still discussing the conditions of short-period equilibrium. Let us suppose identity of *ex post* and *ex ante*, my theory remains.   [P. 183]

In a letter to E. S. Shaw in 1938, Keynes wrote: "I am not concerned with instantaneous snapshots, but with short-period equilibrium, assuming a sufficient interval for momentary decisions to take effect" (1979, p. 280).[24]

Apparently independently, Hicks too shifted his emphasis from one notion of equilibrium to the other in his two consecutive treatments of the *General Theory*. This is particularly important in view of his role as Keynes's leading interpreter for the new generation of formal theorists. In his review for the June 1936 *Economic Journal*, Hicks stressed the instantaneous notion:

> There thus emerges a peculiar, but very significant, type of analysis. If we assume given, not only the tastes and re-

---

[23] A considerable literature on the effective demand apparatus of chap. 3 has largely ignored both this criticism and Keynes's acceptance of it (the latter may be excused by the very recent publication of the relevant correspondence). A notable exception is an excellent recent paper by Asimakopulos (1982) (see also Tarshis 1978, p. 55).

[24] It is, perhaps, interesting that Kalecki, unlike Keynes, settled immediately on an equilibrium-over-time notion of the relation between investment and income (see Asimakopulos 1983).

sources ordinarily assumed given in static theory, but also
people's anticipations of the future, it is possible to regard
demands and supplies as determined by these tastes, resources and anticipations, and prices as determined by demands and supplies. Once the missing element—anticipations—is added, equilibrium analysis can be used, not only in
the remote stationary conditions to which many economists
have found themselves driven back, but even in the real
world, even in the real world in "disequilibrium".

This is the general method of this book; it may be reckoned the first of Mr. Keynes's discoveries. [1936/1982, p. 86]

However, by the time he came to write "Mr. Keynes and the 'Classics' " for the April 1937 *Econometrica,* Hicks had abandoned completely the instantaneous notion in favor of the equilibrium over time
that he formalized so well in his IS-LM apparatus.[25]

By this time, Keynes was quite ready to find this second interpretation congenial. In March 1937, he wrote to Hicks, referring to a draft
of the IS-LM paper: "At long last I have caught up with my reading
and have been through the enclosed. I found it very interesting and
really have next to nothing to say by way of criticism" (1973b, p. 79).

F.   The Road Not Taken: Sequence Analysis

While equilibrium over time represented one way out of the logical
inconsistencies of Keynes's instantaneous notion of equilibrium, it was
felt by many that some sort of explicit sequence analysis represented a
better, if undoubtedly harder, alternative.[26] Hicks was certainly very
conscious of this and found himself much in sympathy with many of
Robertson's criticisms; in later years, he was to express increasing
dissatisfaction with the equilibrium-over-time approach and increas-

---

[25] While the article itself is never explicit on the type of equilibrium it describes,
Hicks is unequivocal writing in retrospect: "If one is to make sense of the *IS-LM* model,
while paying proper attention to time, one must, I think, insist on two things: (1) that
the period in question is a relatively long period, a 'year' rather than a 'week'; and (2)
that, because the behaviour of the economy over that 'year' is to be *determined* by
propensities, and suchlike data, it must be assumed to be, in an appropriate sense, *in
equilibrium*" (1980–81/1982, p. 326).
[26] For example, Lerner (1939, p. 618) wrote that "[the *General Theory*] is concerned
most of the time with short period equilibrium and with the movement of such an
equilibrium through time. In assuming such equilibrium to be continuously maintained, it gives up, for the sake of simplicity, the process analysis that the Robertson
approach attempts. If successfully carried out the latter would be more complete and
more realistic than Mr. Keynes' equilibrium analysis, but it seems at the moment to be
stalemated by the complexity of the problem and the multiplicity of the time lags which
have to be considered."

ing interest in sequence analysis (see, e.g., Hicks 1974; 1982, chap. 10).

Attempts were made at the time, for example, by Lutz (1938) and Machlup (1939) to synthesize the approaches of Keynes and Robertson, but they did not catch on. Keynes, naturally enough, did not endorse these attempts: he was not about to abandon the simplicity and clarity of the equilibrium method for that same morass of sequence analysis that had condemned neoclassical monetary analysis to ivory-tower obscurity in the past.[27]

IV. Consequences of Keynes's Adoption of the Equilibrium Method

> The unsatisfactory aspects of *The General Theory* largely stem from Keynes's desire to keep equilibrium in the centre. [BURSTEIN 1975, p. 44]

A. *Unemployment Equilibrium*

Before the *General Theory*, neoclassical monetary analysis had been concerned with the *stability* of the economic system about equilibrium; the nature of equilibrium itself, it was generally agreed, was described quite adequately by real analysis.[28] Keynes's adoption of the equilibrium method required him *as a matter of logical consistency* to abandon this view of the respective scope of real and monetary analysis. His new theory described a situation that not only differed from the equilibrium of real analysis but was also *itself* an equilibrium. That is, there could exist no tendency for Keynes's equilibrium to regress toward the standard equilibrium of real analysis. If there did exist such a tendency, then his "equilibrium" would not be an equilibrium, and his whole method of analysis would be undermined. While neoclassical monetary analysis could be seen as a modification or refinement of classical economics, Keynes's new theory had to be understood as a complete break, as an alternative. Thus, what many of Keynes's critics saw as exaggerated claims of novelty or as a desire for self-aggrandizement was in fact a logically necessary consequence of the theoretical method that Keynes adopted.[29]

---

[27] For more recent attempts see Smith (1958), Ackley (1961), Tsiang (1966), and Kohn (1981).

[28] Not completely adequately, however, as discussion of "The Problem of Neutral Money" testifies (see Schumpeter 1954, pp. 1088–93). Monetary factors *in equilibrium*, however, were considered to be secondary complications. The neoclassicals very much saw themselves as *adding* a theory of the short run, of deviations from the long-run norm, to the classical theory, rather than as supplanting that theory.

[29] Cf. Milgate (1982, chap. 6). There are, of course, problems with viewing Keynes's

1214   JOURNAL OF POLITICAL ECONOMY

The far-reaching implications of accepting Keynes's theory as an *equilibrium* theory were noted by Hicks in his review:

> In the *Treatise*, Mr. Keynes was still to a considerable extent under the influence of the traditional approach to problems of the Trade Cycle. Ordinary (static) economic theory, so the old argument went, explains to us the working of the economic system in "normal" conditions. Booms and slumps, however, are deviations from this norm, and are thus to be explained by some disturbing cause. Such theories therefore ran in terms of deviations: deviations between market and natural rates of interest, deviations between the actual money supply and some neutral money, forced saving, deviation between saving and investment.
>
> The present theory breaks away from the whole of this range of ideas. It is no longer allowed that ordinary economic theory can give a correct analysis of even normal conditions; the things it leaves out of account are too important. But if there is no norm which we have understood, it is useless to discuss deviations from it. The changing, progressing, fluctuating economy has to be studied on its own, and cannot usefully be referred to the norm of a static state. [1936/1982, p. 85]

Rather than argue with Keynes about the nature of equilibrium at this general level, most of his critics focused specifically on Keynes's theory of the rate of interest. All the neoclassicals, at least since Wicksell, had held a monetary theory of the rate of interest, believing the market rate of interest to be proximately determined by the supply of and demand for loans of money (the "loanable funds" theory). What was new about Keynes's liquidity preference theory was not, therefore, that it was a monetary theory, but rather that it denied the existence of any "normal" or "natural" rate relative to which the market rate moved. In keeping with the equilibrium nature of his theory, Keynes denied any tendency for the market rate to gravitate toward a "normal" value. Interest was a *purely* monetary phenomenon: there was no "normal" rate.[30]

---

theory as a long-run theory, particularly with respect to the "length" of the long run. See Hicks (1965, pp. 64–65) and n. 26 above.

[30] Leijonhufvud (1981) has argued persuasively that the theory of interest is at the heart of most of the confusion and controversy in modern macroeconomics and that the origin of the problem is Keynes's abandonment of the loanable funds theory for his new liquidity preference theory. The position taken here is that the confusion over the rate of interest is itself the result of a deeper problem: Keynes's attempt to ground monetary analysis in the equilibrium method.

Keynes's new view that the economy was not stable, however loosely, about the equilibrium of real analysis had profound implications, too, for the potential role of economic policy. Instead of merely being able to improve stability—to reduce "inappropriate fluctuations" about real equilibrium—policy was now presumed to be able to determine the position of equilibrium itself:

> On my view, there is no unique long-period position of equilibrium equally valid regardless of the character of the policy of the monetary authority. On the contrary there are a number of such positions corresponding to different policies. Moreover there is no reason to suppose that positions of long-period equilibrium have an inherent tendency or likelihood to be positions of optimum output. A long-period position of optimum output is *a special case* corresponding to a special kind of policy on the part of the monetary authority. [1979, p. 35].

> Thus the remedy for the boom is not a higher rate of interest but a lower rate of interest! For that may enable the so-called boom to last. The right remedy for the trade cycle is not to be found in abolishing booms and thus keeping us permanently in a semi-slump; but in abolishing slumps and thus keeping us permanently in a quasi-boom. [1936, p. 322]

This view of policy provoked strong and immediate opposition. Robertson's attitude is described by Hicks:

> [Robertson] began from fluctuations—the subject of his first book, published in 1915. Fluctuations which he looked at as *temporary* divergences from an "equilibrium". Fluctuations not only of output and employment, but also of prices. The classical, or Victorian, trade cycle, with these fluctuations going together, could then be taken for granted. Moderation, or damping, of these fluctuations, was the central (relevant) objective of policy.
>
> In their work in the twenties, both Robertson and Keynes had shared this outlook. It is apparent in Robertson's *Banking Policy and the Price-Level* (1926) and in Keynes' *Treatise* (1930). . . .
>
> The *General Theory* was certainly taken by Robertson to imply an abandonment of the whole "cyclical" approach to which he remained committed. He still wanted to think of the problem of employment as a problem of fluctuations about an "equilibrium". [1982, p. 130]

1216   JOURNAL OF POLITICAL ECONOMY

The argument about whether policy could affect the *location* of equilibrium as opposed to fluctuations about it remained unresolved. It rumbled on under the surface for many years to emerge first in the guise of the Monetarist-Keynesian controversy and then, most recently, in the rational expectations critique of the Phillips curve.

B. Dependence on the Fixed Money Wage

The necessity of a fixed money wage for the existence of a Keynesian equilibrium over time was first demonstrated by Modigliani (1944): without it the Keynesian solution is not stationary, but rather falls back toward real equilibrium.[31] While Hicks certainly mentioned the fixed money wage in his IS-LM article (1937), he did not make clear that it was a *sine qua non* of his analysis. Keyes never accepted that his own theory depended on a fixed money wage, although he did recognize its importance for the Hicksian model (1973b, p. 80). But as the previous section has shown, with the instantaneous notion of equilibrium abandoned, Hicks's model of equilibrium over time *was* the only logically consistent representation of Keynes's theory. Whether Keynes liked it or not, his equilibrium analysis did depend on a fixed money wage.

The entanglement with the assumption of a fixed money wage was to prove fatal to Keynes's theoretical ambition of replacing the real analysis of classical economics with the monetary analysis of his general theory, because the fixed money wage is not only necessary for Keynesian equilibrium but also *sufficient*. The fixed-money-wage equilibrium over time is entirely capable of description using real analysis alone: the complications of monetary analysis—all the fuss of the circular flow—are no more needed here than they are in the classical equilibrium of the repetitive flow (indeed, the fixed-money-wage Keynesian equilibrium *is* a repetitive flow).[32] Moreover, much of Keynes's message about insufficient aggregate demand, about its being easier to raise prices than lower wages, about the need for fiscal policy, carries over very well to a fixed-money-wage real analysis.

In purely pedagogical or polemical terms—in terms of reaching the ear of the policymaker—this theoretical misfire seemed quite unimportant at the time. Over the years, however, Keynesianism has come to be *identified* with the fixed-money-wage assumption. "Classical economics" assumed flexible prices; Keynes made the more realistic as-

---

[31] Actually, Modigliani left a single loophole that was eventually closed in Kohn (1981).

[32] As Leontief (1936) first pointed out, and as subsequent formulations by Patinkin (1965), Barro and Grossman (1971), Malinvaud (1977), and others have made clear.

sumption that prices were less than perfectly flexible. The *General Theory* was understood to be "general" in the sense—a rather peculiar one—that to assume rigid prices is more general than to assume flexible ones. Indeed, Keynesian economics came to mean little else than a defense of this key assumption (e.g., Phelps and Taylor 1977; McDonald and Solow 1981).

Concentration on the fixed-money-wage assumption led to the neglect and eventual abandonment of the elements of Keynes's theory that he himself considered most important. The speculative demand for money was soon dropped as inconsistent with an equilibrium of fulfilled expectations (Fellner 1946; Leontief 1947). Even the multiplier suffered a steady decline, until it came to be regarded as no more than a picturesque shorthand for quantity-constrained Walrasian equilibrium (e.g., Malinvaud 1977). Precious little remains of the "monetary theory of production."

The weakness of this theoretically degenerate system has been revealed all too clearly by the largely successful attacks on its key assumption, first by the Friedman school and then by the rational expectationists. If wage *rigidity* is weakened to rational inflexibility, the Keynesian policy implications do not survive.[33]

C. *The Keynesian Assault on Monetary Analysis*

In defending his theory against actual and potential criticism, Keynes found himself attacking some of the key concepts of monetary analysis. Ironically and unfortunately, the attacks of Keynes and his disciples on neoclassical monetary analysis proved considerably more effective and longer lasting than did their attacks on classical economics.

Keynes's adoption of the relation $S(Y) = I$ as the basic equilibrium relation of his theory left him with a double problem. First, it left no role for the rate of interest since it was now income that brought saving and investment into balance. That is, the internal logic of his theory demanded a theory of interest that did not involve saving and investment: it remained only for Keynes to "discover" it.[34] Keynes's

---

[33] In Kohn (1985) I show, however, that a model more faithful to neoclassical monetary analysis—one incorporating the speculative demand for money and the multiplier—is *not* susceptible to the rational expectations critique. Policy remains effective even with a Lucas supply function and rational expectations. The basis for policy intervention is not informational advantage, but rather the externalities inherent in the use of money in an economy of indirect exchange (see Colander and Koford 1983). The "monetary theory of production" is, after all, essential.

[34] "The initial novelty lies in my maintaining that it is not the rate of interest, but the level of incomes which ensures equality between saving and investment. The arguments which lead up to this initial conclusion are independent of my subsequent theory of the rate of interest, and in fact I reached it before I had reached the latter theory. *But the*

1218   JOURNAL OF POLITICAL ECONOMY

second problem was that, with output determined and prices assumed given, nominal income was also determined, usurping the traditional role of the "market for money" equation. His liquidity preference theory killed both birds with one stone: it gave him a theory of interest, and it gave the market-for-money equation something to do.

This novel approach to both money and interest required a repudiation of several staples of neoclassical monetary analysis: hoarding, forced saving, the loanable funds theory of interest itself—all had to go.

The dynamic concepts of hoarding and forced saving came into conflict with the static nature of liquidity preference theory.[35] But also, and perhaps more basically, they challenged the fundamental idea that investment always brought forth the saving required to finance it:

> "Forced" saving was regarded as supplementing "voluntary" saving—the value of an economy's physical investment being equal to the sum of the two. This doctrine, together with the concept itself of "forced" saving, Keynes completely rejected. Investment creates the necessary "voluntary" saving quite irrespective of the extent to which it is financed by the banks. [Kahn 1975, p. 7]

> The error connected with the idea of "hoarding" arises, no doubt, from the desire to find where the vanished savings have got to. It is clear enough that if the desire of individuals to save has increased, but the desire of entrepreneurs to invest has not increased, then actually savings do not increase, and the explanation is put forward that the missing savings have somehow got lost on the way by going into money instead of into securities. But this is not a tenable explanation. The savings are nowhere. They have failed to

---

result of it was to leave the rate of interest in the air. If the rate of interest is not determined by saving and investment in the same way in which price is determined by supply and demand, how is it determined?" (1973b, p. 212; emphasis added).

[35] "Of course, the concept of 'hoarding' is not a part of the Keynesian system. This is understandable because the instantaneous approach of the *General Theory* avoids so far as possible specific reference to time periods, while 'hoarding' in its usual meaning must have a time dimension. For 'hoarding' which is timeless becomes identical with holding money; accordingly, as all money must be held by someone at all times if it is to be counted as money, it becomes correct to say that all money is 'hoarded' and that changes in 'hoarding' from one period to the next are the same thing as changes in the quantity of money. From this it follows that 'it is impossible for the actual amount of hoarding to change as a result of decisions on the part of the public, so long as we mean by "hoarding" the actual holding of cash. For the amount of hoarding must be equal to the quantity of money . . . ; and the quantity of money is not determined by the public' " (Villard 1948, p. 333).

come into existence, because as fast as one man increases his saving, by reducing his spending, other men's incomes fall off and they save less as much as he saves more. It is of no use to search for the non-existent savings either in "hoards" or anywhere else. [Joan Robinson 1937, pp. 15–16]

The loanable funds theory was thrice cursed: it involved dynamics, it undermined the saving-equals-investment relation, and it admitted the ultimate importance of real equilibrium, so conflicting with Keynes's own competing notion of equilibrium.[36]

The attacks by Keynes and his followers on neoclassical monetary analysis had the effect, in the euphoria of the Keynesian revolution, of making monetary analysis hopelessly unfashionable. With the Keynesian version of monetary analysis rendered down to a fixed-money-wage real analysis and with all alternative versions condemned as being "un-Keynesian," the elimination of monetary analysis from the consideration of mainstream professional economists could not have been more complete.

V. Conclusion

Our judgment of the *General Theory*'s success *as economic theory* must depend very largely on whether or not we believe that Keynes's new creation—equilibrium monetary analysis—really worked. Of course the book was an enormous success in other ways: Keynes's message—because of the simplicity and clarity given it by the equilibrium method—quickly invaded both undergraduate texts and the minds of policymakers.[37] The *General Theory* undoubtedly contained major theoretical insights, particularly the importance of the savings-income relation. There can be no question that it is one of the Great Books of economics. But in terms of Keynes's larger theoretical ambition—his hope of finally and decisively establishing the primacy of monetary analysis as the general theory, with real analysis "coming into its own" only in a very special case—in those terms, the book was a failure, and a disastrous one at that.

The reason for this failure is simple. Monetary analysis and the

---

[36] For his own repudiation of forced saving, hoarding, and the active balance/idle balance distinction, see Keynes (1936, pp. 79–84, 174; 1973a, p. 233). That Keynes once held other views is clear (e.g., 1973a, pp. 104–8). See also Liang (1984), especially on Keynes's inability, or unwillingness, to distinguish between the loanable funds theory and the classical real theory of the rate of interest.

[37] "Finally, and perhaps most important from the long-run standpoint, the Keynesian analysis has begun to filter down into the elementary text-books; and, as everybody knows, once an idea gets into these, however bad it may be, it becomes practically immortal" (Samuelson 1947, p. 147).

1220   JOURNAL OF POLITICAL ECONOMY

equilibrium method (at least the equilibrium method as it then existed) were mutually incompatible. What Keynes had tried to do, what he had even seemed to do, was just not doable. The internal inconsistencies of the theory could be resolved, essentially, in only one of two ways: throw out the idea of equilibrium or throw out the monetary analysis. Since those who sprang to Keynes's defense—most notably Hicks and Samuelson—were themselves deeply committed to the equilibrium method, it is only natural that equilibrium stayed and monetary analysis went. The resulting rationalization of the *General Theory*—one that *did* resolve its internal inconsistencies, although in a particular way—was the fixed-money-wage real analysis that came to be known as the "Keynesian model."[38]

The Keynesian model is not without its merits. It remains a valuable pedagogical tool, and it focuses attention on wage and price inflexibility as an important fact of life. It does, however, suffer from some fatal flaws as an intellectual basis for macroeconomic policy, and these flaws have been revealed in the most glaring fashion by the rational expectations critique. In the Keynesian model, the money wage is not only inflexible, it is set mechanically and unintelligently. Policy actions can be found, ad hoc, to compensate for this assumed clumsiness in the setting of wages. The rational expectations critique has shown that if wages are set rationally—even if they lack the flexibility to continually clear the labor market—then, in this model, no consistent policy regime can be devised to ameliorate cyclical fluctuations.

As a result, those who continue to believe in a place for stabilization policy must go outside the fixed-money-wage Keynesian model to find a rationale. The natural place to look is neoclassical monetary analysis, of which the *General Theory* is itself a special case. Unlike the *General Theory* and fixed-money-wage Keynesianism, and *like* classical economics, both old and new, neoclassical monetary analysis regarded "real" equilibrium as the only equilibrium. However, it parted company with classical economics in its analysis of stability *about* that equilibrium and of how monetary factors could affect that stability. Policy could be effective in reducing monetary exacerbation of real economic fluctuations.

There are signs today that economics is ready, once again, for a resurgence of monetary analysis.[39] First, some major problems with Walrasian general equilibrium theory—the difficulty of including money in an "essential" way and the unsatisfactory state of stability

---

[38] Cf. Clower (1975) on how the neo-Walrasian revolution jumped onto and then hijacked the Keynesian bandwagon.

[39] There have been several quasi resurgences since the Keynesian revolution: Patinkin's (1965) real-balance effect, the "Keynes-Wicksell" growth models (e.g., Stein 1971), and the "government budget constraint" literature (e.g., Christ 1968).

theory—have pushed in this direction.[40] In the most basic sense, monetary analysis *is* the stability theory of general equilibrium. General equilibrium theory is real analysis, and its legitimate domain is the repetitive flow. Problems of stability, by definition, take us out of the repetitive flow and, therefore, into the domain of monetary analysis. The absence of money from the general equilibrium model and the lack of dynamics are not coincidental: the attraction of real analysis is precisely that it enables us to avoid these very difficult issues. The inescapable price, however, is a restriction on the domain of the theory. To expand the domain, we must face the difficulties of monetary analysis.

A second recent development that heralds a renewed interest in monetary analysis is the rapidly growing literature on the *finance* (or cash-in-advance) *constraint*. Although the idea was recently rediscovered by Clower (1967), it clearly parallels the money flow mechanics of Robertson, and even the circular flow of the Physiocrats.[41]

This modern revival of monetary analysis could proceed more smoothly if those involved would realize that it is indeed a revival. Much of value could be learned from Robertson, Hayek, Lundberg, and others, and much wasteful delay and duplication avoided. In fact, one of those from whom we have the most to learn is Keynes himself. What could be more fitting than that the great champion of monetary analysis should contribute to its reconstruction.[42]

References

Ackley, Gardner. *Macroeconomic Theory*. New York: Macmillan, 1961.
American Economic Association (A.E.A.). *Readings in Business Cycle Theory*. Philadelphia: Blakiston, 1944.
Asimakopulos, Athanasios. "Keynes' Theory of Effective Demand Revisited." *Australian Econ. Papers* 21 (June 1982): 18–36.
———. "Kalecki and Keynes on Finance, Investment and Saving." *Cambridge J. Econ.* 7 (September/December 1983): 221–33.
Barro, Robert J., and Grossman, Herschel I. "A General Disequilibrium Model of Income and Employment." *A.E.R.* 61 (March 1971): 82–93.
Bode, Karl. "Plan Analysis and Process Analysis." *A.E.R.* 33 (June 1943): 348–54.
Burstein, Meyer L. "Some More Keynesian Economics." *Econ. Inquiry* 13 (March 1975): 39–54.
Christ, Carl F. "A Simple Macroeconomic Model with a Government Budget Restraint." *J.P.E.* 76 (January/February 1968): 53–67.

---

[40] See Hahn (1965, 1982) on the former problem and Fisher (1983) on the latter.

[41] See Kohn (1984) for a survey of recent developments in this area.

[42] The work of Leijonhufvud (1968, 1981) has been most notable in this task of theoretical archaeology, trying to reconstruct from remaining fragments the origins of our present theoretical civilization. It is as a contribution to this same goal that the present paper is intended.

1222   JOURNAL OF POLITICAL ECONOMY

Clower, Robert W. "A Reconsideration of the Microfoundations of Monetary Theory." *Western Econ. J.* 6 (December 1967): 1–8.

———. "Reflections on the Keynesian Perplex." *Zeitschrift für Nationalökonomie* 35, nos. 1–2 (1975): 1–24.

Colander, David, and Koford, Kenneth. "Externalities and Macro Economic Policy." Mimeographed. Middlebury, Vt.: Middlebury Coll., 1983.

Ellis, Howard S. "Notes on Recent Business-Cycle Literature." *Rev. Econ. Statis.* 20 (August 1938): 111–19.

Fellner, William J. *Monetary Policies and Full Employment.* Berkeley: Univ. California Press, 1946.

Fisher, Franklin M. *Disequilibrium Foundations of Equilibrium Economics.* Cambridge: Cambridge Univ. Press, 1983.

Haberler, Gottfried. "Mr. Keynes' Theory of the 'Multiplier': A Methodological Criticism." *Zeitschrift für Nationalökonomie* 7 (August 1936): 299–305. Reprinted in A.E.A. (1944).

———. *Prosperity and Depression: A Theoretical Analysis of Cyclical Movements.* Geneva: League of Nations, 1937. Rev. ed. New York: Atheneum, 1963.

———. "The Place of the General Theory of Employment, Interest, and Money in the History of Economic Thought." *Rev. Econ. Statis.* 28 (November 1946): 187–94.

Hahn, Frank H. "On Some Problems of Proving the Existence of an Equilibrium in a Monetary Economy." In *The Theory of Interest Rates,* edited by Frank H. Hahn and F. P. R. Brechling. London: Macmillan, 1965.

———. *Money and Inflation.* Oxford: Blackwell, 1982.

Hansson, Björn A. *The Stockholm School and the Development of Dynamic Method.* London: Croom Helm, 1982.

———. "Keynes' Shift of Method and Object between Treatise on Money and the General Theory." Mimeographed. Lund: Univ. Lund, 1983.

Hawtrey, Ralph G. *Capital and Employment.* London: Longmans, 1937.

Hicks, John R. "A Suggestion for Simplifying the Theory of Money." *Economica* 2 (February 1935): 1–19. Reprinted in Hicks (1982).

———. "Mr. Keynes' Theory of Employment." *Econ. J.* 46 (June 1936): 238–53. Reprinted as "The General Theory: A First Impression" in Hicks (1982).

———. "Mr. Keynes and the 'Classics': A Suggested Interpretation." *Econometrica* 5 (April 1937): 147–59. Reprinted in Hicks (1982).

———. "Methods of Dynamic Analysis." In *25 Economic Essays in English, German and Scandinavian Languages, in Honour of Erik Lindahl.* Stockholm: Ekonomisk Tidskrift, 1956. Reprinted in Hicks (1982).

———. *Capital and Growth.* New York: Oxford Univ. Press, 1965.

———. *The Crisis in Keynesian Economics.* Oxford: Blackwell, 1974.

———. "IS-LM—an Explanation." *J. Post Keynesian Econ.* 3 (Winter 1980–81): 139–54. Reprinted in Hicks (1982).

———. *Money, Interest, and Wages.* Cambridge, Mass.: Harvard Univ. Press, 1982.

Hutchison, Terence W. *On Revolutions and Progress in Economic Knowledge.* Cambridge: Cambridge Univ. Press, 1978.

Kahn, Richard F. "The Relation of Home Investment to Unemployment." *Econ. J.* 41 (June 1931): 173–98.

———. *On Rereading Keynes.* London: Oxford Univ. Press, 1975.

Keynes, John Maynard. *A Treatise on Money.* New York: Harcourt, Brace, 1930.

———. *Essays in Persuasion.* London: Macmillan, 1933. **Reprinted as vol. 9 of**

The Collected Writings of John Maynard Keynes. London: Macmillan (for Royal Econ. Soc.), 1972.

———. *The General Theory of Employment, Interest and Money.* London: Macmillan, 1936.

———. *The General Theory and After: Part I, Preparation.* Edited by Donald Moggridge. Vol. 13 of *The Collected Writings of John Maynard Keynes.* London: Macmillan (for Royal Econ. Soc.), 1973. (*a*)

———. *The General Theory and After: Part II, Defence and Development.* Edited by Donald Moggridge. Vol. 14 of *The Collected Writings of John Maynard Keynes.* London: Macmillan (for Royal Econ. Soc.), 1973. (*b*)

———. *The General Theory and After: A Supplement.* Edited by Donald Moggridge. Vol. 29 of *The Collected Writings of John Maynard Keynes.* London: Macmillan (for Royal Econ. Soc.), 1979.

Kohn, Meir. "A Loanable Funds Theory of Unemployment and Monetary Disequilibrium." *A.E.R.* 71 (December 1981): 859–79.

———. "The Finance (Cash-in-Advance) Constraint Comes of Age: A Survey of Some Recent Developments in the Theory of Money." Mimeographed. Hanover, N.H.: Dartmouth Coll., 1984.

———. "Policy Effectiveness and the Specification of Effective Demand: Keynes Rescued by Robertson." Mimeographed. Hanover, N.H.: Dartmouth Coll., 1985.

Leijonhufvud, Axel. *On Keynesian Economics and the Economics of Keynes: A Study in Monetary Theory.* New York: Oxford Univ. Press, 1968.

———. "The Wicksell Connection: Variations on a Theme." In *Information and Coordination: Essays in Macroeconomic Theory.* New York: Oxford Univ. Press, 1981.

Leontief, Wassily W. "The Fundamental Assumption of Mr. Keynes' Monetary Theory of Unemployment." *Q.J.E.* 51 (November 1936): 192–97.

———. "Implicit Theorizing: A Methodological Criticism of the Neo-Cambridge School." *Q.J.E.* 51 (February 1937): 337–51.

———. "Postulates: Keynes' General Theory and the Classicists." In *The New Economics: Keynes' Influence on Theory and Public Policy,* edited by Seymour E. Harris. New York: Knopf, 1947.

Lerner, Abba P. "Saving and Investment: Definitions, Assumptions, Objectives." *Q.J.E.* 53 (August 1939): 611–19.

Liang, Ming-Yih. "Keynes's Errors in the Liquidity Preference versus Loanable Funds Controversy." *J. Macroeconomics* 6 (Spring 1984): 215–27.

Lucas, Robert E., Jr., and Sargent, Thomas J. "After Keynesian Economics." In *After the Phillips Curve: Persistence of High Inflation and High Unemployment.* Boston: Fed. Reserve Bank Boston, 1978.

Lundberg, Erik. *Studies in the Theory of Economic Expansion.* London: King (for Univ. Stockholm, Inst. Soc. Sci.), 1937.

Lutz, Friedrich A. "The Outcome of the Saving-Investment Discússion." *Q.J.E.* 52 (August 1938): 588–614. Reprinted in *A.E.A.* (1944).

McDonald, Ian M., and Solow, Robert M. "Wage Bargaining and Employment." *A.E.R.* 71 (December 1981): 896–908.

Machlup, Fritz. "Period Analysis and Multiplier Theory." *Q.J.E.* 54 (November 1939): 1–27. Reprinted in *A.E.A.* (1944).

Malinvaud, Edmond. *The Theory of Unemployment Reconsidered.* New York: Wiley, 1977.

Milgate, Murray. *Capital and Employment: A Study of Keynes' Economics.* New York: Academic Press, 1982.

1224   JOURNAL OF POLITICAL ECONOMY

Mill, John Stuart. *Principles of Political Economy, with Some of Their Applications to Social Philosophy.* London: Longmans, 1848.

Modigliani, Franco. "Liquidity Preference and the Theory of Interest and Money." *Econometrica* 12 (January 1944): 45–88.

Ohlin, Bertil G. "Some Notes on the Stockholm Theory of Savings and Investment." 2 pts. *Econ. J.* 47 (March 1937): 53–69; (June 1937): 221–40. Reprinted in A.E.A. (1944).

Patinkin, Don. *Money, Interest, and Prices: An Integration of Monetary and Value Theory.* 2d ed. New York: Harper & Row, 1965.

———. *Keynes' Monetary Thought: A Study of Its Development.* Durham, N.C.: Duke Univ. Press, 1976.

Patinkin, Don, and Leith, J. Clark, eds. *Keynes, Cambridge and "The General Theory": The Process of Criticism and Discussion Connected with the Development of "The General Theory."* Toronto: Univ. Toronto Press, 1978.

Phelps, Edmund S., and Taylor, John B. "Stabilizing Powers of Monetary Policy under Rational Expectations." *J.P.E.* 85 (February 1977): 163–90.

Pigou, Arthur C. *The Theory of Unemployment.* London: Macmillan, 1933.

Quesnay, Francois. *Tableau Économique.* Versailles, 1758.

Robertson, Dennis H. *Banking Policy and the Price Level: An Essay in the Theory of Trade.* London: King, 1926. Rev. ed. London: Staples, 1949.

———. "Some Notes on Mr. Keynes' General Theory of Employment." *Q.J.E.* 51 (November 1936): 168–91.

Robinson, Austin. "Memoir of Maynard Keynes." In *Keynes and the Modern World,* edited by David Worswick and James Trevithick. Cambridge: Cambridge Univ. Press, 1983.

Robinson, Joan. *Introduction to the Theory of Employment.* London: Macmillan,

Salant, Walter S. "Keynes as Seen by His Students in the 1930's." In *Keynes, Cambridge and "The General Theory": The Process of Criticism and Discussion Connected with the Development of "The General Theory,"* edited by Don Patinkin and J. Clark Leith. Toronto: Univ. Toronto Press, 1978.

Samuelson, Paul A. "The General Theory." In *The New Economics: Keynes' Influence on Theory and Public Policy,* edited by Seymour E. Harris. New York: Knopf, 1947.

———. "What Classical and Neoclassical Monetary Theory Really Was." *Canadian J. Econ.* 1 (February 1968): 1–15.

Schumpeter, Joseph A. "Keynes, the Economist." In *The New Economics: Keynes' Influence on Theory and Public Policy,* edited by Seymour E. Harris. New York: Knopf, 1947.

———. *History of Economic Analysis.* London: Allen and Unwin, 1954.

Smith, Warren L. "Monetary Theories of the Rate of Interest: A Dynamic Analysis." *Rev. Econ. and Statis.* 40 (February 1958): 15–21.

Stein, Jerome L. *Money and Capacity Growth.* New York: Columbia Univ. Press,

Tarshis, Lorie. "Keynes as Seen by His Students in the 1930s." In *Keynes, Cambridge and "The General Theory": The Process of Criticism and Discussion Connected with the Development of "The General Theory,"* edited by Don Patinkin and J. Clark Leith. Toronto: Univ. Toronto Press, 1978.

Tsiang, S. C. "Walras' Law, Say's Law and Liquidity Preference in General Equilibrium Analysis." *Internat. Econ. Rev.* 7 (September 1966): 329–45.

Villard, Henry H. "Monetary Theory." In *A Survey of Contemporary Economics,* edited by Howard S. Ellis. Homewood, Ill.: Irwin (for American Econ. Assoc.), 1948.

Winch, Donald. *Economics and Policy: A Historical Study.* New York: Walker, 1969.

Part II
On the Need
for Discretionary
Intervention

Part II

[7]

INTERACTIONS BETWEEN THE MULTIPLIER ANALYSIS AND THE PRINCIPLE OF ACCELERATION

FEW economists would deny that the "multiplier" analysis of the effects of governmental deficit spending has thrown some light upon this important problem. Nevertheless, there would seem to be some ground for the fear that this extremely simplified mechanism is in danger of hardening into a dogma, hindering progress and obscuring important subsidiary relations and processes. It is highly desirable, therefore, that model sequences, which operate under more general assumptions, be investigated, possibly including the conventional analysis as a special case.[1]

In particular, the "multiplier," using this term in its usual sense, does *not* pretend to give the relation between total national income induced by governmental spending and the original amount of money spent. This is clearly seen by a simple example. In an economy (not necessarily our own) where any dollar of governmental deficit spending would result in a hundred dollars less of private investment than would otherwise have been undertaken, the ratio of total induced national income to the initial expenditure is overwhelmingly negative, yet the "multiplier" in the strict sense must be positive. The answer to the puzzle is simple. What the multiplier does give is the ratio of the total increase in the national income to the total amount of investment, governmental and private. In other words, it does *not* tell us how much is to be multiplied. The effects upon private investment are often regarded as tertiary influences and receive little systematic attention.

In order to remedy the situation in some measure, Professor Hansen has developed a new model sequence which ingeniously combines the multiplier analysis with that of the *acceleration* principle or *relation*. This is done by making additions to the national income consist of three components: (1) governmental deficit spending, (2) private consumption expenditure induced by previous public expenditure, and (3) induced

private investment, assumed according to the familiar acceleration principle to be proportional to the time increase of consumption. The introduction of the last component accounts for the novelty of the conclusions reached and also the increased complexity of the analysis.

A numerical example may be cited to illuminate the assumptions made. We assume governmental deficit spending of one dollar per unit period, beginning at some initial time and continuing thereafter. The marginal propensity to consume, α, is taken to be one-half. This is taken to mean that the consumption of any period is equal to one-half the national income of the previous period. Our last assumption is that induced private investment is proportional to the increase in consumption between the previous and the current period. This factor of proportionality or *relation*, β, is provisionally taken to be equal to unity; i.e., a time increase in consumption of one dollar will result in one dollar's worth of induced private investment.

In the initial period when the government spends a dollar for the first time, there will be no consumption induced from previous periods, and hence the addition to the national income will equal the one dollar spent. This will yield fifty cents of consumption expenditure in the second period, an increase of fifty cents over the consumption of the first period, and so according to the *relation* we will have fifty cents worth of induced private investment. Finally, we must add the new dollar of expenditure by the government. The national income of the second period must therefore total two dollars. Similarly, in the third period the national income would be the sum of one dollar of consumption, fifty cents induced private investment, and one dollar current governmental expenditure. It is clear that given the values of the marginal propensity to consume, α, and the *relation*, β, all succeeding national income levels can be easily computed in succession. This is done in detail in Table 1 and illustrated in Chart 1. It will be noted that the introduction of the acceleration principle causes our series to reach a peak at the 3rd year, a trough at the 7th, a peak at the 11th, etc. Such oscil-

[1] The writer, who has made this study in connection with his research as a member of the Society of Fellows at Harvard University, wishes to express his indebtedness to Professor Alvin H. Hansen of Harvard University at whose suggestion the investigation was undertaken.

76   THE REVIEW OF ECONOMIC STATISTICS

TABLE 1.—THE DEVELOPMENT OF NATIONAL INCOME AS A RESULT OF A CONTINUOUS LEVEL OF GOVERNMENTAL EXPENDITURE WHEN THE MARGINAL PROPENSITY TO CONSUME EQUALS ONE-HALF AND THE RELATION EQUALS UNITY

(Unit: one dollar)

Period	Current governmental expenditure	Current consumption induced by previous expenditure	Current private investment proportional to time increase in consumption	Total national income
1	1.00	0.00	0.00	1.00
2	1.00	0.50	0.50	2.00
3	1.00	1.00	0.50	2.50
4	1.00	1.25	0.25	2.50
5	1.00	1.25	0.00	2.25
6	1.00	1.125	−0.125 *	2.00
7	1.00	1.00	−0.125	1.875
8	1.00	0.9375	−0.0625	1.875
9	1.00	0.9375	0.00	1.9375
10	1.00	0.96875	0.03125	2.00
11	1.00	1.00	0.03125	2.03125
12	1.00	1.015625	0.015625	2.03125
13	1.00	1.015625	0.00	2.015625
14	1.00	1.0078125	−0.0078125	2.00
....	...	....	....	....

* Negative induced private investment is interpreted to mean that for the system as a whole there is *less* investment in this period than there otherwise would have been. Since this is a marginal analysis, superimposed implicitly upon a going state of affairs, this concept causes no difficulty.

latory behavior could not occur in the conventional model sequences, as will soon become evident.

For other chosen values of a and β similar model sequences can be developed. In Table 2 national income totals are given for various selected values of these coefficients. In the first column, for example, the marginal propensity to consume is assumed to be one-half, and the *relation* to be equal to zero. This is of special interest because it shows the conventional multiplier sequences to be special cases of the more general Hansen analysis. For this case no oscillations are possible. In the second column the oscillations in the national income are undamped and regular. In column three things are still worse; the oscillations are explosive, becoming larger and larger but always fluctuating around an "average value." In the fourth column the behavior is no longer oscillatory but is explosive upward approaching a compound interest rate of growth.

By this time the investigator is inclined to feel somewhat disorganized. A variety of quali-

tatively different results emerge in a seemingly capricious manner from minor changes in hypotheses. Worse than this, how can we be sure that for still different selected values of our coefficients new and stronger types of behavior will not emerge? Is it not even possible that if Table 2 were extended to cover more periods, new types of behavior might result for these selected coefficients?

Fortunately, these questions can be given a definite negative answer. Arithmetical methods cannot do so since we cannot try all possible values of the coefficients nor compute the endless terms of each sequence. Nevertheless, comparatively simple algebraic analysis can be applied which will yield all possible qualitative types of behavior and enable us to unify our results.

The national income at time t, Y_t, can be written as the sum of three components: (1) governmental expenditure, g_t, (2) consumption expenditure, C_t, and (3) induced private investment, I_t.

$$Y_t = g_t + C_t + I_t.$$

But according to the Hansen assumptions

$$C_t = aY_{t-1}$$
$$I_t = \beta[C_t - C_{t-1}] = a\beta Y_{t-1} - a\beta Y_{t-2}$$

and

$$g_t = 1.$$

Therefore, our national income can be rewritten

$$Y_t = 1 + a[1+\beta]Y_{t-1} - a\beta Y_{t-2}.$$

CHART 1.—GRAPHIC REPRESENTATION OF DATA IN TABLE 1

(Unit: one dollar)

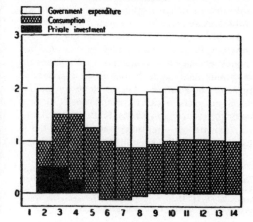

▢ Government expenditure
▨ Consumption
■ Private investment

MULTIPLIER ANALYSIS — PRINCIPLE OF ACCELERATION   77

In words, if we know the national income for two periods, the national income for the following period can be simply derived by taking a weighted sum. The weights depend, of course, upon the values chosen for the marginal propensity to consume and for the *relation*.

This is one of the simplest types of difference equations, having constant coefficients and being of the second order. The mathematical details of its solution need not be entered upon here. Suffice it to say that its solution depends upon the roots — which in turn depend upon the coefficients a and β — of a certain equation.[1]

TABLE 2.—MODEL SEQUENCES OF NATIONAL INCOME FOR SELECTED VALUES OF MARGINAL PROPENSITY TO CONSUME AND RELATION

(Unit: one dollar)

Period	$a = .5$ $\beta = 0$	$a = .5$ $\beta = 2$	$a = .6$ $\beta = 2$	$a = .8$ $\beta = 4$
1	1.00	1.00	1.00	1.00
2	1.50	2.50	2.80	5.00
3	1.75	3.75	4.84	17.80
4	1.875	4.125	6.352	56.20
5	1.9375	3.4375	6.6256	169.84
6	1.9688 *	2.0313	5.3037	500.52
7	1.9844	.9141	2.5959	1,459.592
8	1.9922	− .1172	− .6918	4,227.704
9	1.9961	.2148	−3.3603	12,241.1216

* Table is correct to four decimal places.

It can be easily shown that the whole field of possible values of a and β can be divided into four regions, each of which gives qualitatively different types of behavior. In Chart 2 these regions are plotted. Each point in this diagram represents a selection of values for the marginal propensity to consume and the *relation*. Corresponding to each point there will be a model sequence of national income through time. The qualitative properties of this sequence depend upon whether the point is in Region A, B, C, or D.[2] The properties of each region can be briefly summarized.

[1] Actually, the solution can be written in the form

$$Y_t = \frac{1}{1-a} + a_1[x_1]^t + a_2[x_2]^t$$

where x_1 and x_2 are roots of the quadratic equation

$$x^2 - a[1+\beta]x + a\beta = 0,$$

and a_1 and a_2 are constants dependent upon the a's and β's chosen.

[2] Mathematically, the regions are demarcated by the conditions that the roots of the equation referred to in the pre-

Region A (relatively small values of the *relation*)

If there is a constant level of governmental expenditure through time, the national income will approach asymptotically a value $\frac{1}{1-a}$ times the constant level of governmental expenditure. A single impulse of expenditure, or any amount of expenditure followed by a complete cessation, will result in a gradual approach to the original zero level of national income. (It will be noted that the asymptote approached is identically that given by the Keynes-Kahn-Clark formula. Their analysis applies to points along the a axis and is subsumed under the more general Hansen analysis.) Perfectly periodic net governmental expenditure will result eventually in perfectly periodic fluctuations in national income.

Region B

A constant continuing level of governmental expenditure will result in damped oscillatory movements of national income, gradually approaching the asymptote $\frac{1}{1-a}$ times the constant level of government expenditure. (Cf. Table 1.) Governmental expenditure in a single or finite number of periods will result eventually in damped oscillations around the level of income zero. Perfectly regular periodic fluctuations in government expenditure will result eventually in fluctuations of income of the same period.

Region C

A constant level of governmental expenditure will result in *explosive*, ever increasing oscillations around an asymptote computed as above. (Cf. column 3 of Table 2.) A single impulse of expenditure or a finite number of expenditure impulses will result eventually in explosive oscillations around the level zero.

Region D (large values of the marginal propensity to consume and the *relation*)

A constant level of governmental expenditure will result in an ever increasing national income, eventually approaching a compound interest rate of growth. (Cf. column 4 of Table 2.) A

vious footnote be real or complex, greater or less than unity in absolute value.

CHART 2.—DIAGRAM SHOWING BOUNDARIES OF REGIONS YIELDING DIFFERENT
QUALITATIVE BEHAVIOR OF NATIONAL INCOME

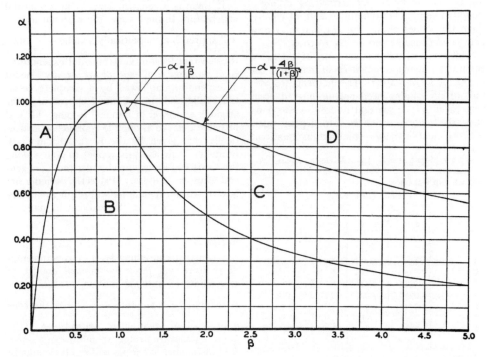

single impulse of net investment will likewise send the system up to infinity at a compound interest rate of growth. On the other hand, a single infinitesimal unit of disinvestment will send the system ever downward at an increasing rate. This is a highly unstable situation, but corresponds most closely to the pure case of pump-priming, where the total increase in national income bears no finite ratio to the original stimulus.

The limitations inherent in so simplified a picture as that presented here should not be overlooked.[1] In particular, it assumes that the marginal propensity to consume and the *relation* are constants; actually these will change with the level of income, so that this representation is strictly a *marginal* analysis to be applied to the study of small oscillations. Nevertheless, it is more general than the usual analysis. Contrary to the impression commonly held, mathematical methods properly employed, far from making economic theory more abstract, actually serve as a powerful liberating device enabling the entertainment and analysis of ever more realistic and complicated hypotheses.

[1] It may be mentioned in passing that the formal structure of our problem is identical with the model sequences of Lundberg, and the dynamic theories of Tinbergen. The present problem is so simple that it provides a useful introduction to the mathematical theory of the latter's work.

PAUL A. SAMUELSON

HARVARD UNIVERSITY

[8]

THE EMPIRICAL SIGNIFICANCE OF THE REAL BALANCE EFFECT*

By Thomas Mayer

I. Introduction

In the early 1940's Professor Pigou developed what was later to be called the "Pigou effect."[1] This idea was presented as a refutation — on a quite abstract level — of the Keynesian underemployment equilibrium thesis. On this level Pigou was successful; Keynesian criticism was limited primarily to a lower level of abstraction. Thus, a frequent criticism was that the Pigou effect required an impractically large price decrease — in spite of the fact that Pigou had admitted that "the puzzles we have been considering in the last section are academic exercises, of some slight use perhaps for clarifying thought, but with very little chance of ever being posed on the chequer board of actual life."[2] This discussion was conducted mainly in short articles and notes in the technical journals with most, though not all, contributors raising a single point or two rather than presenting a detailed formal analysis.

But in 1956 a formal treatise embodying the Pigou effect did appear. Professor Patinkin's *Money, Interest, and Prices*[3] not only worked out the formal aspects of the Pigou effect in a rigorous and beautifully constructed model, but transformed the Pigou effect in three major ways. First, he combined the Pigou effect and the Keynes effect.[4] Second, he returned to Pigou's original high level of abstrac-

* The author is indebted for helpful comments to his colleagues, Martin Bronfenbrenner, Paul Strassmann, Mordechai Kreinin, Victor Smith, Boris Pesek, Frank Child, and Richard Rudner, and to one of his students, Lloyd Orr.

1. "The Classical Stationary State," *Economic Journal*, LIII (Dec. 1943), 343–51. See also "Economic Progress in a Stable Environment," reprinted in American Economic Association, *Readings in Monetary Theory*, pp. 241–51. Although it came to be called the "Pigou effect," the idea was also developed independently by Gottfried Haberler and de Scitovszky. The latter, however, did not consider highly flexible prices to be desirable.

2. "Economic Progress in a Stable Environment," *op. cit.*, p. 251.

3. Evanston, Illinois: Row, Peterson and Co., 1956.

4. The Keynes effect is the change in the demand for money (in nominal terms) resulting from a change in the price level. For example, if prices fall by 50 per cent and liquidity preference and the money supply are constant in real

275

276   *QUARTERLY JOURNAL OF ECONOMICS*

tion, showing little concern with policy aspects. Patinkin's third, and most important innovation, however, was to make the real balance effect (as he called the combined Pigou and Keynes effects) the center of monetary theory. No longer is it treated merely as a qualification to be kept in mind when talking about the stability of the consumption function, but instead it is the factor making the general price level determinate and integrating micro and macro economics.

This paper is an attempt to turn the clock back in two respects. First, the discussion is transferred to a lower level of abstraction by discussing the problem of strength, and second, the real balance effect in the consumption market (the Pigou effect, per se) and the real balance effect in the investment market (the Keynes effect) are treated separately.

Regarding the first of these changes, Patinkin states explicitly that he is concerned not with the strength of the real balance effect, but only with its existence.[5] Given any real balance effect greater than zero, there must be *some* finite price decrease which can restore full employment. But the problem of strength is still important for three reasons. First, on a practical level, the policy implications of the real balance effect depend largely upon how much price flexibility would be needed to restore full employment. Second, there is a more fundamental question. We can build a theory around the real balance effect and then introduce such factors as absolute liquidity preference and wage rigidities as qualifications, or we can build the theory around these factors, and then introduce the real balance effect as a qualification. This choice depends, at least to some extent, upon the strengths of these factors. Third, unless *some* assumption about strength is made, Patinkin's conclusion that price flexibility can restore full employment is of little interest because, *as a formal proposition* it has been known for a long time. Given unlimited price flexibility, and the absence of institutional restraints, the old gold-mining argument suffices to prove the impossibility of involun-

terms, then liquidity preference in money terms is cut in half and the interest rate falls.

The real balance effect is not always sharply distinguished from the original Keynes effect and the Pigou effect. According to Hicks ("A Rehabilitation of 'Classical Economics?'," *Economic Journal*, LXVII (June 1957), 281n.) the Keynes effect is "substantially" the same thing as the real balance effect, but according to Patinkin himself the real balance effect is the same thing as the Pigou effect (*op. cit.*, p. 21n). The position taken here is that the real balance effect includes both the Pigou effect and a Keynes effect.

5. *Op. cit.*, p. 22.

THE REAL BALANCE EFFECT   277

tary long-run unemployment.[6] The fact that Patinkin uses the real balance effect rather than the gold-mining argument is presumably due to an implicit assumption that the real balance effect is stronger.

In other words, there are two ways of interpreting the real balance effect, and the *strength* of the real balance effect is important for one of them. On the one hand, the real balance effect can be taken to mean that, given infinite price flexibility, there is *some* price decrease sufficient to restore full employment. The second interpretation is that price declines act as automatic stabilizers; if prices decline to some extent, this, via the real balance effect, will raise employment.[7] The distinction is important because it is the latter case which is relevant for stabilization policy. If the real balance effect does not operate to raise the level of employment in a reasonable time given a "realistic" degree of price flexibility, then, for practical purposes, we can ignore the fact that completely flexible prices would prevent unemployment. This does not prevent the latter proposition from being important, but it should be sharply distinguished from the former policy question. As will be shown below, it is quite possible that the real balance effect is nonlinear; for small price decreases the real balance effect may at times be close to zero or even negative, even though a sufficiently large price decrease would restore full employment.

The second change, the separation of the original Pigou effect and the Keynes effect, is necessary in a discussion of strength, for, as will be shown below, the two effects have different bases. Moreover, such a separation fits better with the Keynesian consumption-investment dichotomy, and hence makes it easier to compare the Keynesian and Patinkinian theories.

To measure the Pigou effect part of the real balance effect it is necessary to know the change in the real value of assets resulting from a price decline and also the effect of an increase in this real value of wealth on expenditures. The first of these parameters can be obtained by multiplying the net indebtedness of the governmental

6. As prices fall, the cost of mining gold decreases while the price of gold is fixed. Hence output increases, and given a sufficient price decline all the unemployed can be absorbed in gold mining or in the activities induced by its multiplier and accelerator effects. Due to changes in imports and exports of gold-producing countries, this is so even for countries not producing gold.

7. The first position is close to the original argument of Pigou (cf. "Economic Progress in a Stable Environment," *loc. cit.*). The second position is Friedman's "A Monetary and Fiscal Framework for Economic Stability," *American Economic Review*, XXXVIII (June 1948), 245–64.

278   *QUARTERLY JOURNAL OF ECONOMICS*

sector[8] by the percentage decrease in prices. But the increase in
real wealth cannot be estimated directly.[9] However, given certain
assumptions, the increase in expenditures resulting from a given
increase in wealth can be determined deductively. This is the pro-

---

8. For a definition of this concept see the discussion of Herbert Stein and
Don Patinkin (*American Economic Review*, XXXIX (June 1949), 725–28). The
items included are: currency in circulation outside the Treasury and Federal
Reserve, government debt not held by the Federal Reserve, the federal govern-
ment, or state and local governments, member and nonmember deposits in the
Federal Reserve, other Federal Reserve Accounts, postal savings deposits, minus
Federal Reserve credit outstanding and minus Treasury deposits in member and
nonmember banks. (For sources of data see Table I.)

The face value rather than the market value of the public debt was used
here since there is little reason to expect the present ratio of market value to
face value to prevail in the future. In any case, if, as Patinkin advocates, the
market value had been used instead of the face value, the real balance effect
would be smaller. The indebtedness of state and local governments was included
to give the benefit of the doubt to the real balance effect. Fortunately, it is a
small item ($3 billion) so that its inclusion or exclusion does not matter much.
A more important adjustment, however, was the subtraction of the public's
indebtedness to government agencies and government corporations (and the
cash balances of these institutions). Patinkin argued that these institutions
have to balance their books and hence should be treated like members of the
public rather than as part of the government. But since these institutions are
net creditors, they gain rather than lose from price decreases. Moreover, even
if they should be treated as part of the public they could not just be left out of
the computation since they are indebted to the government. Hence, if they are
to be treated as members of the public, their indebtedness to the government
would have to be subtracted. Due to the absence of data not all government
agencies and corporations were included.

Finally following a suggestion of Arthur Okun ("The Effects of Open Inflation on Aggregate Consumer Demand," unpublished Ph.D. thesis, Columbia
University, 1956) government securities held by the major trust funds were
included to make a rough allowance for the public's claim on these funds. (See
also W. Hamburger, "The Relation of Consumption to Wealth and the Wage
Rate," *Econometrica*, Vol. 23 (Jan. 1955), 14.) However, I have not added
the debt of foreigners to the U. S. public as advocated by Okun. To do so one
would have to make allowances for changes in exchange rates, and for the indebtedness of the U. S. public to foreigners. Both of these items present insuperable
difficulties; in the latter case, for example, some of the increase in the wealth of
foreigners would be spent in the United States, but we do not know how much.
To be sure, the omission of international debts is not a good procedure either, but
it seems no worse than any of the alternatives. In any case, it is a relatively
minor item, and hence has no significant effect upon the subsequent argument.

9. Although several consumption function studies have included a wealth
variable, there are serious drawbacks to the use of these studies here. If time
series are used, there are the familiar problems of time series correlation, and if
savings ratios of different wealth, or liquid asset classes are used, there is the
problem that at each income level high savers tend both to save more, and to
have more wealth because of their previous savings. While these factors may not
be important for a study of the MPC, dealing only incidentally with the wealth-
consumption relation, they are crucial for a wealth-consumption relation study
such as this.

cedure followed here. The actual figure for the net indebtedness of the governmental sector is used to obtain the increase in wealth corresponding to various price declines. Given certain special assumptions, it is then possible to convert the increase in wealth into an equivalent increase in income, and hence to derive the corresponding increase in expenditures. As will be shown below, this increase in expenditures is quite small for reasonable price declines. Then the assumptions are removed and it is shown that under more "realistic" conditions no more reliance can be placed on the real balance effect; while the removal of some of the assumptions strengthens the real balance effect, the removal of others weakens it. The effects of the removal of the special assumptions may well be greater than the effects analyzed with the help of these assumptions. Hence, if it is to be argued that the real balance effect is strong after all, this argument would have to stress the favorable effects of the removal of the assumptions.

The special assumptions made are:[1]

1. The net indebtedness of the governmental sector and the money supply are constant in nominal terms.

2. The effects of gains and losses on expenditures are symmetrical and proportional.[2]

3. Falling prices do not cause bankruptcies.

4. Firms distribute all their gains or losses from the operation of the real balance effect to households without delay.

5. There is no money illusion.

6. Households allocate their incomes rationally between current and future consumption.

7. There is no capital rationing (i.e., households can borrow against all their future income at the market rate).[3]

8. There are no consumer durables.

1. In addition there is one minor technical assumption, namely constant income and constant wants.

2. As prices fall, certain businesses and households gain while others lose. Ignoring the government's debt, these gains and losses offset each other. The assumption made here means that each dollar of gain makes gainers raise expenditures by the same amount as a dollar of losses makes losers contract expenditures. Given this assumption, the changes in expenditure must also offset each other and the gains and losses on private debts can be ignored. This assumption is favorable for the real balance effect since bankruptcies may make losers contract expenditures by more than the increase in gainers' expenditures. This was pointed out by Don Patinkin himself. ("Price Flexibility and Full Employment," reprinted in American Economic Association, *Readings in Monetary Theory, op. cit.*, pp. 252–83.) See also Carl Christ, "Patinkin on Money, Interest, and Prices," *Journal of Political Economy*, LXV (Aug. 1957), 350.

3. This is one important assumption. As originally formulated, the Pigou

280   *QUARTERLY JOURNAL OF ECONOMICS*

9. There is no shift of the liquidity preference schedule.

10. The interest rate is 6 per cent.[4]

11. If prices fall, they are expected to remain constant at their new level.

II. CONSUMPTION

The essence of the Pigou effect is, that as prices fall the real value of the net indebtedness of the governmental sector rises and hence consumption increases. Since prices are expected to remain at the new level, this increase in wealth must be considered a once-for-all increase rather than regularly recurring income.

Given these assumptions, how do households react? Since there is no capital rationing, the increase in wealth can be translated into an equivalent increase in income. For example, if the interest rate is 6 per cent, households have the choice of substituting $6 of income for $100 of wealth and conversely. Since, by assumption, they act rationally, they are, at the margin, indifferent between $6 of income and $100 of wealth. Now on the above assumptions, the amount of savings depends on: (1) the relation between present and future wants, (2) the relation between present and expected future income, (3) the interest rate, and (4) the household's total receipts.[5]

An increase in the real value of assets does not change the relation between present and future wants, and present and future income. The rate of interest is constant by assumption, and the only factor which changes is the household's wealth. But a change in wealth by $100 puts the household on the same indifference curve as a change in income of $6, and hence should cause it to increase consumption by the same amount. In other words, a once-for-all increase in the real value of assets represents a capital gain. A rational household will allocate its expenditures over time so that

effect was based almost completely upon the capital rationing assumption. An increase in wealth was taken to increase consumption, even with a zero rate of interest where the increase in wealth would not raise income. Moreover, Carl Christ has pointed out that the real balance effect becomes part of the income effect given a perfect capital market. (*Ibid.*, p. 357.) The procedure adopted in this paper is to treat the Pigou effect not from the cash balance, but from the income theory standpoint.

4. A 6 per cent rate is used as a rough average of a borrower's rate (taken as 12 per cent) and a lender's rate (taken as 3 per cent) with two-thirds of the weight given to the latter. This is done because creditor households (who stand to gain from the real balance effect) are more likely to lend than to borrow. In any case, it is necessarily a hypothetical rate, but the reader can easily recompute Table I using a different rate.

5. Cf. Milton Friedman, *A Theory of the Consumption Function*, National Bureau of Economic Research (Princeton University Press, 1957), Chap. 2.

THE REAL BALANCE EFFECT 281

the marginal utility of expenditures is equal in every year. Hence, if it receives a capital gain, it will not spend the capital gain itself, but will only spend all, or a proportion of the income it can obtain by investing it.[6]

The increase in consumption resulting from the growth in the real value of assets can therefore be found by discounting the increase in the value of assets to obtain the equivalent increase in income, and then applying the marginal propensity to consume to this income increase. This is shown in Table I. Each decrease in the price level

TABLE I

ESTIMATED STRENGTH OF THE REAL BALANCE EFFECT
IN THE CONSUMPTION MARKET, 1956

(1)[1] Price Decline	(2) Equivalent Increase in Income	(3) Increase in Consumption[2]	(4) Increase in Consumption with a Hypothetical 10 Per Cent Drop in Real GNP	
			No Multiplier	Multiplier of 3
%	Billions of Dollars		%	%
	Prices Expected to Stay at the New Level			
5	0.8	0.6	1.4	4.2
10	1.7	1.2	2.8	8.4
15	2.5	1.7	4.2	12.6
20	3.3	2.3	5.6	16.8
25	4.1	2.9	6.9	2).7
50	8.3	5.8	13.9	41.7
	Prices Expected to Return to Their Previous Level in One Year			
5	0.0	0.0	0.1	0.3
10	0.1	0.1	0.2	0.5
15	0.2	0.1	0.2	0.7
20	0.2	0.1	0.3	1.0
25	0.2	0.2	0.4	1.3
50	0.5	0.4	0.8	2.5

1. Sources (of asset data used in column 1): *Economic Report of the President, 1957;* U. S. Treasury Department, *Annual Report for the Fiscal Year Ending June 30, 1956; Combined Statement of Receipts, Expenditures and Balances of the United States Government for the Fiscal Year Ending June 30, 1956; Treasury Bulletin,* Dec. 1956; *Federal Reserve Bulletin,* July, 1956, April, 1957; U. S. Bureau of the Census, *Summary of Government Finances in 1956;* "New Estimates of National Income," *Survey of Current Business,* July, 1958.
2. Marginal propensity to consume taken as 70 per cent of income before taxes.

6. Cf. Milton Friedman, *A Theory of the Consumption Function, op. cit.* This ignores the problem of the limited life span of a household. A rational household may decide to consume all its capital over its life span. But, on the average, households do not act this way; they pass on more capital than they started with. Hence, the assumption can be made that households do not consume their capital in anticipation of death. If the assumption is made that households consume all their capital over their lifespan, the real balance effect would seem larger, but not very much larger. (Cf. Carl Christ, *op. cit.,* p. 352.) Fluctuations in wants and income also create no problems. In the absence of capital rationing households would adjust their borrowing and lending to these fluctuations in any case.

282   *QUARTERLY JOURNAL OF ECONOMICS*

(column 1) results in a certain increase in wealth, and for each of these wealth increases there is an equivalent increase in income which causes an increase in consumption (column 3).

The significance of these increases can then be seen by expressing them as a percentage of a hypothetical 10 per cent decline in real GNP. These figures, (column 4) are, of course, only illustrative, but they indicate that, on the above assumptions, the real balance effect in the consumer goods' market is small. For example, suppose prices are as flexible as they were in the interwar cycles — a 10 per cent drop in output being accompanied by roughly a 10 per cent drop in prices.[7] In this case the real balance effect in the commodity market can offset only 3 per cent of this 10 per cent drop in real GNP without a multiplier, and only 8 per cent of it with a multiplier of three. Even if prices are made twice as flexible as they were in the interwar period, surely a difficult task, the offset rises to only 6 per cent without a multiplier and to 17 per cent with a multiplier of three, thus reducing the original decline to 8.3 per cent.

III. INVESTMENT

As prices fall, the real value of a fixed nominal stock of money rises and interest rates fall. (This part of the real balance effect is called the Keynes effect, and was already recognized and accepted in the *General Theory*.) However, it has a different basis than the real balance effect in the commodity market since it depends on the stock of money as usually defined, i.e., currency and demand deposits, and not on the net indebtedness of the governmental sector.[8]

This increase in the real value of the money supply can be substantial if prices decline enough.[9] How then could the Keynesians

7. During the contraction phase of the five cycles between 1919 and 1938, a 9.1 per cent decline in physical volume was accompanied by only a 10.5 per cent decline in prices (F. C. Mills, *Price Quantity Interactions in Business Cycles*, p. 6).

8. Demand deposits are not relevant for the commodity market aspects of the real balance effect. Falling prices raise the value of demand deposits owned by firms and households, but they also raise the debts owed by banks, and these two effects cancel each other. On the other hand, the stock of government securities, the biggest part of the indebtedness of the governmental sector, is not relevant for the bond market. A falling price level raises the nominal value of the stock of securities, but unless there is a money illusion in the demand for securities (a contingency excluded by assumption) the nominal demand for government securities rises in the same proportion since the real demand is constant. Hence, the interest rate is not affected.

9. Some of the increase in the real money supply is, of course, offset by the increase in the real demand for cash balances resulting from the operation of the Pigou effect. But this seems to be very minor. Milton Friedman and Anna Schwartz have found that in the past the income elasticity of demand for money

THE REAL BALANCE EFFECT   283

brush this effect aside? There are three possible answers. First, as Keynes has pointed out[1] cutting wages to increase the real stock of money can be treated as a remarkably clumsy way to decrease the interest rate. The second approach is to say that the liquidity preference schedule is so elastic, and the marginal efficiency of capital schedule and the savings schedule are so inelastic, that no increase in the real stock of money can stimulate investment significantly.[2] The third possibility is to point out that the Keynes effect is only one of many aspects of a price and wage cut.[3] Some of them (like the Keynes effect) are favorable, but others like the redistribution of income, for example, may be unfavorable, and there is little reason to select for special emphasis a single favorable factor such as the Keynes effect.

How valid are these arguments? Admittedly, price reductions are a clumsy way of increasing the real quantity of money, but this is merely a matter of practical convenience, and does little to justify the Keynesian claim that even with flexible wages and prices, under-employment equilibrium is possible.[4] Moreover, price reductions have one advantage over the usual type of easy money policy. An

has been between one and two ("Trends and Cycles in the Money Supply," in National Bureau of Economic Research, *Thirty-Seventh Annual Report*, New-York, 1957, p. 41). If this proportion is applied to the increase in income shown in Table I then the increase in the demand for money is so small that, for practical purposes, it can be ignored. However, it is possible that an increase in income resulting from an increase in (nonhuman) wealth may lead to a greater demand for money than an increase in income per se — if so there may be a significant increase in the demand for money and the interest rate may fall by less than is indicated above.

1. *The General Theory*, pp. 266–69.

2. Pessimism about monetary policy is, of course, common among Keynesians. Cf. James R. Schlesinger, "After Twenty Years: the General Theory," this *Journal*, LXX (Nov. 1956), 581–602.

3. The author once counted thirteen separate effects of a wage change on employment ("The Effects of a Wage Change Upon Prices, Profits, and Employment," *Economic Journal*, LXI (Sept. 1951), 524). The real balance effect accounts for only two of these, thus leaving eleven other factors to confound the analysis.

4. Patinkin does not claim to have overthrown the Keynesian counter-cyclical remedies. ". . . the propositions of Keynesian monetary theory are much less general than the *General Theory* and later expositions would lead us to believe. But this in no way diminishes the relevance of Keynesian unemployment theory for the formulation of a practicable full-employment policy. . . In brief our interpretation takes the debate on the degree of government intervention necessary for a practical full-employment policy out of the realm of those questions that can be decided by a priori considerations of internal consistency and logical validity, and into the realm of those questions that can be decided only by empirical consideration of the actual magnitudes of the relevant economic parameters." *Money, Interest, and Prices*, pp. 3 and 237.

easy money policy increases the lending power of banks, but in the short run, the loan volume of banks may not increase correspondingly. A price reduction, on the other hand, raises the real money stock of non-bankers directly, and hence avoids any problem of credit-worthy borrowers being reluctant to borrow or banks being unwilling to lend to weak customers. In this respect, price reductions have a considerable advantage over the more orthodox forms of monetary policy.

The second argument is the possibility of a liquidity trap. As will be shown in a subsequent paper by Martin Bronfenbrenner and the author, the total liquidity schedule (including both speculative and idle balances) probably did not become highly elastic at the low interest rates prevailing in the thirties. But at least at a zero rate, liquidity preference would become absolute, and at that point, the Keynes effect would disappear.

The third argument is closely connected with the second. If the Keynes effect is very strong it is then permissible to single it out for analysis. As the preceding paragraph suggests, this may perhaps be permissible at the generally prevailing interest rates. Hence, while cutting prices may be a clumsy way to increase the real money stock, it may none the less have a significant effect on investment. Unfortunately, this effect cannot be quantified. In the paper just mentioned, it will be shown that the elasticity of the liquidity preference schedule varies erratically from year to year; and hence, it is not possible to estimate the size of the Keynes effect.

IV. Removing the Assumptions

Having analyzed the strength of the real balance effect given certain special assumptions, it remains to remove them. First, there is the assumption that the net indebtedness of the governmental sector and the money supply are constant in nominal terms. If the net indebtedness of the governmental sector grows, then the base of the Pigou effect is greater, but if the net indebtedness of the governmental sector falls by a greater percentage than the price level, there is no Pigou effect at all. Similarly, fluctuations in the supply of money can either increase or offset the Keynes effect component of the real balance effect. Given our fractional reserve system and the usual central bank policy, the quantity of money in nominal terms may fall during a depression.

Second, if firms and households gaining from the price decrease have a greater marginal propensity to spend than losing firms and households, then the real balance effect is reinforced; but if they have a lower marginal propensity to spend, this may (at least par-

THE REAL BALANCE EFFECT   285

tially) offset the real balance effect. Such a development is not unlikely.

Third, falling prices may cause bankruptcies, particularly among debtor firms. In this case creditors, as well as debtors, may lose and hence expenditures may be reduced. As Patinkin himself said in an earlier article:

> "If firms are, on balance, debtors with respect to households and government, then a persistent price decline will cause a wave of bankruptcies. This will have a seriously depressing effect upon the economy which may not be offset by the improved status of creditors. Furthermore, in most cases of bankruptcy the creditors also lose. For these reasons it is not at all certain that a price decline will result in a positive net effect on the total expenditures (consumption plus investment) function. On this point much further investigation — of a theoretical as well as an empirical nature — is required.[5]

The fourth assumption is that firms pass on their gains or losses from the real balance effect to households. If firms do not pass their gains on and use them instead to bolster their liquidity position then the Pigou effect is weaker than is indicated in Table I. But firms may use these gains to increase their investment — and in this case the effects on the commodity markets are greater, since this would be an expenditure of the capital sum of the gain rather than just a proportion of the interest received from it.

Fifth, there is the vital assumption that there is no money illusion. If there is a partial money illusion, then the real balance effect is weaker than above indicated.[6] But except in the improbable case

---

5. "Price Flexibility and Full Employment," *op. cit.*, p. 263. On the whole, firms are net creditors rather than debtors (G. L. Bach and Albert Ando, "The Redistributional Effects of Inflation," *Review of Economics and Statistics*, XXXIX (Feb. 1957), 6) but many corporations are debtors and they might be driven into bankruptcy. Nonfinancial corporations, for example, are net debtors (*ibid.*).

6. It is difficult to determine to what extent there is likely to be a money illusion; it probably depends upon the degree of price decline. There is at least one institutional factor likely to create a money illusion — this is the price fixity assumption inherent in depreciation practices. While the better run firms are probably aware of this bias (which has been much discussed in the accounting literature) other firms may not be aware of it. Moreover, lenders may not take it into account when passing on the credit-worthiness of borrowers. On the other hand, some households may have a money illusion in their thinking and still *behave* as though they did not have one. For example, a household may be willing to reduce its bank balance by, say, two hundred dollars to buy a durable good. If prices fall, the real value of this dissaving increases. Moreover, liquid asset holdings are highly concentrated; a ranking of spending units by liquid asset ownership shows that the top two deciles held 83 per cent of selected liquid assets in 1956. ("1956 Survey of Consumer Finances: The Financial Position of Consumers," *Federal Reserve Bulletin*, June, 1956, p. 572.) This concentration tends to reduce the likelihood of a money illusion, since households with extensive holdings are less likely to be ignorant of the real value of these holdings than households with few liquid assets.

of a perverse money illusion (i.e., people thinking the real value of their assets decreases as prices fall) the removal of this assumption cannot make the real balance effect negative.

Sixth, there is the assumption that households act rationally. If instead, households splurge by spending much of the increase in the value of their assets in the initial year, then the real balance effect in the consumption market is much greater in this year than is shown in Table I. On the other hand, if households are irrational they may leave their expenditures completely unchanged in spite of the increase in the real value of their assets.

Seventh, if there is capital rationing then the Pigou effect is greater than shown in Table I. Under capital rationing the inability to borrow at the prevailing interest rate and the imperfection of the markets for household assets limits households in shifting consumption from the future into the present. An increase in the real value of assets partially removes this restraint and allows households to increase their present consumption. The removal of the assumption of no capital rationing therefore strengthens the Pigou effect.[7]

Eighth, if consumer durables are introduced into the model the Pigou effect is also strengthened since consumer durables are a possible investment outlet for a household's gain from the real balance effect. In other words, while it would be irrational for a household to spend all of a capital gain in one period for current consumption, it may not be irrational to spend all of it on goods which will yield services over a longer period.

Ninth, if falling prices reduce the demand for precautionary balances, this reinforces the Keynes effect; but if falling prices increase the demand for precautionary balances this counteracts the Keynes effect part of the real balance effect. The latter case results if falling prices increase uncertainty. But it is by no means clear that falling prices create more uncertainty during a depression than stable ones. If prices are flexible, the seller is uncertain about the price he can obtain for his wares, but he knows that he can sell all his output. If prices are inflexible, on the other hand, there is no uncertainty about future prices, but receipts are still uncertain since sales volume is uncertain. Buyers, on the other hand, are likely to increase their precautionary balances if prices are flexible since there are then more chances of finding bargains.[8]

7. In the original formulation of the Pigou effect capital rationing was a basic assumption, since people save for the amenity of holding wealth. Thus by assuming away capital rationing in the main part of this paper some violence is done to Pigou's original argument. But Patinkin does not make capital rationing a major assumption.

8. Keynes included the holding of cash in the hope of picking up bargains

THE REAL BALANCE EFFECT 287

Tenth, there is the assumption that the interest rate is 6 per cent. If the interest rate is more than 6 per cent, the income to be obtained from a given increase in the real value of assets, and hence the Pigou effect, are greater than shown in Table I; conversely, if the interest rate is below 6 per cent, the Pigou effect is smaller. But there is more than this to the assumption of a 6 per cent interest rate; this is, that the Keynes effect part of the real balance effect is inconsistent with the assumption of a constant interest rate. This inconsistency results in a weakness of the real balance effect. If the rate of interest falls, and at least part of the government debt is refinanced at the lower rate, the public's income from government securities falls, too. Hence, it is conceivable that falling prices may induce a net decline in the real, as well as in the nominal value of the public's interest receipts from the government. Thus, there are two effects on expenditures. On the one hand, the lower interest rate stimulates investment, but on the other, consumption is reduced as the government's contribution to disposable income falls.[9] The decline in disposable income depends upon the proportion of the government debt refinanced and the decline in interest rates; and the resulting decline in expenditures depends on the marginal propensity to consume. On the other hand, the favorable effects on expenditures depend upon the interest elasticity of investment and the percentage decline in interest rates. If the interest elasticity of investment is extremely low, which seems unlikely, the consumption effect might outweigh the investment effect, and the Keynes effect would then be negative. The critical value of the interest elasticity of investment, e, is given by $e = \dfrac{cagx}{I}$, where c is the marginal propensity to consume, a, the proportion of the privately held public debt refinanced, g, the size of this debt, and x, the rate of interest.[1] If all

in the precautionary motive (*General Theory, op. cit.,* p. 196). This practice is also followed by Hart (*Money, Debt and Economic Activity,* 2d ed., p. 203).

9. Since this discussion deals only with the real balance effect rather than with the total effects of price flexibility, the effects of falling prices on tax yields and government expenditures are ignored here, except for this interest rate effect which is directly relevant to the real balance effect.

1. Strictly speaking, x is the average between the previous interest rate and the new lower interest rate. It is this average rate rather than the decline in rates which appears in the equation because in deriving the equation, the latter variable is cancelled out. It is derived as follows: The increase in expenditure resulting from the increase in investment is equal to ΔI, and since $e = \dfrac{\dfrac{\Delta I}{I}}{\dfrac{\Delta x}{x}}$ it

of the government debt is refinanced, and if the rate of interest is taken as 2 per cent, and the marginal propensity to consume as 70 per cent, this critical elasticity becomes approximately 0.05.[2] If the interest elasticity of investment is less than this, then the real balance effect is negative — falling prices then lead to reduced expenditures. Ultimately, however, the real balance effect would have to become positive. After the interest rate has reached zero or any other floor, there is no longer a real balance effect in the bond market to interfere with the real balance effect in the commodity market.

Finally, there is the assumption that the new lower price level is expected to continue indefinitely. If it is assumed instead that prices are expected to fall even further, then (leaving aside for the moment the postponement of expenditures) the real balance effect is *stronger* than it would otherwise be. For example, if prices fall by 5 per cent, and are firmly expected to fall by the same amount again, then the capital gain, both actual and expected, is twice as great as it would otherwise be, and hence the Pigou effect is twice as great. Similarly, the long-term rate of interest declines if a second Keynes effect is expected.

To be sure, if prices are expected to fall, expenditures may be postponed, but this is a separate factor and not part of the real balance effect. Moreover, it can be shown that, if prices fall without a limit and are expected to fall *at a constant rate*, the real balance effect eventually has to outweigh the expectations effect. Assume that prices fall continuously. Wealth increases, and hence consump-

follows that $\Delta I = \dfrac{\Delta x}{x}\, eI$. The decrease in expenditures caused by the decreased interest payments is equal to $cag\Delta x$, so that the net change in expenditure is $\dfrac{\Delta x}{x}\, eI - cag\Delta x$. At the critical point, the net change in expenditure is zero and, rearranging the terms, $e = \dfrac{cagx}{I}$.

2. A 2 per cent rate is used here rather than the previously used 6 per cent rate for two reasons. First, the 6 per cent rate for households is a weighted mean of a 3 per cent lender's rate and a 12 per cent borrower's rate. Second, the interest rate falls as the Keynes effect operates. In mid-1956 g was $223.6 billion (*Economic Report of the President*, 1957, p. 175 and Bureau of the Budget, *Summary of Governmental Finances in 1956*, pp. 33 and 34). This figure includes holdings of state and local governments; if these holdings are excluded, the critical elasticity becomes 0.04. Since g includes the holdings of foreigners and international institutions, g is somewhat overstated and, hence, this tends to raise the critical elasticity, but fortunately, the overstatement is only a small proportion of the total g and hence its effects are minor. I, both foreign and domestic, was $67.3 billion in 1956 (U. S. Department of Commerce, *Business Statistics 1957*, p. 3).

tion tends to rise. If prices are expected to fall further, this increase in consumption may be postponed at first, but eventually current consumption would have to increase. As the amount of postponed consumption rises, the marginal rate of substitution turns in favor of current consumption, and *eventually*, current consumption would rise.

On the other hand, if prices are expected to return promptly to their previous level, the Pigou effect almost disappears. For example, consider a rational man who is convinced that prices will return to their previous level in one year. He now receives higher real interest payments on his bonds, but since he expects this to be temporary, he must treat the increase in his real interest receipts as a capital gain. Again, given the previously stated assumptions, it would be irrational to spend it all in the year of receipt — it has to be treated like an increase in capital and only the income obtained by investing it can be spent. The increase in consumption occurring under these conditions is shown in Table I.[3] This increase in consumption is so insignificant that it can almost be ignored. *As a first approximation there is no Pigou effect if prices are expected to return to their previous level in a few years.*[4] This is a serious weakness of Friedman's well-known stabilization model which combines stabilizing expectations and the Pigou effect.[5]

A similar argument applies to the Keynes effect component of the real balance effect. If prices and hence interest rates are expected to fall further, this tends to reduce interest rates in the current period, particularly the important long-term rate. But, if prices and interest rates are expected to rise again, this interferes with the decline in intermediate and long-term interest rates.

Little can therefore be expected from the real balance effect as a countercyclical tool except in the case where prices are falling in the depression but are not expected to rise during the subsequent boom.

V. CONCLUSION

Given the special assumptions made in the beginning of this paper, the strength of the real balance effect can be measured. On these assumptions there is a relatively small effect in the commodity

3. More precisely, the calculation assumes that prices stay at the lower level for one year and then all of a sudden rise back to their previous level. If a gradual movement during the period had been assumed instead, the Pigou effect would be even smaller.

4. A similar point has been made by J. H. Power, "The Economic Framework of a Theory of Growth," *Economic Journal*, LXVIII (Mar. 1958), 42 n.

5. Milton Friedman, "A Monetary and Fiscal Framework for Economic Stability," *op. cit.*

market but in the bond market there may be a more substantial effect.

When the assumptions are removed, the consequences of a relatively limited price decline become less certain. The removal of two assumptions, the absence of capital rationing and of consumer durables, strengthens the real balance effect. The removal of three other assumptions, consumer rationality, constant price expectations, and the passing on of gains and losses by firms, may strengthen or may weaken the real balance effect but, except in extreme cases, does not create any doubt about its direction. If a money illusion is allowed into the model, the real balance effect is weakened, and in the limiting case of a complete money illusion it disappears completely. If the assumption of no bankruptcies is abandoned the real balance effect is also weakened, and the net result could well be a fall in the real value of expenditures as prices fall. This leaves four other assumptions, the constancy, in nominal terms, of the indebtedness of the government and the constancy of the money supply, the symmetrical effect on expenditures of gains and losses, the constancy of the liquidity preference schedule, and a constant interest rate of 6 per cent. When these assumptions are removed, the direction of the real balance effect becomes uncertain. If reliance is to be placed on the real balance effect, it would have to be shown that the abandonment of these assumptions strengthens the real balance effect, or at least does not weaken it significantly.

But this applies only to the second interpretation of the real balance effect — relatively limited price decreases. Suppose prices fall indefinitely, if need be to one tenth of one per cent or even lower. In this case, there is much less uncertainty about the direction of the real balance effect. If prices are falling continuously, it is quite unlikely that the net indebtedness of the governmental sector, or the money supply falls at a faster rate. After some time, all debtor firms become bankrupt, and from then on, falling prices cause fewer losses. Eventually, at least some households shed their money illusion as the price decline becomes more pronounced. The liquidity preference schedule can, however, become completely elastic so that there may be no real balance effect in the bond market, but in this case the nominal value of the government's interest payments can no longer fall. Hence, the real balance effect has to be accepted as a rigorous demonstration that, given complete price flexibility, underemployment equilibrium is impossible.[6] But this is a theory relating

6. But even in this case of unlimited price declines, there is some uncertainty about the applicability of the real balance effect. An economy with

THE REAL BALANCE EFFECT 291

only to the extreme value of a variable. It cannot be argued from this that relatively limited price declines have significant stabilizing effects.[7] If the importance of a factor is considered to be a function both of its size *and* of the frequency with which it occurs then the real balance effect may not be important after all. To show that it is important, Patinkin would have to show that it operates also with relatively limited price declines. These considerations make it possible to evaluate Patinkin's criticisms of Keynesian economics. If the compatability of underemployment equilibrium and fully flexible prices is considered to be the heart of the Keynesian "message,", then Patinkin has indeed disproved the Keynesian theory. But if the Keynesian "message" is interpreted in a much vaguer, but more important way, namely that underemployment equilibrium is compatible with as much price flexibility as we are at all likely to experience, then the real balance argument as currently stated cannot be used to disprove it.[8]

MICHIGAN STATE UNIVERSITY

unlimited price cuts is foreign to our experience, and hence one cannot be certain what would happen to the relevant variables. Quite unfamiliar problems may arise as the general price level approaches zero. On the whole, it is safer to limit discussion to the neighborhood of familiar values of the variables. For a discussion of the general methodological problem involved see C. G. Hempel, "The Function of General Laws in History" in Herbert Feigl and W. Sellars (ed.), *Readings in Philosophical Analysis* (New York, 1949), pp. 459–71. Moreover, as Lerner has pointed out, if wages and prices are completely flexible, the value of money would be so unstable that the monetary system would be inefficient. "The Essential Properties of Interest and Money," this *Journal*, LXVI (May 1952), 191.

  7. It seems that, at least at one point, Patinkin does treat the real balance effect as being significant even with only limited price declines. (*Money, Interest and Prices, op. cit.*, p. 244.)

  8. Lerner can be cited in support of this interpretation of Keynes. "The so-called 'Keynesian Revolution' was nothing but the discovery that the automatic free market mechanism would not work if a vital part of the machinery was jammed by downward wage and price rigidities." (Lerner, *op. cit.*, p. 190.)

[9]

A KEYNESIAN VIEW OF PATINKIN'S THEORY OF EMPLOYMENT [1]

PROFESSOR PATINKIN has recently elaborated his views on the integration of value and monetary theory in a clearer, more comprehensive and even more reflective fashion than before [22]. Undoubtedly this new volume with its masterly command of monetary doctrine will evoke even wider praise and attention—in classrooms and from professional economists— than did the first edition of Patinkin's book [21].

The obvious future influence of this new volume makes a critical examination of certain key elements in it important, especially since some of these fundamental notions have gone unexamined in the intervening years since 1956. Before the dialogue becomes immersed in a critical discussion of the many fine analytical points raised by Patinkin it is essential to start with a statement of the fundamental differences between the analytical system developed by Keynes—and elaborated by others—for a macroeconomic integration of value and distribution theory into employment, output and price-level analysis, and Patinkin's application of value theory in monetary theory and the analyses of a production economy. Accordingly, this paper is not designed as a critical overall review of Patinkin's latest work. Rather it is an attempt to illuminate the basic theoretical concepts that separate modern neoclassical economists (for this is where Patinkin's work must be classified) and at least one branch of post-Keynesian writers, *i.e.*, those who (following Keynes' lead) have restored the aggregate supply function for commodities to a position of equivalence with aggregate demand in the analysis of the equilibrium level of employment and output.

Differences between Patinkin's model and the Keynesian aggregate supply–demand approach are probably overemphasised in the following pages in the interests of providing a clear and sharp contrast. Patinkin's analysis has many admirable aspects, and the areas of agreement between the two approaches are significantly greater than the areas of difference, although it is the latter aspects which, of course, lead to diverse conclusions about important theoretical and policy matters. Consequently, the ultimate purpose of this paper is not merely to get the " right " model; rather it is hoped that by focusing on the difference in the models, professional discussions on the " right " full-employment policy mix may be reoriented. Before examining these areas of disagreement it seems desirable to remind the reader of some of the more important elements of agreement.

[1] The author is professor of economics at Rutgers University. He is grateful to M. Fleming, I. F. Pearce, E. Smolensky, and S. Weintraub for helpful comments on earlier drafts of this paper.

I. Areas of Agreement

First and foremost, one must shout a strong amen to Patinkin's statement that the traditional 45° " Keynesian " cross does not take account " of the supply side of the commodity market " [22, p. 339, also see p. 325]. This popular diagrammatic representation of a simple Keynesian model[1] has inverted Say's law and has led many economists into a position of arguing that (at less than full employment) demand creates its own supply. It should also be clear, however, that *The General Theory* did not ignore commodity supply aspects, and that Keynes believed that " . . . the true law relating the aggregate demand and supply functions . . . is a vitally important chapter of economic theory . . . without which all discussions concerning the volume of aggregate employment are futile " [2] [18, p. 26].

Secondly, the " Savings equal Investment " equilibrium condition can be (and Patinkin suggests should deliberately be) avoided in an analysis of a market-oriented economy [22, p. 271], since this condition is merely an indirect way of stating that, in equilibrium, the revenue expected by the sellers of commodities (aggregate supply) equals the intended expenditures of the buyers of commodities (aggregate demand) [3] [cf. 29, p. 44, no. 24]. When savings is less than (more than) investment, then expected sales revenue is less than (more than) intended purchases and the system is not at rest.

Thirdly, it is true that the real balance effect was commonly ignored in the pre-Patinkin literature. Patinkin, however, has consistently maintained that the real balance effect is irrelevant for policy purposes (*e.g.*, [21, pp. 233, 235] [22, pp. 21, 57, 335]); rather " the significance of the real balance effect for economic theory . . . is [in] being concerned with the stability of an equilibrium position—with the possibility of its being reached by the automatic workings of a market economy " [22, p. 57].

Since Patinkin, however, it is unlikely that economists will ignore the real balance effect in an analytical discussion. It is unfortunate, however, that some writers in their zeal to enshrine automaticity in the economy have underestimated the impracticality of relying on an effect whose magnitude is significant only for rather disastrous price-level movements. From the outset Patinkin has indicated the absurdity of relying primarily on a real balance effect in a full-employment policy. Since he has also suggested that the real

[1] The fact that 100 pages of the September 1965 issue of the *American Economic Review* was devoted to a discussion of the relative predictive value of a simple Keynesian model (essentially based on the 45° diagram) *vis-à-vis* a velocity model is clear evidence of the ubiquitous identification of this traditional 45° cross as representative of Keynesian economics.

[2] Considering the short shrift the aggregate supply function is given in most popular " Keynesian " writings, one may be surprised at the large number of economists who have discussed it (*e.g.*, [3; 4; 5; 8; 9; 11; 13; 18; 19; 21; 22; 24; 25; 28; 29; 32; 33; 34]).

[3] Just as Patinkin deliberately avoids stating the savings–investment equilibrium condition in his book, so has an entire " Keynesian " work been written where the equilibrium emphasis is always on the equality of aggregate supply and aggregate demand, and the savings equal investment condition is avoided (and apparently never missed by the many reviewers and instructors using the text [5]).

balance effect is not sufficient to assure the stability of full-employment equilibrium under all market conditions [22, p. 236], it would appear that Patinkin may be overemphasising this aspect in relation to other factors, *e.g.*, the existence of fixed money contracts and their redistributive effects (when money wages and prices alter) on the spending behaviour of firms and households.   Unfortunately, Patinkin merely assumes away these latter elements [22, pp. 207, 216–17, 220–1, 285, 336].   Concerned with the operation of a " pure " economy, these contractual rigidities are suppressed as apparently bothersome matters which prevent the operation of the *tâtonnement* mechanism for achieving equilibrium [22, p. 534].

Fourthly, it is essential to understand the distinction, as set out by Patinkin, between a demand curve and a market equilibrium curve [22, pp. 48, 50, 265].   Confusion and wrong theoretical inferences abound if the latter is mistaken for the former.   According to Patinkin, a demand curve attempts to explain variations in the dependent variable (usually demand quantities) when the exogenous independent variables—which are not subject to explanation—vary.   In other words, the demand curve explains what the effect of an unexplained change in the independent variable will be on the dependent variable with other things held constant.   A market equilibrium curve, on the other hand, is the locus of intersection points of demand curves and their corresponding supply curves.   The latter is derived from a family of functions as a cross-cut; the former refers to an individual function where the parameters are specified and held constant.

In the circumstances, it is surprising that some confusion over these matters still persists in some parts of Patinkin's argument.   For example, it will be argued below that Patinkin has mistaken the market equilibrium curve in the labour market for the demand curve for labour.   Not unexpectedly, since Patinkin starts with an incorrect representation of the demand curve for labour, he elicits some rather curious conclusions about the equilibrium level of employment and its relationship to the aggregate supply function.

Finally, the invalidity of a dichotomy between the real and monetary sectors in a monetised, production economy is one of the basic tenets of both Patinkin's analysis and *The General Theory* [18, p. 293].   Disagreement can still persist, however, on the principal substantive grounds for this interdependence.[1]

II. PATINKIN *vs.* THE KEYNESIANS

The fundamental disagreement between Keynesians and Patinkin resides in his belief that Keynesian economics " is the economics of unemployment *dis*equilibrium " [22, pp. 337–8].   Keynes and most of the post-" Keynes-

---

[1] Elsewhere I have suggested factors other than the real balance effect which will lead to this interdependence [2; 5, Ch. 13; 6].

ian " writers have argued that underemployment was not only possible but normal. [1]

It is my contention that this divergence between Patinkin and the Keynesians is partly due to a semantic confusion resulting from the fact that Patinkin defines the concept of market equilibrium as identical with that of market clearing [22, p. 11] and partly (and probably more importantly) as a result of Patinkin's mistakenly identifying the market equilibrium curve in the labour market for the demand curve for labour [22, equation (2), p. 203]. As a result, Patinkin spends most of his time analysing the economy under the classical assumption of a constant (full-employment) level of income, where Walras' law *and* the budget restraint are relevant [22, pp. 258, 261]. Once the level of income is a variable, however, Walras' law is no longer applicable, at least in the way that Patinkin wishes to apply it. Neither Walras nor Patinkin allow changes in the level of output (*i.e.*, effective demand) to affect the *tâtonnement* process (*i.e.*, to affect the] shape or position of the excess demand function). In fact, Patinkin admonishes Walras for arguing that a production economy differs from an exchange economy where in the latter the supply volume is fixed. Patinkin insists that Walras failed to realise that all input quantities are fixed (perfectly inelastic?) in a production economy, and therefore, there is no logical difference between the excess-demand functions in the two types of economies [22, pp. 534–5]. Accordingly, Patinkin introduces Walras' law under the assumption of *a fixed level of output* (*i.e.*, a vertical aggregate supply curve), even in a production economy. It is as if, in the Marshallian short-run, output has no flexibility, and consequently, the difference between temporary market equilibrium and short-run equilibrium has been obliterated. This use of Walras' law on the aggregate level in a production economy, however, involves Patinkin in a fallacy of composition, for he implicitly aggregates individual excess demand functions *under a budget restraint* into an aggregate demand function *where* income and therefore effective demand is a variable.[2] The short-comings of this analysis will be elaborated below.

Equilibrium, Clearing and Disequilibrium

In a commodity market the concept of " clearing," as Marshall (among others) long ago taught, implies that at a given market price the quantity demanded by buyers exactly equals the quantity that sellers are willing to supply. On the other hand, equilibrium (merely) implies that the motivation of buyers (for utility maximisation) and sellers (for income maximisation) are, at the given market-price–quantity situation, being just balanced out so that neither the sellers nor the buyers will act to alter the price or quantity

---

[1] The history of the labour market in the United States since the Korean War suggests the ubiquitous nature of unemployment. Can this be disequilibrium? And, if so, how long can it persist?

[2] It is just this aggregation problem which Keynes was addressing himself to in *The General Theory* [18, p. 281].

offered or purchased.   Accordingly, clearing is a sufficient but not a necessary condition for equilibrium.

In the usual case [Fig. 1 (a)] clearing and equilibrium are obtained simultaneously at a price of p_1.   Without at this time inquiring into the setting which causes the buying and selling behaviour to be as represented by Figs. 1 (b) and 1 (c), it can be shown that in these latter cases *equilibrium will be achieved* at a price of p_1, while q_1 will be bought, but *the market will not clear*. In the equilibrium situation suggested in Fig. 1 (b), q_1 will be purchased, but a maximum of q_2 will be offered at a price of p_1, so that $q_2 - q_1$ will remain unsold.   Nevertheless, if the demand and supply schedules actually depict the behaviour of buyers and sellers to alternative *market prices* nothing tends to change in the system [cf. 22, p. 643].   If the commodity in question is durable it may be held over in inventory for a future period.   If, on the other hand, it is perishable, then we normally say that the quantity $q_2 - q_1$ has been lost to the economy (and in the case of labour we would call it involuntary unemployment—and a permanent loss of services that might have been rendered has occurred).

In Fig. 1 (c), on the other hand, at the equilibrium price of p_1, the quantity q_1 will be offered and purchased, although q_2 could be sold if it were forthcoming at a price of p_1.   Thus the market will be in equilibrium at a price of p_1 with q_1 being sold, and consequently some form of non-price rationing (*e.g.*, lengthening of the order books) will develop in equilibrium.

Despite the common textbook practice, which evidences an apparent preference for demand and supply schedules being drawn as in Fig. 1 (a), the horizontal segments of the supply curve in Fig. 1 (b) and of the demand curve in Fig. 1 (c) are representative of some real world markets.   (Compare Figs. 1 (b) and 1 (c) with Patinkin's money demand curve in Fig. IX–7b [22, p. 226] and his representation of other's view of labour supply in Fig. XIV–1 [22, p. 342].)   Thus it is essential that we recognise that *clearing is not a necessary condition for equilibrium*.

Patinkin, however, defines equilibrium as synonymous with clearing [22, p. 11].   In analysing the labour market, therefore, Patinkin asserts that the real " wage rate will not be an equilibrium one unless it equates the amounts demanded and supplied of labour " [22, p. 203], *i.e.*, unless the labour market is cleared.   Obviously, if the labour market is not cleared, that is, if there is involuntary unemployment, then by Patinkin's limited definition of equilibrium,[1] Keynesian economics must be *dis*equilibrium economics.   Disequilibrium becomes merely a definitional matter—in a context where institutional elements are by-passed.

Once the distinction between clearing and equilibrium is recognised, it is possible to demonstrate the existence of unemployment equilibrium, if it can be shown that the demand and/or supply curves for labour are not

---

[1] In his Note K, however, Patinkin admonishes Keynes for not using equilibrium in " the usual sense of the term that nothing tends to change in the system " [22, p. 643].

represented by Fig. 1 (*a*) (Patinkin's Fig. IX–1, [22, p. 204]) but rather by Fig. 1 (*b*) (Patinkin's Fig. XIV–1 [22, p. 342]).

The crux of the Keynesian–Patinkin disagreement, therefore, involves the question of what is the correct formulation of the aggregate demand and supply curves for labour. It is at this stage that Keynes and Keynesians are

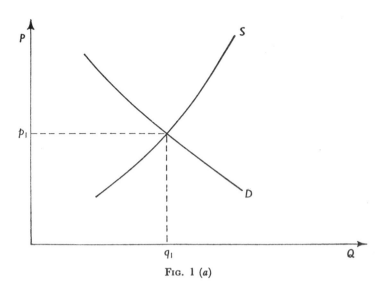

FIG. 1 (*a*)

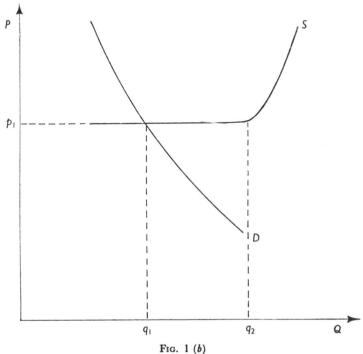

FIG. 1 (*b*)

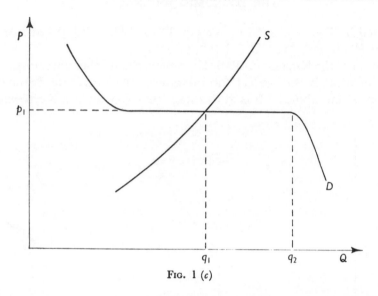

FIG. 1 (*c*)

at loggerheads with Patinkin. The former group have argued that the demand for labour is derived directly from the effective demand for goods. Patinkin, on the other hand, has interpreted an equation relating the level of employment to the real wage-rate (*i.e.*, to the marginal product of labour) as the aggregate demand for labour function [22, p. 203]. This divergence of views involves a much more substantial matter than the confusion between the concepts of clearing and equilibrium.

The Demand for Labour Function

Since the 1930s innumerable writers have argued that the marginal product curve *cannot* be the demand curve for labour as long as the level of output is a variable. (For example, [4, Ch. 3, 4; 5, Ch. 11; 15, p. 95 n. 2; 18, Ch. 2, 20; 20; 29, Ch. 6; 30].) What is rather disappointing is that Professor Patinkin, who has displayed a mastery of so much of the Keynesian literature, and who has spent so much energy in making the profession aware of the difference between demand curves and market equilibrium curves, has not realised that the curve relating the real wage-rate and the level of employment (the inverse of the marginal product curve) may be a market equilibrium curve; *it is not*, as he describes it, *an aggregate demand curve for labour* [22, p. 203].

Patinkin explicitly assumes that in a production economy the demand for productive factors by business firms is based *solely* on relative prices, the rate of interest and the initial level of real assets [22, p. 77], which in turn, implies (*a*) that excess demand functions of households are independent of the quantity of factors demanded by business firms [22, pp. 76–77] (and *consequently the aggregate demand for commodities must be unrelated to total factor incomes!*), and (*b*) the aggregate demand for labour schedule is independent of the level of output, *i.e.*, independent of the level of effective demand [22, p. 319]. Moreover, Patinkin asserts that the absence of output (*i.e.*, effective demand) as a determinant in the demand for labour function is the result of deriving the labour supply function from the usual principle of profit-maximisation [22, p. 319]. Inevitably, Patinkin decides that there is no difference in the market-excess demand functions of an exchange economy where output is fixed (and the above-mentioned assumptions may be applicable) and the market-excess demand functions in a production economy where effective demand *and* labour supply quantities are variable [22, pp. 76–7] (and where, therefore, Keynesians argue these assumptions are inapplicable). In essence *Patinkin has revived the classical position that the Marshallian-type demand schedules (i.e.,* Patinkin's excess demand curves) *can be assumed to remain unchanged as aggregate income and effective demand varies.* This, of course, implies that factor prices and factor incomes can vary without altering the demand for commodities; in Patinkin's terminology, factor incomes can change without altering excess-demand curves. Consequently, there can be a change in total factor income without any change in initial endowments (*i.e.*, in real income).

In a production economy, however, the level of employment and output can vary, and therefore the level of real income cannot be part of the " givens " of the system. Accordingly, an analysis which aggregates excess-demand curves based on the assumption of fixed initial endowments is inapplicable in an economy where output and employment, as well as prices, are variable [cf. 15, p. 95 n. 2; 29, Ch. 1; 5].

Without reviewing the entire analytical argument further, it is interesting to quote Mishan, the most recent of many writers who have argued that even though in perfect competition price equals marginal cost,

> " and, therefore, that—since a common wage prevails—marginal physical product equals the real wage, this condition holds not only in some full-employment equilibrium but for any amount of labor that happens to be employed. The most we could say of the marginal product curve in this connection is that it traces a locus of all possible equilibrium positions in which this condition obtains . . . a decline in the real wage being properly regarded as the *result* of an expansion of aggregate demand; the wage decline is not the " cause " of the expansion " [20, p. 610].

Thus, to paraphrase Patinkin's description of market equilibrium curves [22, pp. 266–7], the real wage-rate and the level of employment are dependent variables in the analysis (hence the equilibrium values cannot be dependent on each other, but only on the independent variables). Accordingly, Patinkin's demand for labour curve is not a demand curve at all; rather it is best to interpret this market equilibrium curve as a real-wage determining function, *i.e.*, *given* the level of employment, it indicates what the equilibrium real wage will be.

Patinkin's model is therefore devoid of a useful, complete analysis of the labour market.   Since he has not presented any demand function for labour, all his conclusions about equilibrium in the level of employment must be suspect.   But then, the reader might ask, if the marginal product curve is not the demand curve, what is the *correct* specification of the demand function for labour?   As Mishan suggests, the demand curve for labour in either a classical or Keynesian framework is " primarily derivable from the effective demand for goods " [20, p. 610].   Elsewhere I have adopted what I believe is the simplest geometric apparatus for analysing the demand and supply curves of labour when the demand is derived from the effective demand for commodities as output varies, and the supply of labour is based on real wage-rate (*i.e.*, there is no money illusion) [5, Ch. 11; also see 29, Ch. 6].   Mishan provides a different geometrical apparatus to display the same market phenomena [20].   While this is not the place to compare these alternative geometric systems, the point remains that Patinkin's model does not have an explicit complete demand for labour function.   Consequently, his claim that Keynesian economics is the economics of unemployment disequilibrium is illusory.

The Aggregate Supply Function

Patinkin's mislabelling of the market equilibrium curve as the demand curve for labour leads him to an inadequate specification of the aggregate supply function for commodities.   According to Patinkin, the aggregate supply function " indicates the amount of commodities the firms of the economy would like to supply in order to maximize the profits at the given real wage with which they are confronted in the market " [1] [22, p. 210]. Since Patinkin has not identified the demand for labour function, he incorrectly indicates that there is only one equilibrium real wage-rate, the rate which clears the labour market—the full-employment rate.   Consequently, he concludes that the aggregate commodity supply function must appear as a vertical line, Y_0, on the 45° diagram [22, p. 211].

If Patinkin had recognised that his equation (3) on p. 203 was not the market demand curve for labour (rather it is the real-wage-rate determining equation), then his own definition of the aggregate supply function would have forced him to introduce a non-vertical aggregate supply curve on the 45° diagram.   Moreover, he might have noticed that a vertical aggregate commodity supply function is inconsistent with his assumption of profit-maximising firms in a perfectly competitive economy.   This latter assumption im-

[1] At this stage it must be pointed out that firms are *not* confronted with real wage-rates in the labour market.   What is relevant to the firm's hiring decision is the relationship between the money wage-rate (assumed equal in each industry) and the price of the firm's product, *i.e.*, the real cost in terms of the own-product of the firm.   *This is not the same as real wage-rate*, which relates the money wage to the price of wage goods, *i.e.*, to the price of consumption goods [cf. 26, p. 356].   The difference between the real cost in terms of own-product and the real wage is most obvious in the hiring decision of a firm where its workers do not buy any of its products, *e.g.*, in an investment-goods industry.

plies, of course, that increasing levels of employment can occur only under conditions of diminishing returns, and consequently for each level of employment and output there will be a different real wage-rate. In other words, at each given level of output on the 45° diagram there is a unique

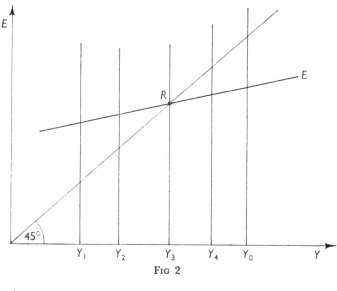

FIG 2

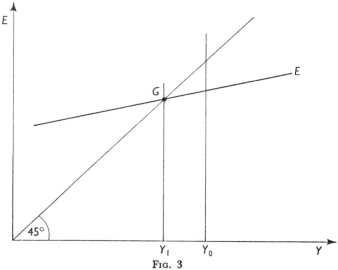

FIG. 3

real wage, and consequently a unique vertical " Patinkin-type " aggregate supply curve (Fig. 2). Only one of this family of vertical supply curves, Y_0, represents supply at full employment, *i.e.*, when the labour market has cleared. The equilibrium level of employment, however, would occur when the aggregate demand function (E in Fig. 2), a vertical aggregate supply line, and the 45° line have all intersected at a single point (R in Fig. 2).

If Patinkin had introduced aggregate supply conditions correctly into his model he would have noted some patent inconsistencies in his system. For example, in a perfectly competitive world the relationship between commodity prices and the money wage-rate varies at each level of output because of diminishing returns. Consequently, the assumption of constant prices as output varies (which underlies Patinkin's aggregate demand curve, E [22, p. 206]) could be applicable only if the money wage-rate declined as the level of employment expanded—a situation which is not usual in the " classical system " and which is obviously not what Patinkin intended to imply.

Similarly, Patinkin's statement of the classical position " as seen with Keynesian eyes " appears odd and unrecognisable [22, p. 357]. In his Keynesian version of Say's law, Patinkin interprets it as meaning that the 45° line becomes the aggregate demand for commodities function. What is surprising is that he then argues that aggregate demand will intersect with aggregate supply only at the full-employment level of output! This is not only inconsistent with his own statement [22, p. 356], but it is also in conflict with Keynes' interpretation of the statement that " Supply creates its own Demand " [18, pp. 25–6]. Keynes argued that under Say's law aggregate demand accommodates itself to the commodity output supplied by firms, *i.e.*, *that the aggregate demand and supply curves are coincident with the 45° line throughout their entire length.* On this, Keynes wrote, " effective demand, instead of having a unique equilibrium value, is an infinite range of values all equally admissible; and the amount of employment is indeterminate except in so far as the marginal disutility of labour sets an upper limit " [18, p. 26]. According to Keynes, therefore, at any level besides full employment the economy is in *neutral* equilibrium and there is no obstacle to full employment. This is obviously quite a different view of Say's law than the one Patinkin interprets " through Keynesian eyes."

Another inconsistency suggests itself when Patinkin indicates that his aggregate supply function

> " assumes the more familiar form of an upward-sloping curve if it is drawn within the [price and quantity] coordinate system of Figure III–Ia (p. 42). For the higher the price level, the lower the real wage rate, the greater the input of labour, and *the greater, therefore, the aggregate amount of commodities supplied.* Similarly it is clear from the discussion on p. 41 that the aggregate demand function for commodities (9) can be represented in Figure III–Ia (*as of a given level of Y* and *r*) by the negatively sloping curve which now appears there " [22, p. 211, italics mine].

Thus Patinkin suggests a diagram similar to our Fig. 1 (*a*) above.

The placing on the same price–quantity coordinate system of a supply curve which allows for changing levels of aggregate output with a demand curve explicitly based on a constant output level is strongly incongruous to one reared on Keynesian economics. Similarly, the representation of an aggregate demand curve which depicts desired expenditure at alternative levels of output, with a vertical aggregate supply curve which assumes a given (full-employment) level of output, in the same 45° diagram [22, p. 212] entails some contradiction.

Since Patinkin has not properly introduced aggregate supply phenomena into his model, it is inevitable that he tends to emphasise excess demand *at full employment* as the primary cause of price changes, and to ignore those " homely but intelligible " supply concepts of marginal costs and the elasticity of short-period supply in the determination of the money-price level [cf. 18, pp. 292 ff.]. What is so vexatious about Patinkin's painstaking efforts to integrate value theory with monetary theory is his almost complete neglect of the supply aspects of value theory. For example, he states that in a purely competitive economy an actual decline in output will occur *without changing the full-employment money wage–price structure* [22, p. 325]. The classical economists, however, recognised that diminishing returns (*i.e.*, a less than infinitely elastic supply condition) must affect the price level when output levels change—a proposition which Patinkin implicitly denies (although this same phenomenon was the basis for his labelling the inverse of the marginal product curve as the demand curve for labour).

Once prices are allowed to vary with output and employment levels and the aggregate commodity supply function is properly introduced into the system, Patinkin's neatly built model starts to become defective at several points. Patinkin's assumption that redistributive income effects are normally unimportant is acceptable only as long as money wages and prices are assumed constant, since then the presence of fixed money contracts—which are essential for the operation of a production-specialisation economy—do not result in either income or wealth redistribution. Once prices and money wages are permitted to vary, however, then those people who received their income as a result of money contracts—and in the real world a large proportion of personal income is the result of such contracts—will see their income eroded by price rises;[1] and there will be a redistribution of real income from households to business firms and governments [cf. 5, Ch. 11, 12]. Since aggregate spending by these latter two sectors is not as closely related to income levels as is the spending of households, the aggregate demand function will not be homogeneous in relation to money price changes, even in the absence of the money illusion. Consequently, the interdependence of the real and monetary sector can be established via redistribution effects and

---

[1] In a modern economy much of personal income is a result of fixed money contracts. Besides the traditional pensioners and coupon-clipping rentiers, government employees, university teachers, individuals engaged in non-commercial research, employees in philanthropic and religious organisations, as well as some salaried workers of business enterprises, receive their incomes as a result of fixed contractual commitments. As footnote 1, p. 577, below indicates, significantly more than 30% of personal income in the United States in any one year may be the result of contracts.

without appeal to the real balance effect.   (This argument and its consequence for labour market analysis has been developed elsewhere [6].)   In
fact, Patinkin ultimately notes that " the real-balance effect is itself a distribution effect " [22, p. 288].   Since the real balance effect is admittedly relatively unimportant for policy, while it is obvious that fixed money contracts
and changing money wages and prices are commonplace in the very nature
of a modern production economy, one may ask why, at this late stage, has
Patinkin spent so much time exploring the intricacy of the former, and ignoring, by assumption, the redistributive aspects of the latter?

Voluntary vs. *Involuntary Unemployment—On* vs. *Off Schedules*

Patinkin indicates that all individuals are acting voluntarily when they
are all on their supply and/or demand schedules simultaneously.   In his
view involuntary unemployment implies that workers and firms are off their
respective supply and demand for labour schedules [22, pp. 313–15].
Patinkin, at this point, finally admits that his demand for labour function is
imperfect in that it does not show the " connection between the firms' output
of commodities and the input of labour . . . .   Indeed, to all outward appearances, this function depends only on the real wage rate, and *not on the
volume of output* " [22, p. 319, italics mine].   In this statement apparently
Patinkin admits that his demand-for-labour curve is not derived from the
effective demand for commodities.   Nevertheless, Patinkin argues that as
effective demand declines, firms will " offer a real wage rate below that indicated by the demand curve . . . or alternatively, at the real wage rate (w/P_0)
they now demand a smaller input " [22, p. 320].   But given technology,
the stock of capital and profit-maximising firms in a perfectly competitive
system, the marginal productivity curve is anchored;   therefore Patinkin's
demand curve *cannot* shift, and Patinkin is forced by the logic of his position
to suggest that firms will *move off* their labour demand schedule.

If the reader becomes a bit incredulous at this stage, Patinkin rebukes
him for having " the ingrained mental habit " of seeing only the points on
the demand or supply curve [1] [22, p. 323].   Nevertheless, this off-schedule
type of analysis does lead to at least one implication which should give
pause and arouse more than a mild suspicion.   According to Patinkin, when
effective demand is deficient firms move off their demand-for-labour curve.

---

[1] My conception of a schedule is that it is a logical representation of the behaviour of buyers or
sellers (given their motivational principles and certain parameters, such as tastes, technology, etc.)
when they are confronted by alternative situations.   If these schedules do represent the observable
behaviour of individuals as they are confronted with alternative situations, then we are involved in
a logical inconsistency when we say that they can be off their schedules.   Either people behave in
the way their schedules say they should or they are operating on a different schedule from the one
shown (perhaps because they are not motivated by the same factors as we assume they are, or something has changed in the environment which is assumed to be constant under the usual *ceteris paribus*
derivation of the schedule).   (See, for example, my discussion of the concept of the aggregate supply
function as a schedule [3, pp. 456–7].)

Market forces are thereby generated which ultimately shift the aggregate-demand-for-commodities curve back to the full-employment intersection [22, pp. 320 ff.]. Thus, given Patinkin's demand-for-labour curve, it is market forces resulting from movements away from the demand curve for labour which ultimately increase aggregate demand. In its most bizarre form, this leads to the conclusion that, in Patinkin's model, the demand-for-commodities is derived from his demand for labour function, and the demand for labour is *not* derived from the demand for commodities.

If Patinkin had recognised that his function was *not* a demand-for-labour curve but rather a real-wage determining equation he would have avoided the difficulty of defining involuntary unemployment as people " being off their schedule." Instead he is forced to twist and turn to avoid the inevitable inconsistencies of his system. He argues, for example, that at point G in Fig. 3 (p. 568 above), although perfectly competitive firms are selling what they are actually producing, it is not an equilibrium situation, for given the relationship between money wages and prices of w/P_0, the firms *desire* to produce Y_0. But this *must* imply that firms are not profit maximising at income level Y_1. Instead, given any money wage-rate, the marginal cost must be less than the market price at Y_1, so that profit-maximisation should lead to an expansion to Y_0. According to Patinkin, however, the market will not purchase the entire Y_0 output at the given relationship between money wages and prices; therefore firms are pressured by the thread of potential unsold, unwanted inventories to remain at the Y_1 level *while the price level relative to money wages remains at the full-employment level.*[1] Firms, however, can maintain the full-employment money-wage and price-level structure in the face of a lower output (and therefore lower marginal costs) only *if either* they do not maximise profits *or* they do not remain in a perfectly competitive market. If either of these latter aspects are true it is not surprising, of course, that firms are conceived as being off their competitive profit-maximising schedules, or that, as Patinkin puts it, " the demand curve ... does *not* describe the actual behaviour of firms " [22, p. 321]. If this curve doesn't describe the actual behaviour of firms to alternative situations, however, why should it be labelled the demand curve for labour?

What is vexing about this Patinkin apparatus for simultaneous departure from Patinkin-type demand and supply curves for labour is not, as he suggests, that " a force majeure " has " coerced " firms and workers off their respective schedules [22, p. 322]; rather it is that Patinkin continues to call this " function " an aggregate-demand-for-labour curve. The confusion is compounded when Patinkin reveals that this analysis results in " a basic analytical problem here whose full solution is still not clear to me " [22, p. 323]. Patinkin will be unable to remove this obscurity from his analytical

---

[1] At this point Patinkin is arguing that market clearing can occur in a disequilibrium situation, —that equilibrium is not a necessary condition for clearing [22, p. 320]—while previously Patinkin defined equilibrium as synonomous with clearing [22, p. 11].

1967]   A KEYNESIAN VIEW OF PATINKIN'S THEORY OF EMPLOYMENT   573

system until he realises that he has yet to derive a demand curve for labour.[1] Until such time as he derives a demand curve to place against his supply curve for labour, Patinkin's theory of employment will remain inchoate and incomplete, and his statement that the " essence of dynamic analysis is involuntariness " will remain an unproven assertion.

Elsewhere I have summarised what I believe to be a reasonably consistent analysis of the labour market [5, Ch. 11].   This is not the place to repeat that analysis nor to argue for its advantages or reveal its limitations.   The burden of the present argument is that the fundamental difference between Patinkin and Keynesian economics is centred on the analysis of the labour market, and that from a Keynesian point of view it appears that Patinkin has reinstated the classical restriction of attempting to derive a demand curve for labour under the implicit assumption of a given level of aggregate effective demand.   In saying this, it should be absolutely clear that nothing has been said here which implies that Patinkin's analysis of the money and bond markets is necessarily faulty.[2]

[1] Others have shown concern over Patinkin's " off schedule " analysis of the labour market [*e.g.*, 1; 10].   They have attempted to rescue Patinkin's conclusion that underemployment is a disequilibrium phenomenon by substituting different explanations for the adjustment process when aggregate demand declines from the full-employment level.   Cross and Williamson assume that unwanted inventories and money-wage and price inflexibility cause firms to move up Patinkin's labour demand curve, so that unemployment disequilibrium is the initial result.   Ultimately, in this model, wages and prices fall, bringing the real balance effect into play, and commodity demand curves shift rightward and employment " re-expands until the process comes to a halt when the [aggregate] demand curve once more intersects the 45° line at B [full employment] " [1, p. 80].

Gogerty and Winston, on the other hand, rightly reject the notion of unwanted inventories and inflexible prices as incompatible with the assumption of pure competition.   Instead, they introduce a *temporary* departure from pure competition in the commodity market when aggregate demand declines, so that firms are no longer on Patinkin's competitive labour demand curve; rather, they are, temporarily, on a monopoly labour demand curve, which, it is asserted, is to the left of Patinkin's curve.   (The complications of introducing monopoly—even temporarily—are not pursued by Gogerty and Winston, and it would divert us from our main purpose to pursue this aspect in detail here.   Suffice it to say that: (1) they ignore the fact that distributive effects of even a temporary monopoly structure will feed back on aggregate demand, and (2) the leftward position of Gogerty and Winston's monopoly labour demand curve is not conclusively demonstrated in the presence of this feedback.)   Nevertheless, if prices and money-wages are flexible, then, according to Gogerty and Winston, equilibrium will be restored when " the demand curve for labour will have returned to its original position—to Patinkin's labor demand curve " [10, p. 125].   Thus, both Cross and Williamson and Gogerty and Winston provide alternative adjusting mechanisms to arrive at the same conclusion as Patinkin, *i.e.*, under-employment is a disequilibrium phenomenon. Patinkin properly rejects both suggestions as unsatisfactory [22, p. 670].   Nevertheless, these alternative models suffer from the same limitation as Patinkin's original system, *i.e.*, they imply that the equilibrium demand curve for commodities is derived from the labour demand curve, and not vice versa.   None of these writers has realised that the marginal productivity curve is *not* the competitive aggregate demand-for-labour schedule, and that therefore their models do not have any explicit demand curve for labour when output and effective demand are variable.

[2] In a future paper I hope to compare the Keynesian view of these markets with Patinkin's analysis.   At this stage one can only point out a surprising assumption underlying Patinkin's capital-market analysis.   Patinkin assumes an imperfection which prevents the supply of bonds from becoming infinite.   This imperfection is an assumption that all debtors operate on the belief that they must repay all their debts by the end of their economic horizon, and therefore they can pay for all

The basic differences between Patinkin and Keynesians, however, hinge on the analysis of the labour market. Perhaps the best way that the arguments developed above can be brought into sharp focus is by concluding with a short discussion of Walras' law, which is the necessary connecting link between the various markets in the Patinkin system.

Walras Law Once More

The crux of Patinkin's entire analysis rests on the applicability of Walras' law, which for him is inextricably connected with the budget restraint. Although Patinkin indicates that one could conceive of an economy where the budget restraint does not imply Walras' law [22, pp. 36, 613], this does not imply that the reverse is true, *i.e.*, that one can have Walras' law in the absence of the budget restraint. In fact, in any number of places in his book Patinkin argues that the budget restraint is necessary for Walras' law [22, pp. 37, 38, 41, 42, 45, 51–3, 70, 201, 211]. Yet the budget restraint is often irrelevant in macroeconomics. *For an economy the budget restraint is full employment.* Thus below the full-employment level the economy is not subject to Walras' law in the sense that Patinkin would have it. Consequently, it does not follow that if there is an excess demand for money there must always be an excess supply of commodities of equal aggregate value [cf. 22, p. 35]. That this is clearly so can be demonstrated by considering an example where the economy starts from a less than full employment position. Assume that there is an increase in investment plans because of improved profit expectations. Accordingly, there will be an increase in the demand for money to finance the additional proposed investment projects (and, *ceteris paribus*, there will be an excess demand for money), even before there is any increase in output (*i.e.*, the supply of commodities is not in excess) [2, pp. 54–6; 17; 23, pp. 10–12; 27, pp. 80–7]. Only if the level of output is constant will money and commodities always be the substitutes suggested by Walras' law. Once income is a variable, the transaction and finance motives for holding money and finance imply that as the demand for goods rises, the demand for money will also rise in a sympathetic relationship.

It *is only when the level of output is predetermined* that Walras' law must lead to the result that flexible prices alone, via the *tâtonnement* process, acts as the equilibrating mechanism. If Patinkin, in his integration of value theory into

their planned borrowing accordingly. Given that some of the major borrowers in the modern economy are business firms and governments which may never retire their outstanding debt, it is surprising that this wholly unrealistic assumption is so readily accepted, whereas the somewhat more realistic imperfections that may exist in the system because of (*a*) the presence of fixed money contracts, and (*b*) the inability of labour to bargain for its own real wage, are dismissed out of hand by Patinkin. Patinkin manages to spend many pages discussing the bond market, and yet he has no fixed money contracts in the system. Walras' law, as Patinkin is well aware, logically requires the ability to recontract [22, p. 534]. Nevertheless, he sweeps aside the fact that bonds themselves are long-term fixed money commitments which do not permit the original debtors to recontract during the life of the bond. Patinkin avoids this problem by neutralising the influence of the firm's initial outstanding bonds [22, p. 217 n. 13].

monetary theory, had followed Keynes' lead and allowed both prices and output to vary concomitantly he would have discovered (as we have always taught in courses in price theory) that *normally both prices and quantities alter when demand changes.* Patinkin develops most of his concepts in an exchange economy where supply is explicitly fixed. When he extends his argument to a production economy Patinkin, recognising that supply may be a variable, states " the essential point is that—according to the marginal productivity theory—once the technical conditions of production are specified, the decisions of a firm with respect to these inputs and outputs are based entirely on relative prices " [22, p. 76]. *This statement is true only if the level of output has been predetermined.* It is indeed surprising that almost thirty years after *The General Theory* an economic model based on the classical assumption of a constant (full-employment) level of output is served up as a refutation of Keynesian underemployment equilibrium analysis.

Patinkin is on weak ground when he argues that " market excess-demand equations of a production economy have exactly the same basic property . . . as do those of our simple exchange economy " [22, p. 77]. In aggregating the former equations, one must explicitly analyse intended expenditures by households as the total factor incomes and their distribution alter; in the aggregation of an exchange economy's excess demand functions the total factor incomes are constant and only their distribution matters (cf. [18, p. 281; 29, pp. 30–2]). Patinkin slurs this point by remarking that " no pretence of showing how this process of aggregation [of individual excess demand functions] is actually carried out " [22, p. 200]. Had Patinkin executed this aggregation exercise with the same extraordinary skill he displays in other portions of his book, he might have become aware that his analytic system was based on the classical obsession with a given income level.

III. POLICY IMPLICATIONS OF PATINKIN *vs.* THE KEYNESIANS

Although the purpose of this paper has been to clarify the conceptual differences between the Patinkin neo-classical model and the Keynesian model, an equally important aspect is to isolate the different policy implications of each model.

Patinkin explicitly recognises that " the necessity of a major price decline " makes reliance on the real balance effect " unacceptable as a primary ingredient of a modern full employment policy " [22, p. 335]. Accordingly, he argues that monetary policy alone can be an efficacious alternative policy for full employment provided the automatic (flexible wage and price) market processes do not subject " the economy to an intolerably long period of dynamic adjustment " [22, p. 339]. Moreover, money-wage rigidities will, according to Patinkin, tend to aggravate the depth and duration of involuntary unemployment [22, p. 342]. Thus, for Patinkin an efficiently operated monetary policy with freely flexible money wages and prices (*i.e.*, inflationary and deflationary price movements) are desirable *and* essential elements for a stable full-employment policy.

Keynesians, and particularly those who use an aggregate supply and demand approach, reach a considerably different policy conclusion. This does not mean that Keynesians do not think that " money matters," for in a monetised production economy it would be foolish to deny the importance of money. After all, it was the neo-classicists and not Keynes who thought money was a veil! Keynes' entire life was devoted to showing that " money matters "—that monetary management was essential. He was essentially a monetary economist, and considered it so important that the words money, monetary, or currency appear prominently in the titles of most of his major works. His legacy to the world includes the I.M.F. and the World Bank. To Keynes money did matter—despite some curious deviations of some Keynesians!

From the policy standpoint, however, it is clear that the *essential* difference between Patinkin and the Keynesians does not lie merely in differing views of the efficacy of monetary policy, for, as Patinkin showed, this is simply a question that can be decided " by empirical consideration of the actual magnitudes of the relevant economic parameters " [22, p. 340].

The basic conceptual difference in the two models involves an analysis of the labour market, and it is therefore not surprising that the fundamental policy difference is found there as well. The intrinsic difference is involved in the Keynesian argument that flexible money wages exert a destabilising influence in a market-oriented production economy. It is essential to the Keynesian model that there be some factor, such as wages, whose value in terms of money is at least sticky (if not fixed) if we are to have " any stability of values in a monetary system " [18, p. 304]. As Keynes observed:

> " The chief result of . . . [a flexible money-wage] policy would be to cause a great instability of prices, so violent perhaps as to make business calculations futile in an economic society functioning after the manner of that in which we live. To suppose that a flexible wage policy is a right and proper adjunct of a system which on the whole is one of *laissez-faire*, is the opposite of the truth " [18, p. 269].

Keynes recommended that a short-run stable money-wage level was the proper policy for a closed system; while a constant money-wage level and fluctuating exchange rates was the desirable policy for an open system. In the long run Keynes suggested that money wages should rise with productivity increments [18, p. 271].

The importance of a wage or incomes policy in both open and closed economies has been recently re-emphasised by some Keynesians [5, Chs. 11, 12; 7; 12, Ch. 2; 32, Ch. 6]. Indeed, for Keynesians short-run stability in the money wage-rate is a desirable policy objective for both efficiency and equity reasons, since: (1) any given monetary measure is likely to be more efficacious in a market economy where wage and price movements are minimised, since changes in money wages will have an impact on liquidity preferences which may offset the effects of changes in the money supply [18, p. 263; 5, Ch. 13], and (2) as long as many people have their personal incomes

> " contractually fixed in terms of money, in particular the rentier class and persons with fixed salaries on the permanent establishment of a firm, an institution, or the State ... social justice and social expediency are best served if the remunerations of *all* factors are somewhat inflexible in terms of money " [1] [18, p. 268].

Clearly Keynes' original ideas on the desirability of stability in wages and prices with changes in demand underlies both the Council of Economic Advisors " wage-guidelines " in the United States and the Labour Government's incomes policy in the United Kingdom.   Indeed, it is the indisputable fact that most economic policy decision-makers in Western market-oriented economies have already chosen between the Keynesian and modern neo-classical models.   Keynes has already won the ideological battle in the world of practical men.   Should not our models and our text-books deal with these facts of life ?

Paul Davidson

Rutgers University, New Brunswick.

References

1. J. G. Cross and J. Williamson, " Patinkin on Unemployment Disequilibrium," *Journal of Political Economy*, February 1962, Vol. 70, pp. 76–81.
2. P. Davidson, " Keynes's Finance Motive," *Oxford Economic Papers*, March 1965, Vol. 17, pp. 47–65.
3. ——, " More on the Aggregate Supply Function," Economic Journal, June 1962, pp. 452–7.
4. ——, *Theories of Aggregate Income Distribution* (New Brunswick, 1960).
5. P. Davidson and E. Smolensky, *Aggregate Supply and Demand Analysis* (New York, 1964).
6. ——, " Modigliani on the Interaction of Real and Monetary Phenomena," *Review of Economics and Statistics*, November 1964, Vol. 46, pp. 429–31.
7. ——, " The Popular Appeal of Five Percent Unemployment " (mimeo).

[1] A cursory examination of the 1962 data on personal income is most revealing. It shows that out of a total personal income of $442·1 billion the compensation to fixed contract groups was as follows:

	$ billion
Employees of Government	55·5
Employees of educational institutions	2·8
Employees of non-profit organisations	3·6
Rentier income (interest and rental income)	42·0
Transfer payments	34·8
	138·7

Thus, excluding salaries paid out to the employees of the profit-making business sector of the economy, we have already accounted for over 30% of personal income. Accordingly, it would not be surprising that if figures on the compensation of this latter group could be obtained as much as 40% or even 50% of personal income could be attributable to contractual commitments.

578   THE ECONOMIC JOURNAL   [SEPT. 1967

8. F. J. DeJong, " Supply Functions in Keynesian Economics," ECONOMIC
   JOURNAL, March 1954, pp. 3–24.   Also see his comments in the December
   1954, September 1955 and September 1956 issues of the ECONOMIC JOURNAL.
9. E. O. Edwards, " Classical and Keynesian Employment Theories: A
   Reconciliation," *Quarterly Journal of Economics*, August 1959, Vol. 73, pp.
   407–28.
10. D. C. Gogerty and G. C. Winston, " Patinkin, Perfect Competition and Un-
    employment Disequilibria," *Review of Economic Studies*, April 1964, Vol. 31,
    pp. 121–5.
11. U. Gruber, " Keynes' Aggregate Supply Function and the Theory of Income
    Distribution," *Jahrbucher fur Nationalokonomie und Statistik*, May 1962, Vol.
    18, pp. 189–219.
12. R. F. Harrod, *Reforming the World's Money* (London, 1965).
13. R. G. Hawtrey, " Comment," ECONOMIC JOURNAL, December 1954, pp.
    834–9.   Also see his note in the September 1956 issue of the ECONOMIC
    JOURNAL.
14. J. R. Hicks, " A Rehabilitation of ' Classical ' Economics? " ECONOMIC
    JOURNAL, June 1957, pp. 278–89.
15. ——, *Value and Capital*, 2nd edn. (London, 1939).
16. J. M. Keynes, " Alternative Theories of the Rate of Interest," ECONOMIC
    JOURNAL, June 1937, pp. 241–52.
17. ——, " The Ex-Ante Theory of the Rate of Interest," ECONOMIC JOURNAL,
    December 1937, pp. 663–9.
18. ——, *The General Theory of Employment, Interest and Money* (New York, 1936).
19. A. L. Marty, " A Geometrical Exposition of the Keynesian Supply Function,"
    ECONOMIC JOURNAL, September 1961, pp. 560–5.
20. E. Mishan, " The Demand for Labor in a Classical and Keynesian Frame-
    work," *Journal of Political Economy*, December 1964, Vol. 72, pp. 610–16.
21. D. Patinkin, *Money, Interest and Prices*, 1st edn. (Evanston, 1956).
22. D. Patinkin, *Money, Interest and Prices*, 2nd edn. (New York, 1965).
23. D. H. Robertson, *Essays on Monetary Theory* (London, 1948).
24. ——, " Two Comments," ECONOMIC JOURNAL, September 1956, pp. 485–7.
25. D. H. Robertson and H. G. Johnson, " Keynes and Supply Functions,"
    ECONOMIC JOURNAL, September 1955, pp. 474–8.
26. J. Robinson, *The Accumulation of Capital* (London, 1956).
27. J. Robinson, *The Rate of Interest and Other Essays* (London, 1952).
28. K. Saito, " Aggregate Supply Function and Income Distribution," *Keizai
    Kenkyu*, October 1962, Vol. 13, pp. 314–21.
29. S. Weintraub, *An Approach to the Theory of Income Distribution* (Philadelphia,
    1958).
30. ——, " A Macroeconomic Approach to the Theory of Wage Determination,"
    American Economic Review, December 1956, Vol. 46, pp. 835–56.
31. ——, " The Micro-Foundation of Aggregate Demand and Supply," ECONOMIC
    JOURNAL, September 1957, pp. 455–70.
32. ——, *Some Aspects of Wage Theory and Policy* (Philadelphia).
33. P. Wells, " Keynes' Aggregate Supply Function: A Suggested Interpretation,"
    ECONOMIC JOURNAL, September 1960, pp. 536–42.
34. J. Vibe-Pederson, *National Income and Aggregate Income Distribution* (Copenhagen,
    1964).

Chapter 1

Unemployment as seen by the Keynesians [1]

RICHARD KAHN

There can be no doubt that Keynes' distinction between 'involuntary' and 'voluntary' unemployment presented in his *General Theory* [2] was the basis for his analysis of the causes of unemployment and for his formulation of the remedies. The unemployment in question was 'involuntary'. Keynes' concept of 'involuntary unemployment' constituted a resounding challenge to the established school of thought. Keynes was entitled to regard Pigou's *Theory of Unemployment* [3] as representative of the classical (now often called 'neo-classical') school.

But here I am confronted by a difficulty. The first use of the term 'involuntary unemployment' of which I am aware occurs in Pigou's popular little book, *Unemployment*, published in the Home University Library series in 1914: 'Unemployment clearly does not include all the idleness of wage earners, *but only that part of it which is, from their point of view and, in their existing conditions at the time, involuntary.*' [4] A few pages further on Pigou wrote: 'The amount of unemployment . . . in any industry is measured by the number of hours' work . . . by which the employment of the persons attached to or occupied in that industry falls short of the number of hours' work that these persons would have been willing to provide at the current rate of wages under current conditions of employment.' [5] Pigou proceeded to base his definition on the drafting of the National Insurance Act. A man is not disqualified from being treated as unemployed because 'in the district where he was last ordinarily employed' he refuses work offered 'at a rate lower, or on conditions less favourable, than those which he habitually obtained in his usual

20   INVOLUNTARY UNEMPLOYMENT

employment in that district, or would have obtained had he continued to be so employed', or if he cannot find work 'in any other district, otherwise than at a rate of wage lower, or on conditions less favourable, than those generally obtained in such district by agreement between associations of employers and of workmen, or, failing any such agreement, then those generally recognised in such district by good employers'.[6]

Excluded under this definition of unemployment. are the incapacitated, the old, those who are idle from choice, including vagrants, and those on strike.

Dennis Robertson also used the term 'involuntary unemployment' in his early book.[7] To me it was a shock when, in the course of preparing this paper, I discovered that the term 'involuntary unemployment' was already in use in 1914, and that of all possible people it was used by Pigou, whom in 1936 Keynes was going rightly to denounce for publishing a book (in 1933) which was exclusively concerned with unemployment which was not involuntary.

I suffered another shock when I reread the first few pages of Pigou's 1933 book. Although Keynes was right in maintaining that the subject of Pigou's book was 'voluntary unemployment', in these opening pages Pigou implicitly denied this. Without actually using the term 'involuntary unemployment', Pigou wrote: 'A man is only unemployed when he is *both* not employed and *also* desires to be employed. . . . The desire to be employed must be taken to mean desire to be employed at current rates of wages. . . . A man is not unemployed because he would like to work if the current wage were £1,000 a day but does not so like when the current wage is 5s a day.'[8]

By taking the ridiculous figure of £1,000 a day, Pigou seriously obscured the argument. What about a man who would like to work if the current wage were 6s a day but does not so like when the current wage is 5s a day?

Pigou's book is, in fact, largely devoted to unemployment of that kind of man. Apart from frictional and cyclical unemployment, unemployment is due to the real wage being maintained – usually through collective bargaining or State action – at a level above that at which everybody would be employed.[9] As Keynes pointed out, the title of Pigou's book was ' something of a misnomer'. The book is not really concerned with unemployment but with the question of 'how much employment there will be . . . when the conditions of full employment are satisfied'.[10]

Pigou appears to have been unaware of the inconsistency between his definition of unemployment in the first few pages of his book and the subject-matter of his book. Keynes appears to have overlooked the first few pages. And even if Pigou became aware of his inconsistency after reading Keynes' criticism of his book, he did not draw attention to it in his review of the *General Theory*.[11]

I come now to Keynes' own treatment in his *General Theory*. Coming back to it after a period of 38 years, I feel that Keynes made unnecessarily heavy weather of the concepts involved. He had said about as much as needed to be said in explanation of the idea of 'involuntary unemployment' in the statement that 'the population generally is seldom doing as much work as it would like to do on the basis of the current wages. . . . More labour would, as a rule, be forthcoming at the existing money-wage if it were demanded.'[12] But Keynes' formal definition of 'involuntary unemployment' ran as follows:

'Men are involuntarily unemployed if, in the event of a small rise in the price of wage-goods relatively to the money-wage, both the aggregate supply of labour willing to work for the current money-wage and the aggregate demand for it at that wage would be greater than the existing volume of employment.'[13]

I am today unable to see why it was necessary to be so complicated. The quotation which I have given from page 7 of the *General Theory* seems perfectly adequate. Or, in slightly different words, there is involuntary unemployment to the extent that, at the current money-wage and with the current price-level, the number of men desiring to work exceeds the number of men for whose labour there is a demand.

There seems to be no need to introduce into the argument the effect of a small fall in the real wage on the supply of labour. (The effect is in either direction according as the supply curve of labour is forward or backward rising.) And the fact that a fall in the real wage is associated with an increase in employment resulting from an increase in demand does not seem to be particularly relevant.[14]

I deliberately concluded my last paragraph but one with the words

22   INVOLUNTARY UNEMPLOYMENT

'the number of men for whose labour there is a demand' rather than with the words 'the number of men employed'. The reason is that apart from 'involuntary unemployment' there is 'voluntary unemployment'. Furthermore, Keynes excluded 'frictional unemployment' – due to 'temporary loss of work of the "between jobs" type' – from his definition of 'involuntary unemployment'.[15] He also excluded the effect of 'intermittent demand for highly specialised resources', and, I suppose, 'seasonal unemployment'.

Keynes did not, in so many words, refer to 'structural unemployment', but clearly he would have included it in 'involuntary unemployment'.

'Full employment' means the absence of 'involuntary unemployment', but not of 'voluntary', 'frictional', or presumably 'seasonal' unemployment. This leads to a simpler definition of 'involuntary unemployment'. It is the kind of unemployment which is non-existent when the situation is such that an increase in effective demand will fail to bring about an increase of output because it will fail to result in additional employment.[16]

'Cyclical unemployment' is, of course, included in 'involuntary unemployment'. Keynes did not use the term; in a letter to Beveridge he referred to it as 'so-called', and pointed out that 'I am mainly concerned with what you call cyclical unemployment.'[17]

In the same letter to Beveridge, Keynes referred to a kind of unemployment which is not, I think, mentioned in the *General Theory* – 'unemployment due to a lack of homogeneity in the units of labour'. Clearly he had in mind the 'unemployability' which arises when an inefficient man is either unable to accept a wage at which it would be worthwhile employing him because the wage system does not permit it, or is unwilling to accept such a wage, possibly because he fares better as an unemployed man. This kind of unemployment is also, of course, excluded from 'involuntary unemployment'. It is, in a sense, part of 'voluntary unemployment'.

Keynes' treatment of 'voluntary unemployment' also seems to me unsatisfactory. It is 'due to the refusal or inability of a unit of labour, as a result of legislation or social practice or of combination for collective bargaining or of slow response to change or of mere human obstinacy, to accept a reward corresponding to the value of the product attributable to its marginal productivity'.[18] That seems reasonably straightforward.

AS SEEN BY THE KEYNESIANS   23

But Keynes seems to me to place too much weight on the idea that a reduction of money-wages 'would lead, through strikes or otherwise, to a withdrawal from the labour market of labour which is now employed'.[19] In criticising Pigou's *Theory of Unemployment*, Keynes stated that 'the whole of Pigou's book is written on the assumption *that any rise in the cost of living, however moderate, relatively to the money-wage will cause the withdrawal from the labour market of a number of workers greater than that of all the existing unemployed.*'[20] It is not clear why it matters whether the withdrawal would be greater or less than the number of existing unemployed. Presumably it would depend on the magnitude of the rise in the cost of living.

But the real obscurity lies in the concept of withdrawal. Presumably Keynes did not mean the withdrawal which is the manifestation of a strike. What he should have said is that the repercussions of a rise in the cost of living would result in a reduction in the demand for labour to the point at which the supply price of the amount of labour demanded is equal to the new real wage. The repercussions would take the form of a wage–price vicious spiral, which brings restraints on demand into operation, monetary and possibly fiscal, automatic as well as possibly discretionary. Keynes emphasised that organised labour is normally unwilling to accept a cut in the money-wage, whereas it often does tacitly accept a moderate fall in the real wage. This after all is the normal procedure between wage settlements, when the cost of living is constantly rising, in all those industries in which wages are governed exclusively by national settlements. But this fact does not need to be cited in order to define voluntary unemployment.

At this point I have to make an apology. It was only in the process of preparing this paper that I discovered – too late for remedial action – that it is not I who should be presenting this paper. Referring to Keynes' new concept of involuntary unemployment, presented in his *General Theory*, David Worswick, in his letter of invitation to me, expressed the hope that I would give an account of how Keynes and my colleagues and I 'saw things at the time and how far this has been borne out by subsequent experience'.

As I have been asked to be personal, I am bound to say – partly in a self-defensive, and partly in a shame-faced, attitude – that the concept of 'voluntary unemployment' left me very cold and that I

24   INVOLUNTARY UNEMPLOYMENT

took no interest in the wording of Chapter 2 of the *General Theory* which I have been criticising. I began the study of economics in June 1927. Between then and the date of publication of the *General Theory* (February 1936), unemployment was always over 10 per cent (the number un.employed was always over 1,200,000) and in the early 1930s rose above 20 per cent (in 1932 unemployment was about 22 per cent – a total of 2,700,000).[21] To my young mind the important thing was to demonstrate analytically the hollowness of the arguments that were used against the adoption of the obvious remedies. I recollect feeling particularly incensed by a talk to the Marshall Society by Sir Horace Wilson, Permanent Secretary of the Ministry of Labour until 1930 and then official Industrial Adviser to the government, in which he purported to show that real unemployment did not amount to much, after you had deducted those whose names appeared on the register only because they had staked out a precautionary claim to unemployment benefit but became absorbed again into industry within a day or two, after you had deducted those changing from one job to another or suffering seasonal or cyclical unemployment, those attached to industries in which 5 per cent or less were unemployed, the 'temporarily stopped' and the 'casuals', after you had deducted those who were of doubtful employment value and were unable or unwilling to accept any alternative employment on offer, and after you had deducted women and juveniles and men over 50 years of age. I was still more incensed by the notorious White Paper of 1929.[22] The contribution of the Ministry of Labour was based on the assumption that the only persons who could benefit from State-aided works were those fitted for heavy manual work, excluding those highly skilled men whose skill would deteriorate as a result of being employed on heavy manual work. In the Memorandum by the Ministry of Labour it was stated that, although the total number unemployed amounted to slightly over one million, in each year the total number who had registered as unemployed was 3 to 4 million. The White Paper also included the Treasury Memorandum in which the notorious Treasury view was expounded.

It seemed clear that, however successfully the problem of unemployment was tackled, there would still remain a considerable amount of 'involuntary unemployment'. It seemed to me unimportant exactly how 'involuntary' and 'voluntary' employment were defined.

Fortunately, Roy Harrod took the matter seriously and, although he did not receive the galley proofs of the *General Theory* until June 1935, his criticisms did result in considerable improvement.[23]

In the course of his friendly review of the *General Theory* published in November 1936,[24] Jacob Viner commented on Keynes' definition and treatment of involuntary unemployment.[25] In his reply Keynes wrote that 'this part of my book is particularly open to criticism. I already feel myself in a position to make improvements.'[26]

Beveridge, in the middle of 1936, read a highly critical paper about the *General Theory* at the London School of Economics.[27] At a time when there were $1\frac{3}{4}$ million unemployed, he completely denied that there was any evidence for the existence of 'involuntary unemployment'. He did, of course, admit the existence of 'cyclical unemployment', but had failed to realise that Keynes included this in 'involuntary unemployment' and that, though he did not use the phrase, it was the main subject of Keynes' book. Beveridge would have preferred to call 'voluntary unemployment' 'wage unemployment'. He utterly rejected Keynes' analysis and conclusions.[28] In 1944 Beveridge published his *Full Employment in a Free Society*, with a motto on the title page – 'Misery generates hate.' He wrote that: 'A new era of economic theorising about employment and unemployment was inaugurated by the publication in 1936 of the *General Theory* – by J. M. Keynes.' And later on: 'There may be unemployment through chronic deficiency of demand for labour, as well as unemployment through fluctuation of demand and through friction.'[29]

While the *General Theory* was going through the press, Joan Robinson wrote her *Essays in the Theory of Employment*, published in 1937. In her first essay, entitled 'Full Employment',[30] she completely broke away from Keynes' definitions and classifications. Keynes read the draft and, as Joan Robinson wrote in 1972, 'it can be taken that he accepted my amendment to his definition of full employment'.[31] Keynes had written to her: 'I like very much indeed the section on full employment and I think your treatment is a considerable improvement.'[32] On the assumption of perfect mobility of labour, Joan Robinson thought it 'plausible to say, in a general way, that in any given conditions of the labour market there is a certain more or less definite level of employment at which money wages will rise, and a lower level of employment at which money wages fall.

26 INVOLUNTARY UNEMPLOYMENT

Between the two critical levels there will be a neutral range within which wages are constant.' 'The point of full employment is the point at which every impediment on the side of labour to a rise in money wages finally gives way.'[33] In her 1972 comment Joan Robinson wrote that, at the time when the essay was written, 'there had been no experience of continuous near-full employment. I certainly would not want to maintain now that there is some particular level of unemployment (say, a statistical record of 3 per cent) at which money-wage rates will remain constant.'[34]

The second essay in Joan Robinson's book was on 'Mobility of Labour'. She wrote: 'No precise meaning can be given to the notion of full employment for a system within which mobility of labour is imperfect, unless it is taken to imply a state of affairs in which there is complete full employment all round, that is to say, in which no available labour is unemployed in any district or in any occupations.'[35] In the course of correspondence with Keynes about a draft of this essay, she wrote: 'I am more doubtful about the idea that the amount of employment which is full employment is increased. This seems to reintroduce the idea of voluntary unemployment, which I tried to get rid of in my other essay (on "Full Employment"). *Individuals* may be voluntarily unemployed if they are holding out for a wage, but it is very hard to make sense of the idea of net voluntary unemployment.'[36]

Joan Robinson was doubtful also about the concept of 'frictional unemployment'. 'It is impossible to . . . give precision to the concept of specifically "frictional" unemployment, because it is impossible to make a hard-and-fast distinction between unemployment which is due to frictions and unemployment which is due to a deficiency of effective demand. . . . It seems preferable to say that full employment, in a precise sense, can never be attained so long as frictions exist, rather than to use "full employment" in an imprecise sense in which it can be said to be attainable, such unemployment as remains being vaguely attributable to frictions.'[37] Keynes did not entirely agree. 'I have found what you have to say about this is very helpful and stimulating, but I still consider that it is a necessary concept to which it is possible to give a useful interpretation.'[38]

David Worswick, in his letter of invitation, asked me to state whether it was conceived at the time that Keynes' new concept of involuntary unemployment 'constituted a step forward in positive economics. Or was the main implication a moral shift, in the sense that an implication of the concept is that, however much he may try, the individual unemployed man can do little to help himself?' My answer is that the concept of involuntary unemployment provided part of the basis of the Keynesian analysis of the causes of unemployment and of his exposition of the remedies. There was very little moral shift. This was partly because even a classical or 'neo-classical' economist could scarcely attach much, if any, blame to the normal unemployed individual for being unemployed.

But on the effect of an all-round rise in money-wages in a closed system Keynes did make an extremely important break-through. . . . He was the first to demonstrate that, apart from the effect of a tightening of the state of credit resulting from the quantity of money being held constant, prices would rise in the same proportion, and neither the real wage nor the levels of output and employment would be altered, except in so far as the rise created an expectation of a further rise, in which case investment would be stimulated and, therefore, output and employment would rise.

The final question which David Worswick addressed to me was how far our feelings at the time about Keynes' concepts 'had been borne out by subsequent experience'. My own answer is that the distinction between 'voluntary' and 'involuntary' unemployment, while important conceptually as a basis for the Keynesian system of analysis, has not proved to have any practical significance, either in terms of statistical measurement or in terms of targets or objectives.

In his own popular writings, such as *Can Lloyd George Do It?*, published in 1929, and *The Means to Prosperity*, published in 1933, Keynes had not found it necessary to make the distinction. In the course of *The Means to Prosperity*, Keynes did, however, comment that 'many people are trying to solve the problem of unemployment with a theory which is based on the assumption that there is no unemployment'. In *How to Pay for the War*,[39] published in *The Times* in November 1939 and in book form in February 1940, Keynes simply stated that output could be increased by absorbing a 'considerable proportion of the $12\frac{3}{4}$ per cent of insured workers who were unemployed (in the fiscal year 1938-9), by bringing into employment . . . boys, women and retired or unoccupied persons, and by more intensive work and overtime'.

In 1937 unemployment was still 1·5 million (over 10 per cent).

28   INVOLUNTARY UNEMPLOYMENT

Nevertheless, in three articles published in *The Times* on the 12th, 13th and 14th January 1937, under the title 'How to Avoid a Slump,'[40] Keynes sounded a note of caution:

'It is widely agreed that it is more important to avoid a descent into another slump than to stimulate . . . still greater activity than we have. . . . It is natural to interject that it is premature to abate our efforts to increase employment so long as the figures of unemployment remain so high. . . . I believe that we are approaching, or have approached, the point where there is not much advantage in applying a further general stimulus at the centre. . . . The economic structure is unfortunately rigid. . . . The later stages of recovery require a different technique. To remedy the condition of the distressed areas, *ad hoc* measures are necessary.'

Keynes was relying, not on the distinction between 'involuntary' and 'voluntary' unemployment, but – in effect, though he did not use the term – on the concept of 'regional unemployment', which had not figured in the *General Theory*. 'We are in more need today of a rightly distributed demand than a greater aggregate demand.'

Keynes' attitude, displayed in these articles, is summarised in the following sentences: 'Three years ago it was important to use public policy to increase investment. It may soon be equally important to retard certain types of investment, so as to keep our most easily available ammunition in hand for when it is more required.'[41]

In September 1930 unemployment amounted to about 2,300,000 – above 19 per cent. In a memorandum addressed to a Committee of Economists of the Economic Advisory Council, Keynes replied to a questionnaire which had been issued to the members. In answering the question 'how much too high are (a) real wages, (b) money wages?' Keynes wrote:

'If we put our present abnormal unemployment at 1,500,000, I should estimate (in order of magnitude) that one third of this is due to the world slump, five-ninths to the emergence of a transfer problem and one-ninth to excessive real wages. . . .'

Thus, in the language of the *General Theory*, 'voluntary unemployment' amounted to about 165,000. Including this 'voluntary un-

AS SEEN BY THE KEYNESIANS   29

employment', 'normal', as opposed to 'abnormal', unemployment amounted to about 800,000 (about 6½ per cent). What Keynes meant by 'normal' unemployment was not made clear.

This order of magnitude, suggested by Keynes in 1930, was confirmed, rather remarkably, in a Memorandum written by Keynes in the Treasury in June 1942 about a draft Paper on 'National Income and Expenditure after the War'. In the course of the Memorandum Keynes wrote:

'Unemployment is due to –
  (a) the hard core of the virtually unemployable (100,000);
  (b) seasonal factors (200,000);
  (c) men moving between jobs (300,000);
  (d) misfits of trade or locality due to lack of mobility (200,000); and
  (e) a deficiency in the aggregate effective demand for labour.

Pre-war statistics are not a useful guide, because at all recent dates before the war (e) played a significant part, whereas the probable heavy demands for labour in excess of the supply indicated below suggest that the most convenient "standard" assumption for the post-war period is the virtual absence of this factor. An attempt which was made by an official committee in 1935 to estimate the probable minimum level of unemployment, excluding factor (e), arrived at a figure of 760,000 or 6 per cent. Subsequent experience suggests that this survey may have overestimated the number of the virtual unemployables, an actual count of insured persons who have been classified as unsuitable for ordinary industrial employment made on March 16th 1942 having brought out a figure below 25,000, compared with 150,000 *plus* 50,000 casuals' unemployment assumed by the Committee. In view of this a "standard" assumption of 800,000 men unemployed (or a somewhat larger aggregate of men and women together, 10 women reckoning as the equivalent of 7 men for the purpose of this calculation), which is about 5 per cent of the insured population, seems quite sufficient, made up as indicated above between brackets. It compares with about 120,000 equivalent men, or less than 1 per cent, unemployed at the present time, when factors (b) and (c) above are virtually inoperative. Experience after the last war shows that, apart from a brief transitional period in the spring of 1919, the above estimate would have been more than enough

30   INVOLUNTARY UNEMPLOYMENT

to cover the facts up to the end of 1920, although Professor Pigou reckons that the slump must be regarded as having commenced in the summer of 1920. This should, however, be regarded as a standard assumption rather than as a prophecy.'

The argument based on an over-estimation of the number of unemployables should have led to a figure less than, rather than greater than, 760,000. If 760,000 represented an unemployment percentage of 6, a percentage of 5 would mean a figure of 635,000. It seems to me that the figure of 800,000 must have been an error, and the correct figure was 600,000.[42]

Beveridge, in his 1944 *Full Employment in a Free Society*, pointed out that between the two wars unemployment had averaged 14 per cent. In the second war unemployment had been reduced to $\frac{1}{2}$ per cent or less. For five months from June to October 1937, at the top of a cyclical fluctuation, the unemployment rate in London (one of the prosperous areas of Britain) was 6 per cent or a little less. 'By this calculation a figure of about 5 per cent is sometimes reached, as the minimum reserve of labour.' Beveridge, however, arrived at 3 per cent 'as a conservative, rather than an unduly hopeful, aim to set for the average unemployment rate of the future under conditions of full employment. In numbers it means about 550,000 persons.'[43]

In December 1944 Keynes wrote to Beveridge warmly congratulating him on his book. In a postscript he mentioned a point of criticism. 'No harm in aiming at 3 per cent unemployment, but I shall be surprised if we succeed.'

So in September 1930 Keynes regarded $6\frac{1}{2}$ per cent unemployed, or 800,000, as 'normal', as opposed to 'abnormal'. In January 1937 he took the rather curious line, defended by his fear that the authorities might run out of ammunition for combating unemployment, that with unemployment at over 10 per cent – over 1 million – only regional measures for reducing it should be adopted. In June 1942 Keynes may have argued that 5 per cent – about 600,000 – was the probable minimum. By this Keynes did not mean that it would be unwise or dangerous to bring the figure down lower, but that this figure probably indicated the maximum success which could be expected from full employment policy. Hence his statement to Beveridge that there was no harm in aiming at an average of 3 per cent but it was an optimistic objective.

AS SEEN BY THE KEYNESIANS   31

I have chosen these three occasions on which Keynes faced the question what, in some sense or other, constituted a quantitatively low level of unemployment – one in 1930, one in 1937 and one in 1942 – to illustrate my contention that the development of Keynes' thinking on the distinction between voluntary and involuntary unemployment, as published in the *General Theory* in 1936, is not matched by any parallel development of his method of arriving at full employment targets in terms of actual levels of unemployment.

POSTSCRIPT

In the course of the conference I became even more convinced that the distinction between voluntary and involuntary unemployment, while very important conceptually, had not proved important in relation to statistical measurement. Some of the time of the conference was devoted to the idea that, while some people did voluntarily give up their jobs, many of these before long became involuntarily unemployed.

NOTES

1 Dr Donald Moggridge (who, in October 1975, became Professor at the University of Toronto), the editor of the later volumes of Keynes' writings published by the Royal Economic Society, has been of great help to me in the preparation of this paper. Those of Keynes' writings to which I refer which have not yet been published will be published in due course in the Royal Economic Society edition.

    For the extract near the end of my paper from a Memorandum written by Keynes in the Treasury, I thank the Controller of Her Majesty's Stationery Office (Public Records Office and Crown Copyright materials).

2 J. M. Keynes, *The General Theory of Employment, Interest and Money*, completed in December 1935 after five years' work (dating from the publication of *A Treatise on Money* in 1930) and published by Macmillan in 1936; republished in 1973 as Volume VII of the Royal Economic Society edition of Keynes' writings.

3 A. C. Pigou, *The Theory of Unemployment*, Macmillan, 1933. The manuscript had been read by Dennis Robertson, more pious in his attitude towards earlier economists than even Pigou, and Robertson had made very valuable suggestions for improvement. It is of interest that at the time when Dennis Robertson wrote his *A Study of Industrial Fluctuation*, published by P. S. King in 1915, his thinking was ahead of that of Keynes, who, criticising an early draft, seemed 'inclined to doubt a fall even in the monetary demand price for

32   INVOLUNTARY UNEMPLOYMENT

consumable goods, and to refer the decline in the consumptive trades to a diversion of productive energy into constructional industry' (Robertson, ibid., p. 221n). Robertson commented on this view on p. xii of his new Introduction to the reprint of his book issued by the London School of Economics in 1948.

4 A. C. Pigou, *Unemployment*, Williams and Norgate, 1914, p. 14. (The italics are Pigou's.)

5 Ibid., p. 16.

6 Ibid., pp. 16, 17. Pigou referred in a footnote to the White Paper, Cd 5991, p. 3.

7 Dennis Robertson, op. cit., p. 210.

8 Pigou, *The Theory of Unemployment*, pp. 3, 4. (The italics are Pigou's.)

9 Ibid., pp. 252, 253.

10 Keynes, *General Theory*, p. 275.

11 Pigou, 'Mr J. M. Keynes' General Theory of Employment, Interest and Money', *Economica*, May 1936. In the course of this review Pigou reaffirmed his own attitude. He wrote (p. 131) that Keynes 'tacitly assumes that his full employment (above which no increase can be brought about by additions to effective money demand) is equivalent, allowance being made for frictions and so on, to maximum possible employment, i.e. to the situation at the peak of a boom. But this need not be so. Wage earners may exercise a continuous pressure directed to keep rates of real wages above what is compatible with maximum possible employment. So far as they do this, enhancements in money demand for labour will not be able to raise employment permanently to the boom level, because they will be offset by rising money wages.'

12 Keynes, *General Theory*, p. 7.

13 Ibid., p. 15. (The italics are Keynes'.)

14 The *General Theory* is based, on the whole, on the economics of the short period. It was assumed that short-period supply curves were rising curves. Work done by J. G. Dunlop and Lorie Tarshis threw doubt on this assumption. Keynes rightly attributed his error to me and pointed out that, if in fact the real wage remains constant when the demand for labour rises, 'it would be possible to simplify considerably the more complicated version of my fundamental explanation', particularly in Chapter 2, in which the concepts of 'voluntary' and 'involuntary' unemployment are explained. And 'my practical conclusions would have, in that case, *a fortiori* force' (*Economic Journal*, March 1939, reprinted in the Royal Economic Society edition of the *General Theory*, p. 401).

15 Keynes, *General Theory*, p. 16.

16 Ibid., p. 26.

17 Volume XIV of the Royal Economic Society edition, p. 56.

18 Keynes, *General Theory*, p. 6.

19 Ibid., p. 8.

20 Ibid., p. 277 (the italics are Keynes'). See also p. 13.

21 As a result of the adoption of a recommendation by an Inter-Departmental Working Party, whose *Report* (Cmnd 5157) was issued in November 1972, the number of those 'temporarily stopped' is now no longer included in the published figures for the total number and for the percentage of the unemployed, but is published separately. Nowadays it is usually a small percentage of the total, but in the early 1930s it was roughly one-quarter of the total.

22 Cmd 3331.

23 See Royal Economic Society edition, Volume XIII, pp. 528, 537 and 543.

24 Jacob Viner, 'Mr Keynes on the Causes of Unemployment', *Quarterly Journal*

of Economics, November 1936; reprinted in R. Lekachman (ed.), *Keynes' General Theory*, Macmillan, 1964.

25 Lekachman, op. cit., pp. 236–8. Incidentally Jacob Viner forestalled J. G. Dunlop and Lorie Tarshis in questioning Keynes' assumption that real wages and volume of output are inversely correlated (ibid., p. 237).

26 *Quarterly Journal of Economics*, February 1937; reprinted in Royal Economic Society edition, Volume XIV, p. 110.

27 It was circulated privately under the title 'Employment Theory and the Facts of Unemployment'. There is a copy among the Keynes papers.

28 For Keynes' comments in a letter to Beveridge, see Royal Economic Society edition, Volume XIV, pp. 56–9. For the 'mass of statistics' referred to in Beveridge's reply see *Economica*, November 1936 and February and May 1937.

29 W. H. Beveridge, *Full Employment in a Free Society*, George Allen and Unwin, 1944, pp. 93 and 97.

30 Reprinted in Joan Robinson, *Collected Economic Papers*, vol. 4, Basil Blackwell, 1973, pp. 176–98.

31 Ibid., p. 174.

32 Royal Economic Society edition, Volume XIV, p. 137.

33 Joan Robinson, *Collected Economic Papers*, Vol. 4, pp. 178, 182.

34 Ibid., p. 175.

35 Joan Robinson, *Essays in the Theory of Employment* (2nd ed.), Macmillan, 1947, p. 41.

36 Royal Economic Society edition, Volume XIV, p. 140. (The italics are Joan Robinson's.)

37 Joan Robinson, *Essays in the Theory of Employment* (2nd ed.), p. 42.

38 Royal Economic Society edition, Volume XIV, p. 142.

39 These three pamphlets are republished in *Essays in Persuasion*, Royal Economic Society edition, Volume IX.

40 When I prepared this paper, I was taken by surprise by these articles, which I had forgotten. Unfortunately I did not have time before delivering the paper to track down the following articles, etc. by Keynes: Chairman's annual address to the National Mutual Life Assurance Society, 24th February 1937; 'Borrowing for Defence', *The Times*, 11th March 1937; 'Borrowing by the State', *The Times*, 24th and 25th July 1939; 'Crisis Finance', *The Times*, 17th and 18th April 1939; 'Will Rearmament Cure Unemployment?', *The Listener*, 1st June 1939. These articles will be reprinted in due course in one of the volumes of the Royal Economic Society edition. This will also include relevant papers of the Economic Advisory Council, about which a book by Mrs Susan Howson and Professor Donald Winch will be published in 1976.

41 It thus becomes clear that one of the considerations in Keynes' mind in January 1937 was the importance of retaining a reserve army of unemployed to meet the requirements of a higher rate of rearmament, which Keynes thought it impolitic to advocate until the end of the following month, by which time the government had indicated a readiness somewhat to speed up rearmament.

42 These figures have been carefully checked against a xerox copy of the original stencilled version. The difficulty of reconciliation is enhanced if the 760,000 included women and the 800,000 was a 'male equivalent', indicating a considerably higher actual aggregate, ten women being reckoned equivalent to seven men.

34   INVOLUNTARY UNEMPLOYMENT

43 This figure is based on a consistently higher post-war level for the insured
population than existed in the 1930s. In his official Report, *Social Insurance
and Allied Services*, Cmd 6404, 1942, Beveridge had assumed an average unemployment percentage of $8\frac{1}{2}$. This was partly due to caution. But in addition
Beveridge had not yet appreciated the possibilities of a successful full employment policy.

[11]

KEYNESIAN EMPLOYMENT THEORY IS NOT DEFUNCT

BY A. P. THIRLWALL[1]

Professor of Applied Economics at the
University of Kent at Canterbury

Introduction

In the last few years it has become increasingly common to hear and read the claim that Keynesian employment theory is irrelevant for understanding the recent high levels of unemployment in the United Kingdom and other countries, and that governments can no longer spend their way out of unemployment. There have been several lines of argument and attack, but three main camps or schools of thought are discernible which I shall call 'the technological', 'the monetarist' and 'the old classical'. The technological school see the high unemployment as of the structural variety caused by technological change which is not amenable to Keynesian demand management policy. It is this school that is particularly worried about the future, and the unemployment consequences of the micro-processor revolution. The monetarist school, to which the present Conservative government subscribes, believes that government spending is the enemy of employment in two ways. First, government borrowing is inflationary which destroys confidence in the private sector. Secondly, government expenditure 'crowds out' private expenditure. This latter belief is essentially a return to the old Treasury view, originally based on the classical assumption of full employment, that there is a fixed quantum of resources, and that more spending by the government must inevitably mean less spending in real terms by other agents. Obviously, at less than full employment there cannot be resource crowding out, but as we shall see later the argument is now more sophisticated with the distinction made between financial crowding out and resource crowding out. Monetarists invoke support for their views by pointing to the apparently minor impact that budget deficits seem to have had in recent years in reducing unemployment, not fully recognising that the deficits themselves are in large part the result of economic recession and of inadequate spending in the economy as a whole. Monetarists also maintain that in any case there is a 'natural' rate of unemployment below which unemployment cannot be reduced without ever-accelerating inflation. The old classical school believes that unemployment is high because the real

---

[1]The author is grateful for discussion with Charles Kennedy, Richard Disney, David Metcalf and Angus Maddison, who do not necessarily share, however, the opinions expressed.

wage is too high. Acceptance of this view implies an acceptance of the classical belief that it is the real wage that determines employment rather than the reverse, and moreover that owing to diminishing returns to labour an increase in employment and a decrease in unemployment must be associated with a reduction in the real wage. Aggregate demand expansion would simply be inflationary and create no extra employment unless real wages were to fall.

It will be argued in this article that the high level of unemployment that the United Kingdom has been experiencing recently is not primarily structural or technological; that there is no reason why government expenditure should inevitably crowd out private expenditure—on the contrary there could equally well be "crowding-in"; that the natural rate of unemployment is a theoretical construct with no operational significance; and that to argue that unemployment is high because the real wage is too high is an unfortunate and unwarranted return to classical modes of thinking, which are based on shaky theoretical and empirical foundations and which would make the nature of high unemployment voluntary, a concept which is very hard to accept.[2] I shall conclude by arguing that there is no reason why Keynesian demand management should not reduce unemployment provided the growth of money wages is not so excessive as to invoke government restraint on demand (which would put Keynesian policies into reverse) and provided the real wage does not rise so much faster than the productivity of labour as to impair the profitabililty of investment. This latter caveat is not a contradiction of the criticism of the classical view that the real wage is too high. There is a fundamental distinction to be made between the level of real wages on the one hand and their rate of growth in relation to productivity growth on the other. To recognise that real wages rising faster than labour productivity will squeeze profits, and probably investment and jobs, is not to deny a Keynesian explanation of, or solution to, high unemployment. The classical view denies involuntary unemployment; the argument that unemployment may result from real wages rising faster than productivity does not.

Furthermore, it can be argued that Keynesian policies will ultimately reduce the public sector borrowing requirement by the increase in tax revenue and fall in social security payments linked to the expansion of income. At current levels of government expenditure, the full employment, inflation-adjusted government budget is probably not in deficit at all,[3] and it is by this criterion that the real fiscal impact of a budget needs to be judged. As Professor Williamson has remarked (in what must become the quote of the decade)

---

[2]As a rough guess, there are probably more than a million unemployed willing to work at the going money wage given the opportunity.
[3]See, for example, J. Alexander and S. Toland, Measuring the Public Sector Borrowing Requirement, *Economic Trends*, August 1980.

'to treat a nominal, inflation unadjusted, cyclically unadjusted Public Sector Borrowing Requirement (PSBR) target as a constraint on economic policy (let alone as an objective) is economic barbarism',[4] yet it is precisely this target that has been guiding the country's economic fortunes since 1979. I shall further argue that provided money wage rate increases are held at a reasonable level, the major economic (as opposed to a doctrinaire or political) constraint on reducing unemployment in the years to come will be the balance of payments because this constitutes the major constraint on the expansion of demand in an open economy whatever the exchange rate regime. The United Kingdom economy has found it increasingly difficult ever since the Second World War, and the obstacles seem to be growing, to convert unemployed domestic resources into foreign exchange. These various constraints on demand, however, do not mean that the present level of unemployment is not explicable in Keynesian terms and that Keynesian theory is somehow suspect and lacking in explanatory power. A simple defence of Keynesian employment theory seems long overdue given the onslaught of recent years.

Technological unemployment

The claim that the current high level of unemployment in the United Kingdom, and for that matter in other industrialised countries, is the result of technological change just does not stand up to historical scrutiny. Only seven years ago, in 1974, registered unemployment in the United Kingdom stood at little more than 600,000 compared with over 2.5 million in June 1981. Even if technical progress is a potential cause of unemployment, it does not occur that quickly to create 2 million extra unemployed in the space of seven years. No, the current high level of unemployment is primarily the product [16] of a deficiency of demand for goods and services brought about by the shift in purchasing power since 1974 between the oil consuming and oil producing countries, which still leaves the oil producing countries in massive balance of payments surplus and most of the oil consuming countries in massive deficit. This deficiency of demand would be rectified, and jobs would be created, if the countries in surplus would (could?) spend more, which at the same time would help to relieve the constraint on internal demand in the deficit countries. The fact that the United Kingdom is now self sufficient in oil and is running a balance of payments surplus makes no difference to the argument because at full employment the current account would still be in substantial deficit. If technological progress is a major source of unemployment, and the

---

[4]Memorandum by John Williamson, in Treasury and Civil Service Committee of the House of Commons, *Memoranda on Monetary Policy*, 17th July 1980, HMSO.

major cause of high unemployment now, why have industrialised societies not witnessed growing unemployment through time? Technological progress has been rapid since the advent of the industrial revolution, and if anything it accelerated after the Second World War, and yet since 1945 unemployment has been at historically low levels. There are three powerful reasons why technological progress is not the enemy of employment. The first is that workers remaining in industries experiencing technological change become more productive, and through their extra spending more jobs are created. It is possible, in fact, that the products on which the extra income is spent are sufficiently labour intensive as to create more jobs than are lost in the industries experiencing technological change. Secondly, by no means all technical change is labour saving. Much technical change is labour using because it creates new products and new demands. One need point no further than to the technical changes that have taken place in the household and in transport to appreciate the point. The washing machine, the vacuum cleaner, the refrigerator, the automobile and the aeroplane have created many more jobs than they have destroyed. Technological change also requires investment for its embodiment and thus, whether it is labour saving or labour using, it adds to aggregate demand. This leads to the third point, that labour displaced by technological change is much more amenable to demand policy than is sometimes supposed. Some men have very specific skills and may have difficult in adapting to new employment opportunities, but the majority of the workforce is relatively versatile and adaptable, and provided there is sufficient overall demand in the economy there is no reason why structural unemployment need be a serious problem, particularly if retraining facilities are also readily available. The declining coal industry has one of the lowest unemployment rates of any industry because its redundant employees are assisted in finding alternative employment; and 7] in war time unemployment falls virtually to zero because the demand for labour is so strong. A mismatch between the supply of and demand for labour is not the inevitably by-product of technological change; it is more likely the symptom of a slack economy. When unemployment approached 10 per cent in the United States in the 1950s, a debate raged between the so-called 'structuralists' and the 'Keynesians', the former camp arguing that the cause of the high unemployment was automation and the computer revolution. And yet when demand was expanded in the early 1960s under the impetus of a tax cut and the Vietnam war, unemployment fell to historically low levels. The experience settled the debate—the high unemployment was primarily the result of a deficiency of aggregate demand. We shall be hearing more about the technological unemployment argument in the coming years with the advent of micro-processors. It is thoroughly alarmist, however, to talk in terms of massive unemployment resulting from the technological change alone. Some labour will be displaced, while new jobs will be created. Provided adequate demand for labour is maintained, and labour released from one activity can move with relative ease to others, there is no cause for pessimism. Even if there is a threat to jobs, the employment consequences of *not* participating in this technological revolution would be even greater because of an inability to compete in world markets and to export enough to pay for imports. The forecasts of future unemployment, made by such bodies as the Institute of Manpower Studies at Sussex University and the Cambridge Economic Policy Group, are extremely sensitive to the assumptions made about the rate of growth of output. A 0.5 per cent difference in the rate of growth of output between now and 2001 can make a two million difference to the forecast level of unemployment in 2001. The debate on unemployment should centre not on what to do with three (four, five?) million unemployed in the year 2000, as if these figures are inevitable, but on why demand and output cannot be expanded at the rate which would at least prevent unemployment from rising, if not reduce it to more acceptable levels. There is no justification for the view that unemployment is no longer responsive to the pressure of demand.

The monetarist argument

Monetarists and latter-day believers in the old "Treasury View' would, of course, take exception to the above statement if the demand expansion were to come from government. This school argues that government spending crowds [18] out private spending, and thus it is impossible for government to create extra jobs. It has never been entirely clear whether the point being made is a purely theoretical one or an empirical one, or a mixture of both. First of all, a distinction needs to be made between financial crowding out and the crowding out of real resources. In conditions of spare capacity and unemployed resources, it is logically impossible for public spending to preclude the use of resources by the private sector; by definition there is a surplus of resources for use by all agents. Indeed, one of the prime roles of Keynesian demand management policy is for the government to add to the demand for resources to *encourage* the private sector to claim more resources itself by improving the business climate and prospective yields which depend so heavily on the buoyancy of demand. Keynesian policies should 'crowd in' real resources not crowd them out, both indirectly as just described and also directly through the Keynesian multiplier if the increased saving generated by increased income is used for private investment purposes. No one could surely claim today that government spending must preclude the use of real resources by the private sector when unemployment is so high and when capital, which in any case is a produced means of production, is working on average less than eight hours a day in manufacturing industry. There can be financial crowding out at any level of employment but it is not inevitable, and to my knowledge there is no empirical evidence which shows that the private sector has been unable or unwilling to borrow as a *direct* result of government borrowing (as distinct from being discouraged by a depressed business climate). If the quantity of money and the velocity of circulation of money are unchanged, it is true that deficit spending cannot increase total expenditure and there would be complete financial crowding out. Under the same extreme assumptions, the same would be true of any increase in *private* spending by one sector; it would crowd out private expenditure by other sectors. In this respect there is nothing especially pernicious about government expenditure as such. If the velocity of circulation of money increases permitting some increase in total expenditure there may be some financial crowding out from public expenditure if interest rates have to rise to service new debt, but if private spending is not sensitive to interest rate changes, or is less sensitive to interest rates than the initial expansion of demand, there is no reason why aggregate expenditure should not increase. In any case, the government can hold interest rates steady by expanding the money supply so that financial crowding out does not arise. The whole crowding out debate hinges on what happens to the money supply. In an ideal world the supply of funds should be made elastic (and actually probably *will* be 9] elastic if the economy *demands* credit) up to the point where crowding out would take place in real terms. The debate then becomes, as Professor Wilson[5] reminds us, where is the point of full employment located?

Monetarists insist on replying to this line of argument by saying that expanding the money supply will not create jobs but will simply cause inflation. But why should increases in the money supply *cause* inflation when most, if not all, markets are in excess supply? The classical quantity theory of money school did not subscribe to this view in conditions of unemployment, and even in conditions of full capacity working surely no-one believes any more that the prices of industrial goods are determined by the free forces of supply and demand in perfectly competitive markets. In the markets for manufactured goods (though not in the markets for primary commodities) prices are based on variable costs per unit of output plus a relatively fixed percentage mark-up on those costs, and if costs do not rise prices will not rise either. The major cause of inflation is strong, autonomous, institutional forces pushing up the cost of labour and raw material inputs to which the money supply responds through a variety of mechanisms. The money supply is demand determined

---

[5]T. Wilson, Crowding out: the Real Issues, *Banca Nazionale del Lavoro Quarterly Review*, September 1979.

and essentially endogenous to the economic system.[6] That is why it is so difficult to control. Money and credit are needed by manufacturers to finance working capital and production before the sale of final output, and they borrow because they know that with the injection of purchasing power, they can pass on higher costs in the form of higher prices. Thus monetary control cannot itself cure inflation unless all sources of credit dry up or the threat of unemployment dampens cost increases. The threat of inflation from government spending in conditions of unemployment comes from wage demands which may start to accelerate as soon as demand pressure increases, particularly in bottleneck sectors, despite the existence of overall surplus capacity. Keynes recognised this full well in the *General Theory* in his discussion in chapter 21 on the Theory of Prices of why prices may rise before the full employment level of output is reached. He gave three main reasons: first, diminishing returns to labour as employment expands because of the non-homogeneity of labour; [20] secondly, bottlenecks in particular sectors of the economy, and thirdly a tendency for the wage unit to rise with the increased bargaining position of trade unions. On the basis of Keynes's pamphlet *How to Pay for the War* (Macmillan 1940) there is a tendency to think of the Keynesian explanation of inflation in terms of an inflationary gap, or excess demand, and yet in the *General Theory* we have modern cost-push and structural theories of inflation precisely anticipated. Indeed, it is not at all difficult to explain and represent stagflation within the Keynesian framework. Rising costs rising prices, and rising prices cause demand to be depressed for a variety of reasons such as real balance effects;[7] a deteriorating foreign balance; cutbacks in government expenditure, and so on.

Another important element in the monetarist model is the idea of a 'natural' rate of unemployment below which unemployment cannot be reduced without ever-accelerating inflation. One must always be careful in economics not to be blinded by words and apparent scientific precision. There is nothing natural about the 'natural' rate of unemployment. It is a theoretical construct without operational significance because it can only be ascertained ex-post and is not a fixed number. It is formally defined as that rate of unemployment at which the actual and expected rates of inflation are equal, which could be any rate of inflation at any level of unemployment. The natural rate is certainly not

---

[6]The best critical assault on monetarism along these lines is still that by Lord Kaldor in 'The New Monetarism', *Lloyds Bank Review*, July 1970. See also his Memorandum to the Treasury and Civil Service Committee on monetary policy, *Memoranda on Monetary Policy*, 17th July 1980, HMSO, and N. Kaldor and J. Trevithick, A Keynesian Perspective on Money, *Lloyds Bank Preview*, January 1981.

[7]i.e. the desire of people to maintain the *real* value of their money holdings in the face of inflation which requires the accumulation of more nominal holdings of money and a reduction in consumption relative to income.

something that policy makers could know in advance; nor is the rate invariant with respect to the pressure of demand as it is sometimes assumed. The degree of structural unemployment and the rate of productivity growth, which are two of the determinants of the natural rate of unemployment, depend partly on the strength of aggregate demand. Unfortunately for the monetarist position, the concept of the natural rate of unemployment, and the predictions that follow from it, are also premised on the doubtful assumption that a reduction in real wages is necessary to increase employment and to reduce unemployment; a reduction that workers will resist if policy makers attempt to reduce unemployment below the natural rate by expanding demand and raising the price level. But if labour productivity increases as employment increases (see the later discussion), an increase in employment is quite compatible with an increase in real wages, and there is no need for workers to resist. In any case, in conditions of *involuntary* unemployment where workers are off their supply curve (i.e. with the utility of the wage in excess of the marginal disutility [1] of work) there will be many unemployed willing to work at a lower real wage if necessary, given the opportunity.

If industrial prices are not determined by the forces of supply and demand in free markets, and there is generalized excess supply anyway, and if the natural rate of unemployment hypothesis is suspect, how can monetary contraction cure inflation? It must be seen primarily as a policy to weaken the market power of the trade unions by creating and threatening unemployment. The monetarists have a traditional (Keynesian) Phillips curve, showing the relationship between the rate of inflation and unemployment, in the back of their minds, although they may deny it. But how much unemployment must be created for the sake of steadying wage costs and inflation, before permanent damage is done not only to industrial relations and social harmony, but to the long run productive potential of the economy while output and investment are stagnant and declining? There are contradictions in the monetarist policy itself. Attempting to cut the money supply by cutting the public sector borrowing requirement and raising interest rates may so dampen economic activity that tax revenues fall by more than government expenditure is cut, thus increasing the borrowing requirement and the potential money supply unless interest rates are raised still further and government expenditure is cut still more. Keynesians appreciate that budget deficits are bound to vary counter-cyclically and can help to stabilise both the money supply and the economy; monetarists have seemed reluctant to concede this fundamental point, and some still do not. It is misunderstanding of this point that leads some economists and politicians to argue that budget deficits seem to have had little impact on the problem of unemployment (when recession and unemployment are themselves a cause of the large deficits), and that therefore unemployment must be voluntary and not of the Keynesian, involuntary variety.

Real wages and unemployment

This return to the idea that the present level of unemployment is voluntary is a return to the classical view that the real wage is too high and that unemployment is due to a refusal of workers to accept a reduction in their real wage.[8] The classical theory, which Keynes attacked and undermined in the 1930s, rests on two fundamental assumptions: first, that the theory of employment [22] determination applicable at the level of the individual firm applies equally to the determination of the level of employment in the aggregate; secondly, that the marginal product of labour falls as employment increases so that an increase in employment and a decrease in unemployment requires a reduction in the real wage. Unfortunately, Keynes accepted in the *General Theory* the classical and neoclassical orthodoxy of an inverse relation between employment and the level of real wages (although reversing the direction of causation), but he rightly exposed the first assumption as a fallacy of composition. The payment of wages is both a cost and a component of aggregate demand. Cutting money wages to increase employment would therefore probably be self-defeating unless aggregate expenditure on either investment, consumption or exports were to rise. There are mechanisms by which this may happen but they are tenuous and uncertain to say the least. Even if wage cuts could increase aggregate demand, however, Keynes did not believe such a policy would be feasible because they would be resisted by workers who felt their relative position in the pay hierarchy jeopardised. The revolutionary break that Keynes made with classical theory was to turn it on its head. At the aggregate level, it is not the real wage that determines employment; rather, it is the level of employment, determined by aggregate demand, which determines the real wage. I see no reason for rejecting this fundamental insight.

Keynes accepted, however, the short-period 'Marshallian' economics based on diminishing returns to the variable factor of production, labour, and conceded that the increase in employment and reduction in (involuntary) unemployment brought about by the expansion of demand would be accompanied by a fall in real wages owing to the rising supply price of output.[9] Keynesian involuntary unemployment is measured as the extra amount of demand for and supply of labour forthcoming at the same money wage as the price level

[8]See Professor G. Maynard in his article 'Keynes and Unemployment Today', *Three Banks Review*, December 1978.
[9]It is not entirely clear that Keynes based his belief in diminishing returns to labour on the law of variable proportions because in some sections of the *General Theory* (e.g. p. 295) he mentions that if labour were homogenous there would be constant returns. This would imply a belief in diminishing returns based on the use of 'inferior' labour the greater the volume of employment.

rises: 'Men are involuntarily unemployed if, in the event of a small rise in the price of wage-goods relatively to the money wage, both the aggregate supply of labour willing to work for the current money wage and the aggregate demand for it at that wage would be greater than the existing volume of employment.'[10] This definition of involuntary unemployment, premised as it is on the classical orthodoxy of an inverse relation between employment and the real wage, is unnecessarily complicated and is now, paradoxically, undermining the essential Keynesian message. The classical theory of the real wage is really an irrelevant element of the *General Theory* and ought to be discarded. Keynes himself remarked in his famous 1939 paper on 'Relative Movements in Real Wages and Output',[11] that the conclusion of an inverse relation between real wages and employment was inconvenient for his own theory because 'it had a tendency to offset the influence of the main forces which I was discussing and made it necessary for me to introduce qualifications which I need not have troubled with if I could have adopted the contrary generalisation'[12] (*i.e.* of a *positive* relation between employment and the real wage). It is now doing harm because, as the late French economist, Jean de Largentayne, persuasively argues in his Introductory Notes to the second edition of his French translation of the *General Theory*, the inclusion of the classical view of diminishing marginal productivity makes it possible to invoke the authority of the *General Theory* in favour of opinions directly contrary to its essential teaching; in particular the idea that a fall in unemployment requires a reduction in real wages and that because workers will resist this there is a 'natural' rate of unemployment below which there will be ever-accelerating inflation.[13] But if there is not diminishing returns to labour because capacity becomes more fully utilised, what does it mean to say that the real wage is too high when an expansion of employment would actually permit an increase in the real wage because the marginal product of labour is rising and marginal cost is falling? If there are increasing returns to labour the very basis of the classical belief that unemployment is high because the real wage is too high collapses. There is now enough empirical evidence to question seriously the orthodox assumption that diminishing returns to labour prevail in manufacturing industry over the range of unemployment relevant to policy debate. Over the trade cycle it is now well established that labour productivity falls during recession and rises during

[23] (margin)

---

[10] *General Theory*, p. 15.
[11] *Economic Journal*, March 1939.
[12] *Ibid.*, p. 40.
[13] An English translation is published in the *Journal of Post-Keynesian Economics*, Spring 1979, with an introduction by Lord Kaldor.

the recovery.[14] In the long run, when all factors of production are variable, there are increasing returns to scale in a wide range of economic activities. If the capital-output ratio is roughly constant, these returns must accrue to [24] labour. Again labour's marginal product rises, and its marginal cost falls as more of it is used. The results of these phenomena are that we witness through time production, employment, real wages and consumption per capita all rising together.

Keynes's own reappraisal in 1939 of the orthodoxy on which he was brought up was prompted by the statistical work of two of his former students, Mr J. Dunlop and Mr L. Tarshis, which showed for Britain and the United States a positive relation between money wages, real wages and employment. When Keynes looked at the historical evidence himself between 1880 and 1914 he also found a positive relation in the booms and slumps, except over the cycle 1880–1886. He was forced to admit: 'It seems we have been living all these years on a generalisation which held good, by exception, in the years 1880–1886, which was the formative period in Marshall's thought on the matter, but has never once held good in the fifty years since he crystallised it!' (p. 38). In his theoretical reappraisal, Keynes distinguishes between conditions of high and low unemployment. Keynes rejects the orthodoxy when he says 'we should all agree that if we start from a level of output very greatly below capacity, so that even the most efficient plant and labour are only partially employed, marginal real cost may be expected to decline with increasing output, or, at the worst, remain constant' (p. 44). On the other hand he believed that the curve must turn up at some point: 'it is of great practical importance that the statisticians should endeavour to determine at what level of employment and output the short-period marginal cost curve for the composite product as a whole begins to turn upwards and how sharply it rises after the turning point has been reached' (p. 45). He concludes by saying that 'if we tend to be living . . . more often to the left than to the right of [the] critical point, the *practical case for a planned expansionist policy is considerably reinforced* (my italics)' (p. 45). Even Pigou, the upholder of the classical faith in Cambridge, conceded in his debate with Kaldor and Keynes in 1937 and 1938 on the relation between money wages and employment, that the expansion of employment brought about money wage cuts and reduction in the rate of interest may not be accompanied by diminishing marginal physical returns if a good deal of equipment is idle: 'Thus we must not say, as I said in December, that, apart from cases of neutral equilibrium, the cut in money wage rates

[14]R. R. Neild, *Pricing and Employment in the Trade Cycle*, Cambridge University Press, 1963: W. A. H. Godley and W. D. Nordhaus, 'Pricing in the Trade Cycle', *Economic Journal*, September 1972.

acts on employment *through* the rate of real wages.'[15] What happens to real wages as economies come out of recession depends on productivity and on businesses' attitude to the restoration of profit rates. Productivity certainly rises, and the increase is probably split between a rise in real wages and a restoration of profit rates. The point is that it is not the case that a fall in real wages is a prior condition for the rise in employment. It is very difficult to believe, in the depressed economic conditions currently prevailing, that an expansion of economic activity would not lower the marginal cost of production.

Constraints on demand expansion

Whether the marginal product of labour rises or falls as employment expands, the fundamental Keynesian proposition remains that it is the level of aggregate demand which determines the level of employment, which in turn determines the real wage. What has happened to employment and unemployment in the 1970s in the United Kingdom and in other countries is quite explicable in conventional Keynesian terms. The rise in commodity prices in the early 1970s, and particularly the continuous increase in the price of oil since December 1973, has done two things to deflate aggregate demand. It has redistributed world income to a group of oil producing countries which lack the capacity to spend their income on goods produced by those countries which use oil. The estimated surplus of the oil producing countries in 1980 alone amounted to a staggering £60,000 million. This situation has made it impossible for the industrialized countries to grow at the same rate as hitherto without the willingness and ability to finance massive balance of payments deficits. Secondly, the rising cost of commodities and oil in the first half of the 1970s led to domestic inflation, and also caused a contraction in demand for domestically produced goods. The increased expenditure on necessary imports itself diverted monetary expenditure from domestic goods. A real balance effect encouraged personal saving,[16] and the fear of fuelling inflation made governments reluctant to counter deflation in the normal way. These are not the ingredients of classical voluntary unemployment, and their consequences cannot be cured with any certainty by cutting money wages to cut real wages since this may reduce aggregate demand still further.

It is perfectly true, of course, that if a country suffers a deterioration in its terms of trade, it must accept a decline in real living standards if the balance of payments is not to worsen. If it does not accept a decline then

---

[15] A. C. Pigou, Money Wages in Relation to Unemployment, *Economic Journal*, March 1938.
[16] See footnote 7, p. 21.

either the balance of payments deficit must be financed or it must be rectified
[26] by demand contraction in which case employment would fall and living
standards would be reduced 'compulsorily'. But if it is argued from this that
too high a real wage is the *cause* of the high unemployment, it may as well
be argued that too high a real wage was the initial cause of the balance of
payments deficit, which would be absurd.

All this is not to say that what is happening to the *growth* of the real
wage through time is not important. Its relation to the rate of growth of
labour productivity is very important because it is this relationship which
determines the distribution of income between wages and profits and hence
determines the rate of profit and the ability and encouragement to invest.
If the rate of growth of real wages exceeds the rate of growth of labour
productivity (including the effect of any increasing returns to labour), the
rate of profit will fall and there will be less encouragement to investment
on which future employment opportunity depends. This is the real threat to
employment. Keynesian theory recognises this danger full well. Although we
know, contrary to Keynes's original assumption, that more employment and
higher real wages can go hand in hand, the employment increase will be choked
if real wages rise faster than productivity. If trade unions could be persuaded
to moderate money wage rate increases for some time, and then not attempt
to bid for *real* wage increases in excess of productivity growth, I see no reason
why Keynesian demand management should not get the United Kingdom
economy back to the levels of employment enjoyed in the 1960s. The economy
would also enjoy reasonable price stability, which might in turn help to improve
the balance of payments—although there is much more to the United Kingdom
balance of payments problem than a lack of price competitiveness. This conclusion is similar to that of a recent study by Maurice Scott who concludes
'we can get back to full employment if, when the government follows a macroeconomic policy which gradually reflates demand, the share of profits gradually
increases, labour-using investment is encouraged, some cyclical and all structural unemployment is gradually absorbed and, despite the rise in profits and
fall in unemployment, wage increases remain moderate, that is, not much
in excess of the average rate of growth of labour productivity'.[17] Scott's major
[27] policy recommendation is that there must be some form of wage fixing machinery to moderate the growth of money wages.

The Balance of payments constraint

The second major threat to jobs in a Keynesian framework of analysis comes

---

[17]Maurice Scott, *Can We Get Back to Full Employment?*, Macmillan 1978.

from the balance of payments. It is true that Keynes's original model was for a closed economy, and that is another of its unfortunate features, but it is not difficult to extend the model to an open economy in which the imbalance between exports and imports at full employment becomes a much more stubborn gap to rectify than the gap between investment and full employment saving which was Keynes's concern. If the ability to export does fall short of full employment imports and other sectors of the economy are in overall balance, income and employment will decline through the workings of the foreign trade multiplier. If income and employment are maintained by an excess of spending over 'saving' in other sectors, the balance of payments will be in deficit, and the empirical question is then how long the deficit can be financed without corrective action having to be taken of an expenditure reducing type. There is strong evidence that the working of the foreign trade multiplier has been a powerful determinant of inter-country growth rate differences in the world economy in the post-war years, and that the major reason for the United Kingdom's slow growth relative to the other countries is its slow rate of growth of exports relative to the income elasticity of demand for imports.[18]

Some economists in the United Kingdom are still sanguine that exchange rate depreciation can achieve simultaneous internal and external equilibrium. But the absolute size of the full employment deficit is now so large, and the underlying trend deterioration on the non-oil account is so serious, that even if the price elasticities of demand for imports and exports were favourable, and money wage increases could be controlled, a major exchange rate adjustment would be required, followed by *continuous* depreciation to maintain a balance through time to offset the unfavourable effects of the low income elasticity of demand for United Kingdom exports compared with the much higher United Kingdom income elasticity of demand for imports.

Thus, even if one dismisses the inevitability of technological change causing unemployment, and of government spending 'crowding out' private spending, there must still be pessimism that the economy can sustain the rate of growth of output required to keep unemployment down without getting into balance of payments difficulties, notwithstanding the substantial balance of payments gains from North Sea oil. And when North Sea oil no longer makes a contribution to the balance of payments, one shudders to contemplate the consequences

---

[18]For an exposition of the workings of the foreign trade multiplier (or more accurately, the Harrod trade multiplier) as a determinant of the level and growth of output, I have a paper available on request entitled 'The Harrod Trade Multiplier and the Importance of Export Led Growth.' On the empirical evidence, see my paper, 'The Balance of Payments Constraint as an Explanation of International Growth Rate Differences', *Banca Nazionale del Lavoro Quarterly Review*, March 1979.

for the balance of payments and unemployment if the non-oil balance of payments does not improve. Already with over 2.5 million unemployed and oil making a £6.0 billion contribution to the balance of payments, the annual current account is in surplus by only £2.0 billion, and the underlying trend at a given level of output is one of deterioration. The 'full' employment balance of payments is probably in deficit to the tune of £6 to £7 billion.[19] By 1985, when oil is supposed to be contributing £8 billion to the balance of payments (at 1977 prices), this will probably be insufficient to cover the non-oil deficit, let alone allowing the economy to expand to reduce unemployment. The argument put forward by some[20] that there must be an absolute decline in the manufacturing sector of the economy because of the balance of payments gain from North Sea oil is unconvincing. It assumes a fully employed, static economy in which the exchange rate must rise. There are so many ways in which the foreign exchange gains from oil production can be dissipated, however, including overseas investment and demand expansion, that the argument need not detain us further. The fundamental task of economic policy, as I argue elsewhere,[21] must be to improve the non-oil balance of payments by reducing the income elasticity of demand for imports and raising the 'world' income elasticity of demand for United Kingdom exports. Only if policies are successful in this regard can the United Kingdom raise its growth rate consistent with balance of payments equilibrium and tackle unemployment at the same time. If there is no improvement in the balance of payments constraint on the growth of demand, I fear that forecasts of higher future unemployment may well come true. It will not be, however, because the nature of unemployment has changed, or because Keynesian employment theory is defunct, but because the balance of payments imposes a constraint on demand

[29] preventing Keynesian policies from being implemented.

---

[19]Defining full employment as 1 million unemployed, a 1.5 million reduction in unemployment would imply increased output of £15 billion and an increase in the import bill of approximately £7 billion.

[20]See J. Kay and P. Forsyth, The Economic Implications of North Sea Oil Revenues, *Fiscal Studies*, July 1980. See also *The Guardian*, 14th July 1980.

[21]A. P. Thirlwall, *Balance of Payments Theory and the United Kingdom Experience*, Macmillan, 1980.

[12]

Keynesian Models of Recession and Depression

Keynes's *General Theory* attempted to prove the existence of equilibrium with involuntary unemployment, and this pretension touched off a long theoretical controversy. A. C. Pigou, in particular, argued effectively that there could not be a long-run equilibrium with excess supply of labor. The predominant verdict of history is that, as a matter of pure theory, Keynes failed to prove his case.

Very likely Keynes chose the wrong battleground. Equilibrium analysis and comparative statics were the tools to which he naturally turned to express his ideas, but they were probably not the best tools for his purpose. For one thing, he explicitly confined the *General Theory* to a time period in which are given "the existing skill and quantity of available labor, quality and quantity of available equipment, the existing technique" and other factors. As he said (p. 245), "in this place and context, we are not considering or taking into account the effects and consequences of changes in them." But his model produces a solution in which, in general, the stock of capital, and other stocks, are not constant. Changes in these stocks will in turn alter investment, saving, and other behavior. For this reason alone, the solution of Keynes's model cannot be stationary, even in its own endogenous variables; and on this ground alone, it fails to qualify as an equilibrium. The evolution of Keynesian equilibrium as stocks change is receiving a great deal of attention these

days and I shall not dwell on this point here. (See, however, A. S. Blinder and R. M. Solow and J. Tobin and W. Buiter.)

The second important point, the one on which Pigou insisted, is that excess supply of labor must cause money wages to decline. Even if this did not succeed in eliminating unemployment, one might not call a situation in which money wages and prices are persistently falling an equilibrium. But of course Pigou went further in contesting Keynes's claim that a "trap" might exist from which the economy could not be rescued, however low the wage and price level.

Keynes tried to make a double argument about wage reduction and employment. One was that wage rates were very slow to decline in the face of excess supply. The other was that, even if they declined faster, employment would not—in depression circumstances—increase. As to the second point, he was well aware of the dynamic argument that *declining* money wage rates are unfavorable to aggregate demand.[1] But perhaps he did not insist upon it strongly enough, for the subsequent theoretical argument focused on the statics of alternative stable wage levels.

The real issue is not the existence of a

---

[1] ". . . it would be much better that wages should be rigidly fixed and deemed incapable of material changes, than that depression should be accompanied by a gradual downward tendency of money-wages, a further moderate wage reduction being expected to signalise each increase of, say, 1 percent in the amount of unemployment. For example, the effect of an expectation that wages are going to sag by, say, 2 percent in the coming year will be roughly equivalent to the effect of a rise of 2 percent in the amount of interest payable for the same period. The same observations apply *mutatis mutandis* to the case of a boom." (See Keynes, p. 265.)

* Sterling Professor of Economics, Yale University. The research described in this paper was undertaken by grants from the National Science Foundation and the Ford Foundation.

196   **AMERICAN ECONOMIC ASSOCIATION**   *MAY 1975*

long-run static *equilibrium* with unemployment, but the possibility of protracted unemployment which the natural adjustments of a market economy remedy very slowly if at all. So what if, within the recherché rules of the contest, Keynes failed to establish an "underemployment equilibrium"? The phenomena he described are better regarded as disequilibrium dynamics. Keynes's comparative statics were an awkward analytical language unequal to the shrewd observations and intuitions he was trying to embody. If the purity of neoclassical equilibrium is preserved, this verdict is no real blow to Keynes or solace for Pigou. The Great Depression is the Great Depression, the notorious "Treasury View" is still ridiculous, whether mass unemployment is a feature of an equilibrium or of a prolonged disequilibrium.

The issue is by no means dead. Today "full employment" has become the "natural rate," and "equilibrium" often allows for any steady rate of deflation or inflation, not just zero. But the proposition which Keynes was questioning is once again strongly argued in the profession and in public debate. Once again it is alleged that the private market economy can and will, without aid from government policy, steer itself to full employment equilibrium. This is the basis for advocacy of fixed rules of monetary growth and fiscal policy, as against active discretionary policy responding to information fed back from the private economy. At this very moment it is the basis for a policy of letting the recession run its course, in confidence that in a relatively short run—two or three years—equilibrium will be restored at full employment with reduced or even zero inflation.

I. Keynesian and Marshallian Price Dynamics

Milton Friedman (p. 18) has pointed out that Keynes was a "Marshallian in method" and translated the supply-demand framework of Alfred Marshall from individual markets to the whole economy. "Where he deviated from Marshall, and it was a momentous deviation, was in reversing the roles assigned to price and quantity. He assumed that, at least for changes in aggregate demand, quantity was the variable that adjusted rapidly, while price was the variable that adjusted slowly, at least in a downward direction." Friedman is correct that this was a momentous deviation, and one way to appreciate the point is to look explicitly at the dynamic stability implications of Walrasian vs. Marshallian assumptions about quantity adjustment.

Marshallian adjustment in a particular market is that quantity adjusts to the difference between demand price and supply price for existing quantity. Walrasian adjustment is that quantity adjusts to the difference between demand and supply at existing price.

Let us now apply these two adjustment assumptions to a simple macroeconomic model. Let Y be aggregate real output, and Y^* its value at full employment, i.e., at the "natural rate" level of unemployment. Let E be aggregate real effective demand, which can differ in short-run disequilibrium both from Y and from Y^*. Given the nominal stock of outside money M and other exogenous or policy-set variables, effective demand E is a function $E(p, x, Y)$ of three variables: p the price level, x its expected rate of change, and Y the level of output and real income.

In finer detail, E is the sum of consumption C, private investment I, and government purchases G:

$$(1) \quad E = C\left(Y, Y^*, -T, -R, x\frac{M}{p}, W\right)$$
$$+ I(Y, Y^*, -K, -R) + G$$

VOL. 65 NO. 2   KEYNESIAN MODEL   197

Here the C and I functions have positive derivatives in all their arguments. T represents taxes, a function of Y and Y^*. W is private wealth, equal to

$$\frac{M}{p} + qK,$$

where the coefficient q is the ratio of market valuation of capital equity to replacement cost. An increase in the real interest rate R relative to the marginal efficiency of capital makes q fall, and makes investment fall. The marginal efficiency of capital depends positively on Y and Y^*, negatively on K. The real interest rate R depends inversely on both M/p and x, and rises with Y and W.

The *price level effect* E_p on demand is negative, for the following familiar combination of reasons. First is the Keynes effect. A given nominal quantity of money will be a larger real quantity at a lower price level. Consequently the interest rate may be lower, and investment demand higher. The Keynes effect is expected to be weaker the larger the real supply of money relative to output Y, and to vanish altogether in the "liquidity trap." This will tend to make E_p smaller in absolute value at low levels of Yp/M.

Second is the Pigou effect, the wealth effect on consumption. The lower the price level, the higher the real value of those components of net private wealth fixed in nominal value. The relevant components are outside money (and some part of any nonmonetary public debt in existence). Consumption demand is expected, *ceteris paribus*, to respond positively to increases of wealth.

The short-run Pigou effect is very likely weaker than the long-run effect and may not even have the same negative sign. And it is the short-run effect which is relevant for Keynesian theory and for the dynamics of this paper. The difference arises as follows: among the stocks fixed in the short

run are private debts in the unit of account. These are a heavier burden to debtors the lower the price level, and there are good reasons why transfer of real income and wealth to creditors spells a net deficit of aggregate demand. Debtors are debtors because they have high propensities to spend. Many of them are liquidity-constrained, and as their debt/equity ratios increase their credit lines dwindle or, in case of bankruptcies, disappear. Although these are "only" distributional effects, they may be more important than the real value of outside money and debt.

The long-run comparative-static Pigou effect, in contrast, assumes that each alternative price level has prevailed for a sufficiently long time so that inside debts are scaled to that price level—although strangely enough exogenous outside money is not. In this counterhistorical "as if" mental experiment, debtors are no more burdened at one price level than at another.

As for *the price change effect* E_x, there are several effects. A decrease in the expected inflation rate raises the real rate of interest. This increase discourages investment, and it also deters consumption both directly and by lowering the market value of equity capital, one component of wealth. On the other hand, expected capital gains on money holdings xM/p are favorable to consumption. This is a "flow Pigou effect," to be distinguished from the stock effect. The question here involves the size of the marginal propensity to spend from expected real capital gains. Econometric evidence has been that this marginal propensity is small, although capital gains eventually affect consumption via the wealth effect. I have assumed that the other effects of expected inflation dominate the flow Pigou effect.

The *marginal propensity to spend* E_y is taken to lie between 0 and 1 on usual Keynesian grounds. As is well-known, a

198   **AMERICAN ECONOMIC ASSOCIATION**   **MAY 1975**

high response of investment demand to contemporaneous income could easily make E_y exceed one. But Keynes typically regarded investment as determined more by long-run sales and profit expectations than by current business activity. The likelihood that, in prolonged departures from full employment, investment will come to be governed more by contemporaneous than by full employment sales and profits is a source of possible instability and of prolonged disequilibrium to which I shall return later in the paper.

In equilibrium, the following three conditions hold:

$$(2.1) \qquad E(p, x, Y) - Y = 0$$

$$(2.2) \qquad Y - Y^* = 0$$

$$(2.3) \qquad x = \dot{p}/p = 0.$$

(I shall also denote $\dot{p}/p$ as π.)

I shall call the first dynamic version of this model the *WKP* model (Walras-Keynes-Phillips). All the adjustment functions which follow will conform to the notation $A_y z$, where y is the variable adjusting, z the variable on which the adjustment depends, and A_y a positive constant.

The *WKP* model is as follows:

The WKP Model

$$(2.1.1) \qquad \dot{Y} = A_y(E - Y)$$

$$(2.2.1) \qquad \pi = A_p(Y - Y^*) + x$$

$$(2.3.1) \qquad \dot{x} = A_z(\pi - x)$$

Equation (2.1.1) says that production Y moves in response to discrepancies of E and Y. This implements the Keynesian view that in the very short run money wages and prices are set and output responds to variations of demand.

How can E and Y diverge even for an instant? Many words have been spilled, both by Keynes himself and by others, on this question, usually posed in terms of the possibility of inequality of Saving and Investment. In our present context, let D be

the demand which must always equal Y to preserve the national income identities. Let D be a function of $\dot{Y}$ as well as of x, p, and Y. Then $D(\dot{Y}, x, p, Y) = Y$, $E(x, p, Y) = D(0, x, p, Y)$. Equation (2.1.1) follows from a negative value of $\partial D/\partial \dot{Y}$, which means that demand is lower, at given Y, when Y is increasing. Lags in consumption spending lead to this sign and so does *unintended* inventory decumulation. The investment accelerator works in the other direction, but for the reason already given it is not a Keynesian idea.

Equation (2.2.1) is a natural-rate version of the Phillips curve. The short-run Phillips curve is the obvious Keynesian version of price dynamics. Throughout this paper I am condensing product and labor markets into one sector and assuming with Keynes that prices are determined by marginal variable costs, i.e., by labor costs. Excess labor supply and $Y - Y^*$, the "Okun gap," are linked,—when one is zero so is the other. So it is the gap which causes wage rates to fall. But to "fall" does not mean to decline absolutely; it means to decline relative to x, the accustomed and expected rate of inflation of both labor costs and prices. This is the more modern wrinkle. By here assuming (2.2.1) I do not mean necessarily to associate myself—much less Keynes!—with the natural-rate hypothesis in all its power and glory.

The third equation (2.3.1) is the well-known model of adaptive expectations. There is nothing particularly Keynesian about this equation, and the same formulation will carry over to the non-Keynesian dynamic model. Keynes himself would scorn it and stress instead the stochastic and historical sources of expectations. But like so many of his observations, these do not lend themselves to simple formal analysis.

As two extremes of interest I shall wish to consider:

$$(2.3.2) \qquad\qquad x = \pi$$

KEYNESIAN MODEL

(extrapolation of current rates of price *change*)

(2.3.3) $x = 0$

(extrapolation of current price *level*)

The alternative dynamic version may be called the M model (Marshall). The equations are:

The M Model

(2.1.2) $\pi = B_p(E - Y) + x$

(2.2.2) $\dot{Y} = B_Y(Y^* - Y)$

(2.3.2) $\dot{x} = A_x(\pi - x)$ (or 2.3.1 or 2.3.3)

As compared with the WKP model, the adjustment roles of the first two equations are interchanged. The first equation now says that the immediate impact of excess demand for goods and services is to raise prices, or more strictly to raise them faster than they had been expected to rise. (It is not entirely accurate to regard (2.1.2) as non-Keynesian. When there is an inflationary gap $(E>Y^*,\ Y=Y^*)$, this looks very much like the Keynesian model of inflation. But in Keynes's inflation theory, Y^* is considered an absolute short-run constraint on production, as in wartime. In normal conditions, Keynes would, I think, regard Y^* as a medium-run labor market equilibrium with normal margins of excess capacity and of frictional unemployment, a level of output which could be at least temporarily exceeded.)[2] In any event, equation (2.1.2) is one way to inject into the model the view that prices respond quite flexibly to changes in excess demand for goods, whether or not the economy is close to full employment.

The non-Keynesian partner of this price adjustment equation is (2.2.2), where the gap between potential and actual output

inspires adjustments of production and employment. This is because they are associated with gaps of the same sign between the demand price for labor (the value of its marginal product) and its supply price.[3] The idea is that when Y^* exceeds Y the real wage is less than marginal productivity. Competitive employers therefore add to their work forces and their production. In Keynesian theory, on the other hand, production increases only when demand at existing prices expands.

II. Local Stability of the Two Models

Let us now consider the local stability of the WKP and M models, around their equilibrium values $Y=Y^*,\ p=p^*,\ x=0$. For this purpose it is convenient to substitute in the third equation the value of $\pi-x$ drawn from the second or first equation. Thus the third equations in the WKP and M models become respectively:

(3.1) $\dot{x} = A_x A_p(Y - Y^*)$

(3.2) $\dot{x} = A_x B_p(E - Y)$

For the WKP model, the linearized equations are:

(3.3)
$$\begin{bmatrix} \dot{Y} \\ \dot{p} \\ \dot{x} \end{bmatrix} = \begin{bmatrix} A_Y(E_y-1) & A_Y E_p & A_Y E_x \\ A_p p^* & 0 & p^* \\ A_x A_p & 0 & 0 \end{bmatrix}$$
$$\cdot \begin{bmatrix} Y - Y^* \\ p - p^* \\ x \end{bmatrix}$$

The critical necessary condition for stability is:

(3.4) $p^* E_p + A_x E_x < 0$

The first term of (3.4) is negative and the second term positive. As would be expected, a strong negative price-level effect on aggregate demand, a weak price-

---

[2] In the *General Theory*, Keynes discusses frictional and involuntary unemployment on p. 6 and, in defining involuntary unemployment on p. 15, says, "Clearly we do not mean by 'involuntary' unemployment the mere existence of an unexhausted capacity to work."

[3] This is true even if the labor supply curve is downward sloping, provided it is closer to vertical than the schedule of marginal productivity of labor.

expectation effect, and a slow response of price expectations to experience are conducive to stability. In one extreme case (2.3.3), where $x=\dot{x}=0$, the system is of course stable. In the other extreme case (2.3.2), where $x=\pi$, the first term of (3.4) drops out and the system is necessarily unstable.

The M model is quite different. It is separable into output and price equations. Equation (2.2.2) is a stable differential equation in the single variable Y. The stability of the price system depends on (3.4), in the same way as the stability of the WKP model. The formal system is:

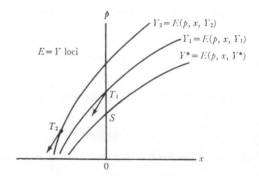

$$(3.5) \quad \begin{bmatrix} \dot{Y} \\ \dot{p} \\ \dot{x} \end{bmatrix} =$$

$$\begin{bmatrix} -B_Y & 0 & 0 \\ B_p(E_Y-1)p^* & B_p p^* E_p & B_p p^* E_x + p^* \\ A_x B_p(E_y-1) & A_x B_p E_p & A_x B_p E_x \end{bmatrix}$$

$$\cdot \begin{bmatrix} Y-Y^* \\ p-p^* \\ x \end{bmatrix}$$

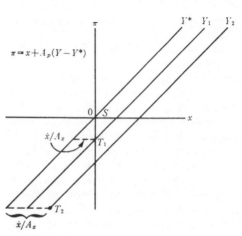

FIGURE 1

As Friedman surmised, Keynes's choice of adjustment mechanisms is a crucial element of his theory. In particular, the Walras-Keynes-Phillips adjustment model allows the distinct possibility that lapses from full employment will not be automatically remedied by market forces. Keynes could also be interpreted to hold the view that price-level effects E_p are weak relative to speculative effects E_x. I shall discuss this interpretation further in the next section.

III. Irreversible Recessions and Deep Depressions

Let us take a more global look at the equilibrium condition $E=Y$ (2.1). In Figure 1 are shown in (p, x) space several loci

along which the condition is met. The slope of such a locus, $-E_x/E_p$, is positive. Each locus is for a given value of Y; a reduction in Y shifts the locus to the left. In the Figure, the right-most locus is for full employment output Y^*. The weakening or vanishing of the "Keynes effect" at low values of Y and p tends to reduce E_p in absolute value. This is reflected in the curvature of the loci.

Consider an initial position T_1 at levels of E and Y short of Y^*. Prices begin to decline because Y_1 is less than Y^*. To a degree that depends on the speed of adaptation, expectations of price change become negative. The arrow indicates the direction of movement. As drawn, the movement is

VOL. 65 NO. 2   KEYNESIAN MODEL   201

stabilizing, taking the economy to higher E and Y, toward Y^* and the equilibrium S.

The lower panel of Figure 1 concerns the direction of the arrow, the relationship of π and x. The horizontal axis matches in origin and scale that of the upper panel. The lines are parallel 45 degree lines, for Y^*, Y_1, and Y_2, the same output levels as in the upper diagram. The points S, T_1, T_2 correspond to the similarly labeled points above. At S, $\pi = 0$. At T_1, π is negative. So is $\dot{x}$, by an amount proportional to the difference between π and x, shown horizontally as $\dot{x}/A_x$.

Consider instead an initial position T_2 in the two panels. At T_2 both the slope of the $E = Y$ locus and that of the arrow are steeper. The reason that the arrow is steeper can be seen in the lower panel: $\dot{x}/A_x$ has doubled, but π has more than doubled. The net outcome could go either way. The possibility illustrated is that at T_2 the locus $E = Y$ is so steep that the movement is destabilizing. The system might be stable for small deviations from its equilibrium but unstable for large shocks.[4] The failure of automatic market processes to restore full employment would be reinforced if large and prolonged recession caused investors to gear their estimates of the marginal efficiency of capital more to current than to equilibrium demand and profitability.

Under these adverse circumstances, and in the absence of countercyclical policy, the economy could slip into a deep depression.

In nonlinear nonmonetary business cycle models like those of M. Kalecki, R. Goodwin, and Sir John Hicks, a long depression phase occurs with the economy at a floor. At this floor the capital stock is excessive

and gross investment is zero; production is solely to meet minimal private and social consumption requirements, which are independent of income and wealth. The depression phase lasts a long time, while depreciation slowly whittles the capital stock down to the amount needed for floor level production.

It is not part of this paper to provide a model of such a floor. The relevant question is whether deflation will by itself lift the economy from the floor. Will deflation so augment private wealth that consumption rises above its floor level? Clearly this will not happen unless condition (3.4) is met at the depression income level.

But at the floor, E_x is higher than in the normal regime. An increase in the deflation rate $-x$ lowers the value of the capital stock. The physical capital stock declines slowly. But its value—its *real* value— can decline rapidly; when no gross investment is taking place, the existing stock will be valued well below replacement cost. At the liquidity trap, the real interest rate is the irreducible nominal rate $\bar{r}$ plus the expected rate of deflation $-x$. The value of a unit of capital is $(\rho - \delta/(r - x))$ where $\rho - \delta$ is the marginal productivity of capital net of depreciation. Although the attrition of the stock slowly raises ρ, deflation rapidly raises $\bar{r} - x$.

IV. Concluding Remarks

God may have made the world so that full employment equilibrium exists and is stable. Perhaps the divine design guarantees that capitalist market economies will never be trapped in depressions with involuntary unemployment and will never need to depart from fixed no-feedback rules of fiscal and monetary policy. But Keynes had good empirical and theoretical reason to suspect otherwise. He did not establish an underemployment equilibrium. But he did not really need to. Even with stable monetary and fiscal policy,

---

[4] Robert Solow has pointed out to me that the possibility illustrated by T_2 is only suggestive of a global instability. The global properties of the system require further investigation.

202   **AMERICAN ECONOMIC ASSOCIATION**   *MAY 1975*

combined with price and wage flexibility, the adjustment mechanisms of the economy may be too weak to eliminate persistent unemployment.

REFERENCES

A. S. Blinder and R. M. Solow, "Does Fiscal Policy Matter?," in *J. of Pub. Econ.*, 1973, **2**, 319–37, and *Econ. of Pub. Fin.*, Brookings Institution, 1974, 452–58.

M. Friedman, *A Theoretical Framework for Monetary Analysis*, Nat. Bur. of Econ. Res. occas. pap. 112, New York 1971.

J. M. Keynes, *The General Theory of Employment, Interest, and Money*, 1st ed., London 1936, 245.

J. Tobin and W. Buiter, "Long-Run Effects of Fiscal and Monetary Policy on Aggregate Demand," Cowles Foundation disc. pap. no. 384, Dec. 1974.

[13]

The Monetarist Controversy or, Should We Forsake Stabilization Policies?

By Franco Modigliani*

In recent years and especially since the onset of the current depression, the economics profession and the lay public have heard a great deal about the sharp conflict between "monetarists and Keynesians" or between "monetarists and fiscalists." The difference between the two "schools" is generally held to center on whether the money supply or fiscal variables are the major determinants of aggregate economic activity, and hence the most appropriate tool of stabilization policies.

My central theme is that this view is quite far from the truth, and that the issues involved are of far greater practical import. There are in reality no serious analytical disagreements between leading monetarists and leading nonmonetarists. Milton Friedman was once quoted as saying, "We are all Keynesians, now," and I am quite prepared to reciprocate that "we are all monetarists"—if by monetarism is meant assigning to the stock of money a major role in determining output and prices. Indeed, the list of those who have long been monetarists in this sense is quite extensive, including among other John Maynard Keynes as well as myself, as is attested by my 1944 and 1963 articles.

In reality the distinguishing feature of the monetarist school and the real issues of disagreement with nonmonetarists is not monetarism, but rather the role that should probably be assigned

*Presidential address delivered at the eighty-ninth meeting of the American Economic Association, Atlantic City, New Jersey, September 17, 1976. The list of those to whom I am indebted for contributing to shape the ideas expressed above is much too large to be included in this footnote. I do wish, however, to single out two lifetime collaborators to . whom my debt is especially large, Albert Ando and Charles Holt. I also wish to express my thanks to Richard Cohn, Rudiger Dornbusch, and Benjamin Friedman for their valuable criticism of earlier drafts, and to David Modest for carrying out the simulations and other computations mentioned in the text.

to stabilization policies. Nonmonetarists accept what I regard to be the fundamental practical message of *The General Theory*: that a private enterprise economy using an intangible money *needs* to be stabilized, *can* be stabilized, and therefore *should* be stabilized by appropriate monetary and fiscal policies. Monetarists by contrast take the view that there is no serious need to stabilize the economy; that even if there were a need, it could not be done, for stabilization policies would be more likely to increase than to decrease instability; and, at least some monetarists would, I believe, go so far as to hold that, even in the unlikely event that stabilization policies could on balance prove beneficial, the government should not be trusted with the necessary power.

What has led me to address this controversy is the recent spread of monetarism, both in a simplistic, superficial form and in the form of growing influence on the practical conduct of economic policy, which influence, I shall argue presently, has played at least some role in the economic upheavals of the last three years.

In what follows then, I propose first to review the main arguments bearing on the *need* for stabilization policies, that is, on the likely extent of instability in the absence of such policies, and then to examine the issue of the supposed destabilizing effect of pursuing stabilization policies. My main concern will be with instability generated by the traditional type of disturbances—demand shocks. But before I am through, I will give some consideration to the difficult problems raised by the newer type of disturbance—supply shocks.

I. The Keynesian Case for Stabilization Policies

A. *The General Theory*

Keynes' novel conclusion about the need for

2   **THE AMERICAN ECONOMIC REVIEW**   **MARCH 1977**

stabilization policies, as was brought out by the early interpreters of *The General Theory* (for example, John Hicks, the author, 1944), resulted from the interaction of a basic contribution to traditional monetary theory—liquidity preference—and an unorthodox hypothesis about the working of the labor market—complete downward rigidity of wages.

Because of liquidity preference, a change in aggregate demand, which may be broadly defined as any event that results in a change in the market clearing or equilibrium rate of interest, will produce a corresponding change in the real demand for money or velocity of circulation, and hence in the real stock of money needed at full employment. As long as wages are perfectly flexible, even with a constant nominal supply, full employment could and would be maintained by a change of wages and prices as needed to produce the required change in the real money supply—though even in this case, stability of the price level would require a countercyclical monetary policy. But, under the Keynesian wage assumption the classical adjustment through prices can occur only in the case of an increased demand. In the case of a decline, instead, wage rigidity prevents the necessary increase in the real money supply and the concomitant required fall in interest rates. Hence, if the nominal money supply is constant, the initial equilibrium must give way to a new stable one, characterized by lower output and by an involuntary reduction in employment, so labeled because it does not result from a shift in notional demand and supply schedules in terms of real wages, but only from an insufficient real money supply. The nature of this equilibrium is elegantly captured by the Hicksian *IS-LM* paradigm, which to our generation of economists has become almost as familiar as the demand-supply paradigm was to earlier ones.

This analysis implied that a fixed money supply far from insuring approximate stability of prices and output, ·as held by the traditional view, would result in a rather unstable economy, alternating between periods of protracted unemployment and stagnation, and bursts of inflation.

The extent of downward instability would depend in part on the size of the exogenous shocks to demand and in part on the strength of what may be called the Hicksian mechanism. By this I mean the extent to which a shift in *IS*, through its interaction with *LM*, results in some decline in interest rates and thus in a change in income which is smaller than the original shift. The stabilizing power of this mechanism is controlled by various parameters of the system. In particular, the economy will be more unstable the greater the interest elasticity of demand for money, and the smaller the interest responsiveness of aggregate demand. Finally, a large multiplier is also destabilizing in that it implies a larger shift in *IS* for a given shock.

However, the instability could be readily counteracted by appropriate stabilization policies. Monetary policy could change the nominal supply of money so as to *accommodate* the change in real demand resulting from shocks in aggregate demand. Fiscal policy, through expenditure and taxes, could *offset* these shocks, making full employment consistent with the initial nominal money stock. In general, both monetary and fiscal policies could be used in combination. But because of a perceived uncertainty in the response of demand to changes in interest rates, and because changes in interest rates through monetary policy could meet difficulties and substantial delays related to expectations (so-called liquidity traps), fiscal policy was regarded as having some advantages.

B. *The Early Keynesians*

The early disciples of the new Keynesian gospel, still haunted by memories of the Great Depression, frequently tended to outdo Keynes' pessimism about potential instability. Concern with liquidity traps fostered the view that the demand for money was highly interest elastic; failure to distinguish between the short- and long-run marginal propensity to save led to overestimating the long-run saving rate, thereby fostering concern with stagnation, and to underestimating the short-run propensity, thereby exaggerating the short-run multiplier. Interest

VOL. 67 NO. 2   *MODIGLIANI: MONETARIST CONTROVERSY*   3

rates were supposed to affect, at best, the demand for long-lived fixed investments, and the interest elasticity was deemed to be low. Thus, shocks were believed to produce a large response. Finally, investment demand was seen as capriciously controlled by "animal spirits," thus providing an important source of shocks. All this justified calling for very active stabilization policies. Furthermore, since the very circumstances which produce a large response to demand shocks also produce a large response to *fiscal* and a small response to *monetary* actions, there was a tendency to focus on fiscal policy as the main tool to keep the economy at near full employment.

C. *The Phillips Curve*

In the two decades following *The General Theory*, there were a number of developments of the Keynesian system including dynamization of the model, the stress on taxes versus expenditures and the balanced budget multiplier, and the first attempts at estimating the critical parameters through econometric techniques and models. But for present purposes, the most important one was the uncovering of a "stable" statistical relation between the rate of change of wages and the rate of unemployment, which has since come to be known as the Phillips curve. This relation, and its generalization by Richard Lipsey to allow for the effect of recent inflation, won wide acceptance even before an analytical underpinning could be provided for it, in part because it could account for the "puzzling" experience of 1954 and 1958, when wages kept rising despite the substantial rise in unemployment. It also served to dispose of the rather sterile "cost push"– "demand pull" controversy.

In the following years, a good deal of attention went into developing theoretical foundations for the Phillips curve, in particular along the lines of search models (for example, Edmund Phelps et al.). This approach served to shed a new light on the nature of unemployment by tracing it in the first place to labor turnover and search time rather than to lack of jobs as such: in a sense unemployment is all frictional—at least in de-

veloped countries. At the same time it clarified how the availability of more jobs tends to reduce unemployment by increasing vacancies and thus reducing search time.

Acceptance of the Phillips curve relation implied some significant changes in the Keynesian framework which partly escaped notice until the subsequent monetarists' attacks. Since the rate of change of wages decreased smoothly with the rate of unemployment, there was no longer a unique Full Employment but rather a whole family of possible equilibrium rates, each associated with a different rate of inflation (and requiring, presumably, a different long-run growth of money). It also impaired the notion of a stable underemployment equilibrium. A fall in demand could still cause an initial rise in unemployment but this rise, by reducing the growth of wages, would eventually raise the real money supply, tending to return unemployment to the equilibrium rate consistent with the given long-run growth of money.

But at the practical level it did not lessen the case for counteracting lasting demand disturbances through stabilization policies rather than by relying on the slow process of wage adjustment to do the job, at the cost of protracted unemployment and instability of prices. Indeed, the realm of stabilization policies appeared to expand in the sense that the stabilization authority had the power of choosing the unemployment rate around which employment was to be stabilized, though it then had to accept the associated inflation. Finally, the dependence of wage changes also on past inflation forced recognition of a distinction between the short- and the long-run Phillips curve, the latter exhibiting the long-run equilibrium rate of inflation implied by a *maintained* unemployment rate. The fact that the long-run tradeoff between unemployment and inflation was necessarily less favorable than the short-run one, opened up new vistas of "enjoy-it-now, pay-later" policies, and even resulted in an entertaining literature on the political business cycle and how to stay in the saddle by riding the Phillips curve (see for example, Ray Fair, William Nordhaus).

4   THE AMERICAN ECONOMIC REVIEW   MARCH 1977

II. The Monetarists' Attack

A. *The Stabilizing Power of the Hicksian Mechanism*

The monetarists' attack on Keynesianism was directed from the very beginning not at the Keynesian framework as such, but at whether it really implied a need for stabilization. It rested on a radically different empirical assessment of the value of the parameters controlling the stabilizing power of the Hicksian mechanism and of the magnitude and duration of response to shocks, given a stable money supply. And this different assessment in turn was felt to justify a radical downgrading of the *practical relevance* of the Keynesian framework as distinguished from its *analytical validity.*

Liquidity preference was a fine contribution to monetary theory but in practice the responsiveness of the demand for money, and hence of velocity, to interest rates, far from being unmanageably large, was so small that according to a well-known paper by Milton Friedman (1969), it could not even be detected empirically. On the other hand, the effect of interest rates on aggregate demand was large and by no means limited to the traditional fixed investments but quite pervasive. The difficulty of detecting it empirically resulted from focusing on a narrow range of measured market rates and from the fact that while the aggregate could be counted on to respond, the response of individual components might not be stable. Finally, Friedman's celebrated contribution to the theory of the consumption function (1957) (and my own work on the life cycle hypothesis with Richard Brumberg and others, reviewed by the author, 1975) implied a very high short-run marginal propensity to save in response to transient disturbances to income and hence a small short-run multiplier.

All this justified the conclusion that (i) though demand shocks might qualitatively work along the lines described by Keynes, quantitatively the Hicks mechanism is so strong that their impact would be *small* and *transient*, provided the stock of money was kept on a steady growth path; (ii) fiscal policy actions, like other demand

shocks, would have *minor* and *transitory* effects on demand, while changes in money would produce *large* and *permanent* effects on money income; and, therefore, (iii) the observed instability of the economy, which was anyway proving moderate as the postwar period unfolded, was most likely the result of the unstable growth of money, be it due to misguided endeavors to stabilize income or to the pursuit of other targets, which were either irrelevant or, in the case of balance of payments goals, should have been made irrelevant by abandoning fixed exchanges.

B. *The Demise of Wage Rigidity and the Vertical Phillips Curve*

But the most serious challenge came in Friedman's 1968 Presidential Address, building on ideas independently put forth also by Phelps (1968). Its basic message was that, despite appearances, wages were in reality perfectly flexible and there was accordingly *no* involuntary unemployment. The evidence to the contrary, including the Phillips curve, was but a statistical illusion resulting from failure to differentiate between price changes and *unexpected* price changes.

Friedman starts out by reviving the Keynesian notion that, at any point of time, there exists a unique full-employment rate which he labels the "natural rate." An unanticipated fall in demand in Friedman's competitive world leads firms to reduce prices and also output and employment along the short-run marginal cost curve—unless the nominal wage declines together with prices. But workers, failing to judge correctly the current and prospective fall in prices, misinterpret the reduction of nominal wages as a cut in *real* wages. Hence, assuming a positively sloped supply function, they reduce the supply of labor. As a result, the effective real wage rises to the point where the resulting decline in the demand for labor matches the reduced supply. Thus, output falls not because of the decline in demand, but because of the entirely voluntary reduction in the supply of labor, in response to erroneous perceptions. Furthermore, the fall in employment can only be temporary, as expectations must soon catch up with the facts, at least in the absence of new shocks. The very same mechanism works in the case of an increase in demand, so that the responsiveness of wages and prices is the same on either side of the natural rate.

The upshot is that Friedman's model also implies a Phillips-type relation between inflation, employment or unemployment, and past inflation,—provided the latter variable is interpreted as a reasonable proxy for expected inflation. But it turns the standard explanation on its head: instead of (excess) employment causing inflation, it is (the unexpected component of) the rate of inflation that causes excess employment.

One very basic implication of Friedman's model is that the coefficient of price expectations should be precisely unity. This specification implies that whatever the shape of the short-run Phillips curve—a shape determined by the relation between expected and actual price changes, and by the elasticity of labor supply with respect to the perceived real wage—the long-run curve *must be vertical.*

Friedman's novel twist provided a fresh prop for the claim that stabilization policies are not really needed, for, with wages flexible, except possibly for transient distortions, the Hicksian mechanism receives powerful reinforcement from changes in the real money supply. Similarly, the fact that full employment was a razor edge provided new support for the claim that stabilization policies were bound to prove destabilizing.

C. *The Macro Rational Expectations Revolution*

But the death blow to the already badly battered Keynesian position was to come only shortly thereafter by incorporating into Friedman's model the so-called rational expectation hypothesis, or *REH*. Put very roughly, this hypothesis, originally due to John Muth, states that rational economic agents will endeavor to form expectations of relevant future variables by making the most efficient use of all information provided by past history. It is a fundamental and fruitful contribution that has already found many important applications, for example, in connection with speculative markets, and as a basis for some thoughtful criticism by Robert Lucas (1976) of certain features of econometric models. What I am concerned with here is only its application to macro-economics, or *MREH*, associated with such authors as Lucas (1972), Thomas Sargent (1976), and Sargent and Neil Wallace (1976).

The basic ingredient of *MREH* is the postulate that the workers of Friedman's model hold rational expectations, which turns out to have a number of remarkable implications: (i) errors of price expectations, which are the only source of departure from the natural state, cannot be avoided but they can only be short-lived and random. In particular, there cannot be persistent unemployment above the natural rate for this would imply high serial correlation between the successive errors of expectation, which is inconsistent with rational expectations; (ii) any attempts to stabilize the economy by means of stated monetary or fiscal rules are bound to be totally ineffective because their effect will be fully discounted in rational expectations; (iii) nor can the government successfully pursue *ad hoc* measures to offset shocks. The private sector is already taking care of any anticipated shock; therefore government policy could conceivably help only if the government information was better than that of the public, which is impossible, by the very definition of rational expectations. Under these conditions, *ad hoc* stabilization policies are most likely to produce instead further destabilizing shocks.

These are clearly remarkable conclusions, and a major *re*discovery—for it had all been said 40 years ago by Keynes in a well-known passage of *The General Theory*:

> If, indeed, labour were always in a position to take action (and were to do so), whenever there was less than full employment, to reduce its money demands by concerted action to whatever point was required to make money so abundant rela-

6   THE AMERICAN ECONOMIC REVIEW   MARCH 1977

tively to the wage-unit that the rate of interest would fall to a level compatible with full employment, we should, in effect, have monetary management by the Trade Unions, aimed at full employment, instead of by the banking systems.
[p. 267]

The only novelty is that *MREH* replaces Keynes' opening "if" with a "since."

If one accepts this little amendment, the case against stabilization policies is complete. The economy is inherently pretty stable—except possibly for the effect of government messing around. And to the extent that there is a small residual instability, it is beyond the power of human beings, let alone the government, to alleviate it.

III. How Valid Is the Monetarist Case?

A. *The Monetarist Model of Wage Price Behavior*

In setting out the counterattack it is convenient to start with the monetarists' model of price and wage behavior. Here one must distinguish between the model as such and a specific implication of that model, namely that the long-run Phillips curve is vertical, or, in substance, that, in the long run, money is neutral. That conclusion, by now, does not meet serious objection from nonmonetarists, at least as a first approximation.

But the proposition that other things equal, and given time enough, the economy will eventually adjust to any indefinitely maintained stock of money, or *n*th derivative thereof, can be derived from a variety of models and, in any event, is of very little practical relevance, as I will argue below. What is unacceptable, because inconsistent with both micro and macro evidence, is the specific monetarist model set out above and its implication that all unemployment is a voluntary, fleeting response to transitory misperceptions.

One may usefully begin with a criticism of the Macro Rational Expectations model and why Keynes' "if" should not be replaced by "since." At the logical level, Benjamin Fried-

man has called attention to the omission from *MREH* of an explicit learning model, and has suggested that, as a result, it can only be interpreted as a description not of short-run but of long-run equilibrium in which no agent would wish to recontract. But then the implications of *MREH* are clearly far from startling, and their policy relevance is almost nil. At the institutional level, Stanley Fischer has shown that the mere recognition of long-term contracts is sufficient to generate wage rigidity and a substantial scope for stabilization policies. But the most glaring flaw of *MREH* is its inconsistency with the evidence: if it were valid, deviations of unemployment from the natural rate would be small and transitory—in which case *The General Theory* would not have been written and neither would this paper. Sargent (1976) has attempted to remedy this fatal flaw by hypothesizing that the persistent and large fluctuations in unemployment reflect merely corresponding swings in the natural rate itself. In other words, what happened to the United States in the 1930's was a severe attack of contagious laziness! I can only say that, despite Sargent's ingenuity, neither I nor, I expect, most others at least of the nonmonetarists' persuasion are quite ready yet to turn over the field of economic fluctuations to the social psychologist!

Equally serious objections apply to Friedman's modeling of the commodity market as a perfectly competitive one—so that the real wage rate is continuously equated to the *short-run* marginal product of labor—and to his treatment of labor as a homogenous commodity traded in an auction market, so that, at the going wage, there never is any excess demand by firms or excess supply by workers. The inadequacies of this model as a useful formalization of present day Western economies are so numerous that only a few of the major ones can be mentioned here.

Friedman's view of unemployment as a voluntary reduction in labor supply could at best provide an explanation of variations in labor force—and then only under the questionable assumption that the supply function has a significantly positive slope—but cannot readily account for changes in unemployment. Furthermore, it cannot be reconciled with the well-known fact that *rising* unemployment is accompanied by a fall, not by a *rise* in quits, nor with the role played by temporary layoffs to which Martin Feldstein has recently called attention. Again, his competitive model of the commodity market, accepted also in *The General Theory*, implies that changes in real wages, adjusted for long-run productivity trend, should be significantly negatively correlated with cyclical changes in employment and output and with changes in money wages. But as early as 1938, John Dunlop showed that this conclusion was rejected by some eighty years of British experience and his results have received some support in more recent tests of Ronald Bodkin for the United States and Canada. Similar tests of my own, using quarterly data, provide striking confirmation that for the last two decades from the end of the Korean War until 1973, the association of trend adjusted real compensations of the private nonfarm sector with either employment or the change in nominal compensation is prevailingly positive and very significantly so.[1]

This evidence can, instead, be accounted for by the oligopolistic pricing model—according to which price is determined by *long-run* mini-

---

[1] Thus, in a logarithmic regression of private nonfarm hourly compensation deflated by the private nonfarm deflator on output per man-hour, time, and private nonfarm employment, after correcting for first-order serial correlation, the latter variable has a coefficient of .17 and a *t*-ratio of 5. Similar though less significant results were found for manufacturing. If employment is replaced by the change in nominal compensation, its coefficient is .40 with a *t*-ratio of 6.5. Finally, if the change in compensation is replaced by the change in price, despite the negative bias from error of measurement of price, the coefficient of this variable is only −.09 with an entirely insignificant *t*-ratio of .7. The period after 1973 has been omitted from the tests as irrelevant for our purposes, since the inflation was driven primarily by an exogenous price shock rather than by excess demand. As a result of the shock, prices, and to some extent wages, rose rapidly while employment and real wages fell. Thus, the addition of the last two years tends to increase spuriously the positive association between real wages and employment, and to decrease that between real wages and the change in nominal wages or prices.

mum average cost up to a mark-up reflecting entry-preventing considerations (see the author, 1958)—coupled with some lags in the adjustment of prices to costs. This model implies that firms respond to a change in demand by endeavoring to adjust output and employment, without significant changes in prices relative to wages; and the resulting changes in available jobs have their initial impact not on wages but rather on unemployment by way of layoffs and recalls and through changes in the level of vacancies, and hence on the length of average search time.

If, in the process, vacancies rise above a critical level, or "natural rate," firms will endeavor to reduce them by outbidding each other, thereby raising the rate of change of wages. Thus, as long as jobs and vacancies remain above, and unemployment remains below, some critical level which might be labeled the "noninflationary rate" (see the author and Lucas Papademos, 1975), wages and prices will tend to accelerate. If, on the other hand, jobs fall below, and unemployment rises above, the noninflationary rate, firms finding that vacancies are less than optimal —in the limit the unemployed queuing outside the gate will fill them instantly—will have an incentive to reduce their relative wage offer. But in this case, in which too much labor is looking for too few jobs, the trend toward a sustained decline in the rate of growth of wages is likely to be even weaker than the corresponding acceleration when too many jobs are bidding for too few people. The main reason is the nonhomogeneity of labor. By far the largest and more valuable source of labor supply to a firm consists of those already employed who are not readily interchangeable with the unemployed and, in contrast with them, are concerned with protecting their earnings and not with reestablishing full employment. For these reasons, and because the first to quit are likely to be the best workers, a reduction of the labor force can, within limits, be accomplished more economically, not by reducing wages to generate enough quits, but by firing or, when possible, by layoffs which insure access to a trained labor force when demand recovers. More generally, the inducement to reduce relative wages to eliminate the excess supply is moderated by the effect that such a reduction would have on quits and costly turnover, even when the resulting vacancies can be readily filled from the ranks of the unemployed. Equally relevant are the consequences in terms of loss of morale and good will, in part for reasons which have been elaborated by the literature on implicit contracts (see Robert Gordon). Thus, while there will be some tendency for the rate of change of wages to fall, the more so the larger the unemployment—at least in an economy like the United States where there are no overpowering centralized unions—that tendency is severely damped.

And whether, given an unemployment rate significantly and persistently above the noninflationary level, the rate of change of wages would, eventually, tend to turn negative and decline without bound or whether it would tend to an asymptote is a question that I doubt the empirical evidence will ever answer. The one experiment we have had—the Great Depression—suggests the answer is negative, and while I admit that, for a variety of reasons, that evidence is muddied, I hope that we will never have the opportunity for a second, clean experiment.

In any event, what is really important for practical purposes is not the long-run equilibrium relation as such, but the speed with which it is approached. Both the model sketched out and the empirical evidence suggest that the process of acceleration or deceleration of wages when unemployment differs from the noninflationary rate will have more nearly the character of a crawl than of a gallop. It will suffice to recall in this connection that there was excess demand pressure in the United States at least from 1965 to mid-1970, and during that period the growth of inflation was from some 1.5 to only about 5.5 percent per year. And the response to the excess supply pressure from mid-1970 to early 1973, and from late 1974 to date was equally sluggish.

B. *The Power of Self-Stabilizing Mechanisms: The Evidence from Econometric Models*

There remains to consider the monetarists' initial criticism of Keynesianism, to wit, that even without high wage flexibility, the system's response to demand shocks is small and short-lived, thanks to the power of the Hicksian mechanism. Here it must be acknowledged that every one of the monetarists' criticisms of early, simpleminded Keynesianism has proved in considerable measure correct.

With regard to the interest elasticity of demand for money, post-Keynesian developments in the theory of money, and in particular, the theoretical contributions of William Baumol, James Tobin, Merton Miller, and Daniel Orr, point to a modest value of around one-half to one-third, and empirical studies (see for example, Stephen Goldfeld) are largely consistent with this prediction (at least until 1975!). Similarly, the dependence of consumption on long-run, or life cycle, income and on wealth, together with the high marginal tax rates of the postwar period, especially the corporate tax, and leakages through imports, lead to a rather low estimate of the multiplier.

Last but not least, both theoretical and empirical work, reflected in part in econometric models, have largely vindicated the monetarist contention that interest effects on demand are pervasive and substantial. Thus, in the construction and estimation of the MIT-Penn-Social Science Research Council *(MPS)* econometric model of the United States, we found evidence of effects, at least modest, on nearly every component of aggregate demand. One response to money supply changes that is especially important in the *MPS*, if somewhat controversial, is via interest rates on the market value of all assets and thus on consumption.

There is, therefore, substantial agreement that in the United States the Hicksian mechanism is fairly effective in limiting the effect of shocks, and that the response of wages and prices to excess demand or supply will also work *gradually* toward eliminating largely, if not totally, any effect on employment. But in the view of nonmonetarists, the evidence overwhelmingly supports the conclusion that the *interim* response is still of significant magnitude and of considerable duration, basically because the wheels of the offsetting mechanism grind slowly. To be sure, the first link of the mechanism, the rise in short-term rates, gets promptly into play and heftily, given the low money demand elasticity; but most expenditures depend on long-term rates, which generally respond but gradually, and the demand response is generally also gradual. Furthermore, while this response is building up, multiplier and accelerator mechanisms work toward amplifying the shock. Finally, the classical mechanism—the change in real money supply through prices—has an even longer lag because of the sluggish response of wages to excess demand.

These interferences are supported by simulations with econometric models like the *MPS*. Isolating, first, the working of the Hicksian mechanism by holding prices constant, we find that a 1 percent demand shock, say a rise in real exports, produces an impact effect on aggregate output which is barely more than 1 percent, rises to a peak of only about 2 percent a year later, and then declines slowly toward a level somewhat over 1.5 percent.

Taking into account the wage price mechanism hardly changes the picture for the first year because of its inertia. Thereafter, however, it becomes increasingly effective so that a year later the real response is back at the impact level, and by the end of the third year the shock has been fully offset (thereafter output oscillates around zero in a damped fashion). Money income, on the other hand, reaches a peak of over 2.5, and then only by the middle of the second year. It declines thereafter, and tends eventually to oscillate around a *positive* value because normally, a demand shock requires eventually a change in interest rates and hence in velocity and money income.

These results, which are broadly confirmed by other econometric models, certainly do not support the view of a highly unstable economy in which fiscal policy has powerful and everlasting effects. But neither do they support the monetarist view of a highly stable economy in which shocks hardly make a ripple and the effects of fiscal policy are puny and fast vanishing.

C. *The Monetarist Evidence and the St. Louis Quandary*

Monetarists, however, have generally been inclined to question this evidence. They coun-

tered at first with tests bearing on the stability of velocity and the insignificance of the multiplier, which, however, as indicated in my criticism with Albert Ando (1965), must be regarded as close to worthless. More recently, several authors at the Federal Reserve Bank of St. Louis (Leonall Andersen, Keith Carlson, Jerry Lee Jordan) have suggested that instead of deriving multipliers from the analytical or numerical solution of an econometric model involving a large number of equations, any one of which may be questioned, they should be estimated directly through "reduced form" equations by relating the change in income to current and lagged changes in some appropriate measure of the money supply and of fiscal impulses.

The results of the original test, using the current and but four lagged values of M^1 and of high Employment Federal Expenditure as measures of monetary and fiscal impulses, turned out to be such as to fill a monetarist's heart with joy. The contribution of money, not only current but also lagged, was large and the coefficients implied a not unreasonable effect of the order of magnitude of the velocity of circulation, though somewhat higher. On the other hand, the estimated coefficients of the fiscal variables seemed to support fully the monetarists' claim that their impact was both small and fleeting: the effect peaked in but two quarters and was only around one, and disappeared totally by the fourth quarter following the change.

These results were immediately attacked on the ground that the authors had used the wrong measure of monetary and fiscal actions, and it was shown that the outcome was somewhat sensitive to alternative measures; however, the basic nature of the results did not change, at least qualitatively. In particular, the outcome does not differ materially, at least for the original period up to 1969, if one replaces high employment outlays with a variable that might be deemed more suitable, like government expenditure on goods and services, plus exports.

These results must be acknowledged as disturbing for nonmonetarists, for there is little question that movements in government purchases and exports are a major source of demand disturbances; if econometric model estimates of

10   **THE AMERICAN ECONOMIC REVIEW**   *MARCH 1977*

the response to demand disturbances are roughly valid, how can they be so grossly inconsistent with the reduced form estimates?

Attempts at reconciling the two have taken several directions, which are reviewed in an article coauthored with Ando (1976). Our main conclusion, based on simulation techniques, is that when income is subject to substantial shocks from many sources other than monetary and fiscal, so that these variables account for only a moderate portion of the variations in income (in the United States, it has been of the order of one-half to two-thirds), then the St. Louis reduced form method yields highly unstable and unreliable estimates of the true structure of the system generating the data.

The crucial role of unreliability and instability has since been confirmed in more recent work of Daniel O'Neill in his forthcoming thesis. He shows in the first place that different methods of estimation yield widely different estimates, including many which clearly overstate the expenditure and understate the money multipliers. He further points out that, given the unreliability of the estimates resulting from multicollinearity and large residual variance, the relevant question to ask is not whether these estimates differ from those obtained by structural estimation, but whether the *difference is statistically significant*; that is, larger than could be reasonably accounted for by sampling fluctuations.

I have carried out this standard statistical test using as true response coefficients those generated by the *MPS* model quoted earlier.[2] I find that, at least when the test is based on the largest possible sample—the entire post-Korean period up to the last two very disturbed years—the difference is totally insignificant when estimation is in level form (F is less than one) and is still not significant at the 5 percent level, when in first differences.

This test resolves the puzzle by showing that there really is no puzzle: the two alternative estimates of the expenditure multipliers are not inconsistent, given the margin of error of the estimates. It implies that one should accept whichever of the two estimates is produced by a more reliable and stable method, and is generally more sensible. To me, those criteria call, without question, for adopting the econometric model estimates. But should there be still some lingering doubt about this choice, I am happy to be able to report the results of one final test which I believe should dispose of the reduced form estimates—at least for a while. Suppose the St. Louis estimates of the expenditure multiplier are closer to God's truth than the estimates derived through econometric models. Then it should be the case that if one uses their coefficients to forecast income beyond the period of fit, these forecasts should be appreciably better than those obtained from a forecasting equation in which the coefficients of the expenditure variable are set equal to those obtained from econometric models.

I have carried out this test, comparing a reduced form equation fitted to the period originally used at St. Louis, terminating in 1969 (but reestimated with the lastest revised data) with an equation in which the coefficients of government expenditure plus exports were constrained to be those estimated from the *MPS*, used in the above F-test. The results are clear cut: the errors using the reduced form coefficient are not smaller but on the average substantially *larger* than those using *MPS* multipliers. For the first four years, terminating at the end of 1973, the St. Louis equation produces errors which are distinctly larger in eight quarters, and smaller in but three, and its squared error is one-third larger. For the last two years of turmoil, both equations perform miserably, though even here the *MPS* coefficients perform just a bit better. I have repeated this test with equations estimated through the first half of the postwar period, and the results are, if anything, even more one-sided.

The moral of the story is pretty clear. First,

[2]For the purpose of the test, coefficients were scaled down by one-third to allow for certain major biases in measured government expenditure for present purposes (mainly the treatment of military procurement on a delivery rather than work progress basis, and the inclusion of direct military expenditure abroad).

VOL. 67 NO. 2   *MODIGLIANI: MONETARIST CONTROVERSY*   11

reduced form equations relying on just two exogenous variables are very unreliable for the purpose of estimating structure, nor are they particularly accurate for forecasting, though per dollar of research expenditure they are surprisingly good. Second, if the St. Louis people want to go on using this method and wish to secure the best possible forecast, then they should ask the *MPS* or any other large econometric model what coefficients they should use for government expenditure, rather than trying to estimate them by their unreliable method.

From the theory and evidence reviewed, we must then conclude that opting for a constant rate of growth of the nominal money supply can result in a stable economy only in the absence of significant exogenous shocks. But obviously the economy has been and will continue to be exposed to many significant shocks, coming from such things as war and peace, and other large changes in government expenditure, foreign trade, agriculture, technological progress, population shifts, and what not. The clearest evidence on the importance of such shocks is provided by our postwar record with its six recessions.

IV. The Record of Stabilization Policies: Stabilizing or Destabilizing

A. *Was Postwar Instability Due to Unstable Money Growth?*

At this point, of course, monetarists will object that, over the postwar period, we have *not* had a constant money growth policy and will hint that the observed instability can largely be traced to the instability of money. The only way of meeting this objection squarely would be, of course, to rerun history with a good computer capable of calculating 3 percent at the helm of the Fed.

A more feasible, if less conclusive approach might be to look for some extended periods in which the money supply grew fairly smoothly and see how the economy fared. Combing through our post-Korean War history, I have been able to find just two stretches of several years in which the growth of the money stock was relatively stable, whether one chooses to measure stability in terms of percentage deviations from a constant growth or of dispersion of four-quarter changes. It may surprise some that one such stretch occurred quite recently and consists of the period of nearly four years beginning in the first quarter of 1971 (see the author and Papademos, 1976). During this period, the average growth was quite large, some 7 percent, but it was relatively smooth, generally well within the 6 to 8 percent band. The average deviation from the mean is about .75 percent. The other such period lasted from the beginning of 1953 to the first half of 1957, again a stretch of roughly four years. In sharp contrast to the most recent period, the average growth here is quite modest, only about 2 percent; but again, most four-quarter changes fell well within a band of two percentage points, and the average deviation is again .7. By contrast, during the remaining 13-year stretch from mid-1957 to the end of 1970, the variability of money growth was roughly twice as large if measured by the average deviation of four quarter changes, and some five times larger if measured by the percentage deviation of the money stock from a constant growth trend.

How did the economy fare in the two periods of relatively stable money growth? It is common knowledge that the period from 1971 to 1974, or from 1972 to 1975 if we want to allow a one-year lag for money to do its trick, was distinctly the most unstable in our recent history, marked by sharp fluctuations in output and wild gyrations of the rate of change of prices. As a result, the average deviation of the four-quarter changes in output was 3.3 percent, more than twice as large as in the period of less stable money growth. But the first stretch was also marked by well above average instability, with the contraction of 1954, the sharp recovery of 1955, and the new contraction in 1958, the sharpest in postwar history except for the present one. The variability of output is again 50 percent larger than in the middle period.

To be sure, in the recent episode serious exogenous shocks played a major role in the development of prices and possibly output, although the

12   **THE AMERICAN ECONOMIC REVIEW**   *MARCH 1977*

same is not so readily apparent for the period 1953 to 1958. But, in any event, such extenuating circumstances are quite irrelevant to my point; for I am not suggesting that the stability of money was the major cause of economic instability—or at any rate, not yet! All I am arguing is that (i) there is no basis for the monetarists' suggestion that our postwar instability can be traced to monetary instability—our most unstable periods have coincided with periods of relative monetary stability; and (ii) stability of the money supply is not enough to give us a stable economy, precisely because there are exogenous disturbances.

Finally, let me mention that I have actually made an attempt at rerunning history to see whether a stable money supply would stabilize the economy, though in a way that I readily acknowledge is much inferior to the real thing, namely through a simulation with the *MPS*. The experiment, carried out in cooperation with Papademos, covered the relatively quiet period from the beginning of 1959 to the introduction of price-wage controls in the middle of 1971. If one eliminates all major sources of shocks, for example, by smoothing federal government expenditures, we found, as did Otto Eckstein in an earlier experiment, that a stable money growth of 3 percent per year does stabilize the economy, as expected. But when we allowed for all the historical shocks, the result was that with a constant money growth the economy was far from stable—in fact, it was distinctly less stable than actual experience, by a factor of 50 percent.

B. *The Overall Effectiveness of Postwar Stabilization Policies*

But even granted that a smooth money supply will not produce a very stable world and that there is therefore room for stabilization policies, monetarists will still argue that we should nonetheless eschew such policies. They claim, first, that allowing for unpredictably variable lags and unforseeable future shocks, we do not know enough to successfully design stabilization policies, and second, that the government would surely be incapable of choosing the appropriate

policies or be politically willing to provide timely enforcement. Thus, in practice, stabilization policies will result in destabilizing the economy much of the time.

This view is supported by two arguments, one logical and one empirical. The logical argument is the one developed in Friedman's Presidential Address (1968). An attempt at stabilizing the economy at full employment is bound to be destabilizing because the full employment or natural rate is not known with certainty and is subject to shifts in time; and if we aim for the incorrect rate, the result must perforce be explosive inflation or deflation. By contrast, with a constant money supply policy, the economy will automatically hunt for, and eventually discover, that shifty natural rate, wherever it may be hiding.

This argument, I submit, is nothing but a debating ploy. It rests on the preposterous assumption that the only alternative to a constant money growth is the pursuit of a very precise unemployment target which will be adhered to indefinitely no matter what, and that if the target is off in the second decimal place, galloping inflation is around the corner. In reality, all that is necessary to pursue stabilization policies is a rough target range that includes the warranted rate, itself a range and not a razor edge; and, of course, responsible supporters of stabilization policies have long been aware of the fact that the target range needs to be adjusted in time on the basis of forseeable shifts in the warranted range, as well as in the light of emerging evidence that the current target is not consistent with price stability. It is precisely for this reason that I, as well as many other nonmonetarists, would side with monetarists in strenuous opposition to recent proposals for a target unemployment rate rigidly fixed by statute (although there is nothing wrong with Congress committing itself and the country to work toward the eventual achievement of some target unemployment rate through *structural* changes rather than aggregate demand policies).

Clearly, even the continuous updating of targets cannot guarantee that errors can be

VOL. 67 NO. 2   *MODIGLIANI: MONETARIST CONTROVERSY*   *13*

avoided altogether or even that they will be promptly recognized; and while errors persist, they will result in some inflationary (or deflationary) pressures. But the growing inflation to which Friedman refers is, to repeat, a crawl not a gallop. One may usefully recall in this connection the experience of 1965–70 referred to earlier, with the further remark that the existence of excess employment was quite generally recognized at the time, and failure to eliminate it resulted overwhelmingly from political considerations and not from a wrong diagnosis.[3]

There remains then only the empirical issue: have stabilization policies worked in the past and will they work in the future? Monetarists think the answer is negative and suggest, as we have seen, that misguided attempts at stabilization, especially through monetary policies, are responsible for much of the observed instability. The main piece of evidence in support of this contention is the Great Depression, an episode well documented through the painstaking work of Friedman and Anna Schwartz, although still the object of dispute (see, for example, Peter Temin). But in any event, that episode while it may attest to the power of money, is irrelevant for present purposes since the contraction of the money supply was certainly not part of a comprehensive stabilization program in the post-Keynesian sense.

When we come to the relevant postwar period, the problem of establishing the success or failure of stabilization policies is an extremely taxing one. Many attempts have been made at developing precise objective tests, but in my view, none of these is of much value, even though I am guilty of having contributed to them in one of my

[3] Friedman's logical argument against stabilization policies and in favor of a constant money growth rule is, I submit, much like arguing to a man from St. Paul wishing to go to New Orleans on important business that he would be a fool to drive and should instead get himself a tub and drift down the Mississippi: that way he can be pretty sure that the current will eventually get him to his destination; whereas, if he drives, he might make a wrong turn and, before he notices he will be going further and further away from his destination and pretty soon he may end up in Alaska, where he will surely catch pneumonia and he may never get to New Orleans!

worst papers (1964). Even the most ingenious test, that suggested by Victor Argy, and relying on a comparison of the variability of income with that of the velocity of circulation, turns out to be valid only under highly unrealistic restrictive assumptions.

Dennis Starleaf and Richard Floyd have proposed testing the effectiveness of stabilization by comparing the stability of money growth with that of income growth, much as I have done above for the United States, except that they apply their test to a cross section of industrialized countries. They found that for a sample of 13 countries, the association was distinctly positive. But this test is again of little value. For while a negative association for a given country, such as suggested by my *U.S.* test, does provide some weak indication that monetary activism helped rather than hindered, the finding of a positive association across countries proves absolutely nothing. It can be readily shown, in fact, that, to the extent that differential variability of income reflects differences in the character of the shocks—a most likely circumstance for their sample—successful stabilization also implies a positive correlation between the variability of income and that of money.

But though the search for unambiguous quantitative tests has so far yielded a meager crop, there exists a different kind of evidence in favor of Keynesian stabilization policies which is impressive, even if hard to quantify. To quote one of the founding fathers of business cycle analysis, Arthur Burns, writing in 1959, "Since 1937 we have had five recessions, the longest of which lasted only 13 months. There is no parallel for such a sequence of mild– or such a sequence of brief—contractions, at least during the past hundred years in our country" (p. 2). By now we can add to that list the recessions of 1961 and 1970.

There is, furthermore, evidence that very similar conclusions hold for other industrialized countries which have made use of stabilization policies; at any rate that was the prevailing view among participants to an international conference held in 1967 on the subject, "Is the busi-

14   **THE AMERICAN ECONOMIC REVIEW**   *MARCH 1977*

ness cycle obsolete?'' (see Martin Bronfen-brenner, editor). No one seemed to question the greater postwar stability of all Western economies—nor is this surprising when one recalls that around that time business cycle specialists felt so threatened by the new-found stability that they were arguing for redefining business cycles as fluctuations in the *rate of growth* rather than in the *level* of output.

It was recognized that the reduced severity of fluctuations might in part reflect structural changes in the economy and the effect of stronger built-in stabilizers, inspired, of course, by the Keynesian analysis. Furthermore, the greater stability in the United States, and in other industrialized countries, are obviously not independent events. Still, at least as of the time of that conference, there seemed to be little question and some evidence that part of the credit for the greater stability should go to the conscious and on balance, successful endeavor at stabilizing the economy.

V. The Case of Supply Shocks and the 1974–76 Episode

A. *Was the 1974 Depression Due to Errors of Commission or Omission?*

In pointing out our relative postwar stability and the qualified success of stabilization policies, I have carefully defined the postwar period as ending somewhere in 1973. What has happened since that has so tarnished the reputation of economists? In facing this problem, the first question that needs to be raised is whether the recent combination of unprecedented rates of inflation as well as unemployment must be traced to crimes of commission or omission. Did our monetary and fiscal stabilization policies misfire, or did we instead fail to use them?

We may begin by establishing one point that has been blurred by monetarists' blanket indictments of recent monetary policy: the virulent explosion that raised the four-quarter rate of inflation from about 4 percent in 1972 to 6.5 percent by the third quarter of 1973, to 11.5 percent in 1974 with a peak quarterly rate of 13.5, can in no way be traced to an excessive, or

to a disorderly, growth of the money supply. As already mentioned, the average rate of money growth from the beginning of 1970 to the second half of 1974 was close to 7 percent. To be sure, this was a high rate and could be expected sooner or later to generate an undesirably high inflation —but how high? Under any reasonable assumption one cannot arrive at a figure much above 6 percent. This might explain what happened up to the fall of 1973, but not from the third quarter of 1973 to the end of 1974, which is the really troublesome period. Similarly, as was indicated above, the growth of money was reasonably smooth over this period, smoother than at any other time in the postwar period, staying within a 2 percent band. Hence, the debacle of 1974 can just not be traced to an erratic behavior of money resulting from a misguided attempt at stabilization.

Should one then conclude that the catastrophe resulted from too slavish an adherence to a stable growth rate, forsaking the opportunity to use monetary policy to stabilize the economy? In one sense, the answer to this question must in my view be in the affirmative. There is ample ground for holding that the rapid contraction that set in toward the end of 1974, on the heels of a slow decline in the previous three quarters, and which drove unemployment to its 9 percent peak, was largely the result of the astronomic rise in interest rates around the middle of the year. That rise in turn was the unavoidable result of the Fed's stubborn refusal to accommodate, to an adequate extent, the exogenous inflationary shock due to oil, by letting the money supply growth exceed the 6 percent rate announced at the beginning of the year. And this despite repeated warnings about that unavoidable result (see, for example, the author 1974).

Monetarists have suggested that the sharp recession was not the result of too slow a monetary growth throughout the year, but instead of the deceleration that took place in the last half of 1974, and early 1975. But this explanation just does not stand up to the facts. The fall in the quarterly growth of money in the third and fourth quarters was puny, especially on the basis of revised figures now available: from 5.7 percent in the second to 4.3 and 4.1—hardly much larger than the error of estimate for quarterly rates! To be sure, in the first quarter of 1975 the growth fell to .6 percent. But, by then, the violent contraction was well on its way—between September 1974 and February 1975, industrial production fell at an annual rate of 25 percent. Furthermore, by the next quarter, monetary growth had resumed heftily. There is thus no way the monetarist proposition can square with these facts unless their long and variable lags are so variable that they sometimes turn into substantial leads. But even then, by anybody's model, a one-quarter dip in the growth of money could not have had a perceptible effect.

B. *What Macro Stabilization Policies Can Accomplish, and How*

But recognizing that the adherence to a stable money growth path through much of 1974 bears a major responsibility for the sharp contraction does not per se establish that the policy was mistaken. The reason is that the shock that hit the system in 1973–74 was not the usual type of demand shock which we have gradually learned to cope with, more or less adequately. It was, instead, a supply or price shock, coming from a cumulation of causes, largely external. This poses an altogether different stabilization problem. In particular, in the case of demand shocks, there exists in principle an ideal policy which avoids all social costs, namely to offset completely the shock thus, at the same time, stabilizing employment and the price level. There may be disagreement as to whether this target can be achieved and how, but not about the target itself.

But in the case of supply shocks, there is no miracle cure—there is no macro policy which can both maintain a stable price level and keep employment at its natural rate. To maintain stable prices in the face of the exogenous price shock, say a rise in import prices, would require a fall in all domestic output prices; but we know of no macro policy by which domestic prices can be made to fall except by creating enough slack,

thus putting downward pressure on wages. And the amount of slack would have to be substantial in view of the sluggishness of wages in the face of unemployment. If we do not offset the exogenous shock completely, then the initial burst, even if activated by an entirely transient rise in some prices, such as a once and for all deterioration in the terms of trade, will give rise to further increases, as nominal wages rise in a vain attempt at preserving real wages; this secondary reaction too can only be cut short by creating slack. In short, once a price shock hits, there is no way of returning to the initial equilibrium except after a painful period of both above equilibrium unemployment and inflation.

There are, of course, in principle, policies other than aggregate demand management to which we might turn, and which are enticing in view of the unpleasant alternatives offered by demand management. But so far such policies, at least those of the wage-price control variety, have proved disappointing. The design of better alternatives is probably the greatest challenge presently confronting those interested in stabilization. However, these policies fall outside my present concern. Within the realm of aggregate demand management, the only choice open to society is the cruel one between alternative feasible paths of inflation and associated paths of unemployment, and the best the macroeconomist can offer is policies designed to approximate the chosen path.

In light of the above, we may ask: is it conceivable that a constant rate of growth of the money supply will provide a satisfactory response to price shocks in the sense of giving rise to an unemployment-inflation path to which the country would object least?

C. *The Monetarist Prescription: Or, Constant Money Growth Once More*

The monetarists are inclined to answer this question affirmatively, if not in terms of the country's preferences, at least in terms of the preferences they think it should have. This is evidenced by their staunch support of a continuation of the 6 percent or so rate of growth through

16   **THE AMERICAN ECONOMIC REVIEW**   **MARCH 1977**

1974, 1975, and 1976.

Their reasoning seems to go along the following lines. The natural rate hypothesis implies that the rate of inflation can change only when employment deviates from the natural rate. Now suppose we start from the natural rate and some corresponding steady rate of inflation, which without loss of generality can be assumed as zero. Let there be an exogenous shock which initially lifts the rate of inflation, say, to 10 percent. If the Central Bank, by accommodating this price rise, keeps employment at the natural rate, the new rate of 10 percent will also be maintained and will in fact continue forever, as long as the money supply accommodates it. The only way to eliminate inflation is to increase unemployment enough, above the natural rate and for a long enough time, so that the cumulated reduction of inflation takes us back to zero. There will of course be many possible unemployment paths that will accomplish this. So the next question is: Which is the least undesirable?

The monetarist answer seems to be—and here I confess that attribution becomes difficult —that it does not make much difference because, to a first approximation, the cumulated amount of unemployment needed to unwind inflation is independent of the path. If we take more unemployment early, we need to take less later, and conversely. But then it follows immediately that the specific path of unemployment that would be generated by a constant money growth is, if not better, at least as good as any other. Corollary: a constant growth of money is a satisfactory answer to supply shocks just as it is to demand shocks—as well as, one may suspect, to any other conceivable illness, indisposition, or disorder.

D. *Why Constant Money Growth Cannot Be the Answer*

This reasoning is admirably simple and elegant, but it suffers from several flaws. The first one is a confusion between the price level and its rate of change. With an unchanged constant growth of the nominal money stock, the system will settle back into equilibrium not when the rate of inflation is back to zero but only when, in addition, the price level itself is back to its initial level. This means that when inflation has finally returned back to the desired original rate, unemployment cannot also be back to the original level but will instead remain above it as long as is necessary to generate enough deflation to offset the earlier cumulated inflation. I doubt that this solution would find many supporters and for a good reason; it amounts to requiring that none of the burden of the price shock should fall on the holder of long-term money fixed contracts— such as debts—and that all other sectors of society should shoulder entirely whatever cost is necessary to insure this result. But if, as seems to be fairly universally agreed, the social target is instead to return the system to the original rate of inflation—zero in our example—then the growth of the money supply cannot be kept constant. Between the time the shock hits and the time inflation has returned to the long-run level, there must be an additional increase in money supply by as much as the price level or by the cumulant of inflation over the path.

A second problem with the monetarists' argument is that it implies a rather special preference function that depends only on cumulated unemployment. And, last but not least, it requires the heroic assumption that the Phillips curve be not only vertical in the long run but also linear in the short run, an assumption that does not seem consistent with empirically estimated curves. Dropping this last assumption has the effect that, for any given social preference, there will be in general a unique optimal path. Clearly, for this path to be precisely that generated by a constant money growth, would require a miracle—or some sleight of the invisible hand!

Actually, there are grounds for holding that the unemployment path generated by a constant money growth, even if temporarily raised to take care of the first flaw, could not possibly be close to an optimal. This conclusion is based on an analysis of optimal paths, relying on the type of linear welfare function that appears to underlie the monetarists' argument, and which is also a straightforward generalization of Okun's fa-

VOL. 67 NO. 2   *MODIGLIANI: MONETARIST CONTROVERSY*   *17*

mous "economic discomfort index." That index (which according to Michael Lovell appears to have some empirical support) is the sum of unemployment and inflation. The index used in my analysis is a weighted average of the cumulated unemployment and cumulated inflation over the path. The weights express the relative social concern for inflation versus unemployment.

Using this index, it has been shown in a forthcoming thesis of Papademos that, in general, the optimum policy calls for raising unemployment at once to a certain critical level and keeping it there until inflation has substantially abated. The critical level depends on the nature of the Phillips curve and the relative weights, but does not depend significantly on the initial shock—as long as it is appreciable. To provide an idea of the order of magnitudes involved, if one relies on the estimate of the Phillips curve reported in my joint paper with Papademos (1975), which is fairly close to vertical and uses Okun's weights, one finds that (i) at the present time, the noninflationary rate of unemployment corresponding to a 2 percent rate of inflation can be estimated at 5.6 percent, and (ii) the optimal response to a large exogenous price shock consists in increasing unemployment from 5.6 to only about 7 percent. That level is to be maintained until inflation falls somewhat below 4 percent; it should then be reduced slowly until inflation gets to 2.5 (which is estimated to take a couple of years), and rapidly thereafter. If, on the other hand, society were to rate inflation twice as costly as unemployment, the initial unemployment rate becomes just over 8 percent, though the path to final equilibrium is then shorter. These results seem intuitively sensible and quantitatively reasonable, providing further justification for the assumed welfare function, with its appealing property of summarizing preferences into a single readily understandable number.

One important implication of the nature of the optimum path described above is that a constant money growth could not possibly be optimal while inflation is being squeezed out of the system, regardless of the relative weights attached to unemployment and inflation. It would tend

to be prevailingly too small for some initial period and too large thereafter.

One must thus conclude that the case for a constant money growth is no more tenable in the case of supply shocks than it is in the case of demand shocks.

VI. Conclusion

To summarize, the monetarists have made a valid and most valuable contribution in establishing that our economy is far less unstable than the early Keynesians pictured it and in rehabilitating the role of money as a determinant of aggregate demand. They are wrong, however, in going as far as asserting that the economy is sufficiently shockproof that stabilization policies are not needed. They have also made an important contribution in pointing out that such policies might in fact prove destabilizing. This criticism has had a salutary effect on reassessing what stabilization policies can and should do, and on trimming down fine-tuning ambitions. But their contention that postwar fluctuations resulted from an unstable money growth or that stabilization policies decreased rather than increased stability just does not stand up to an impartial examination of the postwar record of the United States and other industrialized countries. Up to 1974, these policies have helped to keep the economy reasonable stable by historical standards, even though one can certainly point to some occasional failures.

The serious deterioration in economic stability since 1973 must be attributed in the first place to the novel nature of the shocks that hit us, namely, supply shocks. Even the best possible aggregate demand management cannot offset such shocks without a lot of unemployment together with a lot of inflation. But, in addition, demand management was far from the best. This failure must be attributed in good measure to the fact that we had little experience or even an adequate conceptual framework to deal with such shocks; but at least from my reading of the record, it was also the result of failure to use stabilization policies, including too slavish adherence to the monetarists' constant money

18   THE AMERICAN ECONOMIC REVIEW   *MARCH 1977*

growth presciption.

We must, therefore, categorically reject the monetarist appeal to turn back the clock forty years by discarding the basic message of *The General Theory*. We should instead concentrate our efforts in an endeavor to make stabilization policies even more effective in the future than they have been in the past.

REFERENCES

L. C. **Andersen** and K. M. **Carlson**, "A Monetarist Model for Economic Stabilization," *Fed. Reserve Bank St. Louis Rev.*, Apr. 1970, *52*, 7–25.

———— and J. L. **Jordan**, "Monetary and Fiscal Action: A Test of Their Relative Importance in Economic Stabilization," *Fed. Reserve Bank St. Louis Rev.*, Nov. 1968, *50*, 11–23.

V. **Argy**, "Rules, Discretion in Monetary Management, and Short-Term Stability," *J. Money, Credit, Banking*, Feb. 1971, *3*, 102–22.

W. J. **Baumol**, "The Transactions Demand for Cash: An Inventory Theoretic Approach," *Quart. J. Econ.*, Nov. 1952, *66*, 545–56.

R. G. **Bodkin**, "Real Wages and Cyclical Variations in Employment: A Reexamination of the Evidence," *Can. J. Econ.*, Aug. 1969, *2*, 353–74.

Martin **Bronfenbrenner**, *Is the Business Cycle Obsolete?*, New York 1969.

A. F. **Burns**, "Progress Towards Economic Stability," *Amer. Econ. Rev.*, Mar. 1960, *50*, 1–19.

J. T. **Dunlop**, "The Movement of Real and Money Wage Rates," *Econ. J.*, Sept. 1938, *48*, 413–34.

O. **Eckstein** and R. **Brinner**, "The Inflation Process in the United States," in Otto Eckstein, ed., *Parameters and Policies in the U.S. Economy*, Amsterdam 1976.

R. C. **Fair**, "On Controlling the Economy to Win Elections," unpub. paper, Cowles Foundation 1975.

M. S. **Feldstein**, "Temporary Layoffs in the Theory of Unemployment," *J. Polit. Econ.*, Oct. 1976, *84*, 937–57.

S. **Fischer**, "Long-term Contracts, Rational Expectations and the Optimal Money Supply Rule," *J. Polit. Econ.*, forthcoming.

B. M. **Friedman**, "Rational Expectations Are Really Adaptive After All," unpub. paper, Harvard Univ. 1975.

Milton **Friedman**, *A Theory of the Consumption Function*, Princeton 1957.

————, "The Role of Monetary Policy," *Amer. Econ. Rev.*, Mar. 1968, *58*, 1–17.

————, "The Demand for Money: Some Theoretical and Empirical Results," in his *The Optimum Quantity of Money, and Other Essays*, Chicago 1969.

———— and A. **Schwartz**, *A Monetary History of the United States 1867–1960*, Princeton 1963.

S. **Goldfeld**, "The Demand for Money Revisited," *Brookings Papers*, Washington 1973, *3*, 577–646.

R. J. **Gordon**, "Recent Developments in the Theory of Inflation and Unemployment," *J. Monet. Econ.*, Apr. 1976, *2*, 185–219.

J. R. **Hicks**, "Mr. Keynes and the "Classics"; A Suggested Interpretation," *Econometrica*, Apr. 1937, *5*, 147–59.

John Maynard **Keynes**, *The General Theory of Employment, Interest and Money*, New York 1935.

R. G. **Lipsey**, "The Relation Between Unemployment and the Rate of Change of Money Wage Rates in the United Kingdom, 1862–1957: A Further Analysis," *Economica*, Feb. 1960, *27*, 1–31.

M. **Lovell**, "Why Was the Consumer Feeling So Sad?," *Brookings Papers*, Washington 1975, *2*, 473–79.

R. E. **Lucas, Jr.**, "Econometric Policy Evaluation: A Critique," *J. Monet. Econ.*, suppl. series, 1976, *1*, 19–46.

————, "Expectations and the Neutrality of Money," *J. Econ. Theory*, Apr. 1972, *4*, 103–24.

M. **Miller** and D. **Orr**, "A Model of the Demand for Money by Firms," *Quart. J. Econ.*, Aug. 1966, *80*, 413–35.

F. **Modigliani**, "Liquidity Preference and the Theory of Interest and Money," *Econo-*

VOL. 67 NO. 2   *MODIGLIANI: MONETARIST CONTROVERSY*   19

metrica, Jan. 1944, *12*, 45–88.

——, "New Development on the Oligopoly Front," *J. Polit. Econ.*, June 1958, *66*, 215–33.

——, "The Monetary Mechanism and Its Interaction with Real Phenomena," *Rev. Econ. Statist.*, Feb. 1963, *45*, 79–107.

——, " Some Empirical Tests of Monetary Management and of Rules versus Discretion," *J. Polit. Econ.*, June 1964, *72*, 211–45.

——, "The 1974 Report of the President's Council of Economic Advisers: A Critique of Past and Prospective Policies," *Amer. Econ. Rev.*, Sept. 1974, *64*, 544–77.

——, "The Life Cycle Hypothesis of Saving Twenty Years Later," in Michael Parkin, ed., *Contemporary Issues in Economics*, Manchester 1975.

—— and A. Ando, "The Relative Stability of Monetary Velocity and the Investment Multiplier," *Amer. Econ. Rev.*, Sept. 1965, *55*, 693–728.

—— and ——, "Impacts of Fiscal Actions on Aggregate Income and the Monetarist Controversy: Theory and Evidence," in Jerome L. Stein, ed., *Monetarism*, Amsterdam 1976.

—— and R. Brumberg, "Utility Analysis and the Consumption Function: Interpretation of Cross-Section Data," in Kenneth Kurihara, ed., *Post-Keynesian Economics*, New Brunswick 1954.

—— and L. Papademos, "Targets for Monetary Policy in the Coming Years," *Brookings Papers*, Washington 1975, *1*, 141–65.

—— and ——, "Monetary Policy for the Coming Quarters: The Conflicting Views," *New Eng. Econ. Rev.*, Mar./Apr. 1976, 2–35.

J. F. Muth, "Rational Expectations and the Theory of Price Movements," *Econometrica*, July 1961, *29*, 315–35.

W. D. Nordhaus, "The Political Business Cycle," *Rev. Econ. Stud.*, Apr. 1975, *42*, 169–90.

A. M. Okun, "Inflation: Its Mechanics and Welfare Costs," *Brookings Papers*, Washington 1975, *2*, 351–90.

D. O'Neill, "Directly Estimated Multipliers of Monetary and Fiscal Policy," doctoral thesis in progress, M.I.T.

L. Papademos, "Optimal Aggregate Employment Policy and Other Essays," doctoral thesis in progress, M.I.T.

Edmond S. Phelps, "Money-Wage Dynamics and Labor-Market Equilibrium," *J. Polit. Econ.*, July/Aug. 1968, *76*, 678–711.

—— et al., *Microeconomic Foundations of Employment and Inflation Theory*, New York 1970.

A. W. Phillips, "The Relation Between Unemployment and the Rate of Change of Money Wage Rates in the United Kingdom, 1861–1957," *Economica*, Nov. 1958, *25*, 283–99.

T. J. Sargent, "A Classical Macroeconomic Model for the United States," *J. Polit. Econ.*, Apr. 1976, *84*, 207–37.

—— and N. Wallace, "'Rational' Expectations, the Optimal Monetary Instrument, and the Optimal Money Supply Rule," *J. Polit. Econ.*, Apr. 1975, *83*, 241–57.

D. Starleaf and R. Floyd, "Some Evidence with Respect to the Efficiency of Friedman's Monetary Policy Proposals," *J. Money, Credit, Banking*, Aug. 1972, *4*, 713–22.

Peter Temin, *Did Monetary Forces Cause the Great Depression?*, New York 1976.

James Tobin, *Essays in Economics: Vol. 1, Macroeconomics*, Chicago 1971.

[14]

EFFECTIVE DEMAND FAILURES

Axel Leijonhufvud

University of California, Los Angeles, USA*

Summary

Part I argues that the central issue in macroeconomic theory today again concerns, as it did in the 1930's, the self-regulatory capabilities of market systems. Our failure to make better progress towards a generally acknowleged resolution of long ongoing controversies seems in large measure due to the relatively underdeveloped state of our knowledge pertaining to this question. The theory of effective demand does not deal with all aspects of it, but it deals with hardly anything else.

Part II sketches three exploratory ventures in effective demand theory. In turn, it discusses (A) The Theory of Markets and Money, (B) Theories of the Consumption Function, and (C) Quantity Theories of Money Income Determination. Effective demand failures impair the economy's ability to restore itself to a state in which economic activities are reasonably well coordinated. The three avenues of approach explored in Part II all point to the relation between the magnitude of the shock or shocks to which the system is exposed and the size of the "buffer-stocks"—particularly of liquid assets, and most particularly of money—that transactors maintain as critical to whether effective demand failures of major consequence will emerge or not.

The theory suggests that the system may be much less able to cope automatically with large than with moderate displacements from its equilibrium time-path. Policy prescriptions for large and for moderate displacements will differ, being—very roughly speaking, indeed—"fiscalist" for the former, "monetarist" for the latter case.

There is no reason why the *form* of a realistic model (the form of its equations) should be the same under all values of its variables. We must face the fact that the form of the model may have to be regarded as a function of the values of the variables involved. This will usually be the case if the values of some of the variables affect the basic conditions of choice under which the behavior equations in the model are

[27] derived. *Trygve Haavelmo*[1]

* This paper draws on work done together with my colleague, Robert W. Clower, for a book to be entitled *The Coordination of Economic Activities*. Still, Clower's responsibility for any stupidities or errors is somewhat less than 50%.

[1] Cf. *A Study in the Theory of Investment*, Chicago, 1960, p. 205.

Introduction

My primary concern over the past several years has been with certain theoretical problems embedded in the Keynesian literature that I believe (of course) to be important, unresolved, and difficult. The ramifications of these problems are such that a few of us cannot hope to deal effectively and satisfactorily with them all. In order to enlist others in the work, one has to convince them that the problems in question have not been satisfactorily solved and have a high claim on their attention relative to other matters currently in professional fashion. To do so in this case, I believed and believe, requires a revision of recent macro-doctrine history. Economists who accept without qualification the inherited image of the Keynesian past will not share our views about either the present or the directions for the future.

In this paper, I provide a sketch, free of doctrine-historical subplots, of a number of issues and problems that stand in need of fresh attempts at theoretical modelling and/or empirical testing. Space, time, and dull wits combine to prevent me from treating any of the problems in detail and with rigor; I have chosen instead to convey to the reader how part of the working agenda for theoretical macroeconomics is perceived by someone with a "revised" perspective of the historical development of the field.

The broad theme of the paper is the theory of Effective Demand. In Part II, the theory of effective demand failures is examined, in turn, from the following vantage-points: (A) The Theory of Markets and Money; (B) Theories of the Consumption Function; (C) Quantity Theories of Money Income Determination. Part I sketches the broader context within which I would presently view the theory, and is correspondingly informal and opinionated. Contrary to what seems to be current professional practice, I make my tentative opinions explicit. There are two reasons for doing so. First, one cannot today presume the kind of consensus in macroeconomics that makes it unnecessary to explain why one regards certain issues and approaches as more significant than others. Second, the reader may well want some hints as to the prejudices and biases that underlie what is to follow.

I

In my opinion, the central issue in macroeconomic theory is—once again—the extent to which the economy, or at least its market sectors, may properly be regarded as a self-regulating system. In what respects does it, or does it not, behave in such fashion? How well, or badly, do its "automatic" mechanisms perform? This issue, to illustrate, lies at the heart of two of the most prominent controversies in the field over the last decade: the Fiscalist vs. Monetarist controversy over income determination and aggregate demand management, and the controversy over the long-run stability of the Phillips curve. The volume of writings on each of these continues to mount steadily with no clear-cut resolution in sight—in large measure because this central issue is not being effectively addressed.

The social problem to which the issue of the system's self-regulatory capabilities pertains we may term "the coordination of economic activities". The reference is to coordination of desired sales and purchases at the market level; "full coordination" for our purposes means simply that existing markets clear; it does *not* mean "efficient allocation". Our central question is to be put in that frame. Does the market system (as presently instituted in the US or in Sweden ... etc.) tend to move "automatically" towards a state where all market excess demands and supplies are eliminated? How strong or weak are those tendencies?[2] The significance of these questions is not affected by the admission that one deems the probability of actually ever observing an economy in a perfectly coordinated state to be zero.

When the issue is put in this very general, diffuse way and with reference to real-world systems rather than particular classes of models, modern economic theory can as yet provide no answer.[3] And the message out of all the empirical work in macroeconomics of the past decades is very largely in the (casual) eye of the beholder. Yet, on almost all economic questions of major importance, systematic inquiry can only proceed on some presumption of what the answer is likely to be. Otherwise determinate results are unobtainable. Few, if any, major questions have the same answer independently of whether the entire system of markets "works" to coordinate activities or whether one or more markets fail to function as homeostatic mechanisms. This is most obviously true of macroeconomic issues,[4] but

---

[2] Note that if the conclusion from the proposed inquiry were to be that the system does tend towards establishing a state of "full coordination", no *laissez faire* implications whatever follow. Our conception of "full coordination" omits most of the criteria for Pareto-optimality—it allows markets to be monopolistic or monopsonistic, sales or income taxes to be present, non-existence of organized markets for certain "goods" and other causes of external effects, and so on. Quite apart from all that, the system's homeostatic mechanisms might be so slow in their operation that policy intervention would be deemed desirable simply to speed up the (in themselves) "automatic" self-regulatory tendencies of the system.

The reader will have observed that the term "equilibrating" is eschewed here in favor of "self-regulatory", "homeostatic" or other more or less cumbersome circumlocutions. The reason, of course, is that our discussion moves in a realm of discourse where the "unemployment equilibrium" notion of textbook Keynesianism unavoidably insinuates itself. Since that is not a "coordinated" state, the stability properties asserted for it are not of the kind to which our central question is addressed.

The term "stability" is also better avoided because of its firm associations with certain classes of models. What should concern us is the dynamic behavior of actual economies—and we do not want to prejudge how that behavior is most appropriately to be modelled.

[3] The current boundary markets on this front are set out in K.J. Arrow and F.H. Hahn, *General Competitive Analysis*, San Franciso and Edinburgh 1972. Cf. esp., Chapters 13 and 14.

[4] A most familiar example concerns the consequences of an increased propensity to save as deduced (*a*) from a neo-classical growth model, or (*b*) from a simple Keynesian ('Paradox of Thrift') model. Most standard conceptual experiments in macroeconomics produce the same disturbing result—qualitative predictions for some of the important variables emerge with opposite signs from the two coexisting bodies of theory.

applies as well to a host of problems to which most economists would affix the "micro" label.[5]

The researcher or instructor must then proceed on some presumption or other with regard to the self-regulating capabilities of economic systems— or find that he has nothing to say. The assumptions made may be backed up to some extent by broad and casual empiricism and by reference to scraps of rigorous theoretical results obtained for a variety of special, simplified cases. But ammunition to compel the agreement of a disbelieving colleague will be lacking. At the same time, the validity of the work that an economist does will ultimately hinge on whether his presumptions on this matter do or do not in some sense approximate reality. If they do not, his work is likely to end up on the scrapheap of forgotten intellectual games. The emotional stakes are high, while solidly based knowledge is at best fragmentary.

Briefly put, then, our situation is one of emotionally charged ignorance with regard to a central issue of the science. In such situations one expects a high incidence of technically qualified men rejecting out of hand the work of other, equally qualified men—or, indeed, spurning entire branches of current inquiry. A's models are but "meretricious games" to B. B.'s regression results only "meaningless numbers" to A. And one also expects, rather sadly, to hear charges flying that "the other's" work can only be understood by drawing the always tempting inference that it is the product of nonscientific, biased motives.

From a history of science point of view, none of this is novel, nor is it by itself unhealthy. It could be said of many episodes in diverse fields that we now look back upon as the gestation period of major advances—but, one feels sure, also of many now forgotten controversies that produced only heat and no light in their time because the issues were never given a "soluble" formulation.

What seems to me unhealthy about the situation in macroeconomics is that the central issue does not occupy center stage. In the unending controversies to which it is critical, it keeps bobbing to the surface only as conflicting declarations of faith. I do not think it has been given "soluble" formulation. It is being avoided, I would infer, because the diffuse nature of the question— itself a result of past neglect—makes it very difficult to address it except

------

[5] Consider a social benefit-cost calculation for a labor-saving government investment project under the alternative assumptions (*a* that the displaced labor will be reabsorbed into other employments, and (*b*) that it will be permanently unemployed. More to the point, perhaps, consider the benefit-cost calculator's utter impotence if he were completely ignorant about which assumption (or combination of the two) is applicable.

in terms that (as here) fall short of present-day standards of precision and rigor in theoretical debate. Still, how can the profession go on for decades with this issue remaining out of focus?

The settled, conventional acceptance of having general economic theory split down the middle is, I believe, very largely to blame. Despite the several alternative ways that we have developed to make the gulf between micro-theory and macrotheory seem plausible to new generations of students, the micro-macro distinction remains basically that between models with "perfectly coordinated" solutions and models where one or more markets reach such solutions only by chance. Both sets of exercises are referred to as "theories", but there could be no real-world economy for which both theories are true at once.[6] One allows oneself the major convenience of static modelling by making one courageous decision (for each market). Either the market has demand-equals-supply equilibria *only*, or it has no tendency to eliminate excess demands *at all*.

A fully adequate characterization of the two alternative visions of what real-world market systems are like, to which neoclassical and Keynesian models give formal representation, would be space-consuming. A crude sketch of the two economic "cosmologies" might run as follows.

Assume that we can define a "fully-coordinated" time-path for the economy. The first cosmology then attributes the following properties to the system. It tends to home in on the ideal path and, in the absence of disturbances, to stay on it. Shocks that displace it from the path will trigger immediate deviation-counteracting feedback control mechanisms. The larger the displacement, generally speaking, the stronger will be the homeostatic tendencies working to bring the system back.[7]

According to the second cosmology, the system has no "automatic" tendency to home in on the ideal path, would reach it only by chance—or through deliberate policy-intervention—and will not maintain itself on it if the path were reached. This system may settle down anywhere "between zero and full employment"[8] with all servo-mechanisms idle. When displaced

[30]

---

[6] In theory teaching, the schizophrenic pressure on young minds can be kept within tolerable bounds by dwelling on self-regulating systems on, say, Mondays, Wednesdays, and Fridays—reserving Tuesdays and Thursdays for the economy that "doesn't work that way". In the applied fields, micro and macro have to coexist. Example: the elasticity and absorption approaches to balance of payments theory.

[7] I.e., price adjustment velocities will be monotonically increasing functions of discrepancies between demand and supply in respective markets—where, in Clower's terminology, it is "notional" demand and supply that are measured. Similarly, adjustment velocities for rates of output and factor employments increase monotonically as functions of discrepancies between supply price and demand price—with these schedules also defined in notional terms. Cf. A. Leijonhufvud, "Notes on the Theory of Markets," *Intermountain Economic Review*, Fall 1970. The last statement in the text also assumes, roughly speaking, that excess demands and excess supply prices increase monotonically with the "displacement" from the equilibrium price- and output-vectors, respectively.

[8] Cf., e.g., Robert Lekachman, *The Age of Keynes*, New York, 1966, p. 90.

by shocks from a previous position, moreover, the system will exhibit endogenous ("Multiplier") tendencies that, instead of counteracting the displacement, amplify it.

These, then, are in brief summary the two opposed visions of how a market economy behaves that we are saddled with. Both are firmly entrenched in the literature. The first goes back, of course, to Adam Smith and was *the* cosmology of economists for more than 150 years—if this was not your belief, you were almost by definition not an economist, but at best an amateur. Then, the Great Depression prepared the ground for [31] a mass conversion of economists to the second. But the Keynesian Revolution did not quite succeed in making a clean sweep. The older view survived and has again grown in strength as the 1930's recede from memory and mass unemployment on that scale has failed to recur. The two are inconsistent images of the world but nonetheless manage to coexist—and in rather implausible comfort at that.

Clower's original venture into the uncomfortable no-man's land between Neoclassicism and Keynesianism[9] sought to provide a microtheoretical foundation for the core concept of Keynesian theory—Effective Demand. For the contesting cosmologies, the ramifications of his success appeared at first rather one-sidedly in favor of Keynesianism. Solid microtheoretical respectability for the most important Keynesian doctrines seemed suddenly within grasp. At the same time, "effective demand failures" had to be perceived as an hitherto unrealized, pervasive malfunction of price-systems, casting grave doubt on the entire neoclassical vision of the self-regulating capabilities and *modus operandi* of market systems.[10]

Time has by now allowed sundry second thoughts on the effective demand doctrine. The result is a less one-sided, more balanced perspective. Whether it is also a truer perspective remains to be seen. If I were to sum up my present views as a "cosmology"—neither more, nor less crude than the preceding ones—it would have the following outlines. The system is likely to behave differently for large than for moderate displacements from the

---

[9] R. W. Clower, "The Keynesian Counter Revolution: A Theoretical Appraisal," in F. H. Hahn and F. P. R. Brechling, eds., *The Theory of Interest Rates*, London 1965.

[10] I should add the following: It *is*, I think, true that the ramifications of Clower's contribution were seen as "one-sided"—by those who focused intently on the purely theoretical implications: Keynesian theory now had to be taken seriously by general equilibrium theorists; *tâtonnement* stability theorems had to be quoted at drastically reduced empirical values, etc.

My own work in the same vineyard, however, confused the picture no end for many people. By my attempts to explain and document in some detail the departure of "Keynesian economics" from the "economics of Keynes", and the prominence that I gave to purely doctrine-historical themes, I was in effect launching an attack on the scholarly repute of (conventional) Keynesianism—albeit from a totally different quarter. (Cf. the review by Harry G. Johnson, "Keynes and the Keynesians," *Encounter*, January, 1970.) Some readers, therefore, have found the book "anti-Keynesian" and see it, even, as "just another Chicago-school attack"— the emphasis on labor-market search behavior and on the significance of the structure of relative prices arouses, it seems, suspicion.

"full coordination" time-path. Within some range from the path (referred to as "the corridor" for brevity), the system's homeostatic mechanisms work well, and deviation-counteracting tendencies increase in strength. Outside that range these tendencies become weaker as the system becomes increasingly subject to "effective demand failures". If the system is displaced sufficiently "far out", the forces tending to bring it back may, on balance, be so weak and sluggish that—for all *practical* purposes—the Keynesian "unemployment equilibrium" model is as sensible a representation of its state as economic statics will allow. Inside the corridor, multiplier-repercussions are weak and dominated by neoclassical market adjustments; outside the corridor, they [32] should be strong enough for effects of shocks to the prevailing state to be endogenously amplified. Up to a point, multiplier-coefficients are expected to increase with distance from the ideal path. Within the corridor, the presumption is in favor of "monetarist", outside in favor of "fiscalist", policy prescriptions. Finally, although within the corridor market forces will be acting in the direction of clearing markets, institutional obstacles of the type familiar from the conventional Keynesian literature may, of course, intervene to make them ineffective at some point. Thus, a combination of monopolistic wage-setting in unionized occupations and legal minimum-wage restrictions could obviously cut the automatic adjustment process short before "equilibrium employment" is reached.[11]

II

A. *Theory of Markets and Money*

Pre-Keynesian views of how activities are coordinated in market systems were based on two broad assumptions; (*a*) that price-incentives are effective in controlling the behavior of transactors (price-elasticities of excess demands are not zero throughout in any market and in principle, market-clearing solutions at non-negative prices exist for all markets); (*b*) prices are "free" to move in response to excess demands and supplies and will move towards their market-clearing values. The Keynesian model posed the spectre of a coordination failure of indefinite duration. How could that possibly be? Until relatively recently, the generally accepted answers interpreted Keynesian theory as necessarily denying either one or the other of the two broad assumptions—or both.[12]

Arguments for denying the pre-Keynesian assumptions can be developed

---

[11] It is generally true of homeostatic mechanisms, studied in other fields than economics, that their self-regulating capacities are bounded. Displacements so large that the system cannot "cope" are always possible. Is it farfetched to hypothesize that this is true also of economic systems?

[12] For amplification of these remarks, cf., my *Keynes and the Classics: Two Lectures*, Institute of Economic Affairs, London 1969, pp. 24 ff.

in a great number of ways, of course, and we cannot comment on all the versions. There are theoretical and/or empirical reasons for being at least "very uncomfortable" about all of the arguments I am familiar with. The inelasticity of saving and investment behavior with respect to intertemporal prices (interest rates) is an instance of denying (*a*). This denial has been argued, for example, on the grounds that theoretical reasons for assuming non-zero elasticities can only be derived from strong underlying assumptions of "rationality" and "foresight". But this argument won't hold water.[13] Similarly, the one-time belief that these strict inelasticities had solid empirical support has not stood up. With regards to denials of (*b*), it is enough to point out that the prime test-case of Keynesian theory must be the Great

[33] Depression. But "rigid wages" due to monopolistic unions could only apply to a relatively small (and shrinking) proportion of the US labor force at the time. And in fact money wages were not "rigid"—there is no more dramatic wage-deflation on record than that of 1930–33. And so on. The long survival and endless repetition of sundry arguments denying (a) and (b) appears in retrospect a product of psychological necessity: On the one hand, economists could *not imagine* the persistence of coordination failures on a large scale if both (*a*) and (*b*) had to be accepted as "true". On the other hand, the horrors of the Great Depression were impossible to ignore.

Clower's explanation of effective demand failures offered a release from this dilemma. Price-incentive may be effective in all markets and all prices may be "flexible"[14] and a market system may still go hay-wire in its groping for the coordinated solution. Conditions are possible, and are not far-fetched, under which some prices may show no tendency to change although desires to sell and to buy do not coincide in the respective markets. Not only that. Prices may be at their "right" (general equilibrium) levels, but amounts transacted differ persistently from the desired rates of sale and purchase in some markets.[15] And not only that. prices that were at their GE values may tend ("automatically") to move *away* from those values so that the

---

[13] Cf. Gary S. Becker, "Irrational Behavior and Economic Theory," *Journal of Political Economy*, February 1962.

[14] The main reasons for insisting on working out the theory of effective demand failures first while assuming atomistic markets and no institutional restrictions on price-adjustments are implicit in—but obvious from—the text. Another one is also of some importance. Even when the main results are more easily obtained by *ad hoc* "rigidity" assumptions, that procedure had better be shunned—since it carries the false suggestion, "Break up the unions and monopolies (if you dare!)—and all will be well with the world!" The insistence on working with atomistic markets, etc., has been misconstrued by some economists as revealing an "anti-Keynesian bias" and what not. Macrotheory would become a positively *charming* occupation could we but regain that state of grace where one professional could understand the work of another even under the restrictive assumption that the latter can be trusted...

As pointed out at the very end of Part I, once the general outlines of the theory have been clarified, empirically verified "rigidities", etc. should of course be put back in.

[15] Cf. e.g., R. J. Barro and H. I. Grossman, "A General Disequilibrium Model of Income and Employment," *American Economic Review*, March, 1971. Check the "B-solutions" to the various cases they consider.

information disseminated by price changes is "false" and makes the coordination failure confusion worse.

It was surely inevitable that the early discussion of effective demand theory would focus almost exclusively on the newly discovered possibilities for system malfunction. The net result of this concentration on all the fascinating ways in which the system conceivably can go wrong, we now think, was to give a rather grossly exaggerated picture of the propensities of actual real-world economies to lose track and fail to home in towards a coordinated state. Second thoughts on effective demand theory suggest that the capabilities for self-regulating behavior of actual market systems are likely to be a good deal more "robust"[16]—even though the *models* we were working [34] with at the time were not robust at all, but instead extremely sensitive to changes in specification that explicitly incorporate the conceptual distinction between "notional" and "effective" excess demands.[17]

The original modelling context for the discussion was that of a standard Walrasian model "without the auctioneer" (as I chose to put it). Two properties should be emphasized here: (i) all quantities appear as *flows* (albeit cumulated over the "period"), and (ii) *none* of the goods is explicitly given the singular attribute of being the only *means of payment*.[18] We began,

[16] I.e., suggest the notion of "the corridor" within which market forces, as they were traditionally conceived, are strong enough to override the disorganizing tendencies arising from "trading at false prices", etc. Perhaps I had better make it explicit that this is *not* in Keynes. Obviously, Keynes' theory envisages a world in which potential deviation-amplifying endogenous mechanisms are as strong (multiplier-coefficients as large) in the immediate neighbourhood of the "perfectly coordinated" state as they are far away from it.

I have not changed my mind on the significance of Keynes' contribution to economic *analysis*. I think it of fundamental importance. I have long since parted company with Keynes on many aspects of his economic *theory*, in the sense of *beliefs* about how real-world systems function. (One hates being otiose like this, but many economists simply have trouble drawing the distinction.)

[17] In this paper we will be dealing only with one branch of the effective demand doctrine, namely that concerned with effective demand failures among current spot-markets. Issues that belong to this branch include: (*a*) the possibility of persistent states of large-scale unemployment; (*b*) the "original" multiplier based on the simple consumption-income relation; and (*c*) the independence of model solution-states of conditions determining the supply of labor.

Point (*c*) is more brief than accurate. Note that, in standard Keynesian models, shifts in the supply of labor function that increase or decrease the excess supply of labor (without, however, making it negative), *never* change the solution obtained. The changes in corresponding planned demands for other goods in the system are always treated as "ineffective".

The other branch of effective demand theory pertains to *intertemporal* effective demand failures. More than half of my 1968 book dealt with topics in this area (Saving-Investment coordination; Wicksellian cumulative processes; the Keynes effect *vs.* the Pigou effect, etc.). Space will not allow second thoughts on this set of problems.

[18] Clower's reasons for *not* considering a *stock-flow* system are given, op. cit., pp. 114–15. The reader who chooses to check this statement will find that the reasons still hold—for the *analytical* problem posed in that essay. He will also find, however, that the very same reasons would compel us to use stock-flow representations whenever the object is to derive theoretical inferences about the self-regulating capabilities of real-world systems.

When it has already been said that we deal with a pure flow model, it is naturally redundant to add that we do not have the stock-good, "money", in it. The reasons for nonetheless emphasizing the point will be apparent shortly.

thus, with a *non-monetary* "pure flow" representation of an economy.[19] Within that setting, the consequences of letting individuals trade at disequilibrium prices ("false trading") were then examined. With the budget-constraints of a pure flow model, it is readily (albeit not immediately!) apparent that, if the transactor fails to realize his desired sales due to excess supply in those markets, he will not have the wherewithal to realize his desired purchases. If the actual price-vector at which trading takes place differs at all from the GE vector, furthermore, some markets must exhibit excess supply and, consequently, some transactors must necessarily fail to realize desired sales at prevailing prices. It follows that, as soon as you have a departure from the GE price-vector, the demands of some transactors must be sales-constrained—in the model stipulated.

35]   Another point about the mental setting of these conceptual experiments is relevant: the consumption-income relation (from which the "multiplier" is obtained, for instance) seems *the nexus* of all the "singularly Keynesian", "obviously anti-Classical" model-properties that concern us here.[20] It is natural, therefore, to concentrate on a particular case of the above conceptual experiment as the very archetype of it—namely, the case of a household failing to realize desired sales of labor and thus finding its consumption demand *income-constrained*.[21] (Note that unsold labor-services cannot be stored for sale in the next period—again the case analyzed tends to direct one's attention away from stocks.) The analytically crucial aspect of Keynesian theory seems thus to have been isolated: *realized transactions* appear as arguments in the excess demand functions of such systems, whereas

---

[19] Since the very simplest Keynesian models (the "45° Keynesian Cross", etc.) do not include the stock of "money", but deal simply in relationships among flows, and since these elemental models exhibit all the properties that one deems singularly and particularly "Keynesian", this seems "the way to go", all right. But ... it turns out to be misleading.

[20] Two notes: I say (i) "seems the nexus" because Keynes' Employment Function (*General Theory*, Chapter 20) expressed the analogous sales-constraint on the demand for labor on the business sector side of the market. But Chapter 20 is pretty far into that book ... and elemental Keynesian models do not make use of either the Employment function or its converse, the aggregate supply-price function: (ii) "all the ... properties that concern us here", because intertemporal effective demand failures we have ruled out of order (in fn. 15 above).

[21] Beyond concentrating on income-constrained consumption demand of labor-suppliers at the expense of the sales-constrained labor demand of commodity suppliers, the same considerations led me to focus on the search-behavior on the supply-side of labor markets at the expense of demand-side behavior. The latter deficiency I share with numerous authors (Stigler, Alchian, etc... good company!)

   Barro and Grossman, *op. cit.*, have two virtues in this context: (*a*) they give equal attention to the sales-constrained demand behavior of producers, and (*b*) in considering explicitly also situations of purchase-constrained supply-behavior, they forcefully remind us that false trading in inflationary situations must also be encompassed by the theory.

   E. S. Phelps, "Money Wage Dynamics and Labor Market Equilibrium" in Phelps et al. *Microeconomics Foundations of Employment and Inflation Theory*, New York 1970, models a system in which demanders of labor do the "groping". The not-so-easy task remains of constructing a model in which *both* sides of the market 'grope'.

they have no place in Classical models belonging to the Lausanne-school ("modern") tradition.[22] The troubles with effective demand failures follow immediately—in the archetype case, we will have no effective excess demand for wage-goods in an unemployment situation even though "notional" household consumption demand exceeds current output. Wage-goods output is too low . . . but the servo-mechanisms of the market system are idle.

In this setting, all we thought we knew about the stability of market system seems suddenly imperiled. Stability theorems proved for systems of notional excess demand equations apparently prove nothing, because notional and effective excess demands coincide only when the system is already in general equilibrium.[23] *Any* trade at false prices might upset the apple-cart. Trade at false prices will surely take place if prices do not move *instantly* to their GE values when a disturbance occurs, etc. For models [36] of the type considered, all of this is true—but getting a balanced perspective on its "relevance" is another matter.[24] The income constraints derived from this type of model are "too tight".

Second thought, if not necessarily wisdom, starts from the observation that realized sales have been made to do heavy, in fact, triple duty in the above context. Realized sales appear (i) as a proxy for *expected income*,[25] (ii) as a constraint on current *purchases*, and (iii) as a constraint on the demand-*signals* that may be currently emitted. These three ideas need to be kept carefully distinct.

(i) If *realized income is expected*, income expectations will be realized. One assumes that sellers know beforehand what sales they will succeed in making. But, strictly speaking, this assumption makes sense only for that subset of the possible states of the system that are Keynesian "income-equilibria". Most of these states are, of course, coordination failures—disequilibria from a neoclassical standpoint. The assumption *allows* the analysis of some of the properties of such states with the aid of essentially static model-constructions—a convenience that recommends it for certain expository purposes. But it also *precludes* analysis of the recursive interaction processes that propel the system from one Keynesian income-equilibrium

---

[22] Clower, *op. cit.*, pp. 111–12, 119–20.

[23] Clower, *op. cit.*, p. 123.

[24] To take just one example, I committed the following: "Income-constrained processes result not only when price-level velocity is zero, *but whenever it is short of infinite.*" Leijonhufvud, *On Keynesian Economics and the Economics of Keynes*, New York 1968, p. 67. A number of other authors have followed suit.

[25] Following Keynes' procedure of collapsing, for convenience, short term expectations with realized results. Cf., *The General Theory of Employment, Interest and Money*, London 1936, pp. 50–51. But, apart from the issue noted in the text below, following Keynes here risks fudging another distinction as well, namely, that between Friedman's concepts of measured and permanent income—an aspect of the issue that we save for the next section.

to another.[26] The inherent limitations on what we might learn about the dynamic behavior of such systems in this way are obvious. But there is also, I think, a not so obvious danger to the procedure. It rather invites making *ad hoc* assumptions about the information available to transactors in making the decisions that, in effect, the steady-state assumption dictates that they make.[27] Having put price-rigidities and price-inelasticities to one side, effective demand theory seeks to explain coordination failures that arise through faulty communication among transactors. Communication [37] takes place through market interactions. Hence, ideally, all statements of the type: "Transactor A is expected to behave in such-and-such a manner at date t, because he has good information on x, no information about y, and false information about z . . ." etc., should be justifiable with reference to a history of market interactions that would reasonably produce such a state of knowledge. This means tracing the recursive process. In my, no doubt overly jaundiced view, therefore, steady-state constructions divert attention away from the fundamentals of the theory.[28]

(ii) *Realized sales as constraint on purchases.* As long as Say's Principle is the well-enforced law of the land, the model obviously must have this property. Nonetheless, it is easy to get one's bearings on the real world wrong at this point, particularly when focusing narrowly on the labor-selling, wage-goods-purchasing household experiment. In the pure *flow* model, realized sales are interpreted as *current income* (from the sale of labor-services). But, whereas it is obviously true that the value of purchases has to be financed by the value of sales, it is not at all true that they must be financed

---

[26] Cf., Leijonhufvud, *op. cit.*, pp. 74–5.

The collapsing of realized and expected income was a feature (albeit not a necessary one) of Clower's original treatment of the "dual decision hypothesis". It remains in use, e.g., in H.I. Grossman, "Money, Interest, and Prices in Market Disequilibrium," *Journal of Political Economy*, Sept./Oct. 1971, as well as in Barro and Grossman, *op. cit.*.

[27] I.e., much the same kind of *ad-hoc*-ery that makes so much of neoclassical micro-theory useless to the macrotheorist. For the purposes of the "new" macroeconomics, models with assumptions of the type "sellers just *know* the demand-schedules they face" can simply not be trusted. It is not that such assumptions do not make sense in context. For the steady state they often do. It is that they avoid the question: *How* did they come to know? Since one does not know the process through which this knowledge was gained, one is hard put to start grappling with the questions that count (in macro). For example: In what circumstances would that process teach him some things "that ain't so"?

[28] Note that "imperfect information" is a rather misleading label for the theories developing in the area under discussion since it is likely to be understood as referring to "generalized probabilistic uncertainty". The rich literature on that topic from Knight through Arrow is not particularly relevant or helpful here. We are concerned with "incomplete information" in the sense of certain specific pieces of information missing—and missing for reasons inherent in the structure of the model. (The weakest postulate here might be: Nobody interacts directly with everybody.)

Situations for which we assume "good information about x, no information on z . . ." etc., will sometimes produce inferences of "*asymmetric* behavior" that are apparently peculiarly offensive to theorists used to steady-state frames of reference. For an example, cf. A. A. Alchian, "Information Costs, Pricing, and Resource Unemployment," in Phelps et al., *op. cit.*, p. 44n.

out of current income. A supplier of x does not have "current x" as his only source of funds; he can (*a*) sell "stored x", and (*b*) other things.

The point here is as simple as it is important to our main theme. In pure flow models, realized sales have the interpretation of "income". Income constrains legal acquisition of goods directly. Any little "blip" in the realized income-flow must show up (100% at that) in purchases—the gearing between income receipts and expenditures being that tight. As soon as some market does not clear and false trading takes place, multiplier repercussions should necessarily be observed. This income constraint is too tight; it lures one to adopt an exaggerated view of the potential instabilty of real-world economies—*stock-flow* economies.

In stock-flow systems, the stocks act as "buffers" between physical inflows and outflows and between financial income and expenditure flows. Stocks of liquid assets—of *cash balances*, in particular—allow expenditures to be maintained when receipts fall off; indeed, they are maintained by traders exactly for the purpose of meeting such contingencies. Modern economies maintain, in normal times, an enormous, elaborate system of physical and financial buffer stocks.

[38]   Conclusions: (*a*) in such economies, we must expect the propagation of shocks impinging on flows to be heavily damped—*as long as* the shocks are not of greater magnitude than anticipated by transactors in making their decisions on the levels of buffer stocks to maintain; (*b*) such economies are, therefore, much more "robust" than pure flow models would suggest—within "the corridor"; (*c*) if disturbances are of unanticipatedly large magnitude, buffer stocks may be exhausted—at which point, the direct gearing of inflows and outflows of the "tight" income-constraint takes over. For such large displacements, effective demand theory in the version considered becomes a better guide to the behavior of the system than "Classical economics."

(iii) *Realized sales as restriction on demand-signals.* Consider a system in which each good may be traded against every other good. Let us have this "barter economy" in the midst of a most un-Walrasian false trading debauch: quantities actually transacted (and produced) are far below what they would be in a coordinated state; exchange ratios differ from the GE vector of relative prices;[29] and resources are unemployed. For our archetypical case, we would explain: workers fail to sell their services, so their purchases of wage-goods are constrained; producers fail to sell wage-goods, so their

---

[29] *Not* redundant for several reasons the most important of which is that establishing the GE price vector is a necessary, but *not sufficient*, condition for "full coordination" of activities. It does not guarantee that transactors will find a way actually to execute all desired trades. This observation has been made the starting point of important work on the pure theory of money by my UCLA colleague, Joseph Ostroy. Cf. his "The Informational Efficiency of Monetary Exchange"(forthcoming). Also Ostroy and R. M. Starr, "Money and the Decentralization of Exchange" (forthcoming).

purchases of labor sevices are constrained, etc. Realized sales of labor (wage-goods) in this setting are in themselves realized purchases of wage-goods (labor); there is no intermediate "money"-commodity to separate sale and purchase. Labor services constitute direct "purchasing power" over wage-goods and *vice versa*.

What are the *signals* that the market homeostat would respond to in such a case? If at the going rate of real wages,[30] the desired supply of labor exceeds employment, producers will *ipso facto* receive the signal that demand exceeds current sales and output; if the desired supply of wage-goods exceeds current sales and output, workers will *ipso facto* receive the message that demand for labor exceeds current employment. Note that, at a particular date, both statements could well apply at once[31]—indicating, simply, that the ongoing rate of transactions does not exhaust the mutual gains from trade realizeable at the going exchange rate. As these gains from trade come nearer to being exhausted, however, the market situation will clarify: it emerges either (*a*) as one of excess supply of goods and excess demand for labor or (*b*) as one of excess supply of labor and excess demand for [39] goods. In case (*a*), real wages will tend up, in case (*b*) down. *In either case*, the observed volume of transactions, output, and employment will rise.[32]

Next for the contrasting case: a regime characterized by Clower's postulate "*Money buys goods and goods buy money; but goods do not buy goods.*"[33] Money and no other good is a *means of payment*. Obligatorily, money separates each sale from corresponding purchases. Suppose we find this system in the "same" type of disequilibrium as the one considered above. Offering to sell now means to ask for money in exchange; offers to buy are no longer "valid" if not backed by ready cash.[34] If the desired supply of labor exceeds employment, producers will be aware of the excess supply in labor markets but receive no valid signal indicating that the demand for wage-goods exceeds output. If desired supply of wage-goods exceeds current sales and output, workers are not informed that demand for labor

[30] For brevity, I fudge matters: the exchange ratio for any pair of goods is bound to vary depending upon what pair of traders are observed; inconsistent cross-rates and corresponding arbitrage opportunities are likely to abound in disequilibrium, etc.

[31] Naturally, markets need not clear continuously in this regime. When shifts of the basic parameters occur, producers and workers will spend time searching the other side of the market for the best bargain, etc., etc.

[32] At disequilibrium prices, the short side of markets is assumed to predominate in determining actual transactions.

[33] R. W. Clower, "A Reconsideration of the Microfoundations of Monetary Theory, *Western Economic Journal*, December 1967, reprinted as "Foundations of Monetary Theory", in Clower, ed., *Monetary Theory: Selected Readings*, London 1969. Cf. pp. 207–08.

[34] Suppliers who are sold out and face a queue of dissatisfied customers *with cash in their pockets* will increase their orders and raise prices; they will do neither when observing lines of starving, out-of-pocket unemployed. (Use of Say's Principle in the construction of the model precludes analytical consideration of acts of mercy.)

exceeds employment. Even if the ratio of money wages to money prices comes out as the GE real wage, we may be caught in the vicious circle where the unemployed cannot make their consumption demand *effective* until they have sold their services for money, and producers with excess capacity cannot bid for labor until they have sold their goods—which the unemployed do not have the cash to purchase, and so on.[35] *This failure of the markets to transmit messages about desired transactions from one side to the other is what we mean by the phrase "effective demand failure".*

The non-clearing market states for both our barter and our money system may be described in virtually identical terms, stressing the simple logic of the equal-value-in-exchange requirement (Say's Principle): since transactors do not succeed in selling more than they do, they cannot be buying more than they do ... etc. But such descriptions of the states are *analytically incomplete*[36] or it would be clear what happens next, namely, the first ("barter") system homes in toward a coordinated state, the second (monetary exchange) system does not.

Since it carries a reminder of this analytical fact, we now prefer the term "cash-constrained" to our earlier usage of "income-constrained"(behavior, 40] process, etc.). For similar reasons, it is sometimes needed to distinguish between situation of "deficient aggregate demand" and those characterized by "effective demand failure", and not treat "effective demand" and "aggregate demand" simply as synonyms.

B. *Theories of the Consumption Function*

This section can be brief; the main ideas I have stated elsewhere,[37] and their underpinnings have just been discussed in some detail.

I referred above to Keynes' simple consumption-income relation as the nexus of all the "singularly Keynesian, obviously anti-Classical" properties of standard macro-models, including the Multiplier and the independence of consumption demand from labor supply. One reason for calling Keynes' consumption function "anti-Classical', we recall, is that it makes the consumption of households depend, not on utility maximization constrained by prices and endowments, but on "realized sales of factor services" (current income).

The so-called "postwar forecasting debacle" in the US was attributed in large part to use of this function to predict the consumption component

---

[35] This is a Barro–Grossman "B-solution" again. The Barro and Grossman paper does not stress the distinction between constrained purchases and constrained demand-signals developed in this sub-section, however.

[36] In the sense that, in mechanics, a description giving only, say, the mass and space-coordinates for a body at a given point of time would be incomplete in omitting information about its (directed) velocity. Cf. the earlier discussion above concerning analysis of non-clearing market states using standard steady-state tools.

[37] Cf. *Keynes and the Classics* . . ., pp. 42–45.

of aggregate demand.[38] Later work on the problem—some of the best work we have seen in macroeconomics—produced the "modern consumption functions" of Modigliani–Brumberg–Ando and Friedman. Theirs is the seminal work, but there have been many important contributions both before and since.

It is impossible to do this literature justice in short compass. Ignoring operational empirical issues altogether, the main theoretical theme is this: current consumption is to be predicted, not from current income, but from what I will call "perceived wealth".[39] If we treat wealth—defined as the present value of current and expected future income—as the main determinant of consumption, and define income as the rate of change of wealth, it is clear that no stable relationship between consumption and income can be predicted for short time periods. Even for consumption and income flows cumulated over, say, a calendar year, the influence of income on consumption should be relatively weak and unreliable. What then remains of the "Keynesian nexus"? A low marginal propensity to spend on consumption goods means weak multiplier effects,[40] ineffective fiscal policy, etc., etc.

[41]

[38] My own hypothesis to account for why the US economy did not lapse back into "great depression" is simple, perhaps naive: it was put back into "the corridor" through the huge balances of liquid assets that war finance allowed the private sector to accumulate and then insured against a new departure from it by pre-Accord monetary policy which, to put it favorably, made certain that the well would not run dry again.

If this hypothesis be "true" (whatever that might mean with reference to a generalization so broad), the conclusions drawn from the forecasting debacle caught only part of the trouble. They were, in effect (1) that what is nowadays the standard Keynesian textbook model was all right, but (2) that its consumption function needed repair. The results of that diagnosis seem to have been a "very nearly" neoclassical consumption function stuck into a Keynesian model.

It just might be that that peculiar combination won't fit *any* state of the world, be it inside or outside "the corridor".

[39] How large a step back towards pre-Keynesian theory this represents does not seem to have been generally appreciated. Although there are some fairly subtle conceptual problems, the wealth concept used here is not all that different from "the value of the endowment" concept that appears in intertemporal neoclassical constructions.

For reasons partially adumbrated in the preceding footnote, these theories do not go all the way back to neoclassicism, but occupy in effect a curious halfway house. Keynes' preoccupation with "involuntary unemployment" states of the system allowed him to split the traditional model of household behavior down the middle, separating the consumption decision from the labor supply decision. Income is not the result of household choice, but "involuntarily" determined. Traditional determinants of the labor supply decision, etc., may then be ignored and the consumption decision treated as determined by income. Modern consumption function theory has not put the theory of household behavior back together again. The generalization of Keynes' current income to (the present value of) current plus expected future income still treats future wage-income as parametric to the household's consumption-accumulation decision.

[40] Admittedly not the same thing as consumption—but we can't go into that. For an up-to-date assessment of empirical work in the Friedman branch of this literature, cf. M. R. Darby, "The Permanent Income Theory of Consumption—A Restatement" (forthcoming). Darby shows that "the econometric procedures which have been utilized in the estimation of permanent income have biased upwards the estimates of the weight of current income . . ."

The transmogrifications of "wealth", in this context, are about as numerous and difficult to deal with as were those of "realized sales" in our earlier discussion.[41] We note just two: (i) wealth represents a "subjective estimate of maintainable living standards," and (ii) wealth constitutes a (presumably objective) intertemporal constraint on expenditure.

Suppose for the moment that the effect of a change in the level of current income (over an undefined, but not indefinite "period") on "wealth" in *both* senses were of the second order of smalls. Consumption should then be unaffected, and secondly (multiplier) effects on aggregate demand should not be observed. Consequently, no effective demand failure would be observed in our archetypical case. But suppose next that a drop in income impinges on a household whose balances of cash and other highly liquid assets are zero; the household has no liquid "buffer stock" at the date of impact of the disturbance. Still its "wealth" is, by assumption, unimpaired. In what ways could it finance a maintained level of consumption? I suggest that the empirically relevant opportunities for so doing can be described as "distress" sales of non-human assets and "distress" borrowing against future income prospects.[42] Either avenue of action would, *if taken* (*a*) reduce "wealth" in sense (ii), and (*b*) reduce "wealth" in sense (i) *by more than is avoidable* by simply cutting current consumption until income starts once more to flow at its "permanent" rate. It appears that situations may occur for which "wealth (ii)" is not the relevant constraint on expenditure.

In such situations, the system exhibits effective demand failures. Its self regulating capabilities are drastically reduced. With cash constraints operative, at least on households, further disturbances will trigger deviation-
[42] amplifying multiplier processes—an opportunity for effective, pump-priming, fiscal action.[43]

When would we then expect to observe effective demand failures, sizeable multiplier coefficients and the rest? In brief, *when liquid buffer stocks have been squeezed out of the system.* This takes a "large displacement"—an *unanticipatedly* large displacement.

We "supposed for the moment" that it was legitimate to discuss whether multiplier effects can occur while holding permanent income constant. It is now clear that this simplifying assumption has to be given up at the same time (if not sooner) that cash/income constraints become binding. We are considering a hypothetical situation in which the transactor has been subjected to an income reduction of larger magnitude and longer dura-

---

[41] This is true quite apart from the fact that the human capital component consists largely of income from "not yet realized" sales of labor services. This helps account for the "imperfect" market in loans secured by human capital collateral which is of importance to our argument, be we cannot enlarge upon it here.

[42] For (badly needed) amplification, see my LSE lectures, *op. cit.*, pp. 43–4.

[43] Cf. Leijonhufvud, "Keynes and the Effectiveness of Monetary Policy," *Western Economic Journal*, March 1968.

tion than he anticipated in planning his liquid asset holdings. This *necessarily* means a drop in income of a magnitude and duration such that he must revise downwards the subjective estimate of his permanent income. He could not otherwise consistently (*a*) regard it as wholly "transitory", and (*b*) not have ensured himself of a buffer stock of liquid assets, credit lines, and unemployment compensation rights larger than our illustration supposes.

Outside the corridor, therefore, effective demand failures come to dominate the dynamic motion of the system due to two factors: (i) the exhaustion of liquid buffers, reinforced (ii) by dysfunctional[44] revisions of permanent income expectations.

A final note is in order under this heading. At this stage, it is clear that our theory implies a *variable width of the corridor.* Transactors who have once suffered through a displacement of unanticipated magnitude (on the order of the Great Depression, say) will be encouraged to maintain larger buffers thereafter—until the memory dims . . .

C. *Quantity Theories of Money Income Determination*

On the topics treated so far, I have enjoyed the customary psychological comforts of an author: I know more than I have said. In this section, I [43] will say more than I know[45]—but there will be less of it. In any case, something needs to be set down under this heading to round out the picture this paper has tried to present.

Since Quantity Theories, ancient or modern, usually do not specify equations for the so-called "real sector," it is clear that they are essentially mute on the subject of effective demand failures. But such failures do not seem to fit in. The Quantity Theory approach to income determination

---

[44] "Dysfunctional" in the sense of being self-fulfilling prophesies of future incomes *below* the incomes that would be earned could the system be returned to the "ideal path". For a turgid elaboration on this sort of thing, cf. my *On Keynesian Economics . . .*, Chapter IV, Section 5.

Note that the same sort of expectations-revision will apply to the earnings of corporations. When this happens, the present value of equity shares in them will—*even if evaluated at the "natural rate" of discount*—fall below the market price required to call forth the rate of investment needed for the system to return to the "full coordination time path". Cf. my "Keynes and the Effectiveness . . .", *op. cit.*

The point is worth enlarging upon. Within the corridor, transactors that either over- or under-estimate the present value of earnings from assets in prospect along the "fully coordinated" time path will, in Knightian fashion, suffer losses or forego profits and tend to be weeded out. This means that transactors who persistently act on "socially dysfunctional" evaluations have a low (private) survival probability.

The opposite tends to be the case outside the corridor. This conclusion applies symmetrically to inflationary and deflationary "large displacements".

I am indebted to Prof. Henry A. Latané for forcing my attention onto this issue.

[45] An inequality that promises to be reversed by Mr. Daniel Benjamin's work on the topic of this section. Given the modelling difficulties and severe data availability problems, he risks investing in an "unpublishable UCLA doctoral dissertation". I am indebted to him for this splendid display of risk preference—as well as for numerous helpful discussions.

and effective demand theory can be brought to confrontation by focusing on the multiplier implications of the latter.[46] Modern Quantity Theory, in its elemental form, predicts income from three equations: (1) a money demand function with income as the independent argument; (2) a money supply equation stating that the money stock is exogenously determined; and (3) a "demand equals supply" equilibrium condition. The Quantity Equation is nowadays invariably interpreted as the reduced form of this little system. To allow Keynesian disturbances to displace it from equilibrium, this closed system has to be opened up; we do so by putting the interest rate in as another unknown in the money demand function. The result is a 'variable velocity" model.

Now, assume a "decline in the marginal efficiency of investment". The impact effects are an excess supply of commodities and an excess demand for securities. The latter is eliminated by a fall in the interest rate. This increases the amount of money demanded as of the initial income, thus producing an excess demand for money (equal to the "remainder" of the excess commodity supply). Standard quantity theory reasoning now applies: income must fall until the excess demand for money is eliminated. Utterly Keynesian so far.[47]

But that is it. The adjustment process should stop right there. To restart it would take another shock to create a new excess demand for money. There is no suggestion here of an ensuing deviation-amplifying multiplier process or of the system's ability to recover being impeded by effective demand failures.

The Quantity Theory could be made to accommodate the *possibility* of "cumulative processes" in various ways, e.g., (i) by making the money supply endogenous in such fashion that the "first-around" decline in income does not remove the excess demand for money; (ii) by assuming money demand dependent not only on "steady-state" income but also on changes in income in such a way that short-run "rachet effects" are obtained. These alternatives I leave aside.

[44]

The revival of the Quantity Theory has been accompanied by much inconclusive debate about the proper operational definition of "money". Which assets and how many should be aggregated in measuring "M"? I have nothing conclusive to add to that debate; the following discussion leaves the choice to the reader. There has been virtually no discussion of the *other* aggregation problem. Granted that stable demand functions of money exist for individual

---

[46] . . . or by listening to my colleague, Earl Thompson, to whom I am indebted for bringing about the confrontation in my own mind.

[47] The version of Keynesianism enshrined in the textbooks invariably assumes a stable aggregate demand function for money. That assumption is as crucial to that construction as it is to any quantity theory. Since it is, to say the very least, unclear that this was the original idea, it might be better to refer to IS–LM models as "variable velocity quantity theories".

transactors, how confident can we be of the existence of a stable aggregative money demand function?[48]

At this point, we must take a drastic short cut. I hate being mathematical about it, but consider the equation:

$$MV = PX, \tag{1}$$

where PX stands for aggregate expenditures on *final goods*. Instead of the modern interpretation of the equation as a reduced form, we adopt an oldfashioned one: V is taken to represent the "average propensity to spend on final goods out of money balances". We will assume (*a*) that stable underlying money-expenditure relations exist for all transactors, and also (*b*) that, within the ranges relevant to our conceptual experiments, all these relations are linear with zero intercepts. For each transactor, the average and marginal propensities to spend out of money balances (APSM and MPSM) are equal and constant.[49]

We have k relations of the simple form

[45] $m_j v_j = P x_j$, where $v_j = APSM_j = MPSM_j$. $\tag{2}$

What assumptions would justify replacing these individual functions, k in number, with equation (1)? The usual first two lines of defence of such aggregations are: (i) that it is permissible to assume that all the v_j's are of equal magnitude so that there can be no distribution effects; (ii) that, although the v_j's differ, the proportional distribution of the m_j's can be justifiably assumed constant over the time-period and population of transactors studied. I will suppose that we can agree that (i) is "obviously untrue".

---

[48] The reason why the question has not been raised even by fervent anti-monetarists is provided, I think, in the preceding footnote. Anyone who is tempted to grasp upon the (empirically unsubstantiated) argument that follows as a new weapon against monetarism should be forewarned that it is double-edged. If there were to be sizeable aggregation errors in one of the functions of the standard model, there must *a fortiori* be corresponding "instabilities" elsewhere in it.

The converse double edge to Friedman's insistence on the instability of the multiplier is, cuttingly, pointed out by F. H. Hahn, "Professor Friedman's Views on Money," *Economica,* February 1971.

[49] Readers already uneasy with this short cut may fortify themselves by interpreting these individual money-expenditure schedules as stock-flow equilibrium loci of the type constructed in G. C. Archibald and R. G. Lipsey, "Monetary and Value Theory: A Critique of Lange and Patinkin," *Review of Economic Studies,* 1958. This type of construction will not support our argument below, however, beyond the point where income account and capital account transactions are separated.

In my argument from this point on, I have been greatly fortified by the theoretical investigations of Peter Howitt and by numerous discussions with him during his 1971–72 stay at UCLA. Two of his papers are particularly relevant: "Stability and the Quantity Theory" and "The Short Run Dynamics of Monetary Exchange" (both to be published). The finite-time dynamics of Howitt's model in the latter paper exhibit "the corridor"—for reasons that, while formally more formidable, are at bottom the same as those loosely sketched below.

I will then infer that the implicit justifying assumption for the aggregation over transactors, in Quantity Theories generally is of type (ii).

We may now proceed directly to the analytical possibility that intrigues me. Note that what follows definitely is a *special case*—and it takes the conjunction of the following, separate assumptions to produce it. Following Gurley and Shaw,[50] we divide all transactors into two groups, referred to as "deficit" and "surplus" units, respectively. We assume (*a*) that, over the period that we focus on, migrations between groups do not occur; units are allowed to proceed, at most to the boundary line of running a balanced income-account budget; and (*b*) that, on the average, the v_j's of the deficit group exceed those of the surplus group. This completes the setting of our special case. It implies the following: if we were to trace all income account transactions in the system, while ignoring those on capital account, we would observe a net cash flow from the deficit group to the surplus group. If that was all there was to it, we should—*vide* assumption (ii)—observe total expenditure on final goods declining in the system. Since the money stock is held constant, this means that observed average velocity declines. Consequently, I enlarge upon the earlier inference concerning the implicit aggregation-justifying assumptions of the Quantity Theory: it assumes that capital account transactions (sales and purchases of existing assets as well as credit transactions) occur so as to offset continuously the tendency of net flows on income account to "upset" the given proportional distribution of cash. For brevity, I refer to these offsetting capital account transactions as "cash reshuffling".

We come then to the point: when should we expect monetarist income predictions to "break down" (and do worse relative to simple Keynesian multiplier predictions than "normally")?[51] Even omitting supporting argument, the answer is, I think, clear: during episodes when conditions in asset and credit markets are so "abnormal", that normal cash reshuffling processes are likely to be seriously impeded.[52] Again, we would look for "large displacements" removing the system from the corridor. The most obvious possibilities involve *the same* conditions as those that we previously suggested should be present when effective demand failures occur. Consider the household. The tight cash/income constraint becomes binding when its income earners have been unemployed long enough to exhaust savings deposits and rights to unemployment compensation—and, of course, the availability of credit on "reasonable terms". In that situation, its *MPSM* should also be high relative to transactor units with healthier balance sheets.[53]

[46]

---

[50] E.g., their "Financial Intermediaries and the Saving-Investment Process," *Journal of Finance*, May 1956.

[51] Cf. M. Friedman and D. Meiselman, "The Relative Stability of Monetary Velocity and the Investment Multiplier in the United States, 1897–1958," in *Stabilization Policies* (Commission on Money and Credit), Englewood Cliffs, N.J. 1963.

[52] Here we can only hint at financial instability themes developed by Professor H. P. Minsky in numerous contributions.

I suggest that those well known conditions of the 1930's that have been widely interpreted (by Keynesian writers) as attributable to a static "liquidity trap" property of a stable aggregative (excess) demand for money function are *at least* equally well accounted for by the hypothesis just outlined. If we can assume that open market operations are transacted between the central bank and units with below average MPSM, monetary policy will be atypically "ineffective" under the conditions assumed. In the same conditions, fiscal policy should be atypically "effective" even if unaccompanied by injections of money. It can be so because of the opportunity to borrow from low-MPSM units and to channel the funds through the budget discriminatively into the hands of high-MPSM units—in a situation where the normal endogenous reshuffling mechanisms are inoperative.

A final proposition regarding the corridor: Cantillon-effects will be strong and relatively long-lasting outside, weak and evanescent inside the corridor.[54]

III

Hopefully, the various themes of this paper will be seen to form an intellectually coherent *theory*. Rigorously consistent, it is not; solid empirical support, it does not have. As advertised in the beginning, it is more than anything else an *agenda* for—and invitation to—*needed* modelling and empirical work by those who find it plausible enough to be worth pursuing. I have little doubt but that the results of such work would sooner or later [47] show the idea of the "corridor" to be too crude a generalization. Meanwhile, however, *some* image of how our contending interpretations of post-World War I experience may be reconciled seems needed. It will not have escaped the reader's attention that many an issue controverted these many years between various "schools" is rather defused if the theory outlined here is [48] judged provisionally acceptable.

---

[53] Interference with the cash reshuffling process could also occur in inflationary situations. Consider, for example, "disintermediation" phenomena consequent upon nominal interest rates piercing legal ceilings. The widely discussed disintermediation problems in the US in the late 1960's apparently coincided with previously relatively reliable monetarist velocity equations producing predictions later found to be *over*-estimates. I am indebted to Sam Peltzman for this observation.

For those taking the fashionable literature on "Optimal Monetary Growth" seriously, there just might be a warning here. The policy suggestion has been made that the rate of return on money balances "ought to" be manipulated into equality with the rate of return on real capital. As pointed out to me by Earl Thompson some 5 or 6 years ago, this entails killing off all intermediary institutions, since no margin between borrowing and lending rates will remain to live on. More generally, it completely eliminates the incentive for surplus units to lend—just letting the cash pile up brings the same return. And so on and so forth. The social optimality of this sort of thing escapes me, but I must confess to having ignored much of the literature on the subject.

[54] I define "Cantillon-effects" as occurring whenever the effects on aggregate money income of increases in the money stock are found to depend upon the *route* by which the injection of money takes place.

Part III
Some Unresolved
Theoretical Issues

[15]

19 R. W. Clower

The Keynesian Counter-Revolution: A Theoretical Appraisal

Excerpt from R. W. Clower (1965), 'The Keynesian counter-revolution: a theoretical appraisal', *The Theory of Interest Rates*, edited by F. H. Hahn and F. Brechling, International Economic Association Series, Macmillan, ch. 5, pp. 103–25.

Twenty-five years of discussion and controversy have produced a large and surprisingly harmonious literature on Keynes and the Classics. Although the series still has not converged to a point of universal agreement, the domain remaining open to dispute has contracted steadily with the passage of time. On one essential issue, however, contemporary opinion is still largely undecided: precisely what are the purely formal differences, if any, between Keynes and the Classics? Perhaps the clearest symptom of our uncertainty is the continued lack of an explicit integration of price theory and income analysis. Equally significant, however, is the ambivalence of professional economists towards the Keynesian counter-revolution launched by Hicks in 1937 and now being carried forward with such vigour by Patinkin and other general equilibrium theorists (1–6).[1] The elegance and generality of this literature makes it most alluring. At the same time, one can hardly fail to be impressed – and disturbed – by the close resemblance that some of its central doctrines bear to those of orthodox economics.

I do not presume at this late date either to improve the views of previous writers on Keynes and the Classics or to transform equivocations into certainties. Things are not that simple. However, I shall attempt to show that the same highly special theoretical presuppositions which led to Keynes' original attack

1. The 'counter-revolution' to which I refer is clearly not a conscious revolt against Keynesian economics, for all of the writers involved are, in a practical sense, strong supporters of what they conceive to be the Keynesian revolution. It is another question whether the same people are Keynesians in a theoretical sense. That is one of the issues on which this paper is intended to shed some light.

270

R. W. Clower

on orthodox economics continue to pervade contemporary price theory and that the Keynesian counter-revolution would collapse without them. Unlike Keynes, who had to deal with doctrines of which no authoritative account had ever been given, we now have an extremely clear idea of the orthodox content of contemporary theory.[2] We thus have a distinct advantage over Keynes in describing what has been said. However, our basic problem is to discover and describe what has not but should have been said – and here we are on all fours with Keynes. Like Keynes, therefore, I must begin by asking 'forgiveness if, in the pursuit of sharp distinctions, my controversy is itself too keen' (7).

I Keynes and Traditional Theory

Our first task is to express in modern idiom those aspects of orthodox economics which were of special concern to Keynes. This may be accomplished most conveniently by considering a two-sector economy comprising households on one side and firms on the other. Corresponding to this division into sectors, we distinguish two mutually exclusive classes of commodities: (a) those which are supplied by firms and demanded by households; (b) those which are supplied by households and demanded by firms. Commodities in class (a) will be distinguished by numerical subscripts $i = 1, \ldots, m$, those in class (b) by numerical subscripts $j = m + 1, \ldots, n$. Thus, quantities supplied and demanded by firms are denoted, respectively, by variables $s_1, \ldots, s_m, d_{m+1}, \ldots, d_n$, while quantities demanded and supplied by households are denoted, respectively, by variables $d_1, \ldots, d_m, s_{m+1}, \ldots, s_n$. Prevailing market prices (expressed in units of commodity n) are then represented by symbols $\mathbf{p}_1, \mathbf{p}_2, \ldots, \mathbf{p}_{n-1} (\mathbf{p}_n \equiv 1)$, or, in vector notation, $\mathbf{P}$.[3]

For ease of exposition, we shall ignore aggregation problems and suppose that the preferences of all households in the economy are adequately characterized by a community utility function,

2. For this, we have mainly to thank the counter-revolutionists, since it is their writings which have revived interest in general equilibrium theory.

3. Here and throughout the remainder of the paper, boldface symbols will invariably be used to refer to magnitudes that are to be regarded as given parameters from the standpoint of individual transactors.

271

Monetary Theory and Keynesian Economics

$U(d_1, \ldots, d_m; s_{m+1}, \ldots, s_n)$. Similarly, we shall assume that technical conditions confronting all business firms in the economy are adequately characterized by an aggregate transformation function $T(s_1, \ldots, s_m; d_{m+1}, \ldots, d_n) = 0$. Needless to say, the functions U and T are assumed to possess all continuity and curvature properties needed to ensure the existence of unique extrema under circumstances to be specified below.

Dealing first with the orthodox theory of the firm, we obtain sector supply and demand functions, $\tilde{s}_i(\mathbf{P})$, $\tilde{d}_i(\mathbf{P})$ as solutions of the problem:

maximize $\qquad r = \sum_i^m \mathbf{p}_i \, s_i - \sum_j^n \mathbf{p}_j \, d_j,$ [4]

subject to $\qquad T(s_1, \ldots, s_m; d_{m+1}, \ldots, d_n) = 0.$ [5]

Underlying both sets of solutions are transactor equilibrium conditions of the form

$$\mathbf{p}_k + \frac{\lambda \partial T}{\partial \bar{v}_k} = 0 \quad (\bar{v} = \bar{d}, \tilde{s}; \, k = 1, 2, \ldots, n).$$

In particular, if $n = 2$ and we interpret s_1 as goods and d_2 as labour, we easily establish Keynes' classical postulate I, namely, 'the [real] wage is equal to the marginal product of labour'. (*General Theory*, p. 5.)

In a similar fashion, the demand and supply functions of the household sector are obtained as solutions, $\bar{d}_i(\mathbf{P}, r)$, $\tilde{s}_i(\mathbf{P}, r)$, of the problem

maximize $\qquad U(d_1, \ldots, d_m; s_{m+1}, \ldots, s_n),$

subject to $\qquad \sum_i^m \mathbf{p}_i \, d_i - \sum^n \mathbf{p}_j \, s_j - \mathbf{r} = 0,$

4. The symbols $\overset{m}{\underset{t}{\sum}}$ and $\overset{n}{\underset{j}{\sum}}$ denote, respectively, the operations $\overset{m}{\underset{i=1}{\sum}}$ and $\overset{n}{\underset{j=m+1}{\sum}}$.

5. Since $\mathbf{p}_n \equiv 1$ by assumption, we have not shown it as an explicit divisor of the price variables included in the vector $\mathbf{P}$; but it is there all the same. Thus, the demand and supply functions of the business sector are homogeneous of order zero in the n price variables $\mathbf{p}_1, \ldots, \mathbf{p}_n$. Provided $d_n \neq 0$, however, the same functions are not in general homogenous in the $n - 1$ *numéraire* prices which are contained in the vector $\mathbf{P}$.

272

R. W. Clower

the profit variable **r** being treated as a fixed parameter in this context.[6]

Underlying these solutions are transactor equilibrium conditions of the form

$$\frac{\partial U}{\partial \bar{v}_k} + \gamma \mathbf{p}_k = 0 \ (\bar{v} = \bar{d}, \bar{s}; k = 1, \ldots, n).$$

Thus, if we consider the case $n = 2$ and adopt an appropriate interpretation of the variables d_1 and s_2, we readily derive Keynes' classical postulate II, namely, 'The utility of the [real] wage when a given volume of labour is employed is equal to the marginal disutility of that amount of employment.' (*General Theory*, p. 5.)

So much for the basic ideas of the orthodox theory of transactor behaviour. Let us turn next to the theory of price formation, again seeking to express matters as Keynes might have expressed them had he been less steeped in Marshallian habits of thought.

At least since the time of Adam Smith, the market mechanism has been regarded by economists as an ingenious device for reconciling the freedom of individuals to trade as they please with the ultimate necessity for individuals in the aggregate to buy neither more nor less of any commodity than is offered for sale. To accomplish this feat, the mechanism must be supplied with information about individual sale and purchase plans, which is precisely what is supposed to be furnished by the supply-and-demand functions of orthodox theory.

Assuming that all business profits accrue to accounts in the household sector, we may assert first of all that the sale and purchase plans of individual transactors at any given instant of time[7] depend only on prevailing market prices.[8] We may then argue as follows.

6. The household demand-and-supply functions are homogeneous of order zero in the $n + 1$ variables $\mathbf{p}_1, \ldots, \mathbf{p}_n$ and **r**, but not in the n variables $\mathbf{p}_1, \ldots, \mathbf{p}_{n-1}$ and **r** (provided $s_n \neq 0$).

7. I have chosen to regard 'time' as a continuous rather than a discrete variable, and to confine discussion to current values of all magnitudes, in order to discourage both myself and readers from playing meretricious games with alternative lag assumptions. No part of the present or subsequent argument is affected in any essential way if time is made discrete, lags are introduced, etc.

8. Since we are performing market rather than individual experiments (Patinkin, 1, p. 15), the parameter **r** which appears in the household

Monetary Theory and Keynesian Economics

If prevailing prices are such that demand differs from supply in any market, this means that individual trading plans, taken as a whole, are mutually inconsistent, which, in turn, means that at least some individual plans cannot be carried into effect at prevailing market prices. In these circumstances, it is plausible to suppose that prevailing prices tend to vary over time, rising in markets where demand exceeds supply, falling in markets where supply exceeds demand. Accordingly, the economy may be said to be in a state of disequilibrium. On the other hand, if prevailing market prices at any given instant happen to be such that demand is equal to supply in every market simultaneously, this means that individual trading plans, considered as a whole, are mutually consistent; hence, that all transactions planned at prevailing prices can, in principle, actually be carried out. In these circumstances, it is plausible to suppose that there are no extraneous forces at work tending to alter either individual trading plans or prevailing market prices, and the economy may be said to be in a state of equilibrium.

The only snag in this argument is the familiar one about the number of equations being one greater than the number of prices to be determined. From the theory of household behaviour, however, we know that

$$\sum_i^m \mathbf{p}_i \, \bar{d}_i - \sum_j^n \mathbf{p}_j \, \bar{s}_j - \mathbf{r} = 0, \qquad\qquad 1$$

and from the theory of business behaviour, we know that

$$\sum_i^m \mathbf{p}_i \, \bar{s}_i - \sum_j^n \mathbf{p}_j \, \bar{d}_j - \bar{r} = 0. \qquad\qquad 2$$

Subtracting **2** from **1**, therefore, we have

$$\sum_{k=1}^n \mathbf{p}_k \, [\bar{d}_k - \bar{s}_k] \equiv \mathbf{r} - \bar{r}. \qquad\qquad 3$$

Since in general the variables **r** and $\bar{r}$ refer to completely independent individual experiments, we cannot assume that $\mathbf{r} \equiv \bar{r}$.[8] In

---

demand and supply functions is now replaced by the function the value of

$$\bar{r} = \sum_i^m \mathbf{p}_i \, \bar{s}_i - \sum_j^n \mathbf{p}_j \bar{d}_j,$$

which depends only on the price vector **P**.

274

R. W. Clower

the case of market experiments, however, it does seem plausible to suppose that $\mathbf{r} = \bar{r}$ provided that the variables $s_1, \ldots, s_m$ and $d_{m+1}, \ldots, d_n$ have assumed their equilibrium values. If this is granted, then **3** leads immediately to Walras' law (in the sense of Lange, 8, pp. 49–68).[9]

$$\sum_{k=1}^{n} \mathbf{p}_k[\bar{d}_k(\mathbf{P}) - \bar{s}_k(\mathbf{P})] \equiv 0. \qquad\qquad \mathbf{4}$$

Walras' law obviously implies that the *numéraire* value of one of the excess demands can be inferred from the values of the others, which rids us of the extra supply-and-demand equation. Rewritten in the form

$$\sum_k \mathbf{p}_k\, \bar{s}_k \equiv \sum_k \mathbf{p}_k\, d_k,$$

Walras' law might also be said to assert that 'supply creates its own demand' (cf. *General Theory*, p. 18) – and we shall hear more of this in the sequel. For the time being, however, it may merely be remarked that Walras' law must be valid under the circumstances assumed here.

This account of orthodox doctrine accords well enough, I think, both with modern analysis and with Keynes' conception of classical theory. For the special case $n = 2$, in particular, it is apparent that Keynes' views, as expressed in chapter 2 of the *General Theory*, are exactly equivalent to what is presented above. Granted that this is so, we may reasonably assert that orthodox economics provides a general theory of equilibrium states – that is, an adequate account of the factors determining equilibrium prices and equilibrium transaction plans in a market economy. Moreover, the same analysis may be said to provide the beginnings of a theory of disequilibrium prices and disequilibrium transaction plans. Clearly, however, orthodox analysis does not provide a general theory of disequilibrium states: firstly, because it yields no direct information about the magnitude of *realized* as distinct from *planned* transactions under disequilibrium conditions; secondly, because it tacitly assumes that the forces tending at any instant to change prevailing market prices are independent

9. The distinction drawn by Lange between Walras' law and Say's law is not relevant here; from a formal point of view, the two propositions are equivalent.

Monetary Theory and Keynesian Economics

of realized transactions at the same moment (this includes as a special case the assumption, made explicitly in all '*tâtonnement*', 'recontract' and 'auction' models, that no disequilibrium transactions occur).[10]

It is instructive to compare these views with those of Keynes, as represented by the following assortment of quotations (not all of them torn out of context):

I shall argue that the postulates of the classical theory are applicable to a special case only and not to the general case . . . (*General Theory*, p. 3).

The question . . . of the volume of the *available* resources, in the sense of the size of the employable population, the extent of natural wealth and the accumulated capital equipment, has often been treated descriptively [in orthodox writings]. But the pure theory of what determines the *actual employment* of the available resources has seldom been examined in any detail. . . . I mean, not that the topic has been overlooked, but that the fundamental theory underlying it has been deemed so simple and obvious that it has received, at the most, a bare mention. (*General Theory*, pp. 4–5.)

A theory cannot claim to be a *general* theory, unless it is applicable to the case where (or the range within which) money wages are fixed, just as much as to any other case. Politicians are entitled to complain that money wages *ought* to be flexible; but a theorist must be prepared to deal indifferently with either state of affairs. (*General Theory*. p. 276.)

. . . the classical theory . . . is wholly unable to answer the question what effect on employment a reduction in money wages will have. For it has no method of analysis wherewith to attack the problem. (*General Theory*, p. 260.)

Clearly, there is nothing very novel in any of this; up to this point, at least, the belief that Keynes is 'saying nothing new' need not be confined to those '. . . who are strongly wedded to . . . the classical theory' (cf. *General Theory*, p. v). Like us, Keynes does not in any way deny the generality of orthodox equilibrium analysis; he only denies that orthodox economics provides an adequate account of disequilibrium phenomena.

10. J. R. Hicks (3), note to ch. 9, pp. 127ff. Also Patinkin (1) supplementary note B, pp. 377–85.

276

R. W. Clower

II The Keynesian Indictment of Orthodox Economics

Grounds for theoretical controversy first begin to emerge when we come to the stage in Keynes' argument (*General Theory*, chapter 2) at which he seeks to isolate specific instances in orthodox economics of 'lack of clearness and of generality' (*General Theory*, p. v).

The first item in his bill of particulars is embedded in a lengthy discussion of wage bargains between entrepreneurs and workers (*General Theory*, pp. 1–15). Outwardly, this item represents little more than a vigorous attack on orthodox preconceptions about the stability of a market economy. For the burden of his argument seems to be that if labour is ever forced to move 'off its supply curve' it may be unable to get back on again. If this is an accurate interpretation, we may say immediately that Keynes' criticisms are not of fundamental theoretical significance, for there is no reason to suppose that Keynes was more expert at stability analysis than his orthodox predecessors. However, the same argument might also be interpreted as a direct attack on the orthodox theory of household behaviour. This would certainly put labour off its supply curve and would also explain Keynes' categorical rejection of classical postulate II. But if this is what Keynes intended, i.e. to deny the validity of the orthodox theory of household behaviour, one can only say that he was singularly unsuccessful in providing a rationale for his attack.

The second item in Keynes' bill of particulars is essentially the same as the first: classical theory is charged with failure to recognize the existence of involuntary unemployment (*General Theory*, pp. 15–18). Again, the basic question is: Are 'involuntary unemployment' and 'chronic disequilibrium' synonymous terms for the same objective phenomenon, or is 'involuntary unemployment' a special kind of disequilibrium peculiarly associated with the breakdown of the orthodox theory of household behaviour? Here there is somewhat clearer evidence that Keynes believes his objections to orthodox analysis go very deep indeed:

> . . . if the classical theory is only applicable to the case of full employment, it is fallacious to apply it to the problems of involuntary unemployment – if there be such a thing (and who will deny it?). The classical theorists resemble Euclidean geometers in a non-Euclidean

Monetary Theory and Keynesian Economics

world who, discovering that in experience straight lines apparently parallel often meet, rebuke the lines for not keeping straight – as the only remedy for the unfortunate collisions which are occurring. Yet, in truth, there is no remedy except to throw over the axiom of parallels and to work out a non-Euclidean geometry. Something similar is required today in economics. We need to throw over the second postulate of the classical doctrine and to work out the behavior of a system in which involuntary unemployment in the strict sense is possible. (*General Theory*, pp. 16–17.)

Again, however, we are given no compelling theoretical reason to think that the proposed reconstruction of orthodox economics is really necessary.

The third and final item in Keynes' indictment is a denial of the relevance of Walras' law (*General Theory*, pp. 18–21). Most later writers (e.g. Ohlin, 4, p. 230, footnote; Goodwin, 9; Patinkin, 1, p. 249) have argued either that this portion of Keynes' indictment is wrong, or that the proposition which Keynes attacks is not in fact the one he thought he was attacking. Most economists have opted for the second explanation (10, especially p. 113),[11] partly in deference to Keynes' acknowledged intellectual powers, partly because they recognize that if Keynes seriously meant to question the validity or relevance of Walras' law, he would have to reject the orthodox theory of household behaviour and propose an acceptable alternative – and the alternative would have to include orthodox theory as a special case, valid under conditions of full employment. Walras' law is not, after all, an independent postulate of orthodox analysis; it is a theorem which is susceptible of direct proof on the basis of premises which are typically taken as given in contemporary as well as classical price theory.

III The Post-Keynesian Dilemma

The conclusion which I draw from all this may be put in one phrase: *either Walras' law is incompatible with Keynesian economics, or Keynes had nothing fundamentally new to add to orthodox economic theory.* This may seem an unnecessarily brutal way to confront one sacred cow with another. But what other conclusion is possible? In Keynes' mind, at least, the three items in his bill of

---

11. But see H. Rose's note on Walras' law and the reply by Patinkin (11, 12).

R. W. Clower

particulars 'all amount to the same thing in the sense that they all stand and fall together, any one of them logically involving the other two' (*General Theory*, p. 22). As we have already seen, he could hardly hold this view seriously unless he regarded each of the three items as an attack on the orthodox theory of household behaviour. But suppose that this is not in fact Keynes' view; suppose that Walras' law is both unreservedly valid, relevant and compatible with Keynesian economics. In this event, the recent literature on monetary theory makes it perfectly evident that Keynes may be subsumed as a special case of the Hicks–Lange–Patinkin theory of *tâtonnement* economics, which differs from orthodox theory only in being more detailed and precise. We would then have to conclude that Keynes added nothing fundamentally new to orthodox economic theory.

Thus, we are caught on the horns of a dilemma. If Keynes added nothing new to orthodox doctrine, why have twenty-five years of discussion failed to produce an integrated account of price theory and income analysis? If Keynes did add something new, the integration problem becomes explicable; but then we have to give up Walras' law as a fundamental principle of economic analysis. It is precisely at this point, I believe, that virtually all previous writers have decided to part company with Keynes. I propose to follow a different course. I shall argue that the established theory of household behaviour is, indeed, incompatible with Keynesian economics, that Keynes himself made tacit use of a more general theory, that this more general theory leads to market excess-demand functions which include quantities as well as prices as independent variables and, except in conditions of full employment, the excess-demand functions so defined do not satisfy Walras' law. In short, I shall argue that there has been a fundamental misunderstanding of the formal basis of the Keynesian revolution.

IV Disequilibrium Systems: A Preliminary View

Before attempting to deal directly with the issues raised above, we must say something more about the mechanics of disequilibrium states. In our earlier discussion of orthodox analysis, it was pointed out that the whole of traditional price theory rests on the

279

Monetary Theory and Keynesian Economics

tacit assumption that market excess demands are independent of current market transactions. This implies that *income magnitudes do not appear as independent variables in the demand or supply functions of a general equilibrium model*; for incomes are defined in terms of quantities as well as prices, and quantity variables never appear explicitly in the market excess-demand functions of traditional theory. To be sure, income variables could be introduced by taking factor supplies as given parameters; but this would preclude the formulation of a general equilibrium model containing supply functions of all marketable factor services.[12] The importance of these propositions for Keynesian economics can hardly be over-emphasized, for they imply directly that the Keynesian consumption function and other market relations involving income as an independent variable cannot be derived explicitly from any existing theory of general equilibrium.[13]

The most lucid account of the role which current transactions *might* play in general equilibrium theory has been presented by Professor Hicks in *Value and Capital* (3, pp. 119ff.). The following passages are especially significant in the present connexion (pp. 127–9):

Since, in general, traders cannot be expected to know just what total supplies are available on any market, nor what total demands will be forthcoming at particular prices, any price which is fixed initially can be only a guess. It is not probable that demand and supply will actually be found to be equated at such a guessed price; if they are not, then in

12. This was apparently overlooked by Patinkin when he formulated his 'general theory' of macroeconomics (*Money, Interest and Prices*, ch. 9). It is instructive to notice that this chapter is not supplemented by a mathematical appendix. Some of the consequences of this oversight are evident in the later discussion, see especially the argument beginning at p. 216, including the footnotes to pp. 218 and 220. I do not mean to suggest that authors may not put such variables as they please into their models. My point is that such variables as can be shown to be functionally dependent on others should not then be manipulated independently.

13. Cf. Lange, *Price Flexibility and Employment* (5, ch. 9, p. 53). Lange's usage of the phrase 'propensity to consume' is perfectly legitimate, but the concept invoked by him is not in any sense a consumption function of the sort Keynes worked with since, except on the Keynesian definition, it is not possible to talk about changes in consumption in response to changes in income without at the same time talking about changes in prices.

280

R. W. Clower

the course of trading the price will move up or down. Now if there is a change of price in the midst of trading, the situation appears to elude the ordinary apparatus of demand-and-supply analysis, for, strictly speaking, demand curves and supply curves give us the amounts which buyers and sellers will demand and supply respectively at any particular price, if that price is fixed at the start and adhered to throughout. Earlier writers, such as Walras and Edgeworth, had therefore supposed that demand-and-supply analysis ought strictly to be confined to such markets as permitted of 'recontract'; i.e. markets such that if a transaction was put through at a 'false' price . . . it could be revised when the equilibrium price was reached. Since such markets are highly exceptional, their solution of the problem (if it can be called one) was not very convincing.'

. . . in the general case . . . gains and losses due to false trading only give rise to income effects – effects, that is, which are the same kind as the income effects which may have to be considered even when we suppose equilibrium prices to be fixed straight away. We have seen again and again that a certain degree of indeterminateness is nearly always imparted by income effects to the laws of economic theory. All that happens as a result of false trading is that this indeterminateness is somewhat intensified. How much intensified depends, of course, upon the extent of the false trading; if very extensive transactions take place at prices very different from equilibrium prices, the disturbance will be serious. But I think we may reasonably suppose that the transactions which take place at *very false* prices are limited in volume. If any intelligence is shown in price-fixing, they will be.

It is heartening to know that income effects can be ignored if they are sufficiently unimportant to be neglected; but this is hardly a solution to the problem at issue. The essential question is whether the supply-and-demand functions of traditional analysis are in any way relevant to the formation of market prices in situations where disequilibrium transactions *cannot* be ignored.

To answer this question, we must first define explicit theoretical measures of disequilibrium transaction quantities. Perhaps the simplest way to define such measures is to suppose that actual transactions in any given market are always dominated by the 'short' side of the market; that is to say, market transactions are equal to planned market supply if demand is greater than supply, to planned market demand if supply is equal to or greater than demand (13, p. 203; 14; 1, pp. 157–8). This is, of course, the pro-

Monetary Theory and Keynesian Economics

cedure which has been followed by all previous writers, in so far as they have said anything at all on the subject.

Taken by itself, this addendum to traditional theory has no logical implications; but it opens the way for further analysis. For example, some writers have suggested the desirability of supposing that actual transactions exert a more or less direct influence on price adjustment via 'spillover' effects – changes in prevailing supply and demand conditions to reflect current discrepancies between planned and realized purchases and sales. The most recent expression of this view has been voiced by Patinkin (1, p. 157).[14] His suggestion is to redefine the usual price adjustment functions to make the rate of change of price in one market a function not of excess demand in that market alone, but also of excess demand in all other markets. That this is not an entirely satisfactory vehicle for expressing his basic views, however, is indicated by three considerations.

Firstly, it is not consistent with established preference analysis to suppose that transactors alter their sale and purchase plans before prevailing market prices have already varied in response to the pressure of excess demand somewhere in the economy. Secondly, the supposition that price movements in one market are governed by excess-demand conditions in all markets is logically equivalent to the supposition that individual traders respond not merely to absolute levels of prevailing prices but also to current rates of change of prices. This implies some basic changes in established preference analysis to allow prices as seen by transactors to differ from current market prices (17). Thirdly, from Walras' law (obviously applicable in this instance), the 'money' value of potential 'spillover' from any given market is measured by the aggregate 'money' value of the market excess supply of all other commodities. Thus, if 'spillover' effects from a given market are *fully* reflected in other markets, we are left with effective excess demand in the given market (and, by induction, in all other markets also) identically equal to zero; which is to say that prices never vary. Patinkin does not go to this extreme; he relies instead on a proposition of Samuelson (18, p. 42)[15] and

14. Also see Hansen (15) and Enthoven (16).

15. In fairness to Samuelson, it should be added that his discussion does not refer to spillover effects, but instead to what I have elsewhere called

R. W. Clower

supposes that 'spillover' effects in any given market are only partially reflected in transfers of demand to other markets. But this is simply *ad hoc* theorizing – inventing a solution to a problem which has actually been evaded rather than resolved.

A more promising way to bring current transactions into general equilibrium theory is by way of so-called stock-flow models. Unless we suppose that all commodities traded in the economy are highly perishable, it is clearly plausible to argue that goods will accumulate or decumulate (or both) somewhere in the economic system during periods of market disequilibrium. This forces us to consider possible extensions of traditional theory to deal explicitly with asset-holding phenomena.

There is now a reasonably adequate theoretical literature on this subject, including a number of recent papers on monetary theory and at least one important book on the theory of investment.[16] I think it fair to say, however, that this literature has made little impression on the profession at large; which is perhaps another way of remarking that the equilibrium properties of stock-flow models are essentially the same as those of traditional pure-flow models and that few economists are deeply concerned with anything else. Here, therefore, I shall merely observe that the explicit introduction of asset-holding phenomena into traditional theory entails a redefinition of market excess-demand functions to include asset as well as price arrays among the relevant independent variables and, along with this, an extension of the usual equation systems to include stock-adjustment functions. As a consequence, actual transaction quantities influence market adjustment indirectly, via their impact on existing asset stocks – which creates certain new sources of potential instability (24; 18,

---

'dynamical interdependence' among market excess-demand functions. See Bushaw and Clower (19, ch. 4, pp. 82ff.).

16. Vernon L. Smith, *Investment and Production* (20). This book includes a comprehensive bibliography on the 'real' part of the stock-flow literature. For further details of the 'monetary' part, see George Horwich, 'Money, prices and the theory of interest determination' (21). The latest in this series is the article by Archibald and Lipsey (22, October 1958), the related 'Symposium on monetary theory' (22, October 1960), and Baumol's 'Stocks, flows and monetary theory' (23). The general theory underlying such models is developed at perhaps excessive length in Bushaw and Clower (19).

Monetary Theory and Keynesian Economics

pp. 170–71). Even in this type of model, however, current transactions exercise an influence only after a certain time delay. As in more usual general equilibrium models, therefore, current incomes never appear as independent variables. Thus, this potential road to the *General Theory* also turns out to be a blind alley.

The preceding discussion probably does not exhaust the list of possible ways of introducing current transactions into excess-demand functions, but we have now gone far enough to appreciate that the problem is by no means so transparent as some writers might have us believe. At this point, therefore, let us return to the route which Keynes apparently travelled before us.

V Say's Principle and Walras' Law

In our earlier account of the theory of household behaviour, we did not distinguish between planned and realized magnitudes because to have done so would not in fact have been a meaningful procedure in the context of orthodox equilibrium analysis. However, if we adopt the view that states of transactor disequilibrium are, in principle, just as admissible as states of transactor equilibrium (and how can we do otherwise?) (1, pp. 237–8; 14, pp. 318ff.), the distinction between plans and realizations becomes both meaningful and theoretically relevant. In the discussion that follows, we shall adopt just this point of view; accordingly, we shall henceforth interpret boldface symbols **d**, **s** and **r** as realized or actual magnitudes (hence, given parameters from the standpoint of individual transactors); planned or notional magnitudes will be denoted, as before, by such symbols as d, $\check{s}$, r, etc.

For any individual household (here, we are informally modifying our discussion to recognize that the household sector comprises a multitude of independent decision units), we may clearly assume that the realized *numéraire* value of actual purchases during any given interval of time is identically equal to the aggregate *numéraire* value of realized sales and realized profit receipts during the same interval:

$$\sum_{k=1}^{n} \mathbf{p}_k[\mathbf{d}_k - \mathbf{s}_k] - \mathbf{r} \equiv 0. \qquad\qquad 5$$

R. W. Clower

Indeed, this is just a tacit definition of the concept of a transactor, since what it asserts is that commodities are acquired through market exchange rather than theft, gifts, heavenly favours, etc. The familiar household budget constraint, although similar in form to the truism, equation 5, asserts the rather different proposition that no transactor consciously *plans* to purchase units of any commodity without at the same time *planning* to finance the purchase either from profit receipts or from the sale of units of some other commodity. For later reference, I shall call the last and very general proposition *Say's principle*. This is essentially a rational planning postulate, not a book-keeping identity nor a technical relation. Unlike the market principle known as Walras' law, moreover, Say's principle does not depend on the tacit assumption that values are calculated in terms of current market prices, or on the equally tacit assumption that market prices are independent of individual purchases and sales. Neither does it presuppose that individual behaviour is in any sense optimal. Thus, Say's principle may indeed be regarded as a fundamental convention of economic science, akin in all relevant respects to such basic ideas of physical science as the second law of thermodynamics. Say's principle is not true in the nature of things; but unless we presuppose something of the sort, we have absolutely nothing upon which to build an account of individual decision processes.

Suppose now that we carry through the usual utility maximization procedure to arrive at household demand and supply functions, $\bar{d}_i(\mathbf{P}, \mathbf{r})$, $\bar{s}_j(\mathbf{P}, \mathbf{r})$, interpreting Say's principle to mean what it usually means in this context, namely,

$$\sum_i^m \mathbf{p}_i\, d_i - \sum_j^n \mathbf{p}_j\, s_j - \mathbf{r} = 0.$$

Must we then assert that any reasonable definition of market demand and supply magnitudes will necessarily make use of the functions $\bar{d}_i$, $\bar{s}_j$ so defined? Not necessarily, for the definition of these functions tacitly presupposes something more than Say's principle, namely, that every household expects to be able to buy or sell any desired quantity of each and every commodity at prevailing market prices (24, p. 232ff.).

Now, the rationale of the last presupposition is hardly self-

Monetary Theory and Keynesian Economics

evident. Keynes has been scoffed at on more than one occasion for his dichotomized account of spending and saving decisions (see *General Theory*, p. 166). As far as I can see, the only reason for making humorous comments about this view is that established preference analysis tacitly presupposes that selling, buying and saving plans are all carried out simultaneously. But what if one does not happen to consider the presuppositions of established preference analysis, tacit or otherwise, to be the final word on this subject? (25, 26.) I suggest that the question will bear further examination.

The notion that all household decision are accomplished at a single stroke seems to be an analytically convenient and intuitively plausible procedure as long as we consider each household to be an isolated performer of conceptual experiments. When households are considered to be part of a connected market system, however, the same notion assumes a rather different aspect. What is then presupposed about planned sales and purchases cannot possibly be true of realized sales and purchases, unless the system as a whole is always in a state of equilibrium; that is to say, not every household can buy and sell just what it pleases if supply exceeds demand somewhere in the economy. Do we nevertheless suppose that the facts of life never intrude upon the thought experiments of households?

The answer to this is, I think, that the matter is not of much theoretical significance if, as is usually true when we deal with competitive supply-and-demand models, we are primarily interested in comparative-statics propositions. In this event, differences between realized and planned purchases and sales of individual households may properly be supposed to occur more or less at random. If we entertain the notion of developing market models that will have practical application to situations of chronic disequilibrium, however, we must surely question the universal relevance of the 'unified decision' hypothesis and, by the same token, question whether the usual household supply and demand functions provide relevant market signals.

286

R. W. Clower

VI The Dual-Decision Hypothesis

For the moment, let us imagine ourselves to be involuntarily unemployed in the sense of Keynes. Specifically, imagine that we have a strong wish to satisfy our champagne appetites but that the demand for our services as economic consultants does not in fact allow us to gratify this desire without doing serious damage to our household finances. How do we communicate our thirstiness to producers of champagne; how can they be made aware of our willingness to solve their market research problems in exchange for copious quantities of their excellent beverage?

The answer is that we do so indirectly. We offer more favourable terms to potential buyers of our services (these may include some champagne merchants), leaving it to the market to provide us more employment and income and, in due time, more booze. Do we also signal our craving directly by drawing on money balances and savings accounts and sending our children out to work? In short, do we drink more even before we work more? Or do we become, at least temporarily, involuntarily abstemious and postpone our satisfaction to financially more propitious times? Clearly, this is to pose the question in a highly misleading way, for the issue is not, 'Which do we do?', but 'How much do we do of each?'

But if even this much is granted, we thereby affirm that the demand functions of orthodox theory do not provide relevant market signals. For if realized current receipts are considered to impose any kind of constraint on current consumption plans, planned consumption as expressed in effective market offers to buy will necessarily be less than desired consumption as given by the demand functions of orthodox analysis.

A formal statement of the problem will clarify matters at this point. Following the usual procedure of traditional theory, suppose that the preference function $U(d_1, \ldots, d_m; s_{m+1}, \ldots, s_n)$ is maximized subject to the budget constraint

$$\sum_{i}^{m} \mathbf{p}_i \, d_i - \sum^{n} \mathbf{p}_j \, s_j - \mathbf{r} = 0,$$

and the resulting first-order conditions are used to define the notional demand and supply functions $\bar{d}_i(\mathbf{p}, \mathbf{r})$ and $\bar{s}_j(\mathbf{p}, \mathbf{r})$.

287

Monetary Theory and Keynesian Economics

Provided that realized current income is not less than notional current income, i.e. provided

$$\sum_{j}^{n} \mathbf{p}_j \, \mathbf{s}_j \geqslant \sum_{j}^{n} \mathbf{p}_j \, \bar{s}_j,$$

we may suppose that the functions $\bar{d}_i$ and $\bar{s}_j$ constitute relevant market signalling devices. For this is just to say that current income receipts do not impose an operative constraint on household spending decisions.[17]

In the contrary case, however, i.e. if

$$\sum_{j}^{n} \mathbf{p}_j \, \mathbf{s}_j < \sum_{j}^{n} \mathbf{p}_j \, \bar{s}_j,$$

a second round of decision making is indicated: namely, maximize

$$U(d_1, \ldots, d_m; s_{m+1}, \ldots, s_n),$$

subject to the modified budget constraint

$$\sum_{i}^{m} \mathbf{p}_i \, d_i - \sum_{j}^{n} \mathbf{p}_j \, \mathbf{s}_j - \mathbf{r} = 0.$$

Solving this problem, we obtain a set of *constrained* demand functions,

$$\hat{d}_i(\mathbf{P}, \mathbf{Y}) \quad (i = 1, \ldots, m),$$

where, by definition,

$$\mathbf{Y} \equiv \sum_{j}^{n} \mathbf{p}_j \, \mathbf{s}_j + \mathbf{r}.$$

The values of the constrained functions, $\hat{d}_i$, will then be equal to those of the corresponding notional functions, $\bar{d}_i$, if and only if $\sum_{j}^{n} \mathbf{p}_j (\mathbf{s}_j - \bar{s}_j) = 0$. Except in this singular case,[18] however, the

17. More generally, we might argue that an excess of current income over desired income does affect current expenditure directly; compulsory overtime might be considered a case in point. But we shall not deal with situations of that kind here. In effect, we suppose that individuals are never forced to sell more factor services than they want to sell, though they may be forced for lack of buyers to sell less than they desire.

18. The constrained demand functions are not even defined, of course, when realized income *exceeds* desired income.

R. W. Clower

constrained demand functions $\hat{d}_i(\mathbf{P}, \mathbf{Y})$ and the notional supply functions $\hat{s}_j(\mathbf{P}, \mathbf{r})$, rather than the notional functions $\bar{d}_i$ and $\bar{s}_j$, are the relevant providers of market signals.

Here and elsewhere in the argument, it may be helpful if the reader imagines that a central 'market authority' is responsible for setting all prices (using the nth commodity as an accounting unit), and that this 'authority' maintains continual surveillance over all sale and purchase orders communicated to it by individual transactors to ensure that no purchase order is 'validated' unless it is offset by a sale order that has already been executed (i.e. purchase orders are simply 'cancelled' unless the transactor has a positive balance of 'book credit' with the market authority sufficient to cover the entire value of the purchase order). It must be assumed that the market authority communicates continuously with each transactor to inform it of the precise level of its current credit balance, and further informs each transactor of the precise rate at which previously validated purchase orders currently are being executed. Sale orders are 'validated' automatically, but the rate at which such orders are executed is governed by prevailing demand conditions. It is implicit in this entire line of argument that, at some 'initial' stage in the evolution of market trading arrangements, the market authority advances a nominal quantity of book credit to one or more transactors to set the trading process in motion (without such initial advances, no sale order could ever be executed since no purchase order would ever be validated).

Established preference analysis thus appears as a special case – valid in conditions of full employment – of the present *dual-decision theory*. Considered from this point of view, the other side of involuntary unemployment would seem to be involuntary under-consumption, which should have considerable intuitive appeal to those of us who really do have unsatisfied champagne appetites.

It is worth remarking explicitly that *the dual-decision hypothesis does not in any way flout Say's principle*. It would be more accurate to say that this hypothesis assigns greater force to the principle by recognizing that current income flows may impose an independent restriction on effective demand, separate from those already imposed by prevailing market prices and current

Monetary Theory and Keynesian Economics

transfer receipts. Indeed, it is this theory which is invariably presented in geometrical classroom expositions of the theory of consumer behaviour. It is only in mathematical versions of preference analysis that we lose sight of realized current income as an operative constraint on effective demand.

It is another question whether Keynes can reasonably be considered to have had a dual-decision theory of household behaviour at the back of his mind when he wrote the *General Theory*. For my part, I do not think there can be any serious doubt that he did, although I can find no direct evidence in any of his writings to show that he ever thought explicitly in these terms. But indirect evidence is available in almost unlimited quantity: in his treatment of the orthodox theory of household behaviour, his repeated discussions of 'Say's law', his development of the consumption function concept, his account of interest theory, and his discussions of wage and price determination. It is also significant, I believe, that a year after the appearance of the *General Theory*, Keynes' own evaluation of the theoretical significance of the consumption function concept still differed sharply from that of his reviewers (28):

This psychological law was of the utmost importance in the development of my own thought, and it is, I think, absolutely fundamental to the theory of effective demand as set forth in my book. But few critics or commentators so far have paid particular attention to it.

Finally, it is important to notice that unless the orthodox approach to household behaviour is modified (tacitly if not explicitly) to recognize the dual-decision hypothesis, the Keynesian notion of an aggregate consumption function does not make sense, the distinction between transactions and speculative balances is essentially meaningless, the liquidity-preference theory of interest is indistinguishable from the classical theory of loanable funds, fluctuations in the demand for physical assets cannot be supposed to have more impact on output and employment than fluctuations in the demand for securities, and excess supply in the labour market does not diminish effective excess demand elsewhere in the economy. In short, Keynes either had a dual-decision hypothesis at the back of his mind, or most of the *General Theory* is theoretical nonsense.

290

R. W. Clower

VII From the Classics to Keynes

We remarked above that the dual-decision hypothesis already
has an established position in the oral tradition of established
preference analysis. We have also argued that it plays an important (if tacit) role in income analysis. Thus, it is only when we
turn to contemporary general equilibrium theory that no trace of
the hypothesis is anywhere to be found. Yet it is precisely in this
area that the dual decision approach is most clearly relevant – and
most damaging to orthodoxy.

Referring to our previous account of traditional analysis (Part
I, above), we recall that the business sector supply and demand
functions may, from a market point of view, be so defined as to
depend solely on the price vector **P**, permitting us to write
Walras' law in the form

$$\sum_i^m \mathbf{p}_i[\bar{d}_i(\mathbf{P}) - \bar{s}_i(\mathbf{P})] + \sum_j^n \mathbf{p}_j[\bar{d}_j(\mathbf{P}) - \bar{s}_j(\mathbf{P})] \equiv 0.^{19}$$

In the context of the present discussion, the most interesting
implication of Walras' law is obtained by calling the commodities
$1, \ldots, m$ 'goods' and the commodities $m + 1, \ldots, n$ 'factors'.
We may then assert that excess supply of factors necessarily
implies the simultaneous existence of excess demand for goods.
More generally, we may assert that in any disequilibrium situation, there is always an element of excess demand working directly
on the price system to offset prevailing elements of excess supply.

According to the dual-decision hypothesis, however, the market
relevance of the household functions $\bar{d}_i(\mathbf{P})$ and $\bar{s}_j(\mathbf{P})$ is contingent
on the satisfaction of the condition that realized current income
be not less than planned income.[20] Suppose, however, that

$$\sum_j^n \mathbf{p}_j[\bar{d}_j - \bar{s}_j] < 0;$$

19. Cf. equation **4**, above.

20. Profit receipts do not concern us since we are still proceeding on the
assumption that the condition $\mathbf{r} = \bar{r}$ is satisfied (this is no longer essential to
the argument, but is very convenient). What we are supposing, in effect, is
that household receivers of profit income have perfect information about
profit prospects (they may even be producer-consumers) and react to this
information precisely as if corresponding amounts of *numéraire* profit
were actually being received.

Monetary Theory and Keynesian Economics

i.e. suppose that notational aggregate demand for factors is less than aggregate supply (in the sense indicated). Then involuntary unemployment may be said to exist since realized factor income cannot exceed the aggregate money value of planned demand for factor inputs, that is to say,

$$\sum_{j}^{n} \mathbf{p}_j[\bar{d}_j - \mathbf{s}_j] \geq 0.$$

In this situation, the dual-decision hypothesis requires that we replace the usual household demand functions, $\bar{d}_i$, by the constrained demand functions $\hat{d}_i(\mathbf{P}, \mathbf{Y})$, which, by definition, satisfy the condition

$$\sum_{i}^{m} \mathbf{p}_i \bar{d}_i(\mathbf{P}) \geq \sum_{i}^{m} \mathbf{p}_i \hat{d}_i \,(\mathbf{P}, \mathbf{Y});$$

i.e. the aggregate money value of constrained demand for goods is at most equal to the aggregate money value of planned demand for goods in the sense of traditional preference analysis. It follows immediately that, in a state of involuntary unemployment, Walras' law must be replaced by the more general condition

$$\sum_{i}^{m} \mathbf{p}_i[\hat{d}_i(\mathbf{P}, \mathbf{Y}) - \bar{s}_i(P)] + \sum_{i}^{n} \mathbf{p}_j[\bar{d}_j(P) - \bar{s}_j(P)] \leq 0;$$

i.e. *the sum of all market excess demands, valued at prevailing market prices, is at most equal to zero.* Indeed, since the equality sign applies with certainty only in the absence of factor excess supply, the dual-decision hypothesis effectively implies that Walras' law, although valid as usual with reference to *notional* market excess demands, is in general irrelevant to any but full employment situations. *Contrary to the findings of traditional theory, excess demand may fail to appear anywhere in the economy under conditions of less than full employment.*

The common sense of the preceding analysis may be clarified by a simple geometrical illustration. Let the curve T in the accompanying figure represent the business sector transformation function, let U_1 and U_2 represent alternative household sector indifference curves, and let $L(\mathbf{p}_f/\mathbf{p}_g)$ represent, simultaneously, the profit function of firms and the budget constraint of households. In the situation illustrated, the real wage at time t, $\mathbf{p}_f/\mathbf{p}_g$, is such

292

R. W. Clower

that $\bar{s}_f > \bar{d}_f$; hence, factors are in excess supply. Moreover, since $\bar{d}_g > \hat{s}_g$, goods are simultaneously in a state of notional excess demand. If the real wage rate is assumed to vary inversely with notional excess demand for goods (as is assumed to be the case in orthodox analysis), $\mathbf{p}_f/\mathbf{p}_g$ will tend to fall over time at time t, and the system may therefore be said to tend towards full employment (defined by reference to the point $(\bar{N}, \bar{G})$). However, if the real wage rate is assumed to vary inversely with 'effective' excess

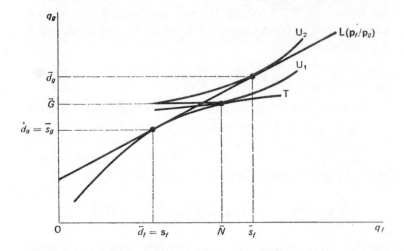

Figure 1

demand for goods, no adjustment of the real wage rate will tend to occur at time t since, as indicated, constrained demand for goods, $\hat{d}_g$, is equal to planned supply of goods at prevailing price and income levels.[21]

This illustration of how effective excess demand may be insufficient to induce price adjustment, despite the obvious sufficiency of notional excess demand, says nothing, of course, about the stability of full employment equilibrium under alternative adjustment hypotheses. For example, if the real wage rate varies in response *either* to constrained excess demand for goods *or* excess demand for factors, then in the situation illustrated the system

21. Compare Keynes' discussion of the same model, *General Theory* (7, p. 261).

Monetary Theory and Keynesian Economics

may still tend towards full employment equilibrium. The point of the example is merely to illustrate that, *when income appears as an independent variable in the market excess-demand functions – more generally, when transactions quantities enter into the definition of these functions – traditional price theory ceases to shed any light on the dynamic stability of a market economy.*[22]

This line of analysis might be carried a good deal further; but I think enough has been said to justify such conclusions as are germane to the present argument:

Firstly, orthodox price theory may be regarded as a special case of Keynesian economics, valid only in conditions of full employment.

Secondly, an essential formal difference between Keynesian and orthodox economics is that market excess demands are in general assumed to depend on current market transactions in the former, to be independent of current market transactions in the latter. This difference depends, in turn, on Keynes' tacit use of a dual-decision theory of household behaviour and his consequent rejection of Walras' law as a relevant principle of economic analysis.

Thirdly, chronic factor unemployment at substantially unchanging levels of real income and output may be consistent with Keynesian economics even if all prices are flexible; this problem has yet to be investigated within the context of a Keynesian model of market price formation.

22. In an unpublished article 'A Keynesian market equilibrium model', my colleague Mitchell Harwitz considers a more general version of the rigid wages case with results that go far to anticipate the dual-decision hypothesis on which the present argument places so much weight. The following passage (Harwitz, p. 40), is particularly significant:

Suppose one market is permanently restrained from full adjustment. What does this mean in terms of the individual participants in the market? *It means that some or all of them face a binding constraint in addition to the budget constraint.* For concreteness, consider the Keynesian labour market. A worker, faced with a certain real wage, can sell *less* labour than is consistent with the usual constrained maximum. In effect, he is in equilibrium, but at a boundary [position] imposed by a quantity constraint on the labour he can sell. . . . It must be granted that these positions are equilibria by our definition; but their stability is a more delicate question. . . . A complete answer would require a theory of the dynamical behaviour of economic units both in and out of equilibrium.

294

R. W. Clower

VIII Conclusion

My original intention in writing this paper was simply to clarify the formal basis of the Keynesian revolution and its relation to orthodox thought. This I think I have done. In a line, Keynesian economics brings current transactions into price theory whereas traditional analysis explicitly leaves them out. Alternatively, we may say that Keynesian economics is price theory without Walras' law,[23] and price theory with Walras' law is just a special case of Keynesian economics. The bearing of my argument on the Keynesian counter-revolution is correspondingly plain: contemporary general equilibrium theories can be maintained intact only if we are willing to barter Keynes for orthodoxy.

This is not the end of the matter, for there is a choice to be made. No one can deny that general equilibrium analysis, as presently constituted, is a useful instrument for thinking about abstract economic problems, and this would hardly be so if it did not omit many realistic frills. The danger in using this instrument to think about practical problems is that, having schooled ourselves so thoroughly in the virtues of elegant simplicity, we may refuse to recognize the crucial relevance of complications that do not fit our theoretical preconceptions. As Keynes has put it, 'The difficulty lies, not in the new ideas, but in escaping from the old ones, which ramify, for those brought up as most of us have been, into every corner of our minds' (*General Theory*, p. viii).

I shall be the last one to suggest that abstract theory is useless; that simply is not so. At the same time, I am convinced that much of what now passes for useful theory is not only worthless economics (and mathematics), but also a positive hindrance to fruitful

23. It is vacuously true, of course, that a proposition similar to Walras' law holds even in Keynesian economics if we *define* the difference between desired sales and realized sales as an excess demand for 'money income'. But the proposition then becomes an empirically meaningless tautology. In conventional value theory, the total value of commodities (goods and money) offered for sale is always equal to the total value of commodities (goods and money) demanded for purchase because all purchase orders are presumed to be effective regardless of prevailing demand-and-supply conditions. But in the present discussion, purchase orders are not validated automatically, sale orders thus do not necessarily generate effective demand for other commodities (effective demands are constrained by purchase orders *executed*, not purchase orders *placed*).

295

Monetary Theory and Keynesian Economics

theoretical and empirical research. Most importantly, however, I am impressed by the worth of Keynesian economics as a guide to practical action, which is in such sharp contrast to the situation of general price theory. As physicists should and would have rejected Einstein's theory of relativity, had it not included Newtonian mechanics as a special case, so we would do well to think twice before accepting as 'useful' or 'general', doctrines which are incapable of accommodating Keynesian economics.

References

1. D. PATINKIN, *Money, Interest and Prices*, Row Peterson, 1956.
2. J. R. HICKS, 'Mr Keynes and the Classics: a suggested interpretation', *Econometrica*, vol. 5, 1937, no. 2, pp. 147–59.
3. J. R. HICKS, *Value and Capital*, Clarendon Press, 1939.
4. B. OHLIN, 'Some notes on the Stockholm theory of savings and investment', *Economic Journal*, vol. 47, 1937, pp. 53–69, 221–40.
5. O. LANGE, *Price Flexibility and Employment*, Principia, 1944.
6. F. MODIGLIANI, 'Liquidity preference and the theory of interest and money', *Econometrica*, vol. 12, 1944, pp. 45–88.
7. J. M. KEYNES, *The General Theory of Employment, Interest and Money*, Harcourt Brace, 1935, pp. v ff.
8. O. LANGE, 'Say's law: a restatement and criticism', *Studies in Mathematical Economics and Econometrics*, edited by Lange, McIntyre and Yntema, University of Chicago Press, 1942, pp. 49–68.
9. R. M. GOODWIN, 'The multiplier as matrix', *Economic Journal*, vol. 59, 1949, pp. 537–55.
10. H. ROSE, 'Liquidity preference and loanable funds', *Review of Economic Studies*, vol. 24, February 1957, pp. 111–19.
11. H. ROSE, 'The rate of interest and Walras' law', *Economica*, vol. 26, 1959, pp. 252–3.
12. D. PATINKIN, 'Reply to R. W. Clower and H. Rose', *Economica*, vol. 26, 1959, pp. 253–5.
13. L. R. KLEIN, *The Keynesian Revolution*, Macmillan, 1952.
14. R. W. CLOWER, 'Keynes and the classics: a dynamical perspective', *Quarterly Journal of Economics*, vol. 74, 1960, pp. 318–20.
15. B. HANSEN, *A Study in the Theory of Inflation*, Allen & Unwin, 1951.
16. A. C. ENTHOVEN, 'Monetary disequilibrium and the dynamics of inflation', *Economic Journal*, vol. 66, 1956, pp. 256–70.
17. F. H. HAHN, 'The Patinkin controversy', *Review of Economic Studies*, vol. 28, October 1960, p. 42, n.l.
18. P. A. SAMUELSON, *Foundations of Economic Analysis*, Harvard University Press, 1947.
19. D. W. BUSHAW and R. W. CLOWER, *Introduction to Mathematical Economics*, Irwin, 1957.
20. V. L. SMITH, *Investment and Production*, Harvard University Press, 1961.

R. W. Clower

21. G. HORWICH, 'Money, prices and the theory of interest determination', *Economic Journal*, vol. 67, 1957, pp. 625–43.
22. G. C. ARCHIBALD and R. G. LIPSEY, 'Monetary and value theory: a critique of Lange and Patinkin', *Review of Economic Studies*, vol. 26, October 1958, pp. 1–22, and 'Symposium on monetary theory', vol. 28, October 1960, pp. 50–56.
23. W. J. BAUMOL, 'Stocks, flows and monetary theory', *Quarterly Journal of Economics*, vol. 76, February 1962, pp. 46–56.
24. T. NEGISHI, 'General equilibrium models of market clearing processes in a monetary economy', *The Theory of Interest Rates*, Macmillan, 1965.
25. W. J. BAUMOL, *Economic Theory and Operations Analysis*, Prentice-Hall, 1961.
26. R. H. STROTZ, 'The empirical implications of a utility tree', *Econometrica*, vol. 25, April 1957, pp. 269–80.
27. I. F. PEARCE, 'A method of consumer demand analysis illustrated', *Economica*, vol. 28, November 1961, pp. 371–94.
28. J. M. KEYNES, 'The general theory of employment', *Quarterly Journal of Economics*, vol. 51, February 1937, pp. 209–23.

[16]

INFORMATION COSTS, PRICING, AND RESOURCE UNEMPLOYMENT

ARMEN A. ALCHIAN*
UNIVERSITY OF CALIFORNIA, LOS ANGELES

Economic theory of exchange often appears to imply that demand changes induce instant wage and price adjustments to maintain full resource use. But unemployment, queues, rationing, and idle resources refute any such implication. And macroeconomic theory does not explain why demand decreases cause unemployment rather than immediate wage and price adjustments in labor *and* nonhuman resources. Instead, administered prices, monopolies, minimum wage laws, union restrictions, and "natural" inflexibilities of wages and prices are invoked.

This paper attempts to show that economic theory is capable of being formulated—consistently with each person acting as an individual utility, or wealth, maximizer without constraints imposed by competitors, and without conventions or taboos about wages or prices—so as to imply shortages, surpluses, unemployment, queues, idle resources, and nonprice rationing with price stability. The theory implies massive correlated fluctuations in employment of both labor and capital in response to aggregate demand decreases—in a context of open market, individual utility maximizing behavior. The theory is general in that it applies to nonhuman goods as well as to human services. Though my primary motivation to explain "unemployed" resources arose from labor market behavior, the analysis is best exposited initially without special reference to labor markets.

The key, which, till recently, seems to have been forgotten, is that *collating information about potential exchange opportunities* is costly and can be performed in various ways.[1] Nobody knows as much as he would like (at zero cost) about everyone else's offers and demands (including the properties of goods offered or demanded), but at a cost, more information can be acquired. Two questions guide our analysis. First, what are the means of providing information more efficiently? Second, given that information is costly, what kinds of substitute arrangements are used to economize on search costs?

1. THEORY OF EXCHANGE, UNEMPLOYMENT, AND PRICE STABILITY

In equilibrium everyone has equal marginal rates of substitution, but how is that equilibrium equality approached? It is not rational to expect a person to exchange with the first person he happens to meet with a different subjective

*Acknowledgement for substantial aid is made to the Lilly Endowment, Inc., grant to UCLA for a study in the behavioral effects of different kinds of property rights.

[1]A study of Stigler [28] will reveal this paper to be a development and application of the fundamentals of that paper. See also, for earlier interest in this problem, Rees [21] [22]. Arrow and Capron [2] used the difficulty of knowing the true market demand and supply as a reason for individual delays in adapting to the equilibrating price and output.

[109] value. It will pay to seek a higher "bid" or a lower "ask". Discovery of the variety of bids and offers and the best path or sequence of actual exchange prices toward an "equilibrium" requires costly search over the population. Institutions facilitate and economize on that search. The marketplace is an example. A large and costly portion of so-called marketing activity is information dissemination. Advertisements, window displays, sales clerks, specialist agents, brokers, inventories, catalogs, correspondence, phone calls, market research agencies, employment agencies, licensing, certification, aptitude testing services (to name a few) facilitate the spread and acquisition of knowledge about potential demanders and suppliers and their goods and about prices they can expect to see prevail.

Marketing includes many activities: (a) "extensive" searching for all possible buyers or sellers; (b) communication of information about characteristics of the goods of each party—the "intensive" search;[2] (c) contract information; (d) contract enforcement; (e) "buffer inventories" by sellers; (f) queueing of buyers, and (g) provision of price predictability. Two propositions about the costs of production or market opportunity information will be critical in the ensuing analysis.

(1) *Dissemination and acquisition (i.e., the production) of information conforms to the ordinary laws of costs of production—viz., faster dissemination or acquisition costs more.* A simple, fruitful characterization of the search for information is sampling from a distribution of "offers" (or "bids") with some mean and dispersion. As the sample is enlarged, the observed maximum value will increase *on the average* at a *diminishing* rate. Assuming search (sampling) at a constant rate, with time thereby measuring size of sample, the expected (mathematical expectation of the) maximum observed value will rise from the median at a diminishing rate toward the upper limit of the distribution.[3] That limit will exceed the past actual price, since there is no necessity for the past sale to have been negotiated at the highest possible price (with exhaustive prior sampling, regardless of cost).

(2) *Like any other production activity, specialization in information is efficient. Gathering and disseminating information about goods or about oneself is in some circumstances more efficiently done while the good or person is not employed, and thus able to specialize (i.e., while specializing) in the production of information.* If seeking information about other jobs while employed is

---

[2] This terminology is taken from Rees [21].

[3] For example, if potential prices are normally distributed with mean, m, and with variance, σ^2, then the expected maximum observed bid $W(n)$ at the n-th observation is approximately $m + \sigma(2 \log n)^{\frac{1}{2}}$. $W(n)$ starts at m and increases at a decreasing rate with n. If we assume one observation every λ units of time, then we can replace n by λt, and obtain W as a function of time of search.

$$W(t) = m + \sigma(2 \log \lambda t)^{\frac{1}{2}}$$

Further, if we increase expenditures on search, the rate of search can be increased per unit time, whatever is the environment of search; in other words, the effective λ is a function of the environment, V, and of the expenditures on search $E(t)$: $\lambda = f[V, E(t)]$. A larger expenditure implies a larger λ and if we let a larger V denote a more costly search environment, then a larger V implies a smaller λ.

[110] more costly than while not employed, it can be economic to refuse a wage cut, become unemployed, and look for job information.[4] The deeper the wage cut in the old job, the cheaper the choice of unemployment in order to ferret information. Without this proposition of *differential* search costs, the theory would not be able, consistently with wealth maximizing choices, to account for the fact that some people refuse to accept a low wage while acquiring and comparing job information.

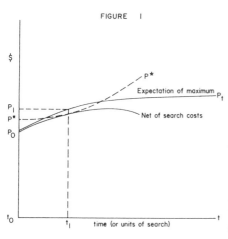

FIGURE I

The fact that being employed is itself a recommendation to a prospective employer does not deny that it may pay to foresake that recommendation in view of the large wage cut required to obtain it. The value of such a recommendation would imply acceptance of greater wage cuts to keep jobs. However, the question here is why anyone would choose to foresake that lower wage and accept unemployment—not why wages are sometimes cut to hold jobs.

Our choice of words is deliberate when speaking of seeking "job information" rather than seeking "jobs." Jobs are always easily available. Timely information about the pay, working conditions, and life expectancy of all available jobs is not cheap. In a sense, *this* kind of unemployment is self-employment in information collection.

This applies to nonhuman resources as well. For example, the automobile on a used car lot—out of "normal" service (unemployed)—facilitates cheaper information to potential buyers. Similarly, unoccupied apartments and houses (like cars and people) are cheaper to show to prospective clients.[5]

A graph of some characteristics of search and its costs is shown in Figure 1. Time is on the horizontal scale and price or wage on the vertical. For any constant rate of search over the population of potential buyers, time and scope of search can both be measured on the horizontal scale. If some good were sold to the first found offerer at t_0, the price would be P_0. The height of curve P_0P_t is the "expectation" of the maximum discerned available [111] contract price found by time t—assuming discerned options do not disappear

[4]This proposition is added to those contained in Stigler and is crucial to much that follows.

[5]We can now identify a "perfect" market—one in which all potential bids and offers are known at zero cost to every other person, and in which contract enforcement costs are zero. Characteristics of every good need to be known perfectly at zero cost. A "perfect" market would imply a "perfect" world in which all costs of production, even of "exchanges," were zero. It is curious that while we economists never formalize our analysis on the basis of an analytical ideal of a perfect world (in the sense of costless production) we have postulated costless *information* as a formal ideal for analysis. Why?

or decay with time. The line rises at a decreasing rate, rather than being horizontal at P_t, as it would be if information about all potential offers were costless (and if all people knew all the characteristics of the good). As the sample (information) increases the expected maximum discerned available price increases by successively smaller increments. In terms of costs, there are increasing marginal costs of unit increments of expected maximum ascertained price.[6] The curve for an unemployed searcher will be above that for an employed searcher—if unemployment is to occur. By identifying characteristics that will affect the shape and position of the curves we can reduce unemployment patterns.

Liquidity. The analogy to liquidity is obvious. Liquidity concepts can be portrayed by the same diagram. The ratio of P^* to P_t is one dimension of the liquidity *vector*. Another, for example, is the time to t_1.

The expectation of discerned maximum offers is a function of amount of expenditures (of all type) for acquiring information up to any moment. A potential (expected maximum discerned) *gross* price will be higher, as of any time t, if more is spent on hastening the information-acquiring process. The seller nets a reward equal to P_1 minus *his* search costs, and the buyer pays P_1 plus his search costs. A perfectly liquid asset is one for which P_0P_t is horizontal at height P_t with no search costs. Money is typically regarded as a resource fulfilling these criteria.[7] It enters into almost every exchange because it provides the most economical vehicle of exchange.

Brokers and Middlemen. The P_0P_t curve reveals an opportunity for exchange with an intermediary broker. Since this analysis is applicable to nonhuman goods as well as to labor, it will be profitable for a "middleman" or "broker" to offer at the initial moment, t_0, a price higher than P_0, if he believes the discerned resale value of the good (net of *his* search costs) will increase at a rate greater than the interest rate and greater than that of the existing possesser of the good. The price he would offer at t_0 would be, at most, the present value of the expected maximum discerned bid price for the time his discerned price line (*net* of *his* search costs) was rising at a rate equal to the interest rate. This can be illustrated by inserting an "iso-net-present value" curve P^*P^*, the height of which *at the vertical* axis ($t = 0$) shows the maximum *present net* discounted value as of t_0 of any future net amount available (net of the *middleman's* search costs). The price that would be offered now by the middleman is P^*. The difference between the present-value price P^*, and the future selling price, P_1, is essentially the retail-wholesale price spread, or the bid-ask spread of brokers, wholesalers or retailers. Since the middleman is a successful specialist in search, his search costs are, by definition, lower, and hence his P^* is higher than for a nonmiddleman, nonspecialist [5].

[112]   *Price Stability: Economizing on Information and Market Adjustment Costs.*

---

[6] If we subtract the *cumulated* search costs over the search interval from the then best observed sales bid price, the *net* price line, now *net* of search costs, will hit a peak after which it will decrease, assuming no "decay" in value of earlier perceived options.

[7] For an illustration of the application of information and search costs to money and liquidity *per se*, see Miller [18].

Aside from the obvious ways to produce information (e.g., advertising and specialist middlemen) there are less well recognized ways involving price stability, unemployed resources, and queues (in which costs are incurred to *reduce* search and other marketing costs even more). Inventories economize on costs of information. Inventories may appear to be idle, excess or unemployed resources, but they can be interpreted as an economical use of resources [26]. An oversimplified but suggestive example is the problem faced by a newsboy who sells an average of 100 copies of a daily paper—but not always 100 each day. The more accurately he tries to predict and the more quickly he adjusts to imperfectly predictable fluctuations in the flow of demand the greater are the costs of his action. Potential customers may prefer that he stock an excessive number on the average with instant availability from inventories, despite higher costs caused by unsold copies. The higher cost may be manifested to customers as a lower quality of product, fewer sellers or a higher price. But this extra cost (of the unsold papers) will be less than if the newspaper sellers attempted to obtain complete information about demands at each future moment, or to make instantaneous adjustments in the number of papers without an inventory. In brief, the costs of unsold items are incurred to reduce even more the information costs in marketing.

Another option exists. The seller could change price instantly to always clear the market when demand fluctuates and thereby never have an inventory of unsold goods awaiting purchasers.[8] Retailers would not be awaiting buyers. Retailers could avoid reservations and queues by varying price instantly with the random fluctuations of appearance of customers. Why don't they? After all, that is what happens, or seems to happen, in the future markets and stock markets.[9]

Consider the consequences. Patrons appear at random intervals, though the probability density of the rate may be predictable. Would patrons prefer to see the market instantly cleared with no queues whatsoever—but only with price fluctuations to do the rationing? Not necessarily. That might *induce more search elsewhere* than under queueing. Customers may prefer more predictable prices with enhanced probability of some queues and less search. [113] Unpredictable prices, as well as queues, impose costs on patrons; there is no reason why *only one* should be avoided regardless of the cost of the other. Retailers must balance (a) costs of search induced by unpredictable prices

---

[8] The expression "demand fluctuation" covers a great amount of mischievousness. For a more rigorous conceptualization, a "probability distribution of latent offers" is better. Reference to the mean and variance of that distribution of potentially discernible or revealed offers would provide some specification of the demand confronting a seller. Furthermore, there is not a *given* flow of *revealed* demanders. Offers could be emitted or received at a slower or faster rate. The analogy to emissions of particles from radioactive elements is apt. The emissions have a "mean" and a "range" of values (voltages) and a random time between emission, i.e., the "rate" of emission. These "randomly spaced" emissions of market offers can be characterized by a probability distribution. The *rate* at which offers are discerned by the seller can be increased or decreased by engaging more information activity (i.e., marketing activity). This paper is not trying to specify some special underlying distribution rigorously. Some progress toward this is to be found in Stigler [28].

[9] As a matter of fact, even on the futures markets and stock exchanges, there are specialists and "scalpers" who stabilize price by providing a buffer inventory [31].

and of inventories against (b) costs of queues and of waiting in queues. If prices of all sellers were known, extensive persistent search could be reduced (there would still be search for small queues), and the gross cost could fall, even though the money price were higher. This is basically one of the economic defenses of manufacturer-imposed retail prices.

A seller who eliminates a nonpredictably fluctuating, transient, market-clearing price could offer his patrons a savings in costs of search. He could make price more predictable by carrying a larger inventory to buffer the transient demand fluctuations, and customers would reduce search costs with the assurance of a stable (i.e., predicted) price if they accepted some costs of waiting in a queue.

The queue length could vary with constant price so long as the *mean* rate of purchases is matched by the production rate. The greater the variance in the transient rate of appearance of shoppers, the greater will be the variation in the length of the queue and *also* the longer will be the average length of the line. An alternative to customer queues is "queueing" of an inventory as a buffer to eliminate customer queues while price is constant. Among these options—transient and instant price changes, customer queues, inventories and continued market search for better options—what determines the efficient extent of each?

Customers engage in repeat purchases; in making purchase plans, predictability of price is conducive to closer adjustment to optional purchases. Revising purchase plans and actions is costly. If one finds a dinner price transiently and unexpectedly high because of randomly high demand at the moment he appears in the restaurant, he will have been led to inappropriate action. *Ex post* his action was not optimal. To avoid such losses, he will, thereafter, prior to concluding a purchase, engage in more search among sellers to discover unusually, transiently low prices. This extra search is less costly than taking one's chances as to what price he will face in a transiently fluctuating market.

In general, smaller and more frequent random fluctuations in demand (i.e., with a fixed expectation in the probability density function), greater search costs, greater value of the buyer's time, and less burdensome forms of queueing or rationing, all will increase the incidence of price stability. If the demand probability density function shifted *predictably*, prices would vary — as they do for daytime and evening restaurants and theaters for example. A lower cost of holding inventories relative to the value of the product will increase the relative size of inventories and increase price stability and shorten queues [114] for any frequency and size of random demand fluctuations.[10]

Accordingly, we should expect to see some prices maintained relatively rigidly over time and among retail stores (with so-called Fair Trade Laws) as *manufacturers* seek to assure final customers of the lower *overall* costs of purchasing their items for high quality, but low value, items purchased by people whose time is relatively valuable (i.e., high wage groups).

An obvious application of the analysis is to shop hours. Stores are open

---

[10]Had this paper been devoted also to the conditions that induce non-market-clearing prices, even with predictable demand, it would have included a discussion of forms of property rights in the goods being sold.

during known hours and stay open even when there are no customers in sight. A store could have lower prices if customers were to ring a bell and wait for the owner to open the store, but this would impose waiting costs on the patrons. I presume the advantage to the store operator (with lower pecuniary prices to customers) in closing his store when no customers are in sight is smaller than the convenience to shoppers.

More apartment units are built than the owner expects on the average to rent. This, of course, assumes that *revealed* demand *to him* for his apartments is neither continuous nor costlessly and perfectly predictable. It pays to build more apartments to satisfy *unpredictable* vagaries in "demand fluctuations" if such demand fluctuations cannot be accommodated by costless reallocation among demanders or "no inconvenience" from immediate rent changes. The apartment owner could always keep apartments fully rented at a lower, quickly revised rental; or at higher stable rentals he could have vacancies part of the time. A landlord, faced with an empty apartment, could cut the rent sufficiently to induce immediate rental to the first person he happened to see, if he ignored marketing (including moving) costs. But in view of costs of transactions, contract revision and displaying and arranging for new higher paying tenants of already *occupied* premises, it sometimes yields greater wealth to forego transient rent revision that would keep apartments *always* rented. In maintaining vacancies, he is responding to renters' preferences (a) to examine apartments, have rental predictability and move more spontaneously rather than (b) to continually adjust to rental changes or (c) to make plans and reservations in advance if there were price predictability *and no* inventory of vacant apartments. The "vacancies" serve as inventories; as such they do not warrant rent reductions.

If instant production were no more costly than slower production or adjustment, people could always produce whatever was wanted only at the moment it was wanted. In fact, however, producing in advance at a less hasty, less expensive rate *and* holding an "excess" for contingent demands economizes in having more services at a cost that is worth paying, taking into account the value of being able to adapt to changed demands without long, advance, "reservations-type" planning. The situation is the same for a home with enough bathrooms and dining space to accommodate more visitors than one will ordinarily have. To say there is "idle," "wasted," or "unemployed" bathroom or dining room capacity is to consider only the cost of that extra capacity while ignoring its infrequent-use value and the *greater* costs of other ways of obtaining equally high convenience or utility.

[115] The foregoing considerations suggest that in a society with (a) costs of obtaining information about sellers' "asking" prices, (b) cost of sellers' obtaining information about customers' demand, and (c) a tendency for unpredicted price changes to induce extra search by buyers and sellers, the "ideal" market will *not* be characterized by prices that instantly fluctuate so as always to clear the market without queues by buyers or sellers. Instead, to reduce the losses consequent to unpredictable delivery times if prices were perfectly stable, it pays: (a) sellers to hold inventories, (b) buyers to accept some queueing—as means of purchasing at predictable prices and avoiding higher search costs

that would be induced if with instant price adjustments there were no queues and inventories, and (c) sometimes to continue shopping before making a contract. The stable price, accompanied by queues and inventories will be slightly higher than if it were not stabilized by queues and inventories—but the higher pecuniary price can save on search and disappointed, incorrect price anticipations. This higher price to the buyer is lower than the sum of the average lower fluctuating price plus search and inconvenience costs to the buyer.

Before leaving the question of price stability as an information economizing device, it is useful to try to complete the catalogue of reasons for price stability in the sense that some prices are *persistently* below or above the market clearing level. This can be done by introducing considerations of the property rights held by the allocator of the goods, of price controls, and of transaction-enforcement costs. Attenuated property rights as prevail in nonprofit enterprises, not-for-profit institutions, or publicly-owned enterprises induce prices below the market-clearing level. They do so because the higher income or wealth derivable with a higher price at a market-clearing level does not become the private property of the allocator or principal to whom it may be responsible. Transactions costs also induce price inflexibility and rationing at a zero price. If the value of the item being rationed is less than the costs of collecting a fee and enforcing the contract (as in parking space or street use) the price will be chronically too low. Or if the change in price to a market clearing level is less valuable than the costs of enforcing that changed price, the price will lag at non-market-clearing levels. See [1, pp. 153–79] [3] [8].

II. LABOR MARKETS

Though most analyses of unemployment rely on wage conventions, restrictions, and controls to retard wage adjustments above market clearing levels, Hicks and Hutt penetrated deeper. Hicks suggested a solution consistent with conventional exchange theory. He stated that "knowledge of opportunities is imperfect" and that the time required to obtain that knowledge leads to unemployment and a delayed effect on wages [9, pp. 45, 58].[11] It is precisely this enhanced significance that this paper seeks to develop, and which Hicks

[116] ignored when he immediately turned to different factors—unions and wage regulations, placing major blame on both for England's heavy unemployment in the 20's and 30's.

We digress to note that Keynes in using a *quantity*, instead of a price, adjusting theory of exchange, merely *postulated* a "slow" reacting price, without showing that slow price responses were consistent with utility or wealth maximizing behavior in open, unconstrained markets. Keynes' analysis was altered in the subsequent income-expenditure models where reliance was placed on "conventional" or "noncompetitive" *wage* rates. Modern "income-expenditure" theorists assumed "institutionally" or "irrationally" inflexible wages

---

[11]And he added another type—"the unemployment of the man who gives up his job in order to look for a better."

resulting from unions, money illusions, regulations or factors allegedly idiosyncratic to labor. Keynes did not assume inflexibility for only wages. His theory rested on a more general scope of price inflexibility.[12] The present paper may in part be viewed as an attempt to "justify" Keynes' presumption about price response to disturbances in demand.

In 1939 W. H. Hutt exposed many of the fallacious interpretations of idleness and unemployment. Hutt applied the analysis suggested by Hicks but later ignored it when discussing Keynes' analysis of involuntary unemployment and policies to alleviate it [10, pp. 165–69]. This is unfortunate, because Hutt's analysis seems to be capable of explaining and accounting for a substantial portion of that unemployment.

If we follow the lead of Hicks and Hutt and develop the implications of "frictional" unemployment for *both* human and *nonhuman* goods, we can perceive conditions that will imply *massive* "frictional" unemployment and depressions in open, unrestricted, competitive markets with rational, utility maximizing, individual behavior. And some tests of that interpretation can be suggested.[13]

Unemployment. The preceding analysis shows why an employee will not necessarily accept a pay cut to *retain* a job, even though some current wage income is better than "none". An employee correctly and *sensibly* believes he can, with some search and evaluation of alternatives, get approximately his old wage at some other job; after all, that is why he was getting what he did at his current job. If looking and "finding out" is more costly while employed, he may have reason to choose temporary unemployment as an efficient form of "producing" or investing in information.

There is reason for rejecting even a "temporary" wage cut. A subsequently restored demand will not be immediately revealed to the employee-seller at zero cost; he will continue at the lower wage than he could get elsewhere, if only he had incurred costs to "find out". Of course, employer competition would not reveal subsequent demand increases instantly; employers also have cost of getting information about alternatives. The cost of learning about all potentially available bids and offers (for employers, as well as employees, and the attributes of the goods being offered) restricts the speed of price adjustments. In sum, refusal to cut wages to retain continuous present employment is neither nonoptimal behavior nor adherence to a convention as to "proper" wages.[14]

[117]

Any firm experiencing a demand decrease could try to lower costs (to maintain output) by offering less to its inputs. But if providers of inputs know, or believe, they have undiminished opportunities elsewhere they will not accept

---

[12]For a thorough exposition and justification of these remarks on Keynes, see Leijonhufvud [14].

[13]Many labor economists have used elements of this approach in their writings. In that sense, nothing said in the preceding is new. But we are attempting to collate and assemble these elements into a general theory of pricing and exchange of goods and service in which labor is included. For example, see [11], [19], [20], [23], [24], [27], [29].

[14]For an indication of the difficulties in formulating as well as solving the optimal search problem, see [15, 16, and especially 17].

the cut.[15] It seems exceedingly unlikely that *all* providers of inputs would know that all their alternatives had deteriorated (if indeed, they had) so as to induce them to accept a cut sufficient to retain their current employment. The larger the portion of the providers of inputs who do not regard their alternative discoverable opportunities as having deteriorated, the larger is the required price cut an employer must ask the complementary inputs to accept if he is to continue their employment in current jobs.[16]

Layoffs. There remains a phenomenon that obscures the present interpretation. For example, General Motors lays off men when demand for cars drops, without any negotiations about a temporary wage cut. It is tempting to blame unions or to conclude that no wage, however low, would enable GM profitably to maintain employment, or that lower wages were impossible because of the pressure from those workers who are not laid off. But suppose there were no such pressure and no union contracts. What would evolve as the "sensible" response when GM's demand fell? Employers learn that wage cuts sufficient to justify profitable maintenance of the prior rate of output and employment would be too low to keep employees, given their beliefs about alternatives. And so layoffs are announced without fruitless wage renegotiations.

If there are job-switching costs, but a man's search costs are not far greater [118] when he is employed than unemployed, a *temporary* wage cut is more likely to be acceptable. If the *temporarily* reduced wage offer is too low to make work worthwhile, the result is a "temporary layoff" taken without an intent of changing jobs. Insofar as onset and duration of "temporary" conditions are *predictable*, the situation is a recognition of normal working hours (e.g., not working at nights or on weekends) at *predictable* intervals because the worker prefers leisure to the wages available during those hours. If the onset of the decreased demand is unpredictable (building workers), but if its probability is believed known, this is again akin to weekend rest—and the wage rate

[15]A seller faced with decreased demand by a buyer does not regard it as a reliable indicator of similar changes in demand by all other demanders for that service. Yet such behavior has been described as an irrational holding of "less than unity (or even zero) elasticity of price expectation." A decrease in price available from *a* buyer does not mean all other buyers have reduced their offer prices. To the extent *we* see only a part of the potential "market" at any one time, it is rational to believe that a decrease in price here does not imply all potential offers will have fallen elsewhere. Keynes, in assuming inelastic price expectations, could have been arguing that a decrease in wages from a current employer or a small set of them is not sufficient to warrant the expectation they are lower every place as well. The contrast with securities is especially striking. Insofar as the securities market is a cheaper market—that is, insofar as it reflects more cheaply a larger, more complete sample of bids and offers of the population, any fall in an observed price is more likely indicative of a decrease in other potential offers as well; the elasticity of expectations about yet-to-be discerned available prices with search should be higher. Thus there is nothing inconsistent in assuming different price expectations elasticities in different markets; in fact there is much to be gained in detecting factors that make them different. See Tobin [30], Fellner [6, pp. 141–51] for example of failures to make the distinction.

[16]The deeper the wage cut necessary to retain the old job, the greater the incentive to embark on job information search while unemployed. The greater the degree of seniority, the greater the wage cut that could be imposed before unemployment, for equally high seniority elsewhere cannot be obtained by a job change. The greater threatened wage cut is fought by the requirement that lower seniority men be dropped first.

is adjusted to reflect that. Building workers are an example; "casual" labor is another. If the demand reduction persists longer than expected, the person will begin a job-information search.

If job-information costs depend upon whether one is employed or unemployed, then unemployment can occur (with or without moving costs). If there are moving costs also, the *length* of unemployment will be longer. But *differential* information costs are necessary for the incidence of unemployment, A *common* (i.e., *un*differentiated) cost of search and job switching would only mean a greater reduction of wealth of employees, not their unemployment as a result of unexpected demand decreases.[17]

Irrelevancy of Atomistic vs. Monopolistic Market Types. Resources sold in atomistic markets (devoid of all monopolistic or "impure" competition) experience unemployment. In any market—even in a price-taker's atomistic market, free of all price "administration" or constraints—if demand falls, some sellers will be unable immediately to sell their output at the price at which others are selling, because marketing (i.e., information) is costly. Although hazardous, it is tempting to push the analysis into the foundation of pure, perfect and monopolistic markets; the idealized polar extreme, pure competition market assumes zero costs of market-information and product identification. If costs of either are significant, some sellers would sell less at a higher price to cater to buyers who deem it not worthwhile looking further for lower price sellers— given the costs of canvassing the population. To attribute unemployment to monopolistic markets or to administered conventional wages and prices is to assume that market information costs the same amount no matter how it is produced.

Job Vacancies: Search by Employers. Information is sought by employers also. Job vacancies, with search for best employees, are the counterpart to unemployment. An employer searching (i.e., competing) for more employees knows that a higher wage will get more employees—or that it costs more to more quickly find out who will work at the same wage with the same talent. Employer search activity will increase the incidence of job changes [119] without the employees' having experienced unemployment, because employers will seek currently employed labor and offer better wages.

Uncertainty of the employer about the quality of a potential employee induces a lower initial wage offer. The best perceived offer to a prospective employee will reflect both the applicant's costs of canvassing all employers *and* the employers' cost of learning more about the applicant. The more homogeneous the class to which the employer believes the applicant belongs—or the less the variance of the possible marginal productivity of the applicant—the

---

[17]Some of the preceding ideas can be summarized in terms of general economic theory by explicitly treating information as a good that is demanded and supplied. The sum of excess demands and supplies for all goods should be zero by definition. We may say that during unemployment there is an increased demand for and supply of information about market opportunities. Or we may say the market for each good is in equilibrium, but the production of market-opportunity-information has increased, leaving other production at equilibrium rates lower than would have existed had resources not been diverted to production of more market-opportunity-information. This method of formulating the structure of the analysis saves Say's Principle that the sum of excess demand equals the sum of excess supplies—always.

closer will the applicant's discerned offers be to the maximum. He will more quickly settle on a new job.

Interproduct Shift vs. "Depression" Unemployment. The greater the rate of interproduct demand shifts, the larger will be unemployment. We could talk of interproduct demand shift unemployment and also of aggregate demand decrease (depression) unemployment, without any reference to *full* employment [10, p. 35]. We shall occasionally use the term "full" employment to admit of unemployment in the absence of *aggregate* demand shifts. In such cases interproduct demand shifts will determine the degree of unemployment that is associated with "full" employment. That source of unemployment is usually called "frictional." But if aggregate demand changes, there is a change in the degree of unemployment, whatever it be called.

Output per Unit of Input. Faced with demand decreases that are regarded as transient, employers will retain employees and equipment because there is a cost of finding new employees as replacements. (Of course, any layoff probably involves loss of some employees.) Keeping "excessive" employees on the payroll is analogous to having empty apartments to allow for economic adjustment to transient unpredictable shifts in demand. Therefore, decreases in demand for an employer's products can imply a less than equivalent reduction in employment and a resultant apparent "higher cost" per output. This is more economical (efficient) than quickly adjusting the size of the work force.

"Depression" Unemployment. It is not necessary here to explain decreases in aggregate demand. Our purpose is to concentrate on the consequences of aggregate demand decreases without attention to feedback effects of unemployment on aggregate demand. A decrease in general demand causes an increase in unemployment because more people will accept unemployment to engage in search and each unemployed person will look longer. Wage earning opportunities will diminish in the sense that lower wages are available elsewhere. People use time to *learn* that the failure to find other equally good job options as quickly as they thought they would, reflects *diminished* alternatives in general, not unlucky search. The discerned maximum offers will be lower than if the structure of alternatives had not decreased. The lower level and slower rate of rise of best observed options is at first taken as an unlucky string of searches, and so unemployment is extended in the expectation of "shortly" finding that elusive best option. And with each person looking longer [120] the total number of unemployed at any one time will be larger. (Incomes fall and feedback effects occur.) Each now has the added task of revising his whole pattern of expectations. Whereas he was formerly searching for a higher clearly formulated expected wage, now he must learn that the "best" has deteriorated.

If the decrease in aggregate demand is a continuing affair (induced, we shall assume for concreteness, by a continuing fall in the quantity of money) unemployment will persist at the higher level during the continuing decrease in demand, which must be continually "discovered". The greater the rate of decrease of general demand, the greater the extent and average duration length of unemployment. Thus a *continuing* decrease in the community's stock of money is associated with a continuing decrease in general demand and with continuing unemployment of human (and nonhuman) resources. Holding general demand at its *new* level would reduce unemployment. But the costs of that mode of recovery may be greater than action designed to increase aggregate demand back to the demand beliefs that people hold.

Conversely, if the rate of increase in the quantity of money accelerates (unanticipated), the general increase in demand will increase job vacancies, increase job information dispersal activity by employers, and increase the search by employers for information about available employable resources. "Jobs are easier to get..." meaning the alternatives are better than they (as well as the present job) formerly were thought to be.

Changes in aggregate demand confuse the public. Each seller notices a changed demand for his current product, but he cannot tell if that is a change also in aggregate demand which affects options elsewhere. Whether he should shift to another option, as he should not if the demand change is general, or stay where he is and change price, is the question to be answered. Should an employee switch jobs upon receipt of a superior offer or should he look over the market more fully? Given interproduct fluctuations, any person who refuses unemployment search for the best alternative option can be misled into accepting another job too soon. He will, because of increasing demand, more easily find a job with higher wages than he now gets. Yet he should have held out longer, since the upward shift means he could have done better. Unemployment will be less than "optimal"—*given* the extent of *interproduct* demand shifts and of the differential costs of knowing other job potentials. In speaking of "optimal" unemployment we are not suggesting that unemployment *per se* is desirable. We mean that *given the fact of different search costs and demand shifts* it pays to engage in some search more economically while not employed. The opportunity to search while not employed is better than the lack of an opportunity to move to unemployment as a more efficient means of search. Given interproduct demand shifts, without unemployment the extent to which resources are in their most valuable uses is reduced, because the public is fooled into believing they have found the best available jobs, when in fact they have failed to invest in enough search to find "best" available jobs.

One cautionary note: Constant per capita aggregate demand is consistent [121] with falling prices of final products. Falling consumer good prices in this case reflect lower costs of production, not reduced profitability of production. Resource prices will not fall. If there is an *un*anticipated inflation trend, the increased (unanticipated) aggregate demand (per capita) will reduce unemployment and maintain it at a lower level. If inflation is correctly anticipated, the change of unemployment implied for any given rate of change of aggregate demand will be lower than for unanticipated inflation, and it will be independent of the anticipated rate.

Lag of What Behind What? The analysis can be expressed more conventionally, but *not* as follows: "A reduction in demand involves a lag of wage rate decreases behind prices—which *is* a rise in real or relative wage rates. This rise implies lower employment because of diminishing marginal returns to labor inputs." That is not contained in the present analysis; wage rates and all other prices can fall at the *same* rate. But the lag that does occur is a lag of the *discernment* of the best available prices behind the new, as yet undiscerned, best (i.e., the new, unascertained lower *equilibrium*) prices which *when* discovered would restore employment. In Walrasian terms, the auctioneer does not instantaneously reveal the new equilibrium price vector. (Even in an actual auction, the time for bidders to reveal the best price is not trivial.) The "lag" is the *time for discovery*. The lag terminology tends to confuse a lag of wages behind other factor or product prices with the "lag" of discernment of the best opportunities behind the (undiscerned) equilibrating price—a price that is not freely or instantly revealed to the world. It follows that a general economy-wide demand decrease does not imply a correlation between real wage rates and depressions (and recoveries). Wage rates can fall as fast as other prices; *that* lag is not necessary for unemploy-

[122] ment.[18]

Reduced employment of human *and nonhuman resources* when coupled with the conventional production function implies nothing about real output per employed input. Suppose that resources when faced with a demand decrease in present jobs *immediately* accepted the first available job—foregoing search for a better job. Job allocations would be "inefficient." Better allocations

---

[18]An intriguing, intellectual historical curiosum may be explainable by this theory, as has been brought to my attention by Axel Leijonhufvud. Keynes' powerful, but elliptical, definition of involuntary unemployment has been left in limbo. He said: men were involuntarily employed if,

> ... in the event of a small rise in the price of wage-goods relative to the money-wage, both the aggregate supply of labour willing to work for the current money wage and the aggregate demand for it at that wage would be greater than the existing volume of employment [11, p. 15].

To see the power and meaning of this definition (not *cause*) of unemployment, consider the following question. Why would a cut in money wages provoke a different response than *if* the price level rose relative to wages—when both would amount to the same change in relative prices, but differ only in the money price level? Almost everyone thought Keynes presumed a money-wage illusion. However, an answer more respectful of Keynes is available. The price level rise conveys *different information*: money-wages everywhere have fallen relative to prices. On the other hand, a cut in one's own money-wage does not imply options elsewhere have fallen. A cut only in one's present job is revealed. The money versus real wage distinction is not the relevant comparison; the wage in the present job versus the wage in all other jobs is the relevant comparison. This rationalizes Keynes' *definition* of involuntary unemployment in terms of price level changes. If wages were cut everywhere else, and *if* employees knew it, they would not choose unemployment—but they would if they believed wages were cut just in their current job. When one employer cuts wages, this does not signify cuts elsewhere. His employees rightly think wages are not reduced elsewhere. On the other hand, with a rise in the price level, employees have less reason to think their current real wages are lower than they are elsewhere. So they do not immediately refuse a lower real wage induced by a higher price level, whereas they would refuse an equal money wage cut in their present job. It is the revelation of information about prospects elsewhere that makes the difference. And this is perfectly consistent with Keynes' definition of unemployment, and it is also consistent with his entire theory of market adjustment processes [12], since he believed wages lagged behind non-wage prices—an unproved and probably false belief [13]. Without that belief a general price level rise is indeed general; it includes wages and as such there is no reason to believe a price level rise is equivalent in real terms to a money wage cut in a particular job.

could be discerned with search, at a cost. The destruction of a former equilibrium is not followed by a costless immediate new equilibrium. But the faster it is sought the greater the costs. There is some optimal rate. Insofar as resources take interim jobs, while "inefficiently" search for better jobs, or failing to search, the "total" output vector will be smaller. In other words there is an optimal rate of unemployment *given* the rate of demand changes and *given* the differential costs of search. Very low unemployment resulting from inflationary forces can be socially inefficient, because resources mistakenly accept new jobs with too little search for better ones.

III. POTENTIAL TESTS OF THE THEORY

Empirical tests of the theory can be sought by identifying characteristics of resources that increase the length and frequency of unemployment. Or situations in which the parameters of search conditions have changed can be compared to see if the implied changes in unemployment are observed. Since the class of alternative theories is open-ended, we shall simply indicate some implications of the present theory, letting the reader conjecture whether any alternative theory contains so broad a class of phenomena.

A discriminatory test of the theory lies not in its implication of "cyclical" labor unemployment fluctuations but in its implication of unemployment, price stability, and queueing for *all* types of resources—as suggested in the preceding pages.

One aggregative unemployment feature that is implied by this analysis is a positive correlation between extent of recovery in employment from a depression with the extent of the preceding decline; a *zero* correlation is implied between the magnitude of an expansion with the subsequent decline. Absence of tendencies to restore employment would imply no correlation between either pair of movements. There is in fact a positive correlation of magnitude of rises with the preceding decrease, and none between contractions and preceding rises [8].

Resources with *less differentiated* costs (while employed or unemployed) of obtaining or dispersing information will have lower incidence, as well as shorter periods, of unemployment. Since an employer knows more about his own employees than those of other employers, the probability of job changes (in tasks and grades) should be greater within a firm than among firms—especially in the upward direction. But the excess probability should decrease in the higher paid tasks, since extra search is more economic the higher the marginal product of an employee's position.

[123] Readily (i.e., cheaply) recognizable, divisible (time, place, etc.), portable (more quickly moveable at a given cost), durable (more long-lived so as to reduce contracting costs) resources, should display shorter length of unemployment.[19] What characteristics of goods yield low costs of information? Market demands and offers of homogeneous goods ("easily and cheaply recognized")

[19]The preceding sentence reminds us of the attributes of money, and who can doubt that money has a very low "unemployment" rate? The suggestive analogy is in fact precisely to the point.

should be cheaper to survey. Tract houses, built by one builder should be easier to sell or rent than custom-built houses. "Easier" to sell or buy means that for given cost of search the realized price is closer (more quickly) to the best possible price obtainable (i.e., to the price that would have resulted if every potential buyer or seller had been canvassed and if each had full information about the product). An observable magnitude correlated with search costs should be the bid-ask spread, or markup, between the buying and selling price [5]. Thus inventories should be a smaller ratio to sales for low than for high information cost items. Frequent, repeated purchases by buyers should be correlated with knowledge about the item and alternative sources of purchases so that the bid-ask spread is lower. Goods sold in a formal market should have lower price spreads, reflecting the lower cost of information provided by formal markets. For example, over-the-counter stocks should have a larger bid-ask spread than stocks on more organized markets [5]. New goods, we conjecture, involve higher information dispersal costs and hence inventories relative to sales and wider price spreads [4].

Apartments built in standard designs will have lower vacancy rates because their characteristics are more cheaply understood, being already commonly known. At one time in Southern California, homes with swimming pools were so unusual as to fall in the higher information cost category. Brokers' fees should therefore be larger in percentage terms.

Corporation stocks and bonds can be categorized by extent of knowledge by the public about the companies. If only a few people are informed, and unless they are more easily discovered, the market will be "thin", implying longer search periods or larger bid-ask spreads. The fewness of buyers or sellers is not *per se* a source of thinness or high information costs. Rather it is the higher cost of finding those few potential buyers among the larger population. Thus new "unseasoned" stocks and bonds should be markedly different in the bid-ask spread from older established stocks and bonds [5].

Price stability with transient demand fluctuations is provided in the commodity and stock exchanges by floor traders. They trade on the "uptick and downtick" out of personal inventories, so as to reduce the variance of prices in response to what these traders regard as transient, random fluctuations in revealed market demands and supplies [31].

The highest and the lowest priced variant of any class of goods will have a longer inventory period and larger retail-wholesale price spread than the typical or modal variant. We assume the extremes are less familiar types; [124] information acquisition and disbursing costs will be larger. Special purpose machine tools should have a longer unemployment period than general purpose widely used types of equipment. Their inventory to sales ratio should be larger.

Standard types of used automobiles should have a shorter inventory interval (and lower ratio of inventory to sales) than do unusual used cars because information about the standard type car is more common among potential buyers.

The larger the dispersion of potential bid prices among buyers, the greater the gross gain from continued search. The *absolute* (not relative) increment of discerned maximum price is larger if the dispersion is larger. Assuming that more unusual items (like paintings or works of art) are subject to a larger variance in valuation by the population, we expect a longer search period or larger markup.

The fewer the major employers in any community the shorter will be the length and the lower will be the incidence of unemployment. Information about jobs is more readily available if there are fewer employers to search and to be told of one's talents. Wages should be more quickly adjusted in areas with only one employer. It has been suggested that the Negro in the South is faced with a fewer number of employers in the small towns than in the North and that he would therefore spend less time in job search in the South.[20].

If the highly skilled worker has a higher ratio of wages per hour to the value of self-generated income from extended job information search, then the highly paid laborer will resort more to employment agencies to economize on his relatively valuable search time. And he will use private more than public employment agencies, because private agencies, by being able to charge higher fees for higher salaried employees, have an incentive to devote more resources to placement of such people than do public agencies. Public agencies are closer competitors of private agencies for lower wage job applicants. (This does not mean low wage workers are not served by private agencies.) Looking at the employment problem from the point of view of the buyer or employer, one implication is that job vacancies for the expensive, heterogeneous executive will be longer-lived than for lower productivity and standard types of laborers. Some evidence of this should be revealed by employment agency fees which, according to the present analysis, should be larger than for lower paying jobs.

Consider an employer looking for a manager and for a janitor. The value of a manager's services are higher than a janitor's so a dollar spent for information about managers has a larger expected net marginal product. Because a better measure of the probability of the marginal product of high marginal product employees is worth more than a better measure of the probability of a lower marginal product employee, the employer will find it profitable to incur greater costs to get information about potential managers than for [125] janitors. If skin color, eye shape or sex is cheaply observable and believed to be correlated with quality of performance, the physical traits provide cheap (though incomplete) information about the quality of the person. For higher salaried jobs an extra dollar of costs for information about the potential employee is more likely to be profitable. The extra information will supplement the skin, eye or sex indicator of quality. As a result, for higher paying jobs, the cheap information will be supplemented by other information. "Discrimination" solely according to only eye shape, sex, skin color and ethnic group is less profitable and hence less probable in higher paying jobs.[21]

[20]Suggested by H. Gregg Lewis.

[21]The example of this paragraph was developed by A. DeVany. The same principle applies to short-versus long-term employees. This test is not relevant for the *differentiated* (according to employed or unemployed) search cost, but instead is derived from presence of search costs as such. One index of discrimination is the extent to which similar types of people work in

If the evidence were to conform to all the foregoing implications, could this interpretation be consistent with the events of 1929–39? There is no doubt that aggregate demand decreased rapidly from 1929–32. Money stocks fell by about 15 per cent in 1939, 1931 and 1932. That does imply decreasing aggregate demand and abnormal unemployment. But it is the prolonged high unemployment after 1932 and the slow recovery, when aggregate demand stopped decreasing that appears inconsistent with the theory. After 1932 national income and money stocks were increasing and it is hard to believe that the rate of unemployment should not have decreased more rapidly. Even if the money stock had not increased, the convergence toward the full equilibrium price vector should have progressed more rapidly, if one is allowed to make *ad hominem* conjectures as to the expected rate of recovery.[22]

One thing that can save the proposed interpretation despite the prolonged unemployment is the imposition of arbitrary restrictions on permissible prices. Another factor that would help to explain the prolonged unemployment without rejecting the proposed interpretation is a sequential injection of depressing policy actions.

In other words a prolonged unemployment—without decreasing aggregate demand—would be consistent with the present interpretation of price behavior and unemployment if actual permissible (not the equilibrium) wages or prices were arbitrarily or exogenously increased. Events that support this interpretation have been chronicled by Roose [25, pp. 45–57] and Friedman [7, pp. 493–99]. A *sequence* of measures by the government (NIRA, Guffey Coal Act, agricultural price support, and the Labor Relations Act, minimum wages) arbitrarily and successively raised prices and wages over the period—not once and for all in 1932. In the absence of these autonomous factors pushing up permissible (though not the equilibrating) wages and prices, 1933–37 would have shown greater employment and output. Roose [25, pp. 45–57] attributes the low recovery to restrictive policies such as higher wages of NIRA codes, National Labor Relations Act, minimum wage enactments, imposition of social security taxes, and unemployment and old age security taxes on employment. In the same interval other policies involving new regulatory agencies are believed to have temporarily restrained capital goods production. Securities and exchange acts, separation of investment from commercial banking, public utility holding company restrictions, the encouragement of labor strikes and

[126]

---

clusters. Janitors are more likely to be mostly of the same types, but managers are more likely to be of a mixed group., Discrimination by cheaply observed traits should be less frequent for managers. My impression is that, in fact, for lower paying jobs there is greater concordance or uniformity of physical types than in higher paying jobs.

[22]There is one restraining factor in the unrestored quantity of money. If the quantity of money is not increased, the recovery of output and employment will imply still lower "full employment" equilibrium prices. The increased real output with constant stock of money requires still lower prices. This continuing deflationary pressure on prices would retard the return of production and employment to "full-use" levels. A sufficient increase in money stocks would have avoided the necessity of a fall in prices and wages and thereby would have speeded the rate of resource reallocation and hence the restoration of employment and output, by eliminating the cost of discerning the continuing *reduction* of potentially available prices and wages in all other opportunities. This was, of course, Keynes' advocated policy.

a general attack on businessmen all contributed to lower capital goods equilibrating price—whatever their merits. To these factors add the 1937 monetary legal reserve debacle. If all of these factors had occurred once and for all in, say, 1932, the subsequent recovery rate should have been more rapid. But they in fact did occur in sequence over several years. If these considerations are accepted, the delayed recovery until 1941 in the face of non-decreasing aggregate demand is consistent with the differential-cost-of-information-about-best-available-job-opportunities theory of unemployment.

REFERENCES

1. A. A. Alchian and W. R. Allen, *Exchange and Production; Theory in Use*. Belmont 1968.
2. —————— and R. A. Kessel, "Competition, Monopoly, and the Pursuit of Pecuniary Gain," *Aspects of Labor Economics*. A Conference of the Universities — National Bureau Committee for Economic Research. New Jersey, 1962, 156–83.
3. K. J. Arrow and W. M. Capron, "Dynamic Shortages and Price Rises: The Engineer Scientist Case," *Quart. Jour. Econ.*, May 1959, 73, 292–308.
4. H. Demsetz, "Exchange and Enforcement of Property Rights, *Jour. Law Econ.*, Oct. 1964, 7, 11–26.
5. ——————, "The Cost of Transacting," *Quart. Jour. Econ.*, Feb. 1968, 82, 33–53.
6. W. Fellner, *Monetary Policies and Full Employment*. Berkeley 1946.
7. M. Friedman, *A Monetary History of the United States, 1867–1960*. Princeton 1964.
8. ——————, "The Monetary Studies of the National Bureau," *The National Bureau Enters Its Forty-Fifth Year, Forty-Fourth Annual Report*. Washington 1964, 14–18.
9. J. R. Hicks, *The Theory of Wages*, 2nd ed. London 1963.
10. W. H. Hutt, *The Theory of Idle Resources*. London 1939.
11. H. Kasper, "The Asking Price of Labor and the Duration of Unemployment," *Rev. Econ. Stat.*, May 1967, 49, 165–72.
12. R. A. Kessel and A. A. Alchian, "The Meaning and Validity of the Inflation-Induced Lag of Wages Behind Prices," *Amer. Econ. Rev.*, Mar. 1960, 50, 43–66.
13. J. M. Keynes, *The General Theory of Employment Interest and Money*. London 1936.
14. A. Leijonhufvud, *The Economics of Keynes and Keynesian Economics*. Oxford 1968.
15. J. MacQueen and R. G. Miller, Jr., "Optimal Persistence Policies," *Oper. Res. Jour.*, Mar. Apr. 1968, 16, 362–80.
16. J. J. McCall, "The Economics of Information and Optimal Stopping Rules," *Jour. Bus.*, July 1965, 38, 300–17.
17. ——————, "Economics of Information and Job Search," RM–5745–OEO. Santa Monica 1968.
18. H. L. Miller, "Liquidity and Transaction Costs," *Southern Econ. Jour.*, July 1965, 32, 43–48.
19. A. C. Pigou, *Lapses from Full Employment*. London 1945.
20. R. V. Rao, "Employment Information and Manpower Utilization," *Manpower Jour.*, July–Sept. 1965, 1, 7–15.
21. A. Rees, "Wage Determination and Involuntary Unemployment," *Jour. Pol. Econ.*, Apr. 1951, 59, 143–144.
22. ——————, "Information Networks and Labor Markets," *Am. Econ. Rev., Supplement*, May 1966, 56, 559–66.
23. L. Reynolds, *Labor Economics and Labor Relations*, 4th ed. New Jersey 1964.
24. A. M. Roose, "Do We Have a New Industrial Feudalism?" *Am. Econ. Rev.*, Dec. 1958, 48, 903–20.
25. K. D. Roose, *The Economics of Recession and Revival*. New Haven 1954.
26. T. L. Saaty, *Elements of Queueing Theory*, New York 1961.
27. H. L. Sheppard and H. A. Belitsky, *The Job Hunt: Job Seeking Behavior of Unemployed Workers in a Local Economy*. Kalamazoo 1965.
28. G. J. Stigler, "Information in the Labor Market," *Jour. Pol. Econ., Supplement*, Oct. 1962, 70, 94–105.

[127]

29. V. Stoikov, "Some Determinants of the Level of Frictional Employment: A Comparative Study," *Intl. Lab. Rev.*, May 1966, 93, 530–49.

30. J. Tobin, "Liquidity Preference as Behavior Towards Risk," *Rev. Econ. Stud.*, Oct. 1957, 25, 65–86.

31. H. J. Working, "Test of a Theory Concerning Floor Trading on Commodity Exchanges," unpublished.

[128]

[17]

TOWARD A RECONSTRUCTION OF KEYNESIAN ECONOMICS: EXPECTATIONS AND CONSTRAINED EQUILIBRIA*

J. Peter Neary and Joseph E. Stiglitz

A two-period model of temporary equilibrium with rationing is presented, paying particular attention to agents' expectations of future constraints. It is shown that with arbitrary constraint expectations many different types of current equilibrium may be consistent with the same set of (current and expected future) wages and prices. and that constraint expectations exhibit "bootstraps" properties (e.g., a higher expectation of Keynesian unemployment tomorrow increases the probability that it will prevail today). In addition, the concept of *rational constraint expectations* (i.e., perfect foresight of future constraints) is introduced and shown to enhance rather than reduce the effectiveness of government policy.

I. Introduction

This paper provides an old answer to an old question: how can we explain unemployment equilibria? The answer, provided both by Keynes and by more recent equilibrium analysts, is that there is some rigidity in prices (of factors or commodities) in the economy. It is well-known that, if all prices are flexible, all factors (which are not in absolute surplus) will be fully employed in equilibrium. Although the precise articulation of the nature of equilibrium when prices are not flexible, including the derivation of demand and supply curves when participants are constrained in their purchases or sales of factors and commodities, is of a more recent vintage,[1] the basic insight that when there is a rigidity in some factor or commodity price, then equilibrium must entail rationing in some markets, remains unaltered.[2]

* An earlier version of this paper, circulated as NBER Working Paper No. 376, was presented at the European Meetings of the Econometric Society at Athens in September, 1979. We are grateful to the Arts and Social Sciences Research Benefaction Fund of Trinity College, Dublin, the Institute for International Economic Studies, Stockholm, and the National Science Foundation for research support, and to C. Azariadis, R. J. Barro, S. Fischer, J. S. Flemming, R. P. Flood, P. T. Geary, M. Gertler, L. Gevers, O. Hart, E. Helpman, M. Hoel, R. King, G. Laroque, J. Muellbauer. D. Newbery, D. Patinkin, T. Persson, D. D. Purvis, Y. Richelle, E. Sheshinski, R. M. Solow, and L. Svensson for helpful comments.

1. See Hansen [1951], Patinkin [1965], Clower [1965], Leijonhufvud [1968], Solow and Stiglitz [1968], Barro and Grossman [1971], Hicks [1974], Benassy [1975], Grandmont [1977], and Malinvaud [1977].
2. The Barro-Grossman-Malinvaud model has been further examined and extended by Hildenbrand and Hildenbrand [1978], Hool [1980], and Muellbauer and Portes [1978]; its dynamic behavior (under tâtonnement-type assumptions) has been studied by Barro and Grossman [1976], Ch. 21; Blad and Kirman [1978]; Böhm [1978]; Dehez and Gabszewicz [1978]; and Honkapohja [1979]; and it or similar models have been applied to public finance by Dixit [1976] and to international economics by Dixit [1978] and Neary [1980].

200   QUARTERLY JOURNAL OF ECONOMICS

However, most recent studies of fix-price macro models have considered a single period only, focusing on the consequences of current wage-price rigidity.[3] This neglects the fact that, in the absence of futures markets, individuals must base their decisions on expectations, and, as Keynes emphasized, expectations of the future have important effects on the nature of the current equilibrium.[4] The objective of this paper is to explore these effects in the context of a two-period model of temporary equilibrium with rationing.

The first point we wish to stress is that, if future prices and wages are not expected to be market-clearing, then individuals will expect to face quantity constraints, and these expected future quantity constraints critically affect current behavior. In particular, we show that, if individuals expect there to be unemployment next period, it is more likely (in a sense to be defined more precisely) that there will be unemployment this period; whereas if individuals expect there to be excess demand for goods next period, then it is more likely that there will be excess demand for goods this period. As a result, for any particular set of current wages and prices, there may exist multiple expectational equilibria that exhibit "bootstraps" properties; e.g., if households expect that they will be unable to sell all their labor both this period and next, then it will turn out that they will be unable to sell all their labor; but had they expected there to be inflationary pressures this period and next, then that would have turned out to be the case instead.

The second major issue that we consider is the effect of alternative assumptions about how expectations are formed. In recent years it has become fashionable, at least on one side of the Atlantic, to focus on a particular set of expectational assumptions—what has come to be called rational expectations (or, perhaps less emotively, perfect stochastic foresight). Without taking sides on either the logical consistency or the behavioral plausibility of this assumption, we investigate the nature of the equilibrium when all households and firms have perfect foresight, not only about future wages and prices and about whether or not they will be constrained in any particular market, but also about the magnitudes of the constraints they will face. We demonstrate that there may still exist equilibria in which there is unemployment. The paper thus serves to clarify the distinctive roles played by the assumptions of rational expectations and price flexi-

---

3. For a detailed examination of the causes and consequences of wage and price rigidities, see Stiglitz [1978].

4. For example, as Grandmont [1982] has noted, if expectations are not sufficiently flexible, a full-employment equilibrium may not exist, even if current wages and prices are perfectly flexible.

bility in some recent models of macroeconomic equilibrium: rational expectations are consistent both with full employment and unemployment equilibria; it is perfect wage and price flexibility that is necessary (but not sufficient) to ensure full employment, in general.

The model we construct also has policy implications that differ significantly from those of the recent rational-expectations literature. The latter, for instance, has emphasized the inefficacy of fully anticipated government policy; we show, on the contrary, that rational expectations actually result, in certain situations, in the multipliers associated with government policy being *greater* than they would be with, say, static expectations: an increase in government expenditure today has a spillover effect in raising national income at a future date; if the equilibrium at that date is also a Keynesian (demand-constrained) equilibrium, then that increases the demand for labor at that date; the anticipation of this increased demand for labor *reduces* savings currently, and hence current aggregate demand rises.

We believe that the model we have constructed, simple as it is, captures much of what was contained in Keynes, but seems to be missing in one-period macroeconomic models of temporary equilibrium with rationing, in which savings and investment, interest rates, and expectation formation play no critical role. Thus, from a technical viewpoint, the present paper may be thought of as an extension of the earlier studies of Solow-Stiglitz, Barro-Grossman, and Malinvaud; by formulating a two-period model that pays explicit attention to households' and firms' expectations of future quantity constraints and in which the real interest rate as well as the wage rate is sticky, we believe we have come much closer to capturing the essence of traditional views concerning the nature of unemployment equilibria. As a side benefit, we believe that the investment and consumption functions that we derive provide a better basis than the neoclassical functions that have become fashionable in the last two decades for future theoretical and empirical work in this area.

The plan of the paper is as follows. In Section II we outline the microeconomic foundations of the model, and in Section III we illustrate the determination of notional equilibrium when all wages and prices are flexible, and examine the various types of effective equilibrium that can prevail when the current and expected future wage rate and output price are sticky. In this section we assume that agents have Walrasian expectations (by which we mean that they do not expect to face any quantity constraints in the future), whereas in Sections IV and V we investigate the consequences of arbitrary and rational constraint expectations, respectively. Sections VI and VII consider the comparative statics properties of the model, paying particular attention to the magnitude of the Keynesian multiplier under different expectational assumptions. Finally, Section VIII summarizes the paper's conclusions and notes some directions for further research.

II. THE MODEL: HOUSEHOLD AND FIRM BEHAVIOR[5]

In the model to be considered, private-sector agents form plans for the remainder of their lifetimes at the beginning of the current period on the basis of their subjectively certain point expectations concerning future prices, wages, and constraint levels. Although the model is thus implicitly a multiperiod one, only the first two periods, labeled "1" and "2," are treated explicitly, while agents' preferences over all subsequent periods are summarized by including as an argument in their objective function their holdings of assets at the end of the second period.

To illustrate this procedure, consider first the household sector. For simplicity, we abstract from distribution effects and so assume that the sector's behavior can be characterized as if it were the outcome of the maximization of a single aggregate utility function. We also assume that total labor supply in each period is fixed.[6] Hence, the sector's utility function (written in additive form) depends on consumption in each period, c_1 and c_2, and on the amount of real money balances held at the end of the second period, m_2/p_2:

$$(1) \qquad\qquad U = u(c_1) + \alpha u(c_2) + \phi(m_2/p_2; \theta).$$

The function $\phi(\cdot)$ indirectly represents the utility derived from consumption in all periods beyond the first two, and so depends on expectations of prices, incomes, and constraint levels in those periods. In the present paper we assume that these expectations, denoted by the vector θ, are independent of all that happens in the first two periods, and so may be treated as exogenous.[7]

5. The present version of the model differs in a number of respects from what appeared in NBER Working Paper No. 376. In particular, profits are now assumed to be redistributed instantaneously to households, and end-of-period-2 asset holdings are included as arguments in both agents' objective functions. These changes make little substantive difference to the properties of the model, and they avoid some implausible artifacts that had to be introduced in the earlier version to avoid a zero price of money in period 2. At the same time, we have reservations about the inclusion of real balances in the household's utility function, for reasons on which we hope to elaborate in a subsequent paper.

6. The simplifying assumption of fixed labor supply precludes the possibility of a Barro-Grossman "supply multiplier" in states of generalized excess demand.

7. This assumption is relaxed in a subsequent paper.

In the absence of any quantity constraints, maximization of (1) is carried out subject only to the budget constraint (2):

$$(2) \qquad p_1 c_1 + p_2 c_2 + m_2 \le Y,$$

where p_1 is the current output price and p_2 is the price that is currently expected to prevail next period. Y is total income received in the first two periods, consisting of households' initial endowment of money balances $\overline{m}_0$, and of their current income in each period, which, since households are the sole owners of firms, equals the total value of output that households expect to be produced each period:

$$(3) \qquad Y = \overline{m}_0 + p_1 y_1 + p_2 y_2.$$

Note that (unlike Malinvaud) we assume that both wages and profits are distributed instantaneously to households,[8] implying (since leisure does not enter the utility function) that the marginal propensity to consume out of each is the same.

Maximization of (1) subject to (2) leads to unconstrained or notional demand functions for current and future consumption:

$$(4) \qquad c_1(p_1, p_2, Y) \quad \text{and} \quad c_2(p_1, p_2, Y).$$
$$\quad - \ ? \ + \qquad\qquad ? \ - \ +$$

These functions are homogeneous of degree zero in all nominal variables, including the prices expected to prevail beyond period 2 that form part of the vector θ. However, since these expectations are treated as parameters, it is more convenient to suppress them and to write the functions in extensive form as shown.

The signs of the partial derivatives of the functions in (4) are as indicated. Naturally, we assume that consumption in each period is a normal good and responds negatively to changes in the price prevailing in that period. However, the effect on current consumption of a change in the price of future output (i.e., the effect on savings of a change in the interest rate) is indeterminate in general, since, as is well-known, the income and substitution effects of such a change work in opposite directions. In the diagrams below we assume for convenience that the substitution effect dominates, so that $\partial c_1 / \partial p_2$ is always positive, but this assumption is not crucial.

Turning next to firms, we see that their behavior is modeled in an analogous manner.[9] We assume that it can be viewed as the outcome of the actions of a representative firm that maximizes the dis-

---

8. Or that there is no "corporate veil," so that it is as if all wages and profits are distributed.

9. The essential difference between households and firms is that the former are assumed to be able to store money but not goods, and conversely for the latter.

counted sum of current and future profits (the latter measured in present value prices), with profits in all periods beyond the second determined by the level of investment in period 2:

$$(5) \qquad \Pi = \pi_1 + \pi_2 + \psi(I_2;\theta).$$

When the firm faces no quantity constraints, it chooses current and future employment levels, e_1 and e_2, as well as I_1 and I_2, the quantities of output in each period that it holds over as investment to augment the productivity of labor in the future. Profits in periods 1 and 2 are therefore given by the following:

$$(6) \qquad \pi_1 = p_1[F(e_1) - I_1] - w_1 e_1$$

$$(7) \qquad \pi_2 = p_2[H(e_2,I_1) - I_2] - w_2 e_2,$$

where $F(e_1)$ is current output and $H(e_2,I_1)$ is output next period.[10] We assume that production is subject to diminishing returns to each factor in both periods: $F_{ee}, H_{ee}, H_{II} < 0$; that labor and investment are complementary in the production of future output: $H_{eI} > 0$; and that the production function for future output is strictly concave: $H_{ee}H_{II} - H_{eI}^2 > 0$ (i.e., that labor and investment are subject to diminishing returns to scale). Under these assumptions, unconstrained profit maximization leads, as shown in the Appendix, to notional employment and investment demand functions:

$$(8) \qquad e_1(p_1,w_1), \quad I_1(p_1,p_2,w_2), \quad e^2(p_1,p_2,w_2), \quad \text{and } I_2(p_2).$$
$$ + - \qquad\quad - + - \qquad\quad - + - \qquad\qquad -$$

These in turn imply notional output supply functions y_i and net corporate sales functions x_i in each period:

$$(9) \qquad\qquad y_1(p_1,w_1) = F[e_1(p_1,w_1)]$$
$$ + -$$

$$(10) \qquad y_2(p_1,p_2,w_2) = H[e_2(p_1,p_2,w_2),I_1(p_1,p_2,w_2)]$$
$$ - + -$$

$$(11) \qquad x_1(p_1,w_1,p_2,w_2) = y_1(p_1,w_1) - I_1(p_1,p_2,w_2)$$
$$ + - - +$$

$$(12) \qquad x_2(p_1,p_2,w_2) = y_2(p_1,p_2,w_2) - I_2(p_2).$$
$$ - + -$$

---

10. If the state of technology is given, the current production function $F(\cdot)$ may be viewed as identical to the future production function $H(\cdot)$ with a predetermined level of investment: $F(e_1) = H(e_1,I_0)$. We explicitly assume that $H(\cdot)$ is strictly concave (thus ruling out, for example, the form $H(e_2,I_1) = F(e_2) + I_1$), since otherwise future-period production levels would be indeterminate, unless firms expected to face a sales or employment constraint next period.

A RECONSTRUCTION OF KEYNESIAN ECONOMICS   205

As in the case of households, equations (8) to (12) are homogeneous of degree zero in all nominal variables, but it is more convenient to write them in extensive form and to suppress the exogenous expectations vector θ. We note that, when firms face no quantity constraints, current employment demand and output supply as given by (9) depend only on the current price and wage rate: a change in expected future wages or prices changes the amount of current output held over as investment and so changes current sales, but (provided that notional output supply does not fall below desired investment) it does not affect current employment and output decisions. Similarly next period's employment and output decisions are independent of the current wage rate.

The third and final agent in the economy is the government, which can make direct transfer payments to households, increasing their initial endowment $\overline{m}_0$, or can make direct purchases of goods in both present and future periods, g_1 and g_2. All of these actions are financed by printing money, so there is no analogue in our model to "pure" or bond-financed fiscal policy.

III. NOTIONAL AND EFFECTIVE EQUILIBRIA WITH WALRASIAN EXPECTATIONS

Having made these assumptions about the individual agents in the economy, we can now characterize a full Walrasian equilibrium by a wage-price vector $(p_1^*, w_1^*, p_2^*, w_2^*)$, which simultaneously satisfies the notional current and future goods-market equilibrium loci (*GMEL*) and the notional current and future labor-market equilibrium loci (*LMEL*):

(13) $GMEL_1(W,W): c_1(p_1,p_2,Y) + g_1 = x_1(p_1,w_1,p_2,w_2)$

(14) $GMEL_2(W,W): c_2(p_1,p_2,Y) + g_2 = x_2(p_1,p_2,w_2)$

(15) $LMEL_1(W,W): L = e_1(p_1,w_1)$

(16) $LMEL_2(W,W): L = e_2(p_1,p_2,w_2),$

where L is the household's full-employment or notional labor supply in both periods.[11] (Here and throughout the paper every equilibrium

---

11. Equations (13) and (14) may be manipulated, along with (2), (3), (9), and (10), to yield a fifth equation, the government budget constraint, which states that total government spending in the two periods must equal the excess of private-sector withdrawals (i.e., net household savings) over injections (i.e., corporate investment): $p_1g_1 + p_2g_2 = (m_2 - \overline{m}_0) - (p_1I_1 + p_2I_2)$. The latter equation must always hold as an ex post accounting identity whether markets are cleared by quantity or price adjustment.

locus refers to a particular period, denoted by a subscript, and is contingent on two regimes, indicated in parentheses: the first is the regime that prevails in the current period, and the second what is expected to prevail next period. W denotes Walrasian equilibrium.) Equations (13) to (16) are completed by specifying that the income which households expect to receive each period is that corresponding to the full-employment level of output (denoted by an asterisk); i.e., (3) is replaced by

$$(17) \qquad\qquad Y = \overline{m}_0 + p_1 \overline{y}_1^* + p_2 \overline{y}_2^*.$$

While equations (13) to (16) determine the full Walrasian wage-price vector, our concern in the remainder of this paper is with the nature of the equilibria that obtain, under different assumptions about constraint expectations, when some prices or wage rates differ from their Walrasian levels. In order to study this, it is desirable to reduce the dimensionality of the model, and we have chosen to confine our attention to variations in w_1 and p_2, assuming that p_1 and w_2 remain equal at all times to their full Walrasian equilibrium values, p_1^* and w_2^*. (It may be checked that our qualitative conclusions continue to hold if p_1 and w_1 are varied, holding p_2^* and w_2^* fixed.) With variations in only two prices under consideration, we may also dispense with two of the equilibrium loci, (13)–(16), and we have chosen to focus on the two first-period equilibrium loci, (13) and (15). Figure I illustrates how these two equations determine the Walrasian market-clearing values of w_1 and p_2. Given p_1^*, the notional $LMEL_1$, equation (15), uniquely defines w_1^*, points above this locus representing excess supply of, and points below representing excess demand for labor, while the notional $GMEL_1$, equation (13), defines a downward-sloping

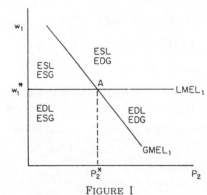

FIGURE I
Notional Equilibria with Walrasian Expectations

A RECONSTRUCTION OF KEYNESIAN ECONOMICS   207

locus, points above it corresponding to excess demand for goods and points below to excess supply of goods. (The assumption that current consumption responds positively to an expected rise in p_2 is sufficient but not necessary to ensure that the $GMEL_1$ is downward-sloping.) It may be noted that the equilibrium at A is globally stable if w_1 and p_2 change according to *tâtonnement* processes. This may be seen more easily by noting that the $GMEL_1$ is a standard IS curve, with points above it representing situations where investment demand exceeds savings, requiring a rise in the "interest rate" implicit in the model (i.e., a fall in p_2) to restore equilibrium and conversely for points below the locus.

When w_1 and p_2 are rigid, however, the division of the space into disequilibrium regions cannot be the same as in Figure I, for the by now well-known reason that a disequilibrium in one market affects decisions in the other market, so affecting the location of the equilibrium loci at all points other than the full Walrasian equilibrium point A. In the remainder of this section we show how the regions are affected when w_1 and p_2 are arbitrarily fixed and so disequilibrium prevails, on the crucial assumption (to be relaxed in the next section) that all agents expect a Walrasian equilibrium to prevail in the next period. We also assume for simplicity that the same expectations of future wage and price levels are held by all agents, and we continue to assume that p_1 is fixed at p_1^* and that expectations of future wages are completely inelastic at the Walrasian level w_2^*.

Consider first the goods-market equilibrium locus under conditions of excess supply of labor (ESL): for all wage rates greater than w_1^* in Figure I, some unemployment prevails, and so households' current income is below the full-employment level $p_1^* y_1^*$. Hence, the effective $GMEL_1$ is not (13), but[12]

(18) $GMEL_1(ESL,W)$: $c_1(p_1^*,p_2,\tilde{Y}) + g_1 = x_1(p_1^*,w_1,p_2,w_2^*)$,

where[13]

(19) $\tilde{Y} = \overline{m}_0 + p_1^* y_1(p_1^*,w_1) + p_2 \overline{y}_2^*$.

12. As in Neary [1980] we adopt the following notational convention throughout: a bar over a variable (e.g., $\bar{e}_1$) indicates that, from the point of view of the agent under consideration, its value is predetermined in the current period; a tilde (e.g., $\tilde{y}_1$) indicates a function or parameter arising from behavior in the face of a labor-market constraint; a circumflex (e.g., $\hat{y}_1$) indicates behavior in the face of a goods-market constraint; and symbols are used to indicate behavior in the face of multiple constraints (e.g., $\hat{y}_1$ denotes behavior in the face of a goods-market constraint in both periods).

13. In this case, unlike (17), there is some ambiguity as to what value should be assigned to $\overline{y}_2^*$, the full-employment level of income that households expect to receive next period. Since investment depends on p_2, a change in this variable affects the capital stock and so the level of full-employment output in period 2. However, it makes little difference to the analysis whether or not households are assumed to take account of this.

208   *QUARTERLY JOURNAL OF ECONOMICS*

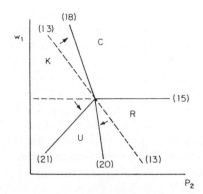

FIGURE II
Effective Equilibria with Walrasian Expectations

Since constrained income $\tilde{Y}$ is less than notional income Y whenever w_1 exceeds w_1^*, it follows that households' effective consumption demand is reduced as a result of the unemployment they face, and so a point of notional goods-market equilibrium in (w_1, p_2) space corresponds to effective excess supply of current output. In passing from notional to effective regions, therefore, the effective $GMEL_1(ESL, W)$ lies to the right of the notional $GMEL_1(W, W)$, as shown in Figure II (where each locus is labeled by the number of the equation that defines it). Of course, the two loci differ only for values of w_1 greater than w_1^*, since it is only in this range that the employment constraint facing households is binding (i.e., $e_1(p_1^*, w_1) < L$ and so $y_1(p_1^*, w_1) < \bar{y}_1^*$).

A similar argument applies to the $GMEL_1$ when the labor market exhibits excess demand (EDL): households are now unconstrained, whereas firms' current production is constrained by the labor they can obtain:

(20) $GMEL_1(EDL, W)$: $c_1(p_1^*, p_2, Y) + g_1 = \tilde{x}_1(\bar{e}_1; p_1^*, p_2, w_2^*)$
$\qquad\qquad\qquad\qquad\qquad\qquad\quad + \ + \ - \ -$

$$= F(\bar{e}_1) - I_1(p_1^*, p_2, w_2^*),$$

(20')

where $\bar{e}_1$ is simply L and is less than the notional demand for labor $e_1(p_1, w_1)$. We may note that, under our assumptions, the excess demand for labor does not affect firms' investment plans (assuming, of course, that the constraint does not become so severe that their maximum output level falls below their desired level of investment). If we compare (20) with (13), it must follow, since the employment constraint bites, that effective supply is less than notional supply, implying that the constrained $GMEL_1$ lies to the left of the notional locus when excess demand for labor prevails (i.e., when w_1 is less than w_1^*), as shown in Figure II.

The $LMEL_1$ is affected in a similar manner when the goods market is out of equilibrium. Thus, in a situation of excess supply of goods, households are unconstrained, but firms are unable to make their notional level of sales. This forces them to recalculate their employment and investment decisions, with the result that the $LMEL_1$ becomes

$$(21) \qquad LMEL_1(ESG,W): L = \hat{e}_1[\bar{x}_1;w_1,p_2,w_2^*]$$
$$+ \ - \ + \ -$$

$$(21') \qquad = F^{-1}[\bar{x}_1 + \hat{I}_1\{\bar{x}_1;w_1,p_2,w_2^*\}],$$
$$- \ - \ + \ -$$

where the current sales constraint facing firms is[14]

$$(22) \qquad \bar{x}_1 = c_1(p_1^*,p_2,Y) + g_1 < x_1(p_1^*,w_1,p_2,w_2^*).$$

We may note that, by contrast with (8), current employment demand now depends on much more than just the current real wage: the demand for labor is determined both by what firms are able to sell and by what they decide to store. The latter is itself in turn affected by the sales constraint, by contrast with an employment constraint that, as equation (20') shows, does not affect the relative profitability of selling and investing. When we compare equations (15) and (21), since constrained employment demand $\hat{e}_1$ is less than notional employment demand e_1 a point of notional labor-market equilibrium must correspond to effective excess supply of labor when excess supply of goods prevails; (21) therefore lies below (15) in Figure II. However, when we compare (21') with (20'), since constrained investment demand $\hat{I}_1$ must be greater than notional investment demand I_1, it follows that these two loci do not coincide and that (21) lies to the left of (20). Allowing investment to be carried out by firms therefore leads to a region of effective excess supply of goods and excess demand for labor, or, in the terminology of Muellbauer and Portes [1978], a region of underconsumption.

14. As with other models of temporary equilibrium with rationing, though unlike the textbook Keynesian model, we assume that firms face a constraint on their sales *net* of investment demand, rather than on their gross sales. Otherwise, with only one representative firm using a single input to produce a homogeneous output, the corporate sector could never face strictly binding rations in both labor and goods markets, and so region U in Figure II would vanish.

Finally, when excess demand for goods prevails and the labor market is in equilibrium, firms are unconstrained, and, though households are rationed in the goods market, the assumption that labor is supplied inelastically ensures that this does not affect their labor supply. The effective $LMEL_1$ therefore coincides with the notional locus (15): as shown in Figure II, the boundary between regions C and R does not pivot around point A.

These shifts from notional to effective equilibrium loci are summarized in Figure II (where the notional loci are shown as dashed lines and the effective loci as solid lines). Following now-standard usage, we may label the four regions K for Keynesian unemployment, C for classical unemployment, R for repressed inflation, and U for underconsumption. The nature of the disequilibrium in the two markets that prevails in each region is the same as in the corresponding notional regions in Figure I.[15]

IV. INTERTEMPORAL SPILLOVERS AND "BOOTSTRAPS" EFFECTS

We now turn to the central focus of this paper: the effects of expectations by households or firms that they will face constraints in the future. One of the central concerns of the recent literature on fix-price models has been to show how a disequilibrium in one market has effects that spill over into other markets. In the light of this, it is not surprising that expectations of future constraints should have a significant effect on the behavior of firms and households in current markets. Our objective here, however, is more than simply to demonstrate that such intertemporal spillovers occur. We wish to show that they exhibit what we call a "bootstraps" property: households' expectations of future constraints on the sale of labor make it more likely that there will be a constraint on their ability to sell labor currently; while expectations by firms of constraints on their ability to sell goods in the future make it more likely that they will face a sales constraint in this period. It is this bootstraps property that leads to the possibility of there being multiple equilibria consistent with the *same* level of current wages and prices, and expected future wages and prices.

In this section we consider the general class of exogenously given

15. Figures I and II are in fact identical to the corresponding diagrams illustrating the regions of notional and effective equilibria in $(w/p, m/p)$ space in the Barro-Grossman-Malinvaud model, provided it is assumed that labor is supplied inelastically and that investment may be carried out by firms.

constraint expectations. In the following section, the techniques that we have developed will be employed to investigate the special case where expectations are rational.[16] Our strategy is to examine the effects of such expectations on the location of the various disequilibrium regions in (w_1, p_2) space. To illustrate the general points, we look in detail at two particularly interesting effects: those of expected Keynesian and classical unemployment on the location of the locus separating regions K and C (i.e., the $GMEL_1$ when current unemployment prevails).

The first point to emphasize is that if agents expect to be constrained next period this may affect their current behavior even if w_1 and p_2 are flexible; in other words, it may shift the notional equilibrium loci in Figure I. Admittedly, this is not true of the $LMEL_1$, equation (15), since labor supply is fixed and, when firms face no constraints in the present period, their current employment decisions are determined only by p_1 and w_1, irrespective of what constraints they expect to face next period. However, the notional $GMEL_1$ is affected. Consider first the case where agents expect regime K (excess supply of both labor and goods) to prevail next period. This displaces the notional locus for two distinct reasons. First, since households expect to be unemployed next period, their expected income is reduced, and so (13) must be replaced by

(23) $GMEL_1(W, ESL): c_1(p_1^*, p_2, \tilde{Y}') + g_1 = x_1(p_1^*, w_1, p_2, w_2^*),$

where

(24) $$\tilde{Y}' = \overline{m}_0 + p_1^* y_1^* + p_2 \overline{y}_2, \quad \overline{y}_2 < \overline{y}_2^*.$$

The lowering of the income that households expect to receive next

---

16. In the context of a nonstochastic fix-price model, the particular sense in which the term rational expectations has come to be understood has extremely strong implications: all individuals have perfect foresight not only concerning the level of wages and prices that will prevail in the future and the constraints that will be binding, but also concerning the magnitude of those constraints. This degree of foresight seems highly implausible. A more general model would take into account explicitly the fact that individuals do not have point estimates of the constraints that they will face, but rather a probability distribution. Since the idiosyncratic components determining the precise distribution of the values of the constraints facing any one household or firm may be relatively large, the individual may have little basis on which to learn when his distribution differs from the "true" distribution. Moreover, since individuals are risk-averse and are typically unable to fully insure against the risks associated with facing particular constraints in the future, the certainty-equivalent value of the constraint may differ markedly from the mean value of the constraint. For these reasons, we conjecture that the discussion of this section may be of greater relevance than the more restricted assumption of rational expectations we employ in the next section. However, not all readers have agreed with us, and, for those readers, the present section should be viewed as simply developing the analytical tools that will be employed in the next.

212   *QUARTERLY JOURNAL OF ECONOMICS*

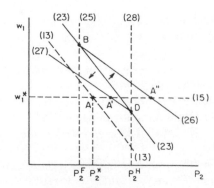

FIGURE III
Notional Equilibria with Arbitrary Expectations of Classical or Keynesian
Unemployment

period to $p_2 \bar{y}_2$ reduces their current consumption, and so shifts the notional locus to the right at all points, expanding the region of current excess supply of goods, as shown in Figure III. (Compare the lines labeled (13) and (23).)

The expectation by all agents that Keynesian unemployment will prevail next period also displaces the notional locus for a second reason, since firms now expect to face a sales constraint $\bar{x}_2$ next period. However, such an exogenous expected constraint is not binding for all wage-price combinations, but only for those that imply a level of notional sales next period which violates the constraint; i.e., for which

$$(25) \qquad \qquad \bar{x}_2 < x_2(p_1^*, p_2, w_2^*).$$

Given p_1^* and w_2^*, (25) written as an equality defines p_2^F, the threshold level of p_2 at which the constraint is just binding on firms, as an increasing function of the expected constraint $\bar{x}_2$. (Clearly, p_2^F must lie below p_2^*, since otherwise the corresponding expected constraint $\bar{x}_2$ would exceed the notional level of sales at the full Walrasian price vector $x_2(p_1^*, p_2^*, w_2^*)$.) For values of p_2 below p_2^F, sales in period 2 are relatively unprofitable, and so the expected constraint is not a binding one, and the locus we are seeking coincides with (23). However, for values of p_2 above p_2^F, firms' notional sales next period exceed $\bar{x}_2$, and so they must recalculate their plans for both periods, which leads to (23) being replaced by (26):

$$(26) \quad GMEL_1(W,K): c_1(p_1^*, p_2, \tilde{Y}') + g_1 = \hat{x}_1(x_2; p_1^* w_1, w_2^*)$$
$$\qquad \qquad \qquad \qquad \qquad - \; + \; - \; -$$

$$(26') \qquad \qquad \qquad \qquad = y_1(p_1^*, w_1) - \hat{I}_1(\bar{x}_2; p_1^*, w_2^*).$$
$$\qquad \qquad \qquad \qquad \qquad \qquad + \; - \; +$$

A RECONSTRUCTION OF KEYNESIAN ECONOMICS   213

The expected sales constraint reduces current investment and so "spills over" into an increase in current sales causing the region of excess supply of goods to expand. This is shown in Figure III by the counterclockwise pivoting of (23) around point B (the point at which the constraint (25) is just binding).

The effect on the notional $GMEL_1$ of the expectation that classical unemployment will prevail next period may be determined in a similar manner, the main difference being that firms do not now expect to face any constraints and so remain on their notional sales function. Households, on the other hand, expect to be constrained in both markets. We assume that their expectation of unemployment is the same as that already assumed in our discussion of expected Keynesian unemployment (i.e., the income they expect to receive in periods 1 and 2 is given by (24)). As before, therefore, this shifts the locus from (13) to (23). In addition, households expect to be rationed in their goods purchases, causing them to recalculate their current demand with the result that (23) must be replaced by (27):

(27) $GMEL_1(W,C)$: $\hat{c}_1(\bar{c}_2;p_1^*,p_2,\tilde{Y}') + g_1 = x_1(p_1^*,w_1,p_2,w_2^*)$.
$$- \quad - \quad ? \quad +$$

The expected goods constraint $\bar{c}_2$ reduces the incentive to save and so raises households' current demand, shifting the notional $GMEL_1$ to the *left* and expanding the region of current excess demand for output. However, as with the expected sales constraint in (26), this does not happen for all (w_1,p_2) combinations but only for those at which the expected constraint $\bar{c}_2$ is binding; i.e., for which

(28) $\bar{c}_2 < c_2(p_1^*,p_2,\tilde{Y})$.

Given p_1^*, (28) written with equality defines p_2^H, the threshold level of p_2 at which the expected constraint $\bar{c}_2$ is just binding on households, as a decreasing function of $\bar{c}_2$. As illustrated in Figure III, p_2^H must lie to the right of p_2^*; for values of p_2 above p_2^H notional demand for consumption in period 2 is less than the constraint, and (23) coincides with (27). However, for lower values of p_2, households expect to be constrained and so the notional $GMEL_1$ pivots to the left around point D (the point on (23) at which p_2 equals p_2^H).

The major conclusion to be drawn from Figure III is that the notional $GMEL_1$ when classical unemployment is expected next period lies strictly to the left of the notional $GMEL_1$ when Keynesian unemployment is expected. Before noting the implications of this, we must recall that our main concern is not with the location of various notional loci in the diagram but rather with the location of the corresponding *effective* loci when different expectations are held about

214   QUARTERLY JOURNAL OF ECONOMICS

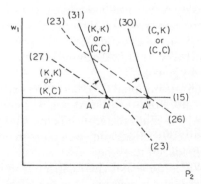

FIGURE IV
Effective Equilibria with Arbitrary Expectations of Classical or Keynesian
Unemployment

future constraints. This is easily done with the help of Figure IV, where the two dashed lines repeat the notional loci derived in Figure III. As with the move from (13) to (18) in Figure II, taking account of current excess supply of labor necessitates replacing $\tilde{Y}$ in both (26) and (27) by $\hat{Y}$, the level of income received when unemployment both prevails in period 1 and is expected to prevail in period 2:

$$(29) \qquad \hat{Y} = \overline{m}_0 + p_1^* y_1(p_1^*, w_1) + p_2 \overline{y}_2, \quad \overline{y}_2 < \overline{y}_2^*.$$

The notional loci (26) and (27) must therefore be replaced by their effective counterparts (30) and (31), which incorporate the effects of current as well as expected future unemployment:

$$(30) \quad GMEL_1(ESL,K): c_1(p_1^*,p_2,\hat{Y}) + g_1 = \hat{x}_1(\overline{x}_2;p_1^*,w_1,w_2^*)$$

$$(31) \quad GMEL_1(ESL,C): \hat{c}_1(\overline{c}_2;p_1^*,p_2,\hat{Y}) + g_1 = x_1(p_1^*,w_1,p_2,w_2^*).$$

Since these loci apply only when w_1 exceeds w_1^* (so that the current employment constraint is binding), they are derived by pivoting the notional loci (26) and (27) clockwise around their points of intersection with the notional $LMEL_1$, i.e., points A' and A''. For the same reasons just given that require the notional $GMEL_1$ when classical unemployment is expected to lie to the left of the corresponding locus when Keynesian unemployment is expected, so the effective locus (31) in Figure IV must lie wholly to the left of (30). The letters in the diagram indicate the combinations of current and expected future regimes that (depending on the state of expectations) may obtain in the three regions bounded by (30), (31), and (15).

This analysis has three important implications. First, *the vector of current and expected future prices consistent with full Walrasian equilibrium is not unique:* when w_1 and p_2 are flexible, there is a continuum of possible Walrasian equilibria lying along the notional $LMEL_1$ defined by equation (15) (including, for example, all points on the segment AA''), each one corresponding to a given configuration of constraint expectations. Second, *effective equilibria are not uniquely determined by current and expected future prices:* when w_1 and p_2 are sticky, there is a large region of (w_1, p_2) space (including the whole of the area between the two solid lines labeled (30) and (31) in Figure IV) which is compatible with *either* regime C or K prevailing today, the only difference being the state of constraint expectations. Third, *exogenous constraint expectations imply a bootstraps effect,* in the sense that, for any arbitrary price vector, regime K is more likely than regime C to prevail today if it is expected to prevail tomorrow, and conversely.

This concludes our examination of how expectations of different types of unemployment affect the location of the locus separating regions K and C. A similar analysis may be carried out for the effects of other constraint expectations on all four effective equilibrium loci, and broadly similar conclusions follow.[17] In particular, the prevalence

17. Two qualifications to this statement must be noted. In the first place, the $LMEL_1$ under conditions of excess demand for goods turns out to be completely independent of the state of expectations about future constraints, just as we found in the last section that with Walrasian expectations it coincides with the notional $LMEL_1$. The reasons for this are simple: the assumption of an inelastic labor supply ensures that households' expectations do not affect their current labor supply; while the assumptions that the labor market is currently in equilibrium and that firms can sell all they currently wish to produce mean that firms' demand for labor depends only on the current real wage and is independent of whether or not they expect to be constrained in the future. A second qualification is that the complementarity assumed to exist between employment and investment in the second-period production function $H(\cdot)$ yields some exceptions to the rule that expectations give rise to a bootstraps effect in the sense defined above. To illustrate this, consider the effective $GMEL_1$ when excess demand for labor prevails. When all agents expect to be unconstrained in the future, this is given by equation (20) above. Now suppose instead that they expect regime R to prevail in the future. This yields an alternative locus:

(32) $$GMEL_1(EDL,R): \hat{c}_1(\bar{c}_2; p_1^*, p_2, Y) + g_1 = \bar{x}_1(\bar{e}_1, \bar{e}_2; p_1^*, p_2)$$
$$\phantom{GMEL_1(EDL,R): \hat{c}_1(\bar{c}_2; p_1^*, p_2, Y) + g_1 = }\begin{matrix} + & - & + & - \end{matrix}$$

(32') $$= F(\bar{e}_1) - \bar{I}_1(\bar{e}_2; p_1^*, p_2),$$
$$\phantom{= F(\bar{e}_1) - \bar{I}_1(\bar}\begin{matrix} + & - & + \end{matrix}$$

where

(33) $$\bar{e}_1 < e_1(p_1^*, w_1) \quad \text{and} \quad \bar{e}_2 < e_2(p_1^*, p_2, w_2^*).$$

As with the case of expected classical unemployment, consumers expect to be constrained in the goods market next period, thus reducing their incentive to save, encouraging them to spend more in the present, and so increasing the likelihood that excess demand for goods will prevail today. However, the fact that firms expect to be unable to hire as much labor as they will wish in the future leads them, because of the complementarity between labor and investment, to *reduce* rather than increase their current investment demand. Since their current output is unaffected, this tends to make it more likely that excess supply of rather than excess demand for goods will prevail today. In this case, therefore, the expectation that regime R will prevail next period leads to two effects, one of which makes it more likely but the other of which makes it less likely that regime R will prevail in the present, and there is no presumption in general as to which of these effects will dominate.

of a given regime today depends on the expectations held about which regimes will prevail tomorrow, and in most cases these expectations give rise to bootstraps phenomena in the sense already discussed.

V. Rational Constraint Expectations

The analysis in the previous section is open to the criticism that, by placing no restrictions on agents' expectations of future constraints, it makes inevitable a considerable degree of arbitrariness in the current regimes that are consistent with a given wage-price vector. In this section we explore an alternative approach that avoids this arbitrariness of expectations by postulating that households and firms have full information concerning each others' intended future actions. Thus, for example, the income constraint that households expect to face in the next period equals the value of output that firms currently intend to produce in that period. By analogy with the widely studied phenomenon of rational expectations of prices, we label this hypothesis one of *rational constraint expectations* (RCE). The concept of rational constraint expectations clearly has a considerable informational requirement. However, it is only assumed that agents know the *aggregate* constraints that they will face next period: for example, from equation (34) below, firms know what the level of aggregate demand will be next period, but they do not know its distribution between different consumers. This assumption is not only plausible but is also necessary if the hypothesis of price-taking behavior in the face of fixed prices is to be maintained, since if firms knew the demands of individual consumers they would have an incentive to enter into bilateral bargaining with them.

We now wish to locate in (w_1, p_2) space the regions that are consistent with different disequilibrium regimes when constraint expectations are rational. As in the previous section we illustrate this construction for one especially interesting case only: namely, the current *GMEL*, assuming that excess supply of labor prevails today and that Keynesian unemployment is rationally expected to prevail tomorrow. This locus is identical to (30), with households' income in the two periods denoted by (29). The new feature is that the expected future constraints, $\bar{x}_2$ and $\bar{y}_2$, are no longer parameters, but instead equal the actual levels of sales and output which, if current plans are realized, will obtain in period 2:

$$(34) \qquad \bar{x}_2 = c_2(p_1^*, p_2, \tilde{Y}) + g_2$$

$$(35) \qquad \bar{y}_2 = \hat{y}_2(\bar{x}_2; p_1^*, w_2^*).$$

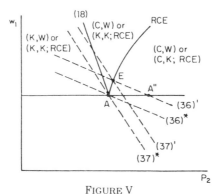

FIGURE V
Effective Equilibria with Rational Expectations of Keynesian Unemployment

The main result we wish to establish concerning the $GMEL_1$ with current unemployment and rational expectations of Keynesian unemployment is that, when this locus exists, *it must lie to the right of* (18), the $GMEL_1$ with current unemployment, and Walrasian expectations. To see this, consider the following algorithm for determining the location of the desired locus: for each value of $\bar{x}_2$, the expected future sales constraint, locate in (w_1,p_2) space the following two loci, which are derived from equations (30) and (34), by using equations (29) and (35) to eliminate $\tilde{Y}$ and $\bar{y}_2$:

(36) $c_1[p_1^*,p_2,\overline{m}_0 + p_1^* y_1(p_1^*,w_1) + p_2 \hat{y}_2(\bar{x}_2;p_1^*,w_2^*)]$

$$+ g_1 = \hat{x}_1(\bar{x}_2;p_1^*,w_1,w_2^*)$$

(37) $\bar{x}_2 = c_2[p_1^* p_2,\overline{m}_0 + p_1^* y_1(p_1^*,w_1) + p_2,\hat{y}_2(\bar{x}_2;p_1^*,w_2^*)] + g_2.$

Now trace out the locus of intersection points of (36) and (37) as $\bar{x}_2$ is varied parametrically. It is clear that this locus is the RCE locus we require, since (36) is the $GMEL_1$ with current unemployment and expected Keynesian unemployment conditional on a given sales constraint being expected by both firms and households, while (37) states that that sales constraint equals planned aggregate demand next period. Thus, every point on the RCE locus must lie on one of the family of loci defined by (36). But, as argued in Section IV, if the expected sales and income constraints, $\bar{x}_2$ and $\bar{y}_2$, are binding, then excess supply of goods in period 1 is increased. Hence every locus defined by (36) for different binding values of $\bar{x}_2$ must lie to the right of (18), the corresponding locus when no binding constraints are expected next period. Thus, the RCE locus itself must lie to the right of (18), as was to be proved.

This reasoning is illustrated in Figure V. The dashed lines labeled

(36)* and (37)* represent the loci defined by equations (36) and (37) where the expected sales constraint equals the value of actual sales next period in the full Walrasian equilibrium: $c_2(p_1^*, p_2^*, \bar{m}_0 + p_1^* \bar{y}_1^* + p_2^* \bar{y}_2^*) + g_2$. These loci intersect at A, since the full Walrasian equilibrium may be interpreted as a "constrained" equilibrium where the values of current and expected future constraints equal the actual values that obtain in the full Walrasian equilibrium itself. Hence point A lies on the $GMEL_1$ with rational constraint expectations. A reduction in the expected sales constraint below its Walrasian level shifts both curves upward to (36)′ and (37)′, whose intersection point E therefore lies on the RCE locus.[18] Successive variations in $\bar{x}_2$ thus trace out the required locus (labeled "RCE" in the diagram) that must lie to the right of (18) if the rationally expected future sales constraint is a binding one.

The implication of this result is of considerable interest: the set of (w_1, p_2) combinations consistent with Keynesian rather than classical unemployment in the current period is *greater* when Keynesian unemployment is rationally expected to prevail next period than when Walrasian equilibrium is expected. In this sense we may say that rational constraint expectations increase the likelihood that Keynesian unemployment will prevail in the current period. At the same time, the requirement that expectations be rational places more restrictions on the types of equilibria consistent with a given wage-price vector than did the exogenous constraint expectations considered in Section IV: for example, many points such as A'' are consistent with Keynesian unemployment in the current period if expectations are allowed to be arbitrarily pessimistic, but not in general if they are required to be rational.

The implications of rational constraint expectations for the location of other equilibrium loci may be considered in a similar fashion, and the same conclusion follows: since every point on a RCE locus must coincide with a point on the locus that represents the same combination of current and expected future regimes but contingent on exogenously given expected constraints, the conclusions in Section IV concerning the location of equilibrium loci when constraint expectations are arbitrary continue to hold when they are rational. Hence, subject to the qualification noted in footnote 17 at the end of Section IV arising from the complementarity between investment and

---

18. It is possible that E lies to the left of (18), in which case the solution to equations (36) and (37) does not satisfy the required inequality constraints; i.e., the effective $GMEL_1$ with rational expectations of Keynesian unemployment does not exist.

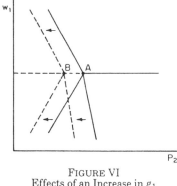

FIGURE VI
Effects of an Increase in g_1

employment in period 2's production function, the bootstraps phenomenon persists with rational constraint expectations.[19]

VI. COMPARATIVE STATICS: SHIFTS BETWEEN REGIMES

Having outlined some of the consequences of exogenous and rational constraint expectations for the location of current disequilibrium regions, we turn to a brief consideration of their implications for the comparative statics responses to exogenous shocks. An analysis of the effects of changes in exogenous variables in a model of temporary equilibrium with rationing must take account of both their effects on the endogenous variables within each region and their effects on the location of the regions themselves. This section considers the latter, while the next examines the Keynesian employment multiplier.

Figures VI and VII illustrate the effects of changes in current government expenditure and the state of technology (or, equivalently, the level of profitability), on the location of the four disequilibrium

19. It should be pointed out that we have *not* established here that rational constraint expectations are consistent with multiple equilibria. Laroque [1981] has shown in a general fix-price model that a necessary and sufficient condition for uniqueness of the fixed-price equilibria in a neighborhood of the competitive equilibrium is that the determinants of the matrices of aggregate spillover effects have the same sign in all states of the markets. Although Laroque's model is a single-period one, it is formally equivalent to ours when constraint expectations are rational. However, the application of his criterion to our model yields ambiguous results: for example in regime (K,K) the relevant determinant equals the denominator of (46), which we have assumed to be positive, whereas in "mixed" regimes such as (C,K) and (K,C) its sign is indeterminate. The more interesting questions of whether price vectors not in a neighborhood of the Walrasian vector are consistent with more than one RCE equilibrium, and whether there are some simple characterizations of those situations in which multiple equilibria arise, must await further research.

220   *QUARTERLY JOURNAL OF ECONOMICS*

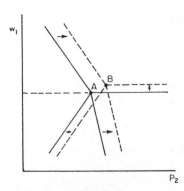

FIGURE VII
Effects of an Exogenous Improvement in Current Profitability

regions, assuming Walrasian expectations. An increase in g_1 shifts the Walrasian equilibrium from A to B in Figure VI, implying that, if the economy is initially in Walrasian equilibrium, a cut in government spending will give rise to Keynesian unemployment, while a rise in government spending will induce excess demand for goods (without immediately disturbing labor market equilibrium). Similarly, Figure VII shows the effects of supply-side shocks on the diagram. An exogenous improvement in profitability (due, for example, to technological progress) affects the loci as shown, assuming (plausibly) that it raises the demand for labor at a given real wage. Hence point A, which represents initial Walrasian equilibrium, moves into a state of Keynesian unemployment, requiring a rise in the real wage if Walrasian equilibrium is to be restored. Conversely, an exogenous decline in profitability (due, for example, to an increase in the price of an imported input) converts an initial state of Walrasian equilibrium into one of classical unemployment, so requiring the classical remedy of a real wage cut.

These effects of changes in current exogenous variables are similar to those that hold in the Barro-Grossman-Malinvaud model. An important additional feature of our two-period model is that it permits an examination of the effects of exogenous changes in expectations, both of future constraint levels and of future wages and prices. The effects of changes in the former have already been considered in Section IV. As for an increase in w_2, the expected future wage rate, this has two effects: First, it has a substitution effect on production, reducing firms' desired employment next period and so (because of the complementarity in the period 2 production function

$H(\cdot)$) reducing current investment demand and therefore raising the current supply of output. Second, to the extent that households foresee the wage increase and the consequent reduction in output next period, their lifetime income is reduced, and so their current demand is lowered. On both counts, therefore, a rise in w_2 expands the region of excess supply of current output. Of course, this conclusion relies heavily on the assumed absence of distribution effects: if the marginal propensity to consume out of wages exceeds that out of nonlabor income, then an increase in w_2 could raise demand for output in period 1. To the extent that this effect dominated, an increase in w_2 would have exactly the same effect on the diagram as an increase in g_1 in Figure VI, implying that an expected future wage *cut* will shift the economy from Walrasian equilibrium into Keynesian unemployment in the current period.

The relationships illustrated in Figures VI and VII between changes in exogenous variables and shifts in the equilibrium loci continue to hold whatever assumptions are made about constraint expectations. In addition, rational constraint expectations permit a further role for demand- and supply-side shocks through the "announcement effects" of perfectly foreseen changes in the levels of future government spending and profitability. Thus, an increase in g_2 relaxes the expected future sales constraint on firms, which both raises their current investment demand and (by raising their planned output next period) relaxes the income constraint facing households. On both counts, the region of excess demand for current output is enlarged, and so with rational constraint expectations a perfectly anticipated increase in g_2 has exactly the same effect on the diagram as an increase in g_1 has in Figure VI. Similarly, an anticipated increase in future profitability enlarges the region of current excess supply of goods, and so has effects similar to those of an increase in current profitability in Figure VII.

VII. COMPARATIVE STATICS: THE KEYNESIAN EMPLOYMENT MULTIPLIER

Turning next to the comparative statics properties of the model within different regions, we show in this section that, when households and firms have rational expectations of future constraints, the employment multiplier following an increase in government spending is *larger* than conventionally assumed.[20] To see this, consider first

---

20. The calculation of other comparative statics results, many of which are similar to those found in earlier studies of the Barro-Grossman-Malinvaud model, is left to the interested reader.

222   *QUARTERLY JOURNAL OF ECONOMICS*

the multiplier when Keynesian unemployment prevails in the current period, but agents make no allowance for future constraints (i.e., they assume that Walrasian equilibrium will prevail next period). Current employment and sales are therefore jointly determined by equations (38), (39), and (40):

$$(38) \qquad \bar{L}_1 = \hat{e}_1(\bar{x}_1; w_1, p_2, w_2)$$

$$(39) \qquad \bar{x}_1 = c_1(p_1, p_2, \tilde{Y}) + g_1$$

$$(40) \qquad \tilde{Y} = \bar{m}_0 + p_1\hat{y}_1(\bar{x}_1; p_1, p_2, w_2) + p_2 y_2^*.$$

These imply a simple one-period multiplier, very similar to the usual textbook expression:[21]

$$(41) \qquad \frac{\partial \bar{L}_1}{\partial g_1} = \left[1 - \frac{\partial c_1}{\partial Y} p_1 \frac{\partial \hat{y}_1}{\partial \bar{x}_1} \right]^{-1} \frac{\partial \hat{e}_1}{\partial \bar{x}_1}.$$

However, if regime K both prevails today and is rationally expected to prevail tomorrow, then since all agents take into account the effect of current events on future behavior, (38), (39), and (40) must be replaced by the following set of four equations:

$$(42) \qquad \bar{L}_1 = \hat{e}_1(\bar{x}_1, \bar{x}_2; w_1, w_2)$$

$$(43) \qquad \bar{x}_1 = c_1(p_1, p_2, \tilde{Y}) + g_1$$

$$(44) \qquad \bar{x}_2 = c_2(p_1, p_2, \tilde{Y}) + g_2$$

$$(45) \qquad \tilde{Y} = \bar{m}_0 + p_1\hat{y}_{11}(\bar{x}_1, \bar{x}_2; w_1, w_2) + p_2\hat{y}_2(\bar{x}_1, \bar{x}_2; w_1, w_2).$$

Routine calculations show that under these circumstances the multiplier is

$$(46) \qquad \frac{\partial \bar{L}_1}{\partial g_1} = \left[1 - \frac{\partial c_1}{\partial Y} A_1 - \frac{\partial c_2}{\partial Y} A_2 \right]^{-1}$$

$$\times \left[\frac{\partial \hat{e}_1}{\partial \bar{x}_1} \left\{ 1 - \frac{\partial c_2}{\partial Y} A_2 \right\} + \frac{\partial \hat{e}_1}{\partial \bar{x}_2} \frac{\partial c_2}{\partial Y} A_1 \right],$$

where

$$(47) \qquad A_1 = \frac{\partial \tilde{Y}}{\partial \bar{x}_1} = p_1 \frac{\partial \hat{y}_1}{\partial \bar{x}_1} + p_2 \frac{\partial \hat{y}_2}{\partial \bar{x}_1}$$

$$(48) \qquad A_2 = \frac{\partial \tilde{Y}}{\partial \bar{x}_2} = p_1 \frac{\partial \hat{y}_1}{\partial \bar{x}_2} + p_2 \frac{\partial \hat{y}_2}{\partial \bar{x}_2}.$$

21. The difference between (41) and the usual textbook expression arises solely from the assumption in our model that the corporate sector faces a constraint on its sales net of investment purchases rather than on its gross sales.

There are three distinct reasons why (46) exceeds (41).[22] First, as shown in the Appendix, $\partial\,\hat{e}_1/\partial\bar{x}_1$ exceeds $\partial\hat{e}_1/\partial\bar{x}_1$ (at least locally); i.e., a relaxation of the current sales constraint faced by firms has a greater impact effect on their current demand for labor when they expect to face a similar constraint in the future than when they expect to be unconstrained. This result, which reflects the Samuelson-Le Chatelier principle, does not arise because expectations are rational but solely because they are "Keynesian": hence government policy has a greater expansionary effect when firms are pessimistic about their future sales prospects. Second, a relaxation of the current sales constraint also causes firms to revise their future employment and output plans upward, but with rational constraint expectations, households know that this raises their lifetime income, and so they increase their consumption in both periods, thus having a further impact effect on firms' current demand for labor. Third, each of these impact effects (represented by $\partial\,\hat{e}_1/\partial\bar{x}_1$ and $\partial\,\hat{e}_1/\bar{x}_2$, respectively) gives rise to a multiplier chain within each period accentuated by accelerator-type effects between the two periods, as the relaxation of a constraint in one period on one group of agents has an enhanced expansionary effect by relaxing the constraints that the other group faces in the current period and expects to face next period.[23] The net effect of these interactions is to raise the multiplier considerably: for example, the coefficient of $\partial\,\hat{e}_1/\partial\bar{x}_1$ in (46) exceeds that of $\partial\hat{e}_1/\partial\bar{x}_1$ in (41).

To summarize, we have demonstrated that when Keynesian unemployment prevails in the current period, the employment multiplier is greater with rational than with static expectations of Keynesian unemployment, and greater still than with Walrasian expectations. These conclusions may be supplemented by two additional observations. First, the efficacy of government policy shown by (46) does not follow from its being unanticipated. On the contrary, a perfectly anticipated increase in government spending in period 2 has a similar expansionary effect. Second, the rigidity of current and expected future prices and wages is not necessary for government spending to have real effects in this model: by changing the division of national output between public and private consumption, a rise

22. The denominator of (46) may reasonably be assumed to be positive, since it equals the responsiveness of income $\bar{Y}$ to a change in initial money balances $\bar{m}_0$. If this were negative, then with fixed prices and wages the model would be unstable under a quantity-*tâtonnement* adjustment process.

23. The effect of expected sales constraints in giving rise to an income-investment accelerator was pointed out in a partial-equilibrium model by Grossman [1972] and in a simple general-equilibrium model by Akerlof and Stiglitz [1965].

224   QUARTERLY JOURNAL OF ECONOMICS

in g_1 has real effects even in the flexible-price equilibrium described by equations (13) to (16). However, the same is not true of monetary expansion: in full Walrasian equilibrium an increase in initial money balances merely raises all nominal magnitudes by the same proportionate amount, leaving output and employment unchanged, whereas when wage and price rigidities give rise to current and rationally anticipated Keynesian unemployment, it has real effects similar to (46):

$$(49) \quad \frac{\partial \bar{L}_1}{\partial \bar{m}_0} = \left[1 - \frac{\partial c_1}{\partial Y} A_1 - \frac{\partial c_2}{\partial Y} A_2 \right]^{-1} \left[\frac{\partial \hat{e}_1}{\partial \bar{x}_1} \frac{\partial c_1}{\partial Y} + \frac{\partial \hat{e}_1}{\partial \bar{x}_2} \frac{\partial c_2}{\partial Y} \right].$$

These findings illustrate the important point that the implications of rational expectations for the effectiveness of government policy depend completely on whether or not they are accompanied by sufficient price flexibility to ensure market clearing without rationing. When prices are rigid, rational constraint expectations, at least in the present model, actually enhance the effectiveness of anticipated government policy.

VIII. Summary and Conclusion

This paper has presented a simple two-period model of temporary equilibrium with rationing that lays considerable stress on agents' expectations of the constraints that they may face in the future. Arbitrary constraint expectations were shown to permit multiple equilibria, with more than one regime in the present period being consistent with a given vector of current and expected future wages and prices. Moreover, such expectations were shown to exhibit a "bootstraps" property, so that, for example, Keynesian unemployment is more likely than classical unemployment to prevail today if it is expected to prevail tomorrow, and vice versa.

It was also shown that Walrasian equilibrium and the impotence of government policy are not guaranteed by *rational constraint expectations*, in the sense of perfect foresight of future constraint levels. On the contrary, such expectations actually increase the probability that Keynesian unemployment will prevail today relative to Walrasian expectations, and they raise the value of the government multiplier. These results suggest that the critique of the effectiveness of government policy presented by "new classical macroeconomists," such as Sargent and Wallace [1975], rests primarily on their assumption that wages and prices move instantaneously to clear markets, and *not* on their use of the rational expectations hypothesis.[24]

One possible objection to our concept of rational constraint expectations is that with so much information available, agents should be able to change prices directly to attain the Walrasian equilibrium. We believe, however, that this type of argument greatly underestimates the difficulties of coordinating individual behavior in a decentralized economy with highly imperfect information. In such an environment the two assumptions of rational expectations and wage-price flexibility are by no means equivalent. Even the assumption of rational constraint expectations alone has an almost unbelievable informational requirement; we defend it not on the grounds of descriptive realism, but because it isolates the role of wage-price rigidities (including rigidities in expected future wages and prices) in giving rise to unemployment, intermarket spillovers, and other such Keynesian phenomena.

Finally, we would argue that even though wage-price flexibility may eventually bring the economy to Walrasian equilibrium, it is unlikely to do so by a swift or easy route. The facts that shifts in expectations may bring about substantial changes in the wage-price vector required to achieve Walrasian equilibrium, and that the market whose price is sticky need not be the one that fails to clear, suggest a sort of "dynamic second-best theorem": with limited flexibility of some prices, increasing the flexibility of other prices may reduce rather than increase the ability of the system to return to Walrasian equilibrium. A fuller consideration of such dynamic problems, as well as an evaluation of the ability of the real-balance effect—excluded from consideration in this paper—to ensure the reattainment of equilibrium, are topics to which we hope to return.

APPENDIX: THE BEHAVIOR OF THE FIRM

The behavior of the firm under different constraint regimes can be derived directly by maximizing (5) subject to (6), (7), and appropriate additional constraints, but it is easier and more illuminating to adopt a dual approach, along with the concept of "virtual" prices used by Neary and Roberts [1980].

Consider first the case of no constraints in either period, where the unconstrained profit function is defined as follows. (To simplify notation, we denote the price-wage vector by (p,w,q,v) in this Ap-

24. Similar criticisms have been made by Fischer [1977] and Phelps and Taylor [1977].

pendix, and not by (p_1, w_1, p_2, w_2) as in the text):

$$(A.1) \quad \pi(p,w,q,v) = \max_{e_1, e_2, I_1, I_2} [p\{F(e_1) - I_1\} - we_1$$

$$+ q\{H(e_2, I_1) - I_2\} - ve_2 + \psi(I_2; \theta)].$$

By Hotelling's Lemma the partial derivatives of this function give the firm's unconstrained net sales and employment demand functions in each period:

$$(A.2) \qquad \pi_p = x_1, \quad \pi_w = -e_1, \quad \pi_q = x_2, \quad \pi_v = -e_2.$$

The properties of these functions may be deduced in standard fashion by noting that π is a convex function of all prices (i.e., $\pi_{\mu\mu} \geq 0$, $\mu = p, w, q, v$). These properties may be further simplified by observing that (in the absence of additional constraints) the firm's decision problem is separable into three distinct subproblems:

$$(A.3) \qquad \pi(p,w,q,v) = \pi^1(p,w) + \pi^2(p,q,v) + \pi^3(q)$$

$$(A.4) \qquad\qquad = \max_{e_1} [pF(e_1) - we_1] + \max_{I_1, e_2} [qH(e_2, I_1)$$

$$- pI_1 - ve_2] + \max_{I_2} [\psi(I_2) - qI_2].$$

Hence current employment demand is independent of period 2 prices and wages and depends only on the current real wage w/p:

$$(A.5) \qquad\qquad \pi_{w\mu} = \pi^1_{w\mu} = 0 \quad \mu = q, v.$$

Suppose now that the firm faces a sales constraint in the current period: $\bar{x}_1 < x_1$. Its behavior in this case may be deduced from the constrained function $\hat{\pi}(\bar{x}_1; p, w, q, v)$, and as in Neary and Roberts [1980], the properties of the latter are most easily determined by relating it to the unconstrained profit function evaluated at the virtual price $\bar{p}$:

$$(A.6) \qquad \hat{\pi}(\bar{x}_1; p, w, q, v) = \max [\pi(p,w,q,v): x_1 \leq \bar{x}_1]$$

$$(A.7) \qquad\qquad\qquad = \pi(\bar{p}, w, q, v) + (p - \bar{p})\bar{x}_1,$$

where the virtual price, that price which would induce an unconstrained firm to produce $\bar{x}_1$, is defined implicitly by

$$(A.8) \qquad\qquad \bar{x}_1 = \pi_p(\bar{p}, w, q, v).$$

It is easily seen that the constrained and unconstrained current employment demand functions coincide when the latter is evaluated at the virtual price $\bar{p}$:

$$(A.9) \qquad \hat{e}_1 = -\hat{\pi}_w = -\pi_w - (\pi_p - \bar{x}_1)\frac{\partial \bar{p}}{\partial w} = -\pi_w.$$

Hence the effect of a change in the sales constraint on current employment demand is found from (A.9) and (A.8) to be

$$(A.10) \qquad\qquad \frac{\partial \hat{e}_1}{\partial \bar{x}_1} = -\pi_{wp}\frac{\partial \bar{p}}{\partial \bar{x}_1}$$

A RECONSTRUCTION OF KEYNESIAN ECONOMICS   227

(A.11) $= -\pi_{wp}\pi_{pp}^{-1} > 0.$

Other properties of the firm's behavior in the face of the sales constraint may be deduced in a similar manner. For example,

(A.12) $\dfrac{\partial \hat{e}_1}{\partial w} = -\pi_{ww} - \pi_{wp}\dfrac{\partial \bar{p}}{\partial w}$

(A.13) $= \dfrac{\partial e_1}{\partial w} + \pi_{wp}\pi_{pp}^{-1}\pi_{pw}.$

Since the second term in (A.13) is positive, this yields a Le Chatelier-type result: *the imposition of a sales constraint reduces* (at least locally) *the responsiveness of employment demand to a change in wages.*

Consider next the case where the firm faces a sales constraint in both periods: $\bar{x}_1 < x_1$ and $\bar{x}_2 < x_2$. We may proceed in an analogous fashion to define a doubly constrained profit function:

(A.14) $\hat{\pi}(\bar{x}_1,\bar{x}_2;p,w,q,v) = \max[\hat{\pi}(\bar{x}_1;p,w,q,v): \hat{x}_2 \leq \bar{x}_2]$

(A.15) $= \hat{\pi}(\bar{x}_1;p,w,\bar{q},v) + (q - \bar{q})\bar{x}_2$

(A.16) $= \pi(\bar{p},w,\bar{q},v) + (p - \bar{p})\bar{x}_1 + (q - \bar{q})\bar{x}_2.$

The two virtual prices, $\bar{p}$ and $\bar{q}$, corresponding to the two constraints, $\bar{x}_1$ and $\bar{x}_2$, are now jointly determined by (A.8) (with $\bar{q}$ replacing q) and (A.17):

(A.17) $\bar{x}_2 = \pi_q(\bar{p},w,\bar{q},v).$

As before, the doubly constrained and unconstrained labor demand functions coincide when the latter is evaluated at $\bar{p}$ and $\bar{q}$:

(A.18) $\hat{e}_1 = -\hat{\pi}_w = -\hat{\pi}_w = -\pi_w.$

Hence,

(A.19) $\dfrac{\partial \hat{e}_1}{\partial \bar{x}_1} = -\pi_{wp}\dfrac{\partial \bar{p}}{\partial \bar{x}_1} - \pi_{wq}\dfrac{\partial \bar{q}}{\partial \bar{y}_1}.$

This may be simplified by recalling from (A.5) that π_{wq} is zero and by solving (A.8) and (A.17) for $\partial \bar{p}/\partial \bar{x}_1$. This yields

(A.20) $\dfrac{\partial \hat{e}_1}{\partial \bar{x}_1} = -\pi_{wp}[\pi_{pp} - \pi_{pq}\pi_{pp}^{-1}\pi_{qp}]^{-1}.$

This is clearly greater than (A.11), which proves that (as was asserted in Section VI) the presence of an expected future sales constraint *increases* the responsiveness of current employment demand to a relaxation of the current sales constraint.

It should be clear how these techniques may be used to deduce the behavior of the firm in the presence of other combinations of constraints.

UNIVERSITY COLLEGE, DUBLIN
PRINCETON UNIVERSITY

228   *QUARTERLY JOURNAL OF ECONOMICS*

REFERENCES

Akerlof, G. A., and J. E. Stiglitz, "Investment and Wages," read at the Econometric Society Meeting, New York, 1965.
Barro, R. J., and H. I. Grossman, "A General Disequilibrium Model of Income and Employment," *American Economic Review*, LXI (1971), 82–93.
——, and ——, *Money, Employment and Inflation* (Cambridge: Cambridge University Press, 1976).
Benassy, J. P., "Neo-Keynesian Disequilibrium in a Monetary Economy," *Review of Economic Studies*, XLII (1975), 503–23.
Blad, M. C., and A. P. Kirman, "The Long-Run Evolution of a Rationed Equilibrium Model," University of Warwick Economic Research Paper No. 128, 1978.
Böhm, V., "Disequilibrium Dynamics in a Simple Macroeconomic Model," *Journal of Economic Theory*, XVII (1978), 179–99.
Clower, R. W., "The Keynesian Counter-Revolution: A Theoretical Appraisal," in F. H. Hahn and F. Brechling, eds., *The Theory of Interest Rates* (London: Macmillan, 1965).
Dehez, P., and J. J. Gabszewicz, "Savings Behaviour and Disequilibrium Analysis," *Colloques Internationaux du C.N.R.S.*, No. 259 (1978), 197–212; CORE Reprint No. 313.
Dixit, A. K., "Public Finance in a Keynesian Temporary Equilibrium," *Journal of Economic Theory*, XII (1976), 242–58.
——, "The Balance of Trade in a Model of Temporary Equilibrium with Rationing," *Review of Economic Studies*, XLV (1978), 393–404.
Fischer, S., "Long-term Contracts, Rational Expectations, and the Optimal Money Supply Rule," *Journal of Political Economy*, LXXXV (1977), 191–210.
Grandmont, J. M., "Temporary General Equilibrium Theory," *Econometrica*, XLV (1977), 535–73.
——, *Money and Value* (Cambridge: Cambridge University Press, 1982).
Grossman, H. I., "A Choice-Theoretic Model of an Income-Investment Accelerator," *American Economic Review*, LXII (1972), 630–41.
Hansen, B., *A Study in the Theory of Inflation* (London: Allen and Unwin, 1951).
Hicks, J. R., *The Crisis in Keynesian Economics* (Oxford: Basil Blackwell, 1974).
Hildenbrand, K., and W. Hildenbrand, "On Keynesian Equilibria with Unemployment and Quantity Rationing," *Journal of Economic Theory*, XVIII (1978), 255–77.
Honkapohja, S., "On the Dynamics of Disequilibria in a Macro Model with Flexible Wages and Prices," in M. Aoki and A. Marzello, eds., *New Trends in Dynamic Systems Theory and Economics* (New York: Academic Press, 1979), pp. 303–36.
Hool, B., "Monetary and Fiscal Policies in Short-Run Equilibria with Rationing," *International Economic Review*, XXII (1980), 301–16.
Laroque, G., "On the Local Uniqueness of the Fixed Price Equilibria," *Review of Economic Studies*, XLVIII (1981), 113–29.
Leijonhufvud, A., *On Keynesian Economics and the Economics of Keynes* (New York: Oxford University Press, 1968).
Malinvaud, E., *The Theory of Unemployment Reconsidered* (Oxford: Basil Blackwell, 1977).
Muellbauer, J., and R. Portes, "Macroeconomic Models with Quantity Rationing," *Economic Journal*, LXXXVIII (1978), 788–821.
Neary, J. P., "Nontraded Goods and the Balance of Trade in a Neo-Keynesian Temporary Equilibrium," this *Journal*, XCV (1980), 403–29.
——, and K. W. S. Roberts, "The Theory of Household Behavior under Rationing," *European Economic Review*, XIII (1980), 25–42.
Patinkin, D., *Money, Interest and Prices: An Integration of Monetary and Value Theory*, 2nd ed. (New York: Harper and Row, 1965).
Phelps, E. S., and J. B. Taylor, "Stabilizing Powers of Monetary Policy with Rational Expectations," *Journal of Political Economy*, LXXXV (1977), 163–90.
Sargent, T. J., and N. Wallace, " 'Rational' Expectations, the Optimal Monetary Instrument, and the Optimal Money Supply Rule," *Journal of Political Economy*, LXXXIII (1975), 241–54.
Solow, R. M., and J. E. Stiglitz, "Output, Employment and Wages in the Short Run," this *Journal*, LXXXII (1968), 537–60.
Stiglitz, J. E., *Lectures in Macroeconomics* (All Souls' College, Oxford: 1978).

[18]

European Economic Review 31 (1987) 288–295. North-Holland

HYSTERESIS IN UNEMPLOYMENT

Olivier J. BLANCHARD*

M.I.T., Cambridge, MA 02139, USA

Lawrence H. SUMMERS*

Harvard University and National Bureau of Economic Research, Cambridge, MA 02138, USA

1. Introduction

Standard macroeconomic models make a sharp distinction between equilibrium and actual unemployment. Equilibrium unemployment is determined by labor market institutions, moves slowly and is unaffected by actual unemployment. Unexpected movements in demand and supply lead to deviations of actual unemployment from equilibrium; these deviations in turn trigger changes in the rate of inflation, which lead eventually to a return to equilibrium unemployment.

The European experience of the last ten years, like the depression of the 1930's, strongly suggests that the standard model may not capture important aspects of reality. As actual unemployment has gone up, equilibrium unemployment, as estimated from Phillips curve relations, has risen in tandem. Today, unemployment in the EEC exceeds 11 percent. But, were it not for the fall in the price of oil and the depreciation of the dollar, inflation would be roughly constant. Put another way, the actual level of unemployment appears to be the equilibrium level. While this could as a matter of logic be due to shocks increasing both the equilibrium and the actual rates, empirical attempts to identify such shocks have failed. Lower productivity growth and higher oil prices may help explain the 70's, but there are very few identifiable adverse shocks which can explain a doubling of equilibrium unemployment in the 80's.

The recent European experience has led to the development of alternative theories of unemployment embodying the idea that the equilibrium unemployment rate depends on the history of the actual unemployment rate. Such theories may be labelled *hysteresis* theories after the term in the physical

*We are grateful to Niels Gottfries for comments on an earlier draft of this paper and to Richard Layard and Steve Nickell for numerous discussions on the subject.

0014-2921/87/$3.50 © 1987, Elsevier Science Publishers B.V. (North-Holland)

sciences referring to situations where equilibrium is path-dependent.[1] Two directions of research on hysteresis appear very promising. Both focus on the labor market and the relation of unemployment to wage setting. First *membership* theories are based on the distinction between insiders and outsiders and explore the idea that wage setting is largely determined by firms' incumbent workers rather than by the unemployed. Second, *duration* theories are based on the distinction between short-term and long-term unemployed and explore the idea that the long-term unemployed exert little pressure on wage setting. This paper shows, using a simple macroeconomic model, how these theories can, singly or together, explain high persistent unemployment.

In what follows, we focus on wage bargaining. To do so, we make the conventional – but not uncontroversial – assumption that wage bargaining determines the nominal wage, with firms being free to choose employment ex post. Therefore we first specify the demand for labor. We then consider the implications of alternative wage setting mechanisms for the persistence of unemployment. We start with the pure insider case, in which the wage is set by insiders, with no pressure from outsiders on wage setting and then consider the more general case where outsiders exert some pressure. Finally, we study the case where not all outsiders exert the same pressure on wage bargains.

2. The derived demand for labor

There are many firms in the economy. The demand facing each firm is a function of aggregate demand, which itself depends on real money balances, and its own price relative to the overall price level. For simplicity, we assume that the only potential source of fluctuations in the economy is nominal money, which, if prices do not adjust, affects aggregate demand and employment. All the variables in what follows are in logarithms and we ignore all unimportant constants. Formally, the demand facing firm i is given by

$$y_i = (m-p) - a(p_i - p), \qquad a > 1, \tag{1}$$

where y_i, p_i are the firm's output and nominal price, and m and p are nominal money and the price level.

---

[1]Strictly speaking, the word hysteresis should be used only in the case where there is path dependence of steady-state equilibrium unemployment. We shall use it more loosely to denote cases where actual unemployment affects equilibrium unemployment for a long time. The idea that the macroeconomy may exhibit hysteresis is not new. Hysteresis effects were for example discussed in Phelps (1972). An analysis of their implications for policy may be found in Sachs (1985). Other recent papers examining hysteresis explanations for the European experience are discussed below.

Each firm operates under constant returns to scale, so that $y_i = n_i$, where n_i is employment in firm i; given constant marginal cost and constant elasticity of demand, profit maximisation implies $p_i = w_i$, where w_i is the nominal wage paid by firm i. Using these relations, and noting that $p = w$, where w is the aggregate nominal wage index, we obtain a derived demand for labor by firm i

$$n_i = (m - w) - a(w_i - w). \tag{2}$$

Employment in each firm depends on real money balances in wage units, and on the relative wage paid by the firm. The determination of employment along this derived demand curve depends on the process of wage setting, to which we now turn. In all cases, we assume that nominal wage bargains are set before nominal money is known.

3. Wage setting in a pure insider model[2]

In the simplest insider model, there is associated with each firm i a group of workers, the insiders or incumbents, with membership n_i^*. They are the only ones whose interests are represented in wage bargaining. Furthermore, they have priority in employment; only when all insiders are employed can the firm hire outsiders.

The assumption that wages are set primarily with regard to the interests of incumbent workers is easily justified. In unionized settings, wage decisions whether made by median voters or senior workers are likely to give little weight to the interests of unemployed members and less to the interests of non-members. In non-union settings incumbent workers are likely to have bargaining power because of the fixed costs of hiring a new worker, and because they can threaten to withhold effort. The differential importance of incumbent workers in wage setting decisions is exemplified by the reluctance of unions to accept two tier contracts. Their reluctance stems from fears that eventually wage decisions will come to be made not in the interests of current members but instead in the interests of new lower tier workers.

Assuming that, in each firm, the group of insiders is sufficiently strong to set the wage unilaterally and sets it so as to make expected employment be equal to the size of the membership we have[3]

---

[2] The idea that wages are the result of a bargain between insiders and the firm has been explored in a series of contributions by Lindbeck and Snower [(1985) for example]. Gregory (1986), looking at Australia, was the first to argue that insider considerations could explain high sustained unemployment. The implications for aggregate unemployment have also been examined by Lindbeck and Snower (1984), Blanchard and Summers (1986a) and Gottfries and Horn (1986). The analysis of this section relies heavily on Blanchard and Summers.

[3] Derivation from first principles yields in general a more complex outcome. In Blanchard and Summers, for example, insiders set the wage so as to make the probability of employment equal to some constant. If insiders set the probability sufficiently high, this implies that expected employment exceeds membership. Although, in average, some outsiders are hired, they are hired to decrease the risk to insiders of being laid off.

$$En_i = n_i^*, \tag{3}$$

This in turn implies, using (2), that the nominal wage satisfies $Em - Ew - a(w_i - Ew) = n_i^*$. Given that all firms and groups of workers are the same, and that the only shocks are aggregate nominal shocks, all groups of workers choose the same nominal wage. Thus, $w_i = w = Ew$. Replacing in (2), and dropping the index i as employment is the same in all firms

$$n = n^* + (m - Em). \tag{4}$$

Employment is equal to membership plus a disturbance, equal to the unanticipated movement in nominal money.

The crucial issue in the context of this model is how membership is determined. If we think of the group of workers as a union, who does the union represent when it sets the wage? Almost surely, the union will care more about the currently employed than about others. If, for example, it cares only about the workers employed at the time of bargaining, n_i^* is equal to $n_i(-1)$. Substituting in the previous equation yields

$$n = n(-1) + (m - Em). \tag{5}$$

The implications of such a membership rule for employment are drastic: employment follows a random walk, with the innovations being due to unexpected movements in aggregate demand. For a given labor force, equilibrium unemployment is equal to last period's value of actual unemployment in the standard terminology. The economy shows no tendency to return to any fixed equilibrium value. The mechanism behind this result is transparent: after an adverse shock which reduces employment, workers who are still employed have no desire to cut the nominal wage so as to increase employment. After a favorable shock which increases employment, some outsiders are now employed and will have no desire to increase wages and to price themselves out of employment.

The connection between membership and employment is probably not as tight as we have portrayed it. Recently laid-off workers may well still be considered insiders; recently hired outsiders may well not be considered insiders. New entrants to the labor force but with family ties to insiders may be treated as insiders. If for example it takes a few periods of unemployment to lose insider status, and a few periods of employment to acquire it, the dynamics of employment are more complex, and in an interesting way. In this case, it takes a longer sequence of unexpected shocks of the same sign, an unlikely event, to change membership. Thus, most of the time, equilibrium employment is stable, and unaffected by movements in the actual rate. But once in a while, a sequence of shocks pushes the equilibrium rate up or down, where it remains until another sequence dislodges it. Such infrequent changes appear to fit quite well with the empirical evidence on unemployment: unemployment seems indeed to be subject to infrequent changes in its mean level.

4. Wage setting with some pressure from outsiders

Assuming, as we have done above, that outsiders have no effect on wage setting, is too strong. First, new firms may hire the outsiders, and through competition in the goods market, force insiders in other firms to accept lower wages. To the extent however that new firms must pay fixed costs to set up production, they may find that, if the economy is depressed and unemployment is high, the size of the market they can enter does not make entry, even at low wages, an attractive option. Indeed, entry seems to occur mostly when unemployment is low, not when it is high.

Even if entry is not an issue, there are two other channels through which unemployment may still affect the wage in existing firms. Higher unemployment means worse re-employment prospects if laid off, and thus should lead the insiders to accept a lower wage and a higher probability of employment. Higher unemployment also implies that replacing the insiders in part or in toto by a new group of lower paid outsider workers is a more attractive option for the firm. Hiring outsiders against the will of the insiders may be costly, as insiders may well harass the outsiders; replacing the whole labor force may also be costly, because of the presence of specific human capital. But a large enough wage differential between the employed and the unemployed may nevertheless make it attractive and stengthen the hand of the firm in bargaining.[4]

We can capture these effects by modifying eq. (3) to read

$$\text{E}n_i - n_i^* = b(\underline{n} - \text{E}n), \qquad b > 0, \tag{3'}$$

where $\underline{n}$ is the labor force and $\text{E}n$ is expected employment,[5] so that $(\underline{n} - \text{E}n)$ is expected unemployment. The stronger the effect of unemployment on wage setting, the larger the expected level of employment in firm i, the lower the nominal wage w_i. Let us assume that $n_i^* = n_i(-1)$, the membership rule, which in the absence of pressure from outsiders, leads to a random walk in employment. Solving, as before, for the level of employment gives

$$n - \underline{n} = (1/(1+b))(n(-1) - \underline{n}) + (m - \text{E}m). \tag{6}$$

---

[4]The implications of the ability of insiders to cooperate or harass outsiders has been explored by Lindbeck and Snower (1986), under the assumption of Nash bargaining between insiders and outsiders.

[5]Actual employment is not known at the time of bargaining.

Employment now follows a first-order process around the level of the labor force. Thus, if the labor force evolves slowly over time, unemployment also follows. approximately a first-order autoregression. The degree of persistence is a function of b. If b is equal to zero, employment follows a random walk. As b increases however, the degree of persistence decreases. After an adverse shock for example, actual unemployment increases, and so does equilibrium unemployment; in the absence of subsequent surprises, unemployment eventually returns to a given value. But, during the transition, short-run equilibrium unemployment is high.

If we look at richer membership rules, the results parallel those of the previous section. If it takes time to lose or acquire membership, only long sequence of shocks of the same sign will change equilibrium unemployment. Once it has changed however, it will only slowly (if b is small) go back to its initial value.

5. Unemployment duration and the wage setting process

The first model we presented assumed that the unemployed had no effect on wage setting while the model of the previous section assumed that all the unemployed exerted some downward pressure on the wage. A plausible intermediate position is that only the short-term unemployed who have worked recently exert downward pressure on wages. Empirical results by Layard and Nickell (1986), and Nickell (1986), suggest that this is indeed the case. Running a variety of wage equations, they conclude that most if not all of the pressure on wages comes in the U.K. from those unemployed one year or less. There is little noticeable effect of the long-term unemployed on wages.

There are a number of complementary explanations for why the long-term unemployed might exert less influence on wage setting than those who have been out of work only briefly. Most obviously, skills may atrophy with protracted unemployment to the point where workers productivity falls below their reservation wage, or the wage which insider workers allow firms to offer. There is however little empirical evidence from either historical or microeconomic data to support this possibility. An alternative possibility is that workers' reservation wage or search intensity may decline as their unemployment spell continues. This may be because they adjust to a lower standard of living, become addicted to living on unemployment insurance benefits, or become discouraged about the prospects for re-employment. This effect and the insider effects discussed above are mutually reinforcing. Inside effects imply that a worker is less likely to be re-employed as his spell of unemployment lengthens. The discouragement of the long-term unemployed in turn strengthens the hand of insiders in wage setting.[6]

---

[6]Another possibility is that the long-term unemployed exert less pressure on wages because employers treat protracted unemployment as an adverse signal. Rational employers will however

Assuming initially that short-term unemployment is roughly equal to the change in unemployment (we return below to the appropriateness of this assumption), eq. (3′) may be modified to read

$$\mathrm{E}n_i - n_i^* = b(n(-1) - \mathrm{E}n). \tag{3''}$$

Thus, we assume that wage pressure from the outsiders depends not on total unemployment, but on (expected) short-term unemployment. Assuming that the membership rule for insiders is still $n_i^* = n_i(-1)$, and solving for aggregate employment gives

$$n = n(-1) + (m - \mathrm{E}m). \tag{7}$$

We recover our initial result that employment follows a random walk. This is now the result of both the behavior of insiders, and the fact that only the short-term unemployed put pressure on wages.

This full persistence result is however too strong. The dynamic relation between short-term and total unemployment is in fact a complex dynamic relation, where the level of short-term unemployment depends both on changes in and the level of unemployment. An increase in the flow into unemployment initially sharply increases the fraction of short-term unemployment, but may eventually be associated with a decrease in this fraction as total unemployment rises.[7] Even taking account of these complications, the general result remains that if the long-term unemployed exert little or no pressure on wages, an increase in long-term unemployment increases equilibrium unemployment for some time. Like the insider model, this implies that short sequences of shocks will have little effect on equilibrium unemployment, while long sequences will increase equilibrium unemployment for some time.

6. Conclusion

While they appear to be able to explain the broad macroeconomic facts of the 80's, hysteresis theories are still in their infancy and need further development and testing. At the theoretical level, it would be desirable to consider more complex bargaining structures than those treated so far. An obvious direction for empirical research is the study of wage behavior at a

---

revise upwards their assessment of the ability of the long-term unemployed when macro-economic developments beyond the control of any single worker increase long-term unemployment.

[7]Because the effect of actual unemployment on equilibrium unemployment is not permanent in this case, Layard and Nickell have privately objected to the use of the word hysteresis to describe their theory.

disaggregated level. If insider and membership considerations are important, wages at the sectoral level should depend for example largely on sectoral conditions as well as on the previous history of employment in the sector.

Even given our current knowledge, hysteresis models point to different policy choices from those implied by models in which equilibrium unemployment is not affected by actual unemployment.[8] They suggest that left to themselves, European economies may remain at high unemployment for the foreseeable future. Regardless of the source of shocks which have led to increased unemployment, they imply that policies to decrease the actual rate, if successful, would probably also lead to decreases in the equilibrium rate. Finally, they suggest that, to succeed, policies must be aimed at re-enfranchising the unemployed, in particular the long-term unemployed.

[8]We elaborate on this point both in Blanchard and Summers (1986a, b). Layard and Nickell (1986) also draw implications of their analysis for policy.

References

Blanchard, O. and L. Summers, 1986a, Hysteresis and the European unemployment problem, in: Stanley Fischer, ed., NBER macroeconomics annual, Vol. 1, Sept. (MIT Press, Cambridge, MA).

Blanchard, O. and L. Summers, 1986b, Fiscal policy, real wages and European unemployment. Mimeo., June (Harvard University, Cambridge, MA).

Gottfries, N. and H. Horn, 1986, Wage formation and the persistence of unemployment, Working paper no. 347 (Institute for International Economic Studies, University of Stockholm, Stockholm).

Gregory, R., 1986, Wages policy and unemployment in Australia, Economica, forthcoming.

Layard, L. and S. Nickell, 1986, The performance of the British labour market, Paper presented at the Chelwood Gate Conference on the British Economy, May.

Lindbeck, A. and D. Snower, 1984, Involuntary unemployment as an insider–outsider dilemma, Seminar paper no. 282 (Institute for International Economic Studies, University of Stockholm, Stockholm).

Lindbeck, A. and D. Snower, 1985, Wage setting, unemployment and insider–outsider relations, Working paper no. 344 (Institute for International Economic Studies, University of Stockholm, Stockholm).

Lindbeck, A. and D. Snower, 1986, Cooperation, harassment and involuntary unemployment, Working paper no. 321 (Institute for International Economic Studies, University of Stockholm, Stockholm).

Nickell, S., 1986, Why is wage inflation in Britain so high?, Mimeo. (Oxford).

Phelps, E., 1972, Inflation theory and unemployment policy (Norton, London).

Sachs, J., 1985, High unemployment in Europe: Diagnosis and policy implications, Mimeo. (Harvard University, Cambridge, MA).

[19]

Aggregate Demand Management in Search Equilibrium

Peter A. Diamond

Massachusetts Institute of Technology

Equilibrium is analyzed for a simple barter model with identical risk-neutral agents where trade is coordinated by a stochastic matching process. It is shown that there are multiple steady-state rational expectations equilibria, with all non–corner solution equilibria inefficient. This implies that an economy with this type of trade friction does not have a unique natural rate of unemployment.

I. Introduction

Some economists attribute fluctuations in unemployment to misperceptions of prices and wages. Others attribute such fluctuations to lags in adjustment of prices and wages (including staggered contracts). It seems to be a shared view that there would be no macroeconomic unemployment problems if prices and wages were fully flexible and correctly perceived. This paper introduces a third cause for macro unemployment problems—the difficulty of coordination of trade in a many-person economy. That is, once one drops the fictional Walrasian auctioneer and introduces trade frictions, one can have macro unemployment problems in an economy with correctly perceived, flexible prices and wages.

Using a barter model with identical, risk-neutral individuals where trade is coordinated by a stochastic matching process, this paper

Valuable discussion with Sidney Winter; helpful comments from Stanley Fischer, Jerry Hausman, James Mirrlees, Richard Schmalensee, Eytan Sheshinski, Robert Solow, and Martin Weitzman; research assistance by Drew Fudenberg and Michael Whinston; and financial support from NSF are gratefully acknowledged.

[*Journal of Political Economy*, 1982, vol. 90, no. 5]

882   JOURNAL OF POLITICAL ECONOMY

examines rational expectations steady-state equilibria. The model is shown to have two properties: multiple steady-state equilibria and local inefficiency of all non–corner solution equilibria. The source of local inefficiency is a trading externality, while the source of multiple equilibria is the positive feedback working through this externality. The externality comes from the plausible assumption that an increase in the number of potential trading partners makes trade easier. The positive feedback is that easier trade, in turn, makes production more profitable.

These results are demonstrated in a model where the trade process is mechanistic, with the production decision as the only control variable. Nevertheless, these results seem robust. Individuals control search intensity and advertising and have reputations for offering good deals. Once all individuals have optimized on these control variables affecting trading opportunities, profitability would still be increased by the availability of more potential trading partners. That is, the externality (and positive feedback) from increased willingness to produce is not correctable by privately available actions given frictions in coordinating trade.

To see the importance of this finding, consider Friedman's (1968) definition of the natural rate of unemployment as the level occurring once frictions are introduced into the Walrasian equations. This paper argues that the result of actually modeling a competitive economy with trade frictions is to find multiple natural rates of unemployment. This implies that one of the goals for macro policy should be to direct the economy toward the best natural rate (not necessarily the lowest) after any sufficiently large macro shock.

The basic model[1] is presented in Sections II–IV. Then, a simple static model is presented in Section V to illustrate the workings of the basic externality. Optimal policy in the dynamic model is analyzed in Sections VI–VIII. An example is worked out in Section IX. A summary description of the model and discussion of its implications are in Section X.

II. Basic Model

We use a highly artificial model of the production and trade processes to highlight the workings of a general equilibrium search model. All individuals are assumed to be alike. Instantaneous utility satisfies

$$U = y - c, \tag{1}$$

---

[1] The model closest to this in structure is that of Hellwig (1976), who shows that his search model converges to a Walrasian model as the rate of arrival of trade opportunities rises without limit.

where y is the consumption of output and c is the cost of production (disutility of labor). The utility function is chosen to be linear as part of the simplification that leads to the conclusion that trade bargains will not vary across pairs who are trading. In addition, the absence of risk aversion permits us to ignore the absence of implicit or explicit wage insurance. Lifetime utility is the present discounted value of instantaneous utility. Since trade and production take place at discrete times, lifetime utility satisfies

$$V = \sum_{i=1}^{\infty} e^{-rt_i} U_{t_i}. \qquad (2)$$

Individuals are assumed to maximize the expected value of lifetime utility, with the times of work and consumption as random variables.

Rather than modeling production as going on continuously, we assume that the arrival of production opportunities is a Poisson process. With arrival rate a, each individual learns of production opportunities. Each opportunity has y units of output and costs c ($c \geq \underline{c} > 0$) units to produce. We assume that y is the same for all projects but that c varies across projects with distribution G. Each opportunity is a random draw from G, with costs known before the decision on undertaking the project. Each project undertaken is completed instantly.

There are two restrictions on individual behavior. (1) Individuals cannot consume the products of their own investment but trade their own output for that produced by others. This represents the advantage of specialized production and trade over self-sufficiency. (2) Individuals cannot undertake a production project if they have unsold produced output on hand. This extreme assumption on the costs of inventory holding is also part of the simplification of the determination of trade bargains. The fact that all trades involve individuals with y units to sell implies that all units are swapped on a one-for-one basis and promptly consumed.[2] It is assumed that there is no credit so that all trade is between individuals with inventories to trade.

Thus individuals have 0 or y units for sale. The former are looking for production opportunities and are referred to as unemployed. The latter are trying to sell their output and are referred to as employed.

The basic difference between individuals in these two different states is that the latter have purchasing power while the former do not.[3] If production were modeled as time consuming, then individuals

---

[2] Dropping the simplifications of risk neutrality, barter, and identical inventory holdings, we would need to solve for a distribution of trade prices, which would complicate the analysis. Assuming that all trade is one-for-one, we do not basically change the model by allowing simultaneous searches for trade and production and thus inventory accumulation.

[3] This is the counterpart in search equilibrium of effective demand considerations in

884   JOURNAL OF POLITICAL ECONOMY

would be in one of three states—unemployed, producing, or trading. Commencing production only adds to demand with a lag. In that sense, those producing are similar to those unemployed. However, it remains the case that the decision to switch from searching for production to engaging in production is the driving force in the model. A similar model can be constructed with no unemployment and varying production intensity. It seems appropriate to associate varying levels of production intensity (coming from varying levels of profitability) with varying levels of unemployment. In a more general setting, there would also be varying hours of work and varying labor intensity on the job.

The trading process is such that for each individual the arrival of potential trading partners is a Poisson process with arrival rate $b(e)$, $b' > 0$, where e is the fraction of the population employed in the trading process, that is, the fraction of the population with inventories available for trade. The presence of lags in the trading process represents primarily the time needed to sell goods. Thus the average length of time of consumer goods in inventories is assumed to increase as the rate of sales declines. For example, a trader might meet with others at a constant rate and find that, for any meeting, there is a probability that the potential trading partner has a unit to sell, that is, is employed. The probability that a potential partner is in the market is a function of the fraction of the population employed, e, with the probability increasing in e. With undirected search for trading partners the probability of finding a trading partner in any meeting would equal e. In a more complicated setting, the greater the stock of available inventories the easier it is to find the particular goods that one wants.

The economy is assumed to be sufficiently large that the expected values of potential production and trade opportunities are realized. The employment rate falls from each completed transaction, as a previously employed person becomes eligible to undertake a production opportunity, and rises whenever a production opportunity is undertaken. Assuming that all production opportunities with costs below c^* are undertaken, we have the time derivative of the employment rate satisfying

$$\dot{e} = a(1 - e)G(c^*) - eb(e). \tag{3}$$

That is, each of the $1 - e$ unemployed (per capita) has the flow probability a of learning of an opportunity and accepts the fraction

---

disequilibrium models (see, e.g., Clower 1965). The large difference in demand between employed and unemployed is a natural consequence of the absence of a capital market. Even with a capital market, there would remain demand differences between individuals in the two states.

$G(c^*)$ of opportunities. Each of the e employed (per capita) faces the probability b of having a successful trade meeting and being freed to seek a new opportunity.[4]

In a steady state, we have the equilibrium rate of unemployment by setting $\dot{e}$ equal to zero. Setting (3) equal to zero, we see that the steady-state employment rate rises with c^*:

$$\left.\frac{de}{dc^*}\right|_{\dot{e}=0} = \frac{a(1-e)G'(c^*)}{b(e) + eb'(e) + aG(c^*)} > 0. \tag{4}$$

We turn next to the determination of c^*.

III. Individual Choice

As modeled, the only decision to be made is which production opportunities to undertake. Assuming a steady-state equilibrium, we can describe this decision as a simple dynamic programming problem. Let us denote the expected present discounted value of lifetime utility for employed and unemployed by W_e and W_u. Then, the utility discount rate times each of these values equals the expected value of the flow of instantaneous utility plus the expected capital gain from a change in status,

$$rW_e = b(y - W_e + W_u),$$
$$rW_u = a\int_0^{c^*} (W_e - W_u - c)dG(c). \tag{5}$$

With probability b, an employed person has a trade opportunity giving rise to instantaneous consumption y and a change in status to unemployed. Each unemployed person accepting a production opportunity has an instantaneous utility $-c$ and a change in status to employed.

An unemployed person accepts any opportunity that raises expected utility. Thus we have the criterion

$$c^* = W_e - W_u = \frac{by + a\int_0^{c^*} cdG}{r + b + aG(c^*)}, \tag{6}$$

where the second equality comes from taking the difference between the two equations in (5) and solving for $W_e - W_u$. The level of aggregate demand, measured as the number of traders seeking to

[4] We are aggregating the individually experienced process, $b(e)$, over all individuals in the process, rather than (equivalently) the rate of meetings, each of which frees two traders to seek new opportunities.

886   JOURNAL OF POLITICAL ECONOMY

purchase, affects production decisions since the probability of a sale increases with the employment rate. Differentiating (6) we have

$$\frac{dc^*}{de} = \frac{(y - c^*)b'}{r + b + aG} > 0,$$

$$\frac{d^2c^*}{de^2} = \frac{(y - c^*)b'' - 2b'(dc^*/de) - aG'(dc^*/de)^2}{r + b + aG}. \tag{7}$$

To see that dc^*/de is positive, we note that (with positive interest) no one would undertake a project with less output than input ($y > c^*$) and $b' > 0$. With $b'' \leq 0$, d^2c^*/de^2 is also negative. Armed with (3) and (6) we can describe steady-state equilibrium.

IV. Steady-State Equilibrium

A steady state is marked by optimal production decisions (6) and a constant rate of employment, with (3) set equal to zero. In each of these equations e and c^* are positively related, which allows the possibility of multiple steady-state equilibria. Except when the shutdown of the economy ($e = 0$) is the unique equilibrium, there will be multiple equilibria. To see this, we note that c^* goes to zero as e (and so b) goes to zero. Also, $c^*(e)$ is bounded above since c^* is less than y for any finite b. Steady-state employment rates are bounded above by the employment level reached if all production opportunities are accepted ($G = 1$). As drawn in figure 1, it is assumed that there is no upper bound to the support of G. The steady-state employment rate equals zero for c^* below $\underline{c}$, the lower bound of possible production costs.

If agents expect the current unemployment rate to be permanent, then the economy is always on the optimal steady-state production decision curve, (6), with movement determined by the $\dot{e}$ equation. Then, the equilibria in figure 1 with the highest employment rate and with a rate of zero are stable. Since G does not necessarily have nice properties, there can be more equilibria than shown.

If the model were extended to allow random shocks to the aggregate economy, the presence of multiple steady-state equilibria implies that the economy can get stuck at the "wrong" steady-state equilibrium after the shock has gone away. Similarly, the presence of multiple steady-state rational expectations equilibria implies the existence of multiple rational expectations paths from some initial positions.

V. Static Model

The dynamic model used above seems useful for understanding both the workings of the externality and the design of policy. Given that

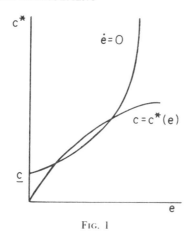

FIG. 1

model to motivate the equilibrium trade possibilities, one can describe the externality more simply in terms of a static model. Let us consider an aggregate cost function

$$c = f(y), \tag{8}$$

with $f' > 0, f'' > 0$. Let $p(y)$ be the probability of making a sale as a function of the aggregate output level. Unsold output is assumed to be wasted, so that welfare satisfies

$$U = yp(y) - c. \tag{9}$$

If individuals view p as a parameter, equilibrium occurs at a level of production satisfying

$$p(y) = f'(y). \tag{10}$$

For efficiency, the aggregate relationship between sales probability and production level must be recognized, which gives an optimality condition

$$p(y) + yp'(y) = f'(y). \tag{11}$$

By subsidizing the cost of production (financed by lump-sum taxation) the decentralized economy can be induced to produce at a point which satisfies the social optimality condition.

It is straightforward to extend this static model to include public goods. This extension will show the presence of a multiplier process and the need to consider multiplier effects in the absence of other demand management policies. Let g be the quantity of output used for public consumption and $V(g)$ the concave addition to social welfare from public consumption. We assume lump-sum tax finance, so the cost of public consumption is added to the cost of production for private consumption. The probability of a sale is assumed to increase with aggregate demand, $y + g$. Private consumption equals total sales less public consumption. Thus, social welfare can be written as

$$U = yp(y + g) - g + V(g) - c. \tag{12}$$

The equilibrium production decision with p taken to be a parameter can now be written as

$$p(y + g) = f'(y). \tag{13}$$

Implicitly differentiating (and thus assuming equilibrium y continuous in g) we have

$$\frac{dy}{dg} = -\frac{p'}{p' - f''}. \tag{14}$$

To sign this expression we need to appeal to the stability argument that the relevant equilibria have the marginal cost of production, $f'(y)$, rising more rapidly than the probability of a sale, $p(y)$. With $p' - f'' < 0$, we have $dy/dg > 0$.

Turning to the first-order condition for the optimal level of public consumption we have

$$\frac{dU}{dg} = yp' - 1 + V' + (p + yp' - f')\frac{dy}{dg} = 0. \tag{15}$$

Using the equilibrium condition, (13), we can write this as

$$V' = 1 - yp'\left(1 + \frac{dy}{dg}\right) = 1 + \frac{yp'f''}{p' - f''} < 1. \tag{16}$$

For a contrast let us consider an economy where the exogenous fraction $(1 - p)$ of output produced is lost in the distribution network. Then dy/dg would be zero and the marginal benefit of public consumption should be equated with the marginal cost of forgone consumption, which is one. Thus there is higher optimal public consumption when the profitability of production increases with increased government demand, and greater production yields a trade externality.

VI. Long-Run Stimulation Policy

To explore policy in the dynamic model we will assume that the government has sufficient policy tools to control production decisions. (In this barter economy, one cannot distinguish between aggregate demand policy and aggregate supply policy.) Below we will consider a production-cost subsidy to induce private decisions that sustain the optimal steady state. In this section we will examine a small permanent change in $c*$ away from a steady-state equilibrium with no intervention. In the next section we will examine the optimal path for $c*(t)$ from an arbitrary initial position. In steady-state equilibrium, we have a flow of utility per capita satisfying

$$Q(t) = eb(e)y - a(1 - e)\int_0^{c*} cdG, \qquad (17)$$

where $eb(e)$ is the rate of sales, with consumption of y per sale, and $a(1 - e)G$ is the rate of production, with an average cost of $\int_0^{c*} cdG/G$ per project undertaken. For social welfare we are interested in the present discounted value of Q:

$$W = \int_0^\infty e^{-rt} Q(t)dt. \qquad (18)$$

When the economy starts at a steady-state equilibrium ($\dot{e} = 0$), the change in W (along the dynamic path of economy) resulting from a permanent change in $c*$ satisfies (for a derivation of [19] see Diamond [1980])

$$r\frac{\partial W}{\partial c*} = -a(1 - e)c*G'(c*)$$

$$+ \left[y(b + eb') + a\int_0^{c*} cdG\right]\frac{a(1 - e)G'(c*)}{r + b + eb' + aG(c*)}. \qquad (19)$$

The first term represents the increase in production costs at the steady-state employment rate, while the second represents the change in both output and production costs along the employment trajectory induced by the change in production rule. At an equilibrium without intervention (where [6] holds), we can write this as

$$r\frac{\partial W}{\partial c*} = -a(1 - e)c*G' + \frac{[yeb' + c*(r + b + aG)]a(1 - e)G'}{r + b + eb' + aG}$$

$$= \frac{a(1 - e)G'eb'}{r + b + eb' + aG}(y - c*) > 0. \qquad (20)$$

Thus, without intervention, there is locally too little activity in the economy.[5] This permanent increase in $c*$ raises expected lifetime utility for every person as well as raising aggregate welfare. The efficiency argument does not apply at the equilibrium with no economic activity ($e = 0$) since $G'(c)$ is zero for $c < \underline{c}$.

---

[5] In a partial equilibrium model of job matching, I have argued (Diamond 1981) that equilibrium has too rapid job filling for efficiency. I have not integrated that model with this one. If such an integration were done in a model with a single decision (by having a be a function of $1 - e$, e.g.), these would be offsetting externalities. If such an integration were done in a model with two decisions, two externalities may prove to be simultaneously present rather than offsetting.

890   JOURNAL OF POLITICAL ECONOMY

VII.   Short-Run Stabilization Policy

Continuing with the assumption that the government can control production decisions, we can examine the optimal policy for an arbitrary initial position. That is, the optimal stabilization policy satisfies

$$\max_{c^*(t)} \int_0^\infty e^{-rt} Q(t)dt,$$

$$\text{where } Q(t) = e(t)b[e(t)]y - a[1 - e(t)]\int_0^{c^*(t)} cdG, \tag{21}$$

$$\dot{e}(t) = a[1 - e(t)]G[c^*(t)] - e(t)b[e(t)],$$

$$e(0) = e_0.$$

Writing the optimal policy as $c^{**}(t)$, we get (the Euler equation)

$$\dot{c}^{**}(t) = rc^{**} - (y - c^{**})(b + eb') + a\int_0^{c^{**}} (c^{**} - c)dG. \tag{22}$$

Setting $\dot{c}^{**}(t)$ equal to zero and differentiating, we have

$$\left. \frac{dc^{**}}{de} \right|_{\dot{c}^{**}=0} = \frac{(y - c^{**})(2b' + eb'')}{r + b + eb' + aG}. \tag{23}$$

With $b'' \leq 0$, this expression is not necessarily positive, except near the origin. The phase diagram is shown in figure 2 under the assumption that the state with lowest unemployment is the optimum for any initial position.

Comparing the equation for $\dot{c}^{**} = 0$, (22), and the private choice of c^* in a steady state, (6), we see that the former is always above the latter as a function of e. That is, superimposing figures 1 and 2, we see that the $\dot{c}^{**} = 0$ curve lies above the $c = c^*(e)$ curve.

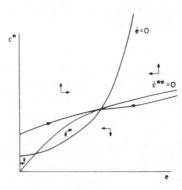

FIG. 2

VIII. Subsidizing Production

The asymptotically optimal steady state is described by setting $\dot{c}^{**}$, in (22), equal to zero (or, alternatively, by setting $\partial W/\partial c^*$, in [19], equal to zero). By subsidizing the cost of production, individuals can be induced to select this cutoff cost. In this section we derive the equation for this subsidy. We assume that the subsidy is financed by a lump-sum tax (payable in labor) that falls on the employed and unemployed equally.

With a subsidy of s per project completed, the individually optimal cutoff rule becomes

$$c^* - s = W_e - W_u = \frac{by + a \int_0^{c^*} (c - s)dG}{r + b + aG(c^*)}. \tag{24}$$

The asymptotically optimal level satisfies

$$c^{**} = \frac{by + eb'y + a \int_0^{c^{**}} cdG}{r + b + eb' + aG(c^{**})}. \tag{25}$$

Equating the expressions for c^* and c^{**} and solving, we have

$$s = \frac{eb'\left[ry + a \int_0^{c^*} (y - c)dG\right]}{(r + b)(r + b + eb' + aG)}. \tag{26}$$

This subsidy level is positive, as can be seen from (22), which implies that $y > c^*$ when $\dot{c}^{**}$ equals zero.[6]

IX. An Example

As an example, assume that $b(e) = eb$ and that all projects cost the same, $\underline{c}$. In this case there will be three steady-state equilibria provided that $\underline{c} < y/[1 + (r/b\bar{e})]$, where $\bar{e}$ is the solution to $b\bar{e}^2 = a(1 - e)$. For this case the curves determining equilibria and optima are shown in figure 3.

It is interesting to consider the optimal plan in more detail. Let the

---

[6] Laurence Weiss suggested calculating the effect of unemployment compensation, financed by a tax on output. Such a policy can be fitted into the model by giving each unemployed person a probability of receiving an output bundle just equal to the after-tax output level of a project. Such a policy moves in the wrong direction, since the incentive to production of having more potential trading partners is smaller than the disincentives coming from the sum of output taxation and unemployment subsidization.

892   JOURNAL OF POLITICAL ECONOMY

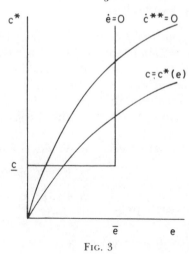

FIG. 3

rate of change of the employment rate be the control variable. Then, social welfare can be written as

$$W = \int_0^\infty e^{-rt}\{b(y - \underline{c})[e(t)]^2 + \underline{c}\dot{e}(t)\}dt, \tag{27}$$

where $\dot{e}(t)$ is constrained by

$$b[e(t)]^2 - a[1 - e(t)] \leq -\dot{e}(t) \leq b[e(t)]^2. \tag{28}$$

Since the objective is linear in $\dot{e}$, there are two possible asymptotic solutions as one or the other of the constraints on $\dot{e}(t)$ is binding. Thus, asymptotically, either no opportunities are accepted or all of them are. For initial condition e_0, let us write the levels of welfare under these plans[7] as $W_0(e_0)$ and $W_1(e_0)$. For some parameter values one or the other of these two functions is larger for all values of e_0 between zero and one. For some parameter values the functions appear as in figure 4. In this case it is optimal to take all opportunities for $e_0 > e_0'$ and optimal to take no opportunities for $e_0 < e_0'$.

X.   Summary and Conclusions

It is common in theoretical economics to use a tropical island metaphor to describe the workings of a model. The island described here has many individuals, not one. When employed, they stroll along the beaches examining palm trees. Some trees have coconuts. All

---

[7] We are ignoring the possibility that for some parameters it might be optimal to take all opportunities for a range of employment rates above $\bar{e}$ and then switch over to taking no further opportunities.

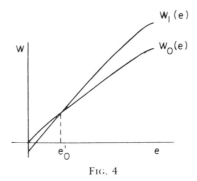

FIG. 4

bunches have the same number of nuts but differ in their height above the ground. Having spotted a bunch, the individual decides whether to climb the tree. There is a taboo against eating nuts one has picked oneself. Having climbed a tree, the worker goes searching for a trade—nuts for nuts—which will result in consumption. This represents, artificially, the realistic aspect of the small extent of consumption of one's own production in modern economies. The ease in finding a trading partner depends on the number of potential partners available. Thus the equilibrium level of production is not efficient if everyone correctly predicts the difficulty of successful trading. Of course, overoptimism can result in the efficient production level. There is no mechanism to ensure that individual by individual, or on average, forecasts of time to completed trade are correct. Errors would be particularly likely on a non-steady-state path.

When a Walrasian auctioneer organizes a competitive equilibrium, there are not unrealized mutually advantageous trading opportunities. In a complex modern economy, there will always remain unrecognized, and so unrealized, opportunities. The complexity of the many-person, many-good trades needed to realize some potential opportunities, together with costs of information, prevent the economy from achieving a full realization. The model employed here has abstracted from the many-good aspect of modern economies. However, the fact of large numbers of different goods should be kept in mind when interpreting the difficulty in completing trades as modeled here. In the presence of unrealized trading opportunities, many government policies will naturally affect the extent to which these opportunities are realized by affecting individual production and trade incentives. Policies can have two distinct goals—inducing small changes in the steady-state equilibrium position to offset externalities and inducing large changes when the economy has settled down at an inefficient long-run equilibrium.

There are several properties of this type of macro search model that seem particularly attractive. Even without lags in the ability of the

894   JOURNAL OF POLITICAL ECONOMY

government to affect private decisions, the government does not have the power to move instantaneously to a full employment position. Recognizing the costs of starting a production process, we see that there is an optimal rate of convergence to the optimally full employment steady state, which reflects the higher real costs of moving too quickly. Knowledge of private forecasts would be essential to the optimal design of tools to alter private decisions but is not necessary for recognizing a situation calling for intervention (except to the extent that the bases of private forecasts might improve the government forecast).

The model presented here is very special. One cannot draw policy conclusions directly from such a model. There are two purposes for its construction. One is to form a basis for further generalization and study. In particular, it would be interesting to introduce varying technological conditions to examine how government policy should vary with the position of the economy. The second is to provide an example to contrast with models that assume, unrealistically, the existence of a frictionless, instantaneous trade-coordination mechanism and thus the absence of the potential for corrective policies.[8] While the construction of realistic models of trade frictions (and wage rigidities) is needed for good policy analysis, the existence of this simple model indicates the feasibility of constructing consistent micro based models with a role for reactive macro policy.

References

Clower, Robert. "The Keynesian Counterrevolution: A Theoretical Appraisal." In *The Theory of Interest Rates*, edited by Frank H. Hahn and F. P. R. Brechling. London: Macmillan, 1965.

Diamond, Peter A. "An Alternative to Steady State Comparisons." *Econ. Letters* 5, no. 1 (1980): 7–9.

———. "Mobility Costs, Frictional Unemployment, and Efficiency." *J.P.E.* 89, no. 4 (August 1981): 789–812.

Friedman, Milton. "The Role of Monetary Policy." *A.E.R.* 58 (March 1968): 1–17.

Hellwig, Martin F. "A Model of Monetary Exchange." Research Memorandum no. 202, Econometric Res. Program, Princeton Univ., 1976.

Lucas, Robert E., Jr. "Expectations and the Neutrality of Money." *J. Econ. Theory* 4 (April 1972): 103–24.

Lucas, Robert E., Jr., and Prescott, Edward C. "Equilibrium Search and Unemployment." *J. Econ. Theory* 7 (February 1974): 188–209.

[8] In Lucas (1972) and Lucas and Prescott (1974) there are physically separate markets, with each market involving perfect coordination. The efficiency of movements between markets is unaffected by aggregate demand management policies. Thus these extensions of the competitive model have trade frictions but not the externalities from trading efforts modeled here.

Name Index

Ackley, G. 97
Akerlof, G.A. 307
Alchian, A.A. 221, 263–82
Alexander, J. 169
Andersen, L. 199
Ando, A. 125, 191, 199, 200, 225
Archibald, G.C. 229, 248
Argy, V. 203
Arrow, K.S. 48, 49, 78, 212, 221, 263
Asimakopulos, A. 75, 95
Azariadis, C. 283

Bach, G.L. 125
Barro, R.J. 41, 100, 217, 219, 221, 224, 283, 285, 288, 294, 304, 305
Baumol, W.J. 198, 248
Becker, G.S. 217
Benassy, J.-P. 53, 283
Benjamin, D. 227
Bentham, J. 11, 20
Beveridge, W.H. 155, 158, 163, 166, 167
Blad, M.C. 283
Blanchard, O.J. 313–20
Blaug, M. 4
Blinder, A.S. 183
Bode, K. 79
Bodkin, R. 197
Böhm, V. 283
Brechling, F.P.R. 215, 235
Bronfenbrenner, M. 115, 124, 204
Brumberg, R. 194, 225
Buiter, W. 183
Burns, A. 203
Burstein, M.L. 97
Bushaw, D.W. 248

Cantillon, R. 79, 231
Capron, W.M. 263
Carlson, L. 199
Cassel, G. 89
Child, F. 115
Christ, C.F. 93, 104, 119, 120, 121
Clark, 113
Clower, R.W. 2, 41–2, 50, 76, 104, 105, 210, 214, 215, 217, 218, 220, 221, 223, 235–62, 283, 324
Coddington, A. 67–74
Cohn, R. 191
Colander, D. 101
Cross, J.G. 146

Cross, R. 4

Danziger, S. 45
Darby, M.R. 225
Davidson, P. 2, 38–52, 132–50
Debreu, G. 78
Dehez, P. 283
Diamond, P.A. 321–34
Disney, R. 168
Dixit, A.K. 283
Dornbusch, R. 191
Dunlop, J.G. 165, 166, 178, 197

Edgeworth, F.Y. 10, 246
Eichner, A.S. 73
Einstein, A. 261
Ellis, H.S. 88
Enthoven, A.C. 247

Fair, R. 193
Feigl, H. 131
Feldstein, M. 197
Fellner, W.J. 101, 272
Fischer, S. 196, 283, 309, 321
Fisher, F.M. 105
Fisher, I. 7, 46, 75, 81
Fleming, M. 132
Flemming, J.S. 283
Flood, R.P. 283
Floyd, R. 203
Forsyth, P. 182
Friedman, B. 44, 50, 191, 196
Friedman, M. 39, 45, 46, 101, 117, 120–2, 129, 184, 191, 194, 195, 202, 203, 220, 225, 229, 230, 280, 322
Frisch, R. 89
Fudenberg, D. 321

Gabszewicz, J.J. 283
Geary, P.T. 283
Georgescu-Roegen, N. 22
Gertler, M. 283
Gevers, L. 283
Godley, W.A.H. 178
Gogerty, D.C. 146
Goldfeld, S. 198
Goodwin, R.M. 53, 189, 243
Gordon, R. 198
Gottfries, N. 313, 315
Grandmont, J.M. 283, 284

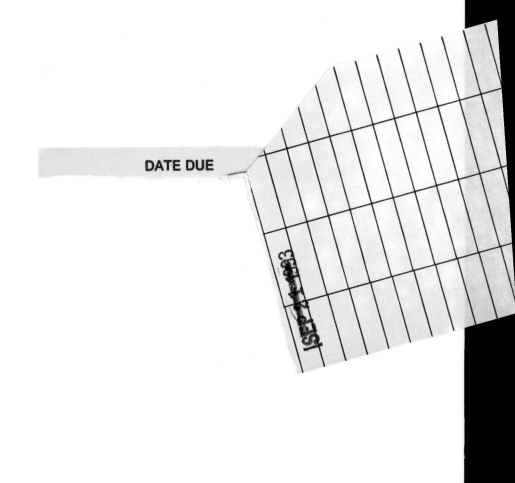